WANDERINGS IN THE GREAT
FORESTS OF BORNEO

Fig. I. VEGETATION ON A NORTH BORNEAN RIVER.

WANDERINGS IN THE GREAT FORESTS OF BORNEO

ODOARDO BECCARI

*With an Introduction by
the Earl of Cranbrook*

SINGAPORE
OXFORD UNIVERSITY PRESS
OXFORD NEW YORK
1989

Oxford University Press

Oxford New York Toronto
Delhi Bombay Calcutta Madras Karachi
Petaling Jaya Singapore Hong Kong Tokyo
Nairobi Dar es Salaam Cape Town
Melbourne Auckland
and associated companies in
Berlin Ibadan

Oxford is a trade mark of Oxford University Press

Introduction © Oxford University Press Pte. Ltd. 1986

Reprinted in Oxford in Asia Hardback Reprints in 1986
from the English translation published by
Archibald Constable & Co. Ltd., London, 1904

Reissued as an Oxford University Press paperback 1989

ISBN 0 19 588923 1

Printed in Malaysia by Peter Chong Printers Sdn. Bhd.
Published by Oxford University Press Pte. Ltd.,
Unit 221, Ubi Avenue 4, Singapore 1440

INTRODUCTION

ODOARDO BECCARI has been described as a man of great intelligence, versatility and intuition, an indefatigable worker, austere and inflexible, courageous and stalwart, proud and almost misanthropic, not an easy character, not afraid of solitude but, on the contrary, finding refuge in it, 'the better to devote himself to his studies and serve his single purpose and sole end: the science of nature' (R. E. G. Pichi Sermolli & C. G. G. J. van Steenis, *Flora Malesiana*, Ser. I, Vol. 9, 1983, p. 29). In the course of a long and productive career, he described many new plant species and made other important contributions to biological knowledge of the Malaysian/Indonesian region. His interest in this part of the world sprang initially from the two and a half years he spent in Sarawak which, looking back in 1902, he still considered the happiest period of his life (p. 354).

For today's reader, *Wanderings in the Great Forests of Borneo* offers an intriguing social picture of Sarawak at the close of James Brooke's rule. Beccari's descriptions of the natural environment at a time when the impacts of modern development were scarcely felt are of enduring biological value. Above all, this book stands as a vivid record of the diversity of tropical plant life, seen through the eyes of a dedicated botanist. Although published many years after the events described, the story is based on detailed notes and a diary made at the time. The narrative holds its youthful freshness, imbued with the author's mature personality and enriched by the reflections of later research and experience.

Beccari was born in the ancient Italian city of Firenze (Florence) on 16 November 1843. His mother, Antonietta, died soon after his birth and his father, Giuseppe, in 1849. He was then, at the age of six, taken into the care of his maternal uncle, Minuccio Minucci. In April 1853, he was sent to school in Lucca. Here, his early love of botany was encouraged by the Abbé Ingnazio Mezzetti and by the Professor of Botany and Director of the Lucca botanic garden, Cesare Bicchi (who, in 1860, went so far as to name *Tulipa beccariana* in honour of his pupil).

Beccari started collecting plants at 13 and at 17 wrote his first professional article, an account of a botanical excursion appearing in the Lucca *Catholic Herald*. Entering the University of Pisa in the autumn of 1861, he excelled in botany to such an extent that he was appointed assistant to the professor (Pietro Savi) in January 1863, while still an undergraduate. This did not deter him from transferring to Bologna University, where he obtained a degree in Natural Sciences in July 1864.

In the same summer, while at Bologna, Beccari met the wealthy young Marquis Giacomo Doria, the great patron of the Civic Museum of Natural History at Genoa which now bears his name. The two young men resolved to combine forces on a scientific expedition and (apparently on the advice of John Ball, a distinguished Anglo-Irish scientist and member of Parliament) chose the exploration of Sarawak as their objective. To prepare himself, Beccari spent February–April 1865 in England, where he visited Kew and the British Museum, and met leading naturalists of the day. He was also introduced to Sir James Brooke who assured him of the support of his nephew Charles, then Tuan Muda and in that capacity in charge of the government of the State.

On 4 April 1865, Beccari sailed from Southampton, joining Doria at Alexandria. They travelled overland to Suez, where they re-embarked for the East. They spent a fortnight in Ceylon, then on via Penang and Singapore, to arrive at Kuching on 19 June. Here they were welcomed by the Tuan Muda, who provided them with accommodation and found staff. It is typical of Beccari that he started to collect at once in the forest that then lay close at hand. Bukit Siul was his first objective, accessible only on foot by a forest path consisting largely of end-to-end tree trunks which he found extremely slippery!

Doria suffered bad health and in March 1866 returned to Italy. Beccari, however, adapted well to life in Sarawak (although he later endured recurrent malaria and an oedema which he identified as filariasis). He soon abandoned his heavy boots for light cotton shoes in which he cheerfully ran down the slopes of Gunung 'Poe'. A photograph of about this period (1864) shows a handsome, dark-haired young man with a high brow, well-shaped mouth and a powerful chin. While in Sarawak, he allowed these features to be obscured by the luxuriant beard (p. 172) which is seen in all later photographs. He appears to have been received in the longhouses with traditional good manners and hospitality. No doubt the backing of the Tuan Muda gave him authority, but we see early symptoms of his forceful personality, not lacking in ruthlessness—as when he persuaded his Chinese hosts at Marop to endure in their home the gruesome processes of skinning, skeletonizing, pickling and preserving his collection of orang-utans (p. 150), broke the taboo (*pemali*) on the Tubau (p. 294), commandeered a boat (p. 341), or tested the efficacy of blowpipe poison on a dog (p. 347).

The montane environment attracted Beccari, and from Kuching he made

INTRODUCTION

trips to most of the accessible peaks. His idyll he created on the flank of Matang (in the area later developed as a tea and coffee plantation). Here he built his house, called 'Vallombrosa' after a monastery in the mountain forest of Pratomagno, east of Florence. He made use of tree climbers and fellers to obtain botanical specimens from the forest, always concentrating on fertile examples. He found that the damp climate obliged him to dry specimens by artificial heat. His efficient methods for doing so undoubtedly accounted for the good condition of his collections. It was only towards the end of 1866 that the persistent rain of the '*Munsim landas*' (p. 259) finally drove him from 'Vallombrosa' back to town.

1867 was largely spent in true wanderings and high adventure, including a *maias* hunt in the Batang Lupar, Undup and Pakit, followed by journeys across to the Kapuas, by sampan to Tanjung Datuk, to Singgi, by launch to Labuan and Brunei, up the Bintulu River and its tributary the Tubau, over to Belaga and down the Rejang to Sibu, a return trip to Kuala Igan, across country from Kanowit via Entebai to Simanggang and finally by Samarahan back to Kuching, ending in the dark and rain, with his stores exhausted, compassless, and almost lost, saved by two resourceful companions who rode a floating nipah crown down the flooded river to find a boat. The rains of November–December once more held him in Kuching and, unfortunately, affected his health. In January 1868, prostrated by a bad attack of fever, Beccari abandoned plans to visit Java and took ship for home.

Back in Italy, Beccari's first preoccupation was the curation and study of his material. Several groups of plants were passed to specialists, for example, lichens to A. von Kremplehuber, mosses to E. Hampe, hepatics to C. de Notaris, ferns to V. Cesati and marine phanerogams to P. Ascherson. His own first reports, in 1868, were published in existing journals: a botanical paper in the *Acta* of the Italian Natural History Society, and an account of his travels in the bulletin of the Italian Geographical Society. In 1869, however, he launched a new periodical, the *Nuovo Giornale Botanico Italiano*, choosing a title deliberately reminiscent of the defunct *Giornale Botanico Italiano*. He edited this journal until 1871, using it as the medium for publication of his own and others' botanical papers based on his Sarawak collections. His successor as editor was T. Caruel who held the post until 1893, when the journal was adopted by the Italian Botanical Society.

We must judge that the urge for further travel remained unassuaged. In 1870, Beccari joined the zoologist O. Antinori and the geologist A. Issel on an expedition to Ethiopia. The following year (November 1871) he set off once more for the East Indies, this time in the company of Count Luigi M. d'Albertis. In a reprise of events in Sarawak, d'Albertis was forced by bad health to return home in October 1872. His departure upset financial arrangements, but in 1874, through the generosity of his friend Giacomo Doria, Beccari received a subvention from Genoa which enabled him to remain in the region until 1876. He made something of a base at Ambon, where he enjoyed the hospitality of Captain P. F. Kraal and his Italian wife, Amalia, but travelled extensively among the islands of eastern Indonesia, including two important collecting trips to the New Guinea mainland.

On his return to Italy, Beccari received a hero's welcome. He was awarded the Freedom of Florence, honorary membership of bodies including the Zoological Society of London, and several gold medals. He still could not resist the offer of another trip to the Indies and beyond, departing in 1877, on this occasion with Enrico A. d'Albertis, cousin of his former companion. In December he paid the brief, nostalgic visit to Kuching recorded in these pages (pp. 354–5), but his main objective was Sumatra where he called on the return journey in 1878 and made rich collections.

During this final trip, Beccari had been appointed Director of the Botanical Collections and Garden of the Florence Museum. Essentially a loner, he was not happy in this post and resigned after a short time, accepting an annuity from the museum in exchange for his botanical collections (for which the Dutch at Buitenzorg had made a similar offer). His zoological collections went largely to the natural history museum at Genoa.

In 1877, Beccari resumed the publication of his collections, with the first parts of his great compendium entitled *Malesia*. Written in Italian, the work was not a commercial success and had to weather serious financial problems before the last fascicule appeared in 1890. At mid career, Beccari then seems to have entered a phase during which he was on bad terms with the museum and his enthusiasm for research waned. From 1893, there was a break in his botanical output.

In 1897, however, the Ranee Margaret of Sarawak (during one of the Brookes' habitual vacations in Italy) visited Florence and was evidently instrumental in persuading him to take up his pen once again and to produce a more elaborate account of his Sarawak days in book form. The Italian text, *Nelle foreste di Borneo*, was published in Florence in 1902. This English language version was based on a translation by the ornithologist E. H. Giglioli, revised and edited by F. H. H. Guillemard. Many of the photographs were provided by the Ranee, as the attributions show, being taken from a presentation album which she gave to Beccari in June 1897 (said to be still extant in the Florence Botanical Museum).

His interest in botanical research was apparently revived by the success of this book, and the wider audience it reached. Beccari thus entered the final

INTRODUCTION

phase of his productive life. He worked in seclusion, making few contacts with his fellow Italian botanists but becoming known world-wide through his studies of palms, a specialization first developed in Sarawak, as these pages show.

Beccari had married in 1882, Nella Gorretti de Flaminj. Four sons (Nello, Dino, Baccio and Renzo) were born to them. After his father's death, aged 77 (on 25 October 1920), Nello—himself also a botanist—arranged the posthumous publication of a companion volume on his journeys in New Guinea, Celebes and the Moluccas (1924) and other botanical papers.

Of all his trips in the East Indies, the time spent by Beccari in Sarawak was the most productive. In two and a half years, he collected over 4,000 botanical specimens, many of them different species and most of them fertile examples. His subsequent prompt publication of scientific reports ensured that these discoveries rapidly became known to the botanical world. His zoological collections went largely to the Civic Museum of Natural History at Genoa where Giacomo Doria was equally assiduous in encouraging publication. T. Salvadori's *Catalogo sistematico degli Uccelli di Borneo* (1874), based largely on Beccari's specimens, was the first comprehensive list of Bornean birds. The beetles were treated by M. Jacoby in 1884. Items of Doria's personal interest, the mammals, were made available to specialists, including W. Peters who reported on the bats in 1868 and shrews in 1870. When, in the 1880s, British collectors (A. H. Everett, C. Hose) began to send material from Sarawak to London, Doria co-operated closely with mammalogists at the British Museum (O. Thomas, K. Andersen), ensuring that Beccari's specimens were available to them. He also provided a medium of publication through his museum's *Annali* (sometimes as co-author himself). Across this wide range of organisms, from marine algae to rain forest dipterocarps, beetles to orang-utans, at that particular juncture in history, the quality and diversity of Beccari's collections were of decisive value. His evolutionary theory, dependent on a process termed 'plasmation', is now a scientific curiosity and much of his nomenclature has since been revised. Yet the account of Bornean forests, appearing as the concluding Appendix to this book, still provides a uniquely comprehensive survey of this fascinating and important biotope.

Great Glemham House
Saxmundham, U.K.
March 1986

CRANBROOK

WANDERINGS IN THE GREAT FORESTS OF BORNEO

TRAVELS AND RESEARCHES OF A NATURALIST
IN SARAWAK

By

ODOARDO BECCARI

Sc.D., F.L.M.S., C.M.Z.S. ETC.

TRANSLATED BY

DR. ENRICO H. GIGLIOLI, C.M.Z.S., M.B.O.U.

Professor of Zoology in the University of Florence

AND REVISED AND EDITED BY

F. H. H. GUILLEMARD, M.A., M.D., ETC.

Late Reader in Geography at the University of Cambridge

LONDON
ARCHIBALD CONSTABLE & CO LTD
16 JAMES STREET HAYMARKET
1904

TO

GIACOMO DORIA

MAECENAS OF NATURALISTS AND BEST OF FRIENDS,

HIS OLD TRAVELLING COMPANION

DEDICATES THIS VOLUME

IN MEMORY OF YOUTHFUL DAYS TOGETHER

IN BORNEO

EDITOR'S PREFACE

TO naturalists generally, but especially to botanists, the author of the following pages stands in no need of introduction. His work in Borneo, which he here describes, was but the prelude to many years of travel and exploration which have found expression, in so far as regards their scientific results, in the pages of various Societies' publications, and the shelves and drawers of the great museums of Italy and other countries—a monument alike to the author's botanical and zoological knowledge and his tireless zeal as a collector. But while his name is thus familiar to the student of science, notably to those who have made the fauna and flora of the Eastern Archipelago a special subject of research, it is probably less so to what an old translator once contemptuously described as " the mere English reader," or—as it would nowadays be phrased— the man in the street. To the latter it is only necessary to say that no one is more fully qualified to act as guide to the great island amidst whose primeval forests he wandered for so long. Whether the scientific reader does or does not admit the validity of all Dr. Beccari's theories concerning species-formation, he cannot call in question his abundant experience of the country, or his knowledge of the subjects of which he treats.

Dr. Beccari tells us that nearly forty years have passed away since the days of which he writes, and deems an apology necessary for so lengthy a hesitation. Certainly, in these days of " steam and speed," a forty-year-old description of a country might seem to a hasty thinker something more than a little out of date. Were he to reject the volume on these grounds, his conclusion would be an erroneous one, and he would miss not a little. These vast primeval groves, through which the author will guide him so pleasantly, secure from mosquito's bite and equatorial temperatures, are to-day as they have been from almost the beginning of things. The stupendous trees which form them have turned from seedling to mould for æons not to be numbered. Beneath the shade of their predecessors the common ancestors of Man and Mayas may have wandered ; and though change is touching even the unchanging East, and there are such things as volcanoes to be reckoned with, the end of the Bornean forest is not, as yet, within sight. It is with nature rather than man that Dr. Beccari deals, and nature needs something more than a generation to get out of date. For those

*

EDITOR'S PREFACE

desirous of information concerning the political and social condition of Sarawak at the present day the author has added a special chapter.

A word is necessary regarding this English presentment of the original *Nelle Foreste di Borneo*. It is not a literal translation of the latter. Somewhat liberally paraphrased by Professor Giglioli, it has at the same time undergone various emendations and additions at the hands of the author, while some appendices of more or less purely botanical interest have been omitted. For the English rendering the present writer is in great measure responsible. He has derived considerable enjoyment from the book, for it recalled pleasant memories of his own experiences as a wandering naturalist in Bornean jungles some twenty years ago. What would he not have given for the companionship in his journeys of so skilled a botanist and so enthusiastic a nature-lover as the author of this volume !

F. H. H. GUILLEMARD.

CAMBRIDGE, *October* 1904.

PREFACE

IN Borneo, the largest island of Malaysia, an English Rajah and an English Ranee rule with pure autocracy a State which in area equals England and Wales, and has its fleet and its army, yet is without telegraphic communication with the rest of the world; possesses not only no railroads, but no roads, and is clothed by dense and interminable forests in which wanders the orang-utan. Here the natives live a primitive life, are in part still mere savages, true man-hunters, who delight in hanging in their houses the smoked skulls of their human victims, as a homage to imaginary supernatural spirits and as a proof of their bravery. This is the kingdom of Sarawak, which owes its origin to a man of great gifts and a born lover of adventure, Mr., afterwards Rajah Sir James Brooke, whose nephew and successor, Sir Charles Brooke, the second European Rajah, now governs with a spirit of the truest philanthropy, leading his subjects rapidly along the path of progress towards civilisation. In this country, when it was in a much more primitive and savage condition, and far less known to the world at large, I landed in June 1865, in company with Giacomo Doria, with the object of investigating its natural history. After the lapse of so many years, I should certainly never have dreamt of putting together the notes and itineraries of my juvenile travels, if a happy chance had not led to my meeting in Florence, with the present Ranee, H.H. Lady Brooke, who urged me to the task, assuring me that the manners and customs of the people and the very localities which I had visited are still to-day what they were then, and, indeed, what they have been from times unknown. I may thus venture to hope that it will not be thought that the publication of this book has been too long delayed, the more so as the subjects to which I paid special attention have, not a temporary, but a permanent interest, and a large portion of the regions which I explored have not been visited since by other naturalists. I have also endeavoured, in a separate chapter, to give the reader an idea—as exact as information from authentic sources can render it—of the present condition of Sarawak. While I am comforted by the hope that I may in no way have to repent of having followed the advice of the charming and gifted Queen of Sarawak, I cannot but feel in duty bound to express to her my gratitude for the help and encouragement which she has so freely given me, and for the permission she has granted me of using and reproducing some of the fine photographs taken by Her Highness during a recent visit to her dominions.

ODOARDO BECCARI.

CONTENTS

CONTENTS

CONTENTS

CHAPTER VII

CHAPTER VIII

CHAPTER IX

CONTENTS

CHAPTER X

CHAPTER XI

CHAPTER XII

CONTENTS

CHAPTER XIII

CHAPTER XIV

CHAPTER XV

CONTENTS

CHAPTER XVI

CHAPTER XVII

CHAPTER XVIII

CONTENTS

CHAPTER XIX

CHAPTER XX

CHAPTER XXI

CONTENTS

CONTENTS

APPENDIX

ILLUSTRATIONS

ILLUSTRATIONS

ILLUSTRATIONS

MAPS

CHAPTER I

ON April 4th, 1865, I embarked at Southampton on the *Delhi*, one
of the fine steamers of the P. and O. Company, and twelve days
later reached Alexandria, where I met my friend Doria, who came
from Genoa. The Suez Canal being then non-existent, we crossed
the Isthmus by rail to join the Indian mail steamer in the Red Sea.

After the usual stop at Aden, and a quiet voyage over the Indian
Ocean, we sighted the high land of Ceylon at dawn on May 5th, and
at 6 a.m. our vessel, the *Candia*, dropped anchor in the small and
not too well protected harbour of Point de Galle. The delight with
which I gazed at this outermost fringe of the continent of Asia—
perhaps more blessed by Nature than any other part of the world
—I can hardly venture to describe. The surprise for the traveller
is all the greater from the fact that, as it were, at a single bound
he finds himself transported from Europe to the tropics. The
memory of the sweltering shores of the Red Sea, and the burnt and
arid crags of Aden, only serve to increase his admiration of the charms
of this island of perennial verdure.

In Ceylon we spent some delightful weeks which I need not
dwell upon here. As a naturalist, finding himself for the first time
in tropic lands, I was greatly disappointed to have to tear myself
away from this enchanted isle. But our aspirations were towards
more distant and less known lands, and on May 20th we bade adieu
to the island, laden with ineffaceable memories of the delightful
days we passed on it. Touching at Penang, we arrived in due course
at Singapore, and on June 15th found ourselves on the *Rainbow*,
the Sarawak Government's steamer, carrying the mails between
Singapore and Kuching, the capital of Rajah Brooke's dominions.

On the morning of June 19th we were early on deck, for with
daylight the mountains of Borneo were sighted. The steamer
had slackened speed in order not to approach the coast before dawn.
As the sun rose, the imposing mass of Santubong appeared, like a
great fortress commanding the entrance to the Sarawak river.

Westward, and not far off, rose the high mountains Gading and Poe, and nearer still were the little islands Satang and Sampadien. Beyond, the coast-line terminates with the bold outline of Tanjong Datu, the frontier of the dominions of Rajah Brooke.[1]

The crests of Mattang command the land, which we rapidly approached, whilst the outlines of new hills and new mountains appeared in the background as the morning mists faded away. Santubong from the sea looks quite inaccessible; but few bare patches of rock were to be seen on its flanks, for it is almost everywhere clothed with dense vegetation. Huge trees rose from the fissures in its rocky sides, and on the enormous branches spreading out from their gigantic trunks lianas climbed up everywhere and hung down in thick festoons of verdure. Before us lay a narrow, sandy beach, covered beyond the water-line with tall casuarinas.

The Sarawak river is about 450 yards wide at its mouth, but at low tide it has a depth of hardly more than nineteen feet on the bar. Once inside the river, the few huts of the Malay fishermen forming the village of Santubong are visible on the mountain side. The Santubong entrance to the river is preferable with fine weather, whilst with bad weather it is easier to enter by the Maratabas channel, where there is greater depth and good anchorage for big ships.

Within the river mouth the scenery is at first highly picturesque, but after passing some hills covered with dense forest this is the case no longer. Both banks are covered down to the water's edge with the vegetation peculiar to these tropical estuaries. Most conspicuous are the mangroves (*Rhizophora*), with bright, shining leaves of an intense green, which reflect the sun's rays on their polished surfaces. Large tracts are entirely covered with the Nipa palm, whose enormous leaves are very like those of the coconut. Beautiful as they are, they become extremely monotonous after a time, packed closely together and without variation either in appearance or height. More elegant are the Nibong palms (*Oncosperma filamentosa*), also very abundant, with straight and slender stems, crowned with a tuft of delicate fronds finely divided and drooping in graceful curves.

The navigation on the Sarawak river is not dangerous for small ships; there are only two rocks to be avoided near the left bank about two and a half miles below the city. From this point the country, hitherto flat, gradually rises. Malay huts, partly hidden by trees, also begin to appear; but although we are very near Kuching, the capital of Sarawak, distant seventeen miles from Santubong, the course of the river is so tortuous that no signs of the town can

[1] The following words, *Tanjong* (cape), *Pulo* (island), *Gunong* (mountain), *Bukit* (hill), *Sungei* (river) and *Danau* (lake), should be noted as Malay geographical terms which of necessity will often occur in these pages.

Fig. 2.—KUCHING, SARAWAK.

yet be seen.   A last point is rounded and a few white houses with wide roofs come into view, next the stores of the Borneo Company near the water's edge, the Chinese bazaar, and a small wooden fort over which waves the Rajah's flag.   All this is on the right bank. On the left are few houses, but conspicuous amongst them the Astana, or palace of the Rajah, painted grey, and situated on a hill which overlooks the river.   Such was our first view of the capital of Sarawak; but since our visit the town has increased very considerably in size, and has now some 25,000 inhabitants.

We were expected at Kuching, and a Government officer boarded the steamer at once with a kind invitation from the *Tuan Muda* for us to land and take up our quarters with him.   The then *Tuan Muda*—for whom we had special letters of introduction from Sir James Brooke, the first European Rajah of Sarawak, whose acquaintance I had made in London before I started—is the present Rajah, H.H. Sir Charles Brooke, nephew of Sir James.[1]   He received us with courteous and kind hospitality, which he extended to us during our residence in Sarawak, and which I shall ever remember with the sincerest gratitude.

We were lodged in a bungalow not far from the Astana or palace, and only a few hundred yards from the primeval forest.   The house was constructed entirely of wood, somewhat in the style of Malay dwellings, resting on piles some five or six feet above the ground, thus enabling a man to walk beneath.   It consisted of two big rooms, with a wide verandah all round, from which we had an extensive view of the town and its surroundings.   The river which flowed at our feet is here about 250 yards in width.   Its waters are turbid and completely influenced by the tides.   The Malay quarter (*Kampong Malayu*) is composed entirely of houses built on piles which encroach upon the water along the muddy bank. A couple of miles away, in the direction of the Mattang range, rises the isolated conical hill known as Gunong Siul.   Across the stream, in a south-easterly direction, the green forest covers the land as far as the eye can reach, with a distant border formed by rugged mountains.   Not a village nor even an isolated hut was to be seen.

Such was the country which was to be the field of our explorations.   Nothing better could be wished for by a naturalist—a wild and virgin country untouched by man, near a populous and civilised centre.   Here we could study at our leisure the natural products of the land, then but little known, and enjoy at the same time most of the advantages of civilisation.   Later, I travelled over a large portion of Borneo, penetrating into its far interior; I visited also

[1] In Malay the title of " *Rajah* " corresponds to king, and that of " *Ranee* " to queen.   The Crown Prince bears the title of " *Rajah Muda* " (young king), the second heir that of " *Tuan Muda* " (young sir)

many of the less known islands of Malaysia and New Guinea; but nowhere did I meet with primeval forests so rich, so varied, and so peculiar in their flora as in the vicinity of Kuching.

The reason why so primeval a forest is to be found so near a populous centre may very naturally be asked. It is more simple than at first sight appears. To begin with, the capital of Sarawak was formerly much lower down the river, where Santubong now lies. Again, it must be remembered that, until lately, the Malay population of the Bornean coast-land lived entirely by piracy, and hardly thought of or attempted anything in the way of agriculture ; while even those Malays who had settled along the rivers of the interior were more often engaged in trying to cheat the Land-Dyaks than in cultivating the soil. With the country in a constant state of war and anarchy, the refuge of pirates from all parts of the Indian archipelago, now siding with the Malays now with the Sea-Dyaks, agriculture was, in fact, impossible. Yet this was the condition of Sarawak before Sir James Brooke came to the rescue. It is therefore not surprising that the forest around Kuching should be still unmodified over an area of many miles towards the interior, and that the Land-Dyaks, more peaceful in their habits than the Sea-Dyaks, found it safer to establish themselves in less accessible localities, far from the sea and from the Malay settlements.

But I must lay aside the past history of Sarawak to complete the description of the neighbourhood of our bungalow, the scene of our first scientific explorations. I have already remarked that the primeval forest was on one side close to our house. No kind of pathway, however, led to it, and in order to reach it a dense scrub had to be crossed which had grown where the old trees of the forest had been destroyed. The flora of this scrub was very uninteresting, and after the first day got none of my attention. Westwards, however, in the direction of Mattang, only a short stretch of bare ground intervened, and a good path led at once into the great forest. Our bungalow was in the midst of park-like ground, the meadow patches being formed by a small grass (*Andropogon aciculatus*, Retz.), the well-known " love grass " of Anglo-Indians, so called because its prickly glumes or ears are easily detached and fasten themselves on the dress of the passer-by in the most tenacious and inconvenient manner. Round the Rajah's palace the gardeners are continually cutting it, and have succeeded in converting it into fine, green, soft and close-cropped lawns. In Sarawak this " love grass " is the only plant with which lawns can be made, and when well kept the inconvenience caused by the seeds and their involucra is much diminished. The plant, which is a stranger to Borneo, as are nearly all the grasses found there, owes its wide diffusion to its tenacious and too affectionate ears.

Around the bungalow, but farther off, where the ground was left uncultivated, other kinds of grasses grew. Of these the most pernicious was the "Lalang" or "Alang-alang," the *Imperata arundinacea* of botanists, which destroys every other plant where it grows. I need not speak of it at present, but on more than one occasion I shall have to mention this pest in the following pages. More interesting were the bushes of the "Onkodok" of the Malays (*Melastoma obvolutum*, Jack.), with big, rosy flowers of great beauty, and, where the soil was damper, clumps of *Dillenia* (*Wormia*), *suffruticosa*, Griff.), the "Simpor" of the Malays, were most conspicuous on account of its large leaves and huge golden flowers, often five and a half inches in diameter.

A little stream, issuing from the jungle and running into the river just below our house, was crossed by a wooden bridge. Following it a pathway led to a hill on which once stood the Rajah's residence, burnt to the ground in 1857, during the historic mutiny of the Chinese, which very nearly overthrew the young kingdom, and in which the Rajah, Sir James Brooke, narrowly escaped with his life. Our bungalow was one of the few European residences which were not destroyed during the revolt.

Some of the land lying between our house and the forest was partially cultivated with plantations of sweet-potatoes, bananas, yam, pineapples, etc., which were evidently recent. These orchards were cared for by the "Orang Boyan,"[1] or more correctly "Bawean"—Javanese who come from a small island north of Madura and are considered in Borneo the best field-labourers. In the midst of these plantations a few trees of the old forest were still remaining, some yet living — giants with their first branches springing from the trunks a hundred feet or more from the ground—but most of them dead, and their bare limbs battered and broken by the winds. On some of these large epiphytes were still growing, such as figs, Pandani and ferns. Amongst the latter the great elk's-horn (*Platycerium grande*), on account of its singular conformation and the diversity in shape of its fronds, was by far the most notable.

The trees which go to form the great forests of Borneo are not adapted to remain isolated, although in most cases provided at their bases with broad expansions in the shape of buttresses which widen considerably below and contribute greatly to the stability of the trunk. If each tree could grow without having others near it its trunk would branch sooner and not grow to so great a height

---

[1] *Orang* in Malay means "man." The "*Orang Boyan*" are thus the natives of the island of Boyan, as "*Orang Ingris*" are the English, "*Orang Blanda*" the Dutch, "*Orang putih*" or "white men," all Europeans, "*Orang Dayak*" the Dyaks, "*Orang Malayu*" the Malays, etc.

as it does, struggling for light and air in the company of its fellows. Thus the enormous height of the trunk is a direct consequence of the number of other trees in its vicinity competing for the ground on a restricted area, each individual striving to outgrow its neighbours in order to place its foliage in the best possible conditions. As long as these giants of the vegetable world are associated in large numbers so as to form a forest, they prop each other up reciprocally and have good stability. But as soon as a forest tree is isolated by the destruction of those which grew around it, it cannot long resist the violence of the winds, and is soon mutilated and perishes. In the forest the roots of the trees are also in a peculiar condition of existence, so that they are unable to withstand the destruction of the surrounding timber. The soil, which before was always damp and shady, becomes abruptly exposed to great variations both in temperature and moisture. Moreover, on account of the thick stratum of rich humus which forms the surface layer of the primeval forest, the roots of the trees grow out superficially instead of downwards. This circumstance, which on the one hand must have contributed to the formation of the basal buttress-like expansions of the trunks, explains on the other how isolated trees can easily be overthrown by the wind, owing to the absence of deep roots.

I was impatient to see something of the country, and the morning after our arrival, followed by a few native lads, I took my way along the path I have mentioned which led directly into the forest— a dense assemblage of trees, some gigantic in size, some slender, cylindrical, and devoid of branches to a considerable height. Their foliage high up, compactly united, formed a dense green vault, occasionally pierced by a stray sunbeam, marking its way across the hot, damp air. Lesser plants and bushes, of many kinds and varied aspect, struggled below for air and light amidst the bigger trees. The ground was covered by an intricate and confused mass of branches and fallen trunks of aged trees, decayed and enveloped with mosses ; and a host of plants, all new to me. Not a single stone did I see uncovered. The fallen leaves heaped together formed a thick layer, which decomposition converts into a rich leaf-mould wherein other plants flourish in the shade caused by the larger ones. It hardly required any botanical experience to recognise a few palms in the multiform vegetable crowd surrounding me. Of these some had fan-like leaves (*Licuala*), and others showed elegant pinnated fronds, springing from a long and slender trunk (*Pinanga*). But few gaudy flowers indeed were to be seen ; only here and there a solitary *Ixora* ventured to colour with its deep red blossoms the pervading dark green of the forest. The big aroids, Freycinetias, and Pandani with long, hanging leaves, together with ferns, orchids and hosts of epiphytes which it is impossible to enumerate, find ways and means of existence, as exiles from the soil, high up in the air, holding on by their roots to the bark of the veterans of the forest.

For a few hundred yards the path was fairly good and dry, but if one wandered from it one was often brought up short by the sharp hooked thorns of the rotangs (*Calamus*), the climbing palms so characteristic of the forests of Malaysia. The ground was undulating, and gradually rose on the right, but on the left it sloped towards the river and soon became marshy. Farther on was a streamlet with sluggish waters, clear, but of the colour of strong tea. In such hollows, where one sinks up to the knees in the black mire formed by the decomposition of the fallen leaves, the types of vegetation were very varied. Numerous lianas with singular stems tightly twisted together ran along the ground, then climbed rampant over the trees, to shoot up far beyond their tops. From the bare trunks of these lianas bunches of flowers and masses of fruit often project, without the least trace of leaves, looking as if they were attached to the ropes of a ship. Here also grew various small trees and singular shrubs, some with stems supported by high roots, as if wishing to be lifted from the miry soil. One amongst them, a new species of *Archytæa*, had a tall but slender stem which appeared as if raised on high stilts, and its head was entirely covered with beautiful blossoms of a camellia-like red. This plant (one of the Ternstrœmiaceæ, P.B., No. 319), not having yet received a name, may be known as *Archytæa* (*Plojarium*) *pulcherrima ;* it is easily distinguished from the well-known species *A. elegans* by its much larger flowers. This was one of the few small trees which, under the shade of the big ones, bore flowers of a bright colour. Another very curious small tree not scarce in that locality belonged to the Anonaceæ (*Polyalthia*, P.B., No. 2,277), with the stem clothed from the base to the bigger branches with stellate flowers of a salmon red. The number of plants new to science which I subsequently found in this small tract of forest was truly wonderful.

Continuing to advance, the path grew worse. Hardly a foot of dry ground was met with, but the pathway was traced out, and was an example of many such in Borneo. It had been made by order of the Tuan Muda not long before, and led to Siul, the small conical hill which could be seen from our house. Where the ground was rising and dry, the forest could be easily crossed; but in the hollows the water accumulates, and the vegetation is so dense as to be quite impenetrable. In order, therefore, to make a pathway, big trees are cut by the natives so as to fall in the direction required ; the branches are then lopped off and the trunks adjusted in a con-tinuous line. Thus a path is laid down over a line of prostrate tree trunks, or " *batang*," as the Malays call them, even for many miles ; but, naturally, it is hardly a level and smooth one, although much can be done in this way by filling the gaps with smaller trunks

and branches tied down with rotangs and fixed with stakes driven
into the ground. Such pathways when recently constructed can be
travelled over rapidly enough when one has learnt how to do so
with bare feet, but a novice can only acquire the art after the
experience gained by frequent falls.

The road to Siul was for the most part of this kind, but being
some months old the trunks, owing to the prevailing damp heat
and frequent rains, were becoming decayed. Many had lost their
bark on the exposed side, and this was rendered extremely slippery
by a thin coating of a minute alga. Such trunks were not at all easy
to cross without slipping off, for they were as greasy as if they had
been well soaped. I soon learnt that thick-soled boots were highly
inconvenient for travelling along the pathways of a Bornean forest,
and found thin-soled cloth shoes better adapted to the task ; for
although they cannot prevent one getting wet feet, they afford a
certain amount of protection against thorns.

The inconvenience and trouble of travelling along these pathways—the only means of crossing the forest marshes—is, however,
amply compensated to a naturalist, and especially an entomologist,
by the abundance of insect life. That narrow luminous streak,
where the sun rays are not intercepted by the dense foliage overhead,
is frequented by myriads of insects, especially butterflies ; too often,
alas ! not easy to catch. Amongst those which were to me particularly tantalising were certain big *Hestias*, with silvery transparent
wings, which kept fluttering some fifty feet or more above my head
without ever coming within reach. At last in despair I fired at
them with dust shot, and was thus able to get one.

On the trunks and branches recently cut down, one was pretty
sure of making large captures of coleoptera of the longicorn and
Curculio families ; and on the damp, rotten surface of trees which
had been long dead, mucilaginous planarians glided along. More
rarely a carab was to be seen, conspicuous by its metallic tints
and slow gait ; and shiny myriapods of a vivid chestnut hue
(*Sphæropœus sulcatulus*), which, on the slightest vibration, curled
themselves up, forming a ball of the size of a large musket bullet,
and thus rolling off to the ground. Under the bark a rich catch of
insects was easily made, mostly of dull colours and with depressed
bodies. The mycologist, too, was sure in such places of a fine collection of *Polyporus, Hypoxylon, Tremella, Xylaria* and other kinds
of cryptogams. At times interminable columns of termites or white
ants (which are, nevertheless, not white but brown) would be met
with, crossing the path in serried ranks in a sinuous line, looking
not unlike a never-ending serpent. It is not improbable that from
these termite processions arose the oft-repeated tale that the
forests of Borneo harbour snakes of such enormous length that
they never come to an end.

Among the greatest pests of these forests are the leeches (*Hemidipsa*) known to the Malays as *lintà* ; they are very numerous in some localities and excessively troublesome. There are two species : one keeps on the bushes and attaches itself to the passer-by on the slightest contact, getting especially on the hands and neck ; the other, which is still more frequent, lives on the ground, and gets on the feet and legs. There is no way of avoiding them ; they get into the shoes and under the stockings, and, fastening especially round the ankle, gorge themselves with blood before one is aware of their unwelcome presence. In Sarawak there are also other kinds of leeches—large aquatic ones. I was told that one species (*Limnotis lowei*, Baird) occasionally gets into the intestine of persons bathing, depositing its eggs there, and causing death, but I cannot guarantee the truth of the assertion. I can only say that the leech in question is very swift in its movements, and adheres strongly to the part where it attaches itself, soon getting enormously distended with blood. It frequents clear running water, and in certain localities on the Upper Sarawak river the natives abstain from bathing on its account. Another species of leech said to be equally dangerous frequents the turbid waters around Kuching. I did not, however, succeed in getting specimens of it.

Our first excursions in the forest were necessarily short, for we very soon collected a sufficient number of specimens to occupy us several hours in their preparation. But I very soon felt impelled to penetrate farther, and one morning I made up my mind not to be tempted by anything along the road, but to reach Siul. I took my gun and went alone, so as to enjoy fully the beauties of the forest. I had now some days' experience in travelling over the tree-trunks, and I confess that I was surprised and gratified to find how rapidly I could get along. Success, however, made me less cautious, and I had several falls before, after about an hour's tramp, I reached the foot of the isolated cone of Siul, happily with no bad consequences. Here, from a solitary hut built in the midst of a small plantation of pineapples, a native came out to meet me. He was dressed in a short jacket and trousers reaching only to the knees, and a long knife or *parang* hung at his side. I thought at first that I had met with a Dyak head-hunter, but I was very much mistaken. How easy it is for the inexperienced traveller to commit such mistakes, and how many such are transmitted to posterity as first impressions in new countries ! On my return, during luncheon with the Tuan Muda, I learnt that my Dyak was no less than a " Sereib " or " Tuan-ku," the title given in Sarawak to supposed descendants of the Prophet.[1] But on meeting him at Siul I fully believed him to be a Dyak, and eyed him with a certain amount of diffidence, for

---

[1] " Tuan-ku " in Malay is in reality a title given to persons of high rank and to princes. " Tuan " merely means sir or master.

the thought struck me that he might take a fancy to my head. Having my gun I felt somewhat reassured; but I very soon found out that the supposed head-hunter was a very civil fellow.

It is well known to travellers in the Far East how courteous and gentlemanly the Malays are. This one, who rejoiced in the name of Tuan-ku Yassim, very soon became my best guide in the forest. He was a good hunter, an excellent shot, and perfectly acquainted with jungle life; [1] quite as much so, indeed, as a Dyak, for to the experience of a true son of the forest he added no small degree of intelligence. His features, except, perhaps, the eyes, scarcely betrayed his Arab descent, but he had no doubt a goodly proportion of Malay and Dyak blood in his veins.

Tuan-ku Yassim, who was always called by us the Tuan-ku of Siul, procured quite a number of animals for our collections: monkeys, squirrels, tupaias, various striking birds, amongst them hornbills and big fruit-pigeons (*Carpophaga ænea*), the *pergam* of the Malays, and many others. Living in the midst of the primeval forest, he had the best possible opportunities for collecting. One cannot easily get natives to collect small birds, however, and these were got by Doria. I also helped in such collections, and always carried my gun during my daily excursions in the forest. We also came to know a Javanese, named Sennen, who lived near us—a patient hunter who added many fine birds to our collection.

Frequently towards evening Doria and I took our guns and went towards the recent clearings, which were full of life at that hour, especially the big isolated trees left standing amongst the pineapple plantations. The waning of the day, usually a silent hour in temperate climes, is in Borneo marked by the commencement of a concert of noisy cicadas, who in legions fill the air with their deafening and varied clamour. One species (*Pomponia imperatoria ;* West.), which the Malays have named "*kriang pokul anam*," or the "six o'clock cicada," is a giant; one of the specimens we got measured nearly $7\frac{1}{2}$ inches across the wings. It begins at sunset, and the noise it makes is not unlike the braying of an ass in high treble, and can be heard at a distance of many hundred yards. As soon as the cicadas begin their concert, flights of elegant long-tailed parakeets (*Palæornis longicauda*) appear in search of a roosting-place on the higher trees. This was also the favourable time for observing a diminutive hawk (*Hierax cærulescens*) which, from the top of one of the highest dry branches of a tree, darted forth ever and anon to seize a passing

---

[1] The "jungle" of Anglo-Indians is not always an exact equivalent for the primeval forest, but often implies a region run wild and covered by secondary forest-growth. The term is not derived from the Malay language, although it is used in the form of "Jangala." but is the Sanscrit word for wild and desert.

insect, returning to its perch to devour its quarry at leisure. It also preys on small birds, showing a boldness hardly in keeping with its lilliputian size. It certainly is one of the smallest of the Raptores, being scarcely larger than a sparrow; its plumage is of a silky black with greenish sheen; the under parts are white, and altogether it is a finer bird than most of its allies.

When the short twilight came on, it was not unusual to see dark creatures jump noiselessly off from the bigger isolated trees, perform a singular reversed parabolic flight, and alight on another tree some thirty yards away, which they struck always lower than the height they had started from, though they at once scrambled up to about the same level. These were the great flying-squirrels (*Pteromys nitidus*). The wide expansions of skin which extend between the fore and hind limbs on either side are spread out when they take their leap, and act as an admirable parachute.

We soon found out that certain trees which appeared to be a great attraction to birds were fig-trees, covered with ripe fruits not bigger than a pea. These trees, which are named "*Kayu ara*," are not only of many species in Borneo, but are all abundant; their fruits afford food to heterogeneous animals, but more especially to birds.[1] The Fici of Borneo show quite a series of adaptations, both in shape and size, to varied biological conditions, and well deserve special investigation.

The species of Ficus mentioned above as a great attraction to birds—a *Urostigma*—had small leaves, and its branches came from a large and very tall trunk, upon which, as an epiphyte, it had originally grown. It spread over an immense area. Flight succeeded flight amidst its wide branches, but we had to wait patiently until a bird showed itself clear to be able to shoot. If one fell the others paid no attention. Many shots were fired without any effect, on account of the great height of the branches, which were for the most part beyond the range of our guns. The birds which frequented these trees were mostly of brilliant colours; amongst them several species of barbet abounded (*Chotorea, Xantholæma,* and *Calorhamphus*), of which we were able to collect many specimens.

There may be exceptions, indeed, possibly many, but it appears to me that birds which frequent the forests of tropical countries and feed mostly on brightly coloured fruits, have a brilliant plumage in which bright yellow and red predominate. Green is also a frequent colour in the plumage of these birds; and perhaps it was originally not merely assumed in defensive mimicry, but as a sort of instinctive sympathy with the surrounding predominant tint.

---

[1] "*Kayu*" means tree in Malay, and is prefixed to the specific name of any kind. The words *Bunga* (flower), *Bua* (fruit), *Akar* (root or liana), are preposed in a similar manner.

Fig. 3.—VIEW IN THE GARDENS OF THE ASTANA, KUCHING.

The Mattang mountain, which I could see clothed in its mantle of green each day from our verandah, was an irresistible attraction to me, and I decided to climb its heights as soon as possible. The Tuan Muda told me that it was no easy task, as in that direction no pathway led through the forest, which was stated to extend for nearly ten miles over low and marshy land, and thus to be most difficult to cross. At the time we did not know that by following certain winding estuaries hidden amongst the mangroves it was possible to reach the foot of the mountain in a canoe. I had suggested to the Tuan Muda to have a pathway laid down by Dyaks. Meanwhile, on the morning of July 9th, with Tuan-ku Yassim and a few Malays, I decided to attempt to explore the forest beyond Siul. We only took our guns and provisions for a meal in the forest. I had already several times travelled the road between Kuching and Siul, and was pretty certain that no important novelty could cause me to delay on the way. But beyond Siul all was unknown country, not only to me, but also to the Tuan-ku, although he lived so near.

We rounded Siul—at whose foot, in several places, the forest had been thinned, and a fine tree-fern, *Alsophila contaminans*, had multiplied—but we soon entered the primeval forest, and then, compass in hand, made our way towards the Mattang mountains, steering for the higher peak, the bearing of which I got by sending one of my men to the top of a tree. The forest could hardly have been wilder and denser. It is possible that Malays or Dyaks had previously gone into it in search of gutta-percha or rotangs, but no trace of any path could be seen, nor that human feet had ever trodden its soil. Even the Malays, however, rarely attempt to penetrate the primeval forest beyond a mile or two from the river banks. The ground was at first rising and dry, and the spaces between the forest giants were covered with young specimens of these big trees, and by an immense and varied host of other plants which could not emulate the latter in the struggle for existence. On the ground lay enormous prostrate trunks which in a few years, or, it may be, in a few months, were once more to give back to the soil that which during hundreds of years they had taken from it. In such a forest our progress was very slow ; obstacles had to be avoided, and we had to cut our way through with parangs. I had early laid aside my European hunting-knife, and had adopted this very handy Malay weapon, which is indeed invaluable in forest travelling. We cut steadily through the intricate mass of vegetation which barred our way, the worst obstacle being the thorny leaves of the Calami (rotangs), with their whip-like appendages covered with hooked spines destructive alike to our skin and dress. In addition to cutting down the bushes and such like, one takes the precaution of bending them down in the direction to be followed—a simple plan of marking the way, but indispensable in forest travelling, to prevent getting lost. Even when such travelling is comparatively easy because the vegetation is less dense, it is prudent to keep marking the way thus. Those who have never known these forests could hardly believe how easy it is to lose oneself.

In the forest, as on the ocean, the horizon closes up behind as one progresses, with this difference, that in the forest the horizon is only a few feet distant. Forest travelling inspires greater fear than sea or desert travelling, for here the sun by day and the stars by night are sure guides. But in the Bornean primeval jungle the sky is invisible, and if a few sun-rays now and then filter through the dense foliage overhead, they are useless in telling the direction to be followed. Again, in deserts or extensive plains it is rare indeed not to find some prominent object which can be used as a sign-post to mark the way. In the forest the world appears to close in behind us, the fear of advancing grows with the thought of not being able to turn back, and the unknown generates a sense of horror. I think it very probable that many animals feel this same impression of fear and horror that man does at the thought of losing himself in a forest. And it is possibly this which causes a marked restriction in the geographical range of the forest fauna when compared with that of deserts, steppes, or plains.

During certain hours of the day a strange and impressive calm pervades the forest. Nature appears to have gone to sleep in her own domain, and hardly a sound or a cry can be heard denoting the presence of living creatures. But the Bornean forest is so varied and so different at different hours and seasons that no description can possibly convey an adequate idea of it to those who have not known it. Infinite and ever changing are its aspects, as are the treasures it hides. Its beauties are as inexhaustible as the variety of its productions. In the forest, man feels singularly free. The more one wanders in it the greater grows the sense of profound admiration before Nature in one of its grandest aspects. The more one endeavours to study it, the more one finds in it to study. Its deep shades are sacred to the devotee of Science. Yet they afford ample food for the mind of the believer, not less than to that of the philosopher.

We proceeded slowly, compass in hand, through the forest, thinking we had made more progress than was actually the case. The marshy nature of the ground and the matted vegetation of rotangs, screw-pines, Mapania, and other big herbaceous plants with spinous leaves, greatly hampered our movements. In these localities *Nepenthes rafflesiana* is frequently met with—one of those singular pitcher-plants for which Borneo is renowned, with large, blood-stained ampullæ filled with water, depending from a thread at the extremities of the leaves.

We had left Siul about three hours when we reached a slightly rising ground covered with a vegetation different from that of the surrounding forest, and especially marked by the presence of two conifers, *Dacrydium elatum* and the umbrella casuarina (*C. sumatrana* ?), besides other shrubs, trees, and ferns which we had not met with previously in the forest, even a few paces off. The Malays name such patches of different vegetation " *Mattang*," and consider them sacred and inhabited by spirits. There are several of them in the neighbourhood of Kuching. One of the ferns always to be found on the mattang is the lovely *Polypodium dipteris*, Bl., and *Nepenthes* are also often met with.

Our progress was almost immediately after this arrested by a watercourse ten or fifteen yards wide and very deep, with singularly dark brown water. On this mattang the trees were less lofty than elsewhere, and the shade, on account of the peculiar foliage of the conifers just mentioned, less dark. The Tuan-ku climbed up a tree, helping himself with a liana, and was thus able to see that we had hitherto followed the right direction, but also that we had hardly got through one third of the distance. We had travelled at the rate of rather over half a mile an hour !

It was near noon, and we took advantage of the dry spot to eat our rice. To push on farther was difficult, for we had to find a means of crossing the stream. My object was, however, in a measure attained, and I had seen enough of the forest to know the sort of difficulties I had to contend with in crossing it. Big streams could hardly be met with ; most probably the one we had seen was the biggest, and this could easily be got over by cutting down one of the trees growing on its banks, so as to make it fall across and act as a bridge. We accordingly turned homewards, laden with a large collection of botanical specimens. Many, however, I had to leave ungathered, it being difficult to reach them ; but these were all noted and destined for collection at some future day, and the completion of my rapidly increasing herbarium.

CHAPTER II

HAVING decided on a prolonged stay in Sarawak, and finding
that Kuching formed an excellent centre whence excursions
could be made in all directions, we took measures to set up house
for ourselves, not wishing to encroach too much on the Tuan Muda's
kind hospitality. We engaged a Chinese cook and a "tukang
ayer," or water-carrier, who was also a Chinaman, and each of
us engaged besides a Malay "boy," or body-servant. Mine was
named Ismael; Doria's, Kassim. We also bought a sampan, or
boat, in order to be able to cross the river whenever we desired,
and hired two Malay boatmen. In addition to these, I had to engage
several men to fell trees when in blossom, this being the only way
of getting botanical specimens of such nature.

In Sarawak the different trades and professions are in the
hands of persons of various nationalities. The best carpenters
and smiths are Chinese, who, it must be said, do many kinds of
work. Thus the principal merchants, vendors of eatables, cooks,
tailors, water-carriers, and porters are all Chinese. The Malays,
true seamen, do the fishing and small maritime trade ; they are
also woodsmen, felling trees and preparing timber, and exploring
the forest in search of its natural products—rotangs, resins, guttapercha, india-rubber, oil-seeds, etc. The washermen, the hair-
dressers for Europeans (tukang chukor), tinkers, and a few
merchants and shopkeepers, are Hindus or Klings.

The best agriculturists in Sarawak are again Chinese; but the
European residents mostly employ as gardeners Javanese and
the already-mentioned Orang Boyan, and Klings (natives of the
Malabar coast), who also act as cow-keepers, taking charge of
the few head of cattle, mostly milch cows, which the country can
boast of. I often admired the splendid pigs bred by Chinese,
who certainly excel in the art of fattening these animals. Amongst
other food they give them an aquatic plant, the so-called water-
lettuce (*Pistia stratiotes*), grown purposely·in swamps and pools,
and boiled.

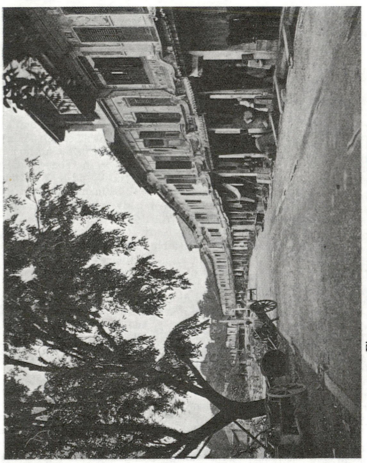

Fig. 4.—THE CHINESE KAMPONG IN KUCHING.

At present the mixed population of Sarawak does not amalgamate, and each minds his own business, looks after his special trade, and professes his own religion. But in time it is hardly possible that no mixture should take place in this heterogeneous assemblage. The Chinese population keeps quite distinct, and especially so from the Malays, partly on account of religious antipathy, and partly because there is a constant immigration of new elements. Otherwise the Chinese mix easily with other people, for they can get only few of their own women, and must therefore intermarry with the natives of the land where they have come to settle. They are beyond doubt the most active, industrious, laborious, and enterprising element in the population of Sarawak; and, foremost in the inveterate vice of opium-smoking, cause more money to circulate than the more sober Malay. They are thus in every way a source of considerable revenue to the local government.

The *Orang Malayu*, or Malays of Borneo, like those settled on the coasts of the Malayan peninsula and of the Indian Archipelago generally, are the result of very different ethnic elements. Every individual who qualifies himself as an *Orang Malayu* is a Mussulman, and speaks Malay. The Mussulmans of Sarawak all belong to the " Sunni," or orthodox sect, and the aristocracy amongst them, the chiefs and their families, show Arab descent. The fact that the Malays are Mussulmans is plain evidence that the Arabs were the original introducers of the religion of Mahomet in these lands.

It appears that Arabs were formerly more numerous in Sarawak than they are at present, and there can be no doubt of the very great influence they have exerted on the littoral populations of Borneo.[1] Low writes that the Arab Sareib-Saib, his brother Sareib-Mulla, and their relations, often used to send parties of Sea-Dyaks into the interior to carry off as many young women of the Land-Dyaks as they could get. It is said that in one such raid as many as 300 were carried off.

And again, these very Arabs who came to settle in Borneo were doubtless by no means always of pure descent, and the blood of negroes and other races probably flowed in their veins. For do not all tradesmen and merchants, from Zanzibar to the Persian Gulf, who profess Islamism call themselves Arabs, and often give themselves the title of " Sareib " or " Seriff," pretending to be descendants of the Prophet ?

This shows how dangerous it is in Borneo to take one of the headmen or chiefs as an ethnic type of a given tribe, as they are often of foreign origin. For instance, it is well known that on the Seribas river the chiefs are nearly all of Arab descent. On

---

[1] Low. *Sarawak: Its Inhabitants and Productions*, pp. 118, 119-23.

the other hand, even the common people in Borneo, on account of prevalent piracy, raids, and slavery, must necessarily be greatly mixed. On large continents and with great masses of population such causes can only act slowly and moderately in changing the general aspect of the people ; but in Borneo, where the population is small and surrounded by different elements, the case is different, and raids and piracy are factors which have to be taken into con-

Fig. 5.—INCHE BAKAR, CLERK AT THE COURT OF JUSTICE (MALAY)
DATU IMAUN, HEAD OF THE MOSQUE AT KUCHING (OF ARAB ORIGIN)
HADJI SUDEN, MEMBER OF COUNCIL, KUCHING (PARTLY ARAB).
(Reading from Left to Right.)

sideration. In such countries, where slavery exists, and more especially where a dominant and superior race is in contact with an inferior one, the ethnic type is soon modified, for the progeny becomes part of the family, and the descendants interbreed.

Returning to the foreign elements which have contributed to form the present Malay population of Sarawak, I may quote Mr.

St. John, who tells us that when the town of Kuching was located nearer the sea at Santubong, it was attacked by a fleet of Pegu pirates, who carried off all the women, the majority of the men being absent on an expedition.[1] But the latter returned in time to pursue the ravishers, and their swift boats quickly overtook the heavy prahus of the Peguans, who were soon defeated and captured. Thus the Malays not only recovered their women, but carried back to Sarawak as slaves the Pegu pirates, with the exception of the chiefs, who were slain. In Sarawak there is still a tradition that some of the Malays of Samarahan, and also of Kuching, are descendants of these Peguans.

It is also undeniable that a certain proportion of the Malays of Sarawak and other parts of Borneo came originally from Sumatra, and from the Malay Peninsula. But the Malays of Malacca, who are considered typical and of pure descent, must undoubtedly have been influenced by the geographical position of the peninsula, along which the people of India, Burma, Siam, and Cochinchina would naturally pass on their way to the islands of the Indian Archipelago.

Sarawak, before being ceded to Sir James Brooke by Rajah Muda Hassim, was one of the principal provinces of the kingdom of Bruni. Thus besides the Arab Sareibs, who, under the cloak of religious hypocrisy, managed to domineer the native population, there were the nobles, or "Pangerangs," of Bruni, who emulated the Sareibs in fleecing the Land-Dyaks and in carrying off their women.

It appears that the Pangerangs of Bruni are the descendants of Mussulman chieftains who came originally from Malacca, and settled at Bruni with the spread of Islamism. But it is believed that the kingdom of Bruni was originally founded by Chinese, and it is asserted that in its capital at the end of the eighteenth century there were no less than 30,000 Chinamen, mostly pepper planters. At present the true Chinese at Bruni are few; but it cannot be doubted that the native population there must have been ethnologically modified by so large an immigration from China. St. John (*Op. cit.* I., p. 290) further asserts that in North Borneo many natives of the Philippine Islands are to be seen ; they were originally captured by the Lanuns and Balignini, sold as slaves, and eventually married native women. Moreover, in the case of a very large island like Borneo, with its peculiar geographical position, it is not enough to take into consideration events which have happened in recent and historical periods, but possible immigrations in remote times must not be overlooked. However, even allowing only for what we know has taken place during the last four or five centuries, one cannot

[1] ST. JOHN. *Life in the Forests of the Far East*, I., p. 126. London, 1862.

speak of the natives of Borneo, and especially of the Malays, in a general way, as unities. Thus Sukadana, Banjarmasin, and, some say, Sarawak (Low, *Op. cit.* p. 94), are Javanese settlements; Pasir and Koti, on the east coast have been peopled by Bugis from Celebes. At Sambas and Pontianak the Arabs predominated, not to mention a large Chinese element and their descendants through unions with Dyak women who for many generations have washed for gold in that region.

The Malays of Borneo, who inhabit the coast and are given to commerce, are thus, I hold, to be considered as the outcome of an ancient and long-continued fusion of numerous and very different ethnic elements, principally Hindus, Burmese, Chinese, Siamese, and Annamites, with a marked infusion of Arab blood, to say nothing of other factors resulting from piratical expeditions, slavery, and the importation of women robbed from other native tribes.

It is not easy to say what race of mankind originally peopled Borneo in remote antiquity; but it is in my opinion not improbable that the Negroid [1] race was spread over all Southern Asia and the numerous dependent islands in the distant past. Of this race more or less unaltered remains are to be found in the Andamanese, and in the Aetas or Negritos of the Philippines; and —less pure—in the Samangs and other Selangian tribes of the Malay Peninsula. The very dark skin and the curly hair of many natives of India are, I think, traces of what remains in them of the Negroid element after the Aryan invasions.

In conclusion, I believe that any Malay submitted to an analytical investigation of an anthropological nature will be found to be the outcome of an amalgamation of various ethnic types. And it is for this reason that I regard them as a secondary, much mixed, and hybrid race.

From what we have seen, then, regarding the origin of the Malays of Sarawak, it is plain that their physical characters must be equally varied, and that it is not easy to give a good comprehensive ethnological description of their appearance. Certain characteristics, however, are pretty constant. They have little or no beard, but when they manage to grow a few hairs with a faint semblance to a moustache they cultivate them with great care, and are very proud of them. It may be said of the Malays that their skin is brown, and that they never have a prominent nose, it being usually depressed. Their eyes are often straight, but as often oblique, like those of the Chinese; the cheek-bones are prominent, the chin is small, the lips regular but full. Their hair is very black and smooth, but, as they generally wear it short

[1] This term, which I consider most appropriate, was first proposed by Professor Henry H. Giglioli.

or very closely shaven, the head is always covered with a piece of cloth variously folded, or, in the case of those of Arab origin, with a turban, the rest of the costume being likewise Arab. The true Malay dress consists of a short jacket or baju, often of silk, and more or less embroidered, and short trousers (*sloár*). The latter might be thought a modern fashion derived from European influence. It appears, however, that this kind of nether garment for men is very ancient in Asia, for in the sculptures of the ancient temples of Boro Budor in Java[1] (Fig. 6) a costume of this nature

Fig. 6.—MAN WEARING THE *Sloar*, OR BREECHES.
(From the Sculptures at the Temple of Boro Budor in Java.)

is represented. Besides the above-mentioned articles of dress, the Malays wear a sarong wrapped round the waist and secured in front ; it supports a kris or dagger, which is always worn. At the present day, Western civilisation has a continual tendency to change the style of dress of the Borneo Malays, as in the past Hindu culture imported amongst even the wilder people of the Indian Archipelago not only the style of dress and ornaments of India, but most of the religious beliefs, superstitions, folklore, industries, and art notions which they now possess.

The sarong is used by both sexes. It is put on in many ways,

[1] LEEMANS. *Boro Boudour dans l'Île de Java*, p. 616.

and can be a substitute for trousers, petticoats, shirt, and waist-cloth, or even serves as a sheet or a bathing costume. Its use is widely spread in Southern Asia and all over the Malay Archipelago (Fig. 7). For women, the sarong is an essential article of dress; they usually wear it as a skirt or petticoat, held by a belt round the waist. Besides the sarong, the wealthy ladies of Kuching wear a sort of chemise of cambric or of coloured silk, whilst on their head an embroidered scarf surrounds the face, recalling the head-dress of certain nuns, and falls down the back. It would take too long to give a minute description of the variations and details

Fig. 7.—WOMAN WEARING *Sarong*.
(From the Boro Budor Sculptures.)

of the toilette of the Sarawak ladies, who also much affect both gold and silver jewellery, which they love to display on every occasion.

The women of Kuching have beautiful black hair, and their complexion is much lighter than that of the men, but the nose is somewhat more flattened. There is, however, a certain vari-ability in the type, a fact which can easily be explained by what I have previously stated regarding the piratical habits formerly practised by the natives of Kuching.

CHAPTER III

The Fruits of Sarawak—The Mangosteen and its Habitat—Origin of Cultivated Fruits—The Pinang—Our Menagerie—Monkeys—The Nasalis and the Shape of the Nose in Man—Birds in Captivity—Snakes—Fascinated Frogs—The Flying Lizard—Flying Animals—The Mammals of Borneo—Big Game in Sarawak.

ON the hill where the former residence of Rajah Brooke used to stand, and in the park around his present residence, are grown most of the cultivated fruit-trees of Malaysia. The Rajah had also endeavoured to introduce various kinds of plants which might, if acclimatised, have proved a source of wealth to the country; amongst these were the nutmeg, the cinnamon, and the cacao. Most of the characteristic fruit-trees were not then in blossom; such, for example, as the durian, rambutan, lansat and mango. We were, however, still able to get some mangosteens, the fruit of *Garcinia mangostana* (Fig. 8), and one of the most delicious within the tropics. It is rarely to be found beyond the limits of the Malayan Islands. Even in Borneo its cultivation is limited. The Malays call it "Manggis," and the Land-Dyaks, "Sekup." The true native land of the mangosteen is unknown. It is true that in Borneo several wild species of *Garcinia* are found, not unlike the mangosteen, and some with edible fruits, but they are always sour. The mangosteen is beyond doubt a native of the Malayan region, but nowhere yet has it been found growing wild. It has been asserted, but without proof, that its native land, like that of the durian, is the Malay Peninsula. The latter tree also is only known as a cultivated species.

Has the sea overwhelmed the land where these originated, or are they still to be found growing wild in some remote forest ? Or, on the other hand, may they not have been produced by cultivation ? But, if the latter hypothesis be true, what is the parental stock from which they have been obtained ? It seems to me probable that certain cultivated plants—wheat, amongst others—have been so long cared for by man that they cannot exist or multiply without his protection. Such plants, I consider, are united to man by a kind of symbiosis, so that they can only be found where he is and can ensure their existence. In the wild state now they cannot, in their modified condition, hold their own in the struggle with destructive agents.

In virtue of its delicious flavour, the mangosteen heads the list of the edible fruits of the tropical world. It is of the size and shape of a small orange. When ripe its skin, or rather rind, is smooth, and of a dark purple or vinous colour. To get at the edible part this rind must be cut through all round. The inner layer of it is nearly half an inch thick, and is highly astringent, containing, probably, a large proportion of tannin. If one has taken

Fig. 8.—FRUIT OF THE MANGOSTEEN, *Garcinia Mangostana* (⅔ NAT. SIZE).

care to cut through to the right depth, the upper half of the rind can be detached, leaving uncovered a central white, glittering mass composed of 5–6 segments, like the " pigs " of an orange. Each of these consists of a seed surrounded by an abundant white, juicy pulp; soft, sweet, slightly acidulated, and with a delicate, delicious flavour, which recalls that of a fine peach, muscatel grapes, and something peculiar and indescribable which no other fruit has.

All the year round ripe soursops (*Anona muricata*) can be obtained at Kuching. They are big heart-shaped fruits, green outside, with a white, juicy flesh, which is very agreeable to the palate. The papaw (*Carica papaya*) is also a perennial fruiter, and grows almost spontaneously in gardens and about houses ; its fruit is not unlike a melon, but less highly flavoured. Both these are of American origin, as are also the sweetsop (*Anona squamata*) and the custard-apple (*Anona reticulata*), both of which grow to perfection in Sarawak.

Of bananas there are many varieties; pineapples are also always to be seen in the market, where, in its season, they also bring for sale the gigantic fruit of the Jack-tree (*Artocarpus integrifolia*).

The coconut palm is found everywhere, but the larvæ of an insect pest (*Rhynchophorus ferrugineus*) damage it greatly at Kuching. There are some plantations in a more flourishing condition on the sandy beaches of the small islands off the coast, but most of the coconuts used in Sarawak are imported from the Natuna Islands.

The *Areca catechu*, or "pinang," is perhaps in strict parlance not a fruit-tree, because its nuts are not eaten, but merely chewed, as all know. It is to the Malay what the camel is to the Arab: it has followed him in all his wanderings. It may be safely asserted that there is not a Malay hut near which at least one of these most elegant of palms is not seen growing Fig. 9). Like the mangosteen, it belongs to that series of cultivated plants whose origin is a mystery.[1] But there can be no doubt that the habit of chewing it, together with *siri*, or betel leaves, and lime, has spread from tropical Asia to the Indian Archipelago, and thence eastwards across Melanesia to Polynesia. In Borneo the pinang nuts have a part in various rites and ceremonies of the Malays and Dyaks. The areca palm itself has often inspired the poetic sentiments of Malay writers, and its flowers are much appreciated by the women for their fragrance. Amongst the Lingga Dyaks and the Balu the marriage ceremony is preceded by that called "*Bla Pinang*," which means the division of areca nuts.

To grow to perfection the pinang requires a rich, somewhat damp soil, moist atmosphere, and a perennial high temperature. Its foliage is always a fresh green, for when a frond is old its immense leaf-sheath splits all down and falls, carrying the frond with it. The tree, therefore, never shows any dried or withered part, but is always in fine condition ; its slender, elegant trunk, straight and smooth

---

[1] The fruit of the areca does not stand in need of human protection, for it does not appear to be eaten by animals. Nevertheless, the tree is not found in a wild state. But although its fruit is not sought after as food, its heart or "cabbage" is so excellent, besides being totally unprotected by spines, that in the forest it would probably soon be devoured, and the death of the palm ensue. Its existence may thus be said indirectly to depend on human protection. Among all the wild species of areca found in the East Indies, the Malay Peninsula, Sumatra, Borneo, the Philippines, etc., that which in its botanic character is closest to the domestic form is the *Areca concinna* of Ceylon. This would seem to indicate that the native country of the pinang must have once been that area which connected Ceylon and the Malay peninsula ; a region of which the Andaman and Nicobar islands may be considered the last remnants. The same may be said for the durian and mangosteen, both of which may also have had their origin on lands now submerged.

as an arrow, is generally of a grey colour, caused by the lichens which grow on it.[1]

Most of the plants and fruit-trees I have mentioned do not grow in and about Kuching with that vigour which the luxuriance of the neighbouring forest would lead one to expect. The soil of the low hills on which Kuching is built, and also that of the adjoining land, is formed of white or yellowish clays, and is far from fertile —which one would hardly suspect, or, indeed, think possible, considering the giant proportions attained by trees on the same area before the forest was cleared. The explanation probably lies in the fact that the forest trees depend mostly for their growth not on the soil formed by the decomposition of rocks, but on the vegetable humus, the result of centuries of accumulation.

The first months of our stay in Sarawak passed rapidly ; many and varied occupations made the time seem short. It was with difficulty that I found time to prepare and dry the numerous plants which I collected daily in the adjacent forest. The number of species

---

[1] In Borneo I found foliaceous lichens excessively rare ; most of those which I collected there, about 140 in number, were encrusting species, which blend with the bark on which they grow. They were principally *Graphideæ, Thelotrema, Ascidineæ* and *Verrucaria.* (Cf. KREMPELHUBER. *Lichenes quos legit O. Beccari in Insulis Borneo,* etc., in *Nuovo Giornale Bot. Ital.,* 1875, p. 6.) A large portion of these lichens were found by me in the grounds of Government House on the trunks of arecas, coconut palms, orange, and shaddock trees. It appears, therefore, that, in Sarawak, trees with a smooth bark, in open localities with plenty of light, are best adapted to support lichens ; for in the shady forest they are much less frequent on tree trunks, but abound, together with various Fungi and Jungermannias, on the leaves of low-growing species. The reason of this predilection shown by lichens for the smooth bark of trees growing in the more open spaces is, I suspect, to be sought in the greater facility of the condensation of aqueous vapour on certain surfaces in preference to others. The non-porous, smooth, and compact surface of the bark on the trunks of coconuts, arecas, and orange trees growing in the open, which becomes much heated during the day, radiates greatly at night, and, in cooling, causes the aqueous vapour with which the atmosphere is laden to condense in abundance. This moisture remains, moreover, better on these smooth barks than on those of a cork-like or porous nature, far less good conductors of heat, and more easily absorbing the aqueous vapour. A smooth and non-porous bark may be compared with a rock, on which encrusting lichens flourish well ; for these organisms require periods of moisture, alternating with seasons of drought, in well-lighted localities, rather than an excess of moisture of a continuous nature in shady places. I imagine that such is the reason why many epiphytes, and amongst them orchids, prefer to take root on naked smooth-barked trees, often in the highest and most exposed parts, where at first sight one would think that their seeds must find great difficulty in germinating. Smooth and coriaceous leaves must likewise condense the aqueous vapour of the air much more easily than leaves which are hairy and soft in texture ; and it is for these reasons, perhaps, that a large number of Hepaticæ, and both encrusting and foliaceous lichens, are often found on the upper surface of such leaves in the low-lying parts of the Malayan forests.

Fig. 9.—THE SARAWAK RIVER FROM THE ASTANA GARDENS.
(Areca palms, *Areca catechu*, in foreground.)

appeared inexhaustible, and many of them—I may say several hundreds—turned out later to be new to science. Doria, on his part, brought home insects, birds, and other animals which his Persian taxidermist Kerim had to skin and prepare. But even the Malays had begun to understand our work, and they often brought us animals, usually alive.

In a short time we had thus got together a fine series of skins and a goodly collection of live animals. Amongst the latter were several " plandoks " (*Tragulus napu*), one of the most diminutive species of the chevrotain tribe. We fed them on the flowers of the Simpor, botanically, *Dillinia suffruticosa*, of which we had an abundance close to the house. The plandok is an extremely timid creature, with eyes so large and beautiful that *mata plandok* (Tragulus-eyed) is an endearing expression used by Malay lovers in praise of the lady of their affections.

Another singular creature which we fed with no great trouble on bananas is the " kongkang " of the Malays (*Nycticebus tardigradus*), one of the lemurs. It is a nocturnal animal, and sleeps all day long with its head between its legs. The Malays regard it with superstition, and believe it to possess various supernatural attributes. It certainly is a weird-looking creature. We had also several " tangling " of the Malays, the singular scaly anteater (*Manis javanica*) ; as well as viverras or " munsangs," wild cats or palm-civets (*Paradoxurus*), and a lot of monkeys, of which there is no lack in Sarawak. These we kept tied up to the bars of the verandah.

The " krah " and the " berok " or " bruk " of the Malays (*Macacus cynomolgus* and *M. nemestrinus*), which of all the Bornean monkeys are most tolerant of captivity, often came in large parties to the trees along the river close to our house. The latter is tamed by the natives and taught to gather coconuts.

The " bidgit " and the " lotong " of the Malays (*Semnopithecus frontatus* and *S. femoralis*), and the " wa-wa," an anthropoid (*Hylobates mülleri*), are also very frequent about Kuching. The latter is, of course, tailless, of a dark grey colour, with soft fur, a small round face, and immensely long arms. In the mornings the adjoining forest echoed with its singular and characteristic call. It is so strange a sound that for a long while I could not believe that it came from a monkey ; it was to me more like the loud harmonious cry of some large bird. It consists of the syllables *wa-wa* many times repeated with great force, dropping in tone and increasing in rapidity. The wa-wa thrives fairly well in captivity, feeding on fruit and boiled rice or " nassi " ; which, strange to say, was eagerly taken by all the animals we kept in our menagerie, whether frugivorous or carnivorous. The wa-wa certainly might excusably be credited with carnivorous propensities to judge by the great development of its canine teeth. It moves with astonishing rapidity from tree to tree,

swinging itself along at such a pace when frightened that it gives
one the impression of a flying mammal.   Apart from the orang
utan,[1] of which at first we were unable to obtain specimens, the
most singular of the Quadrumana in Borneo is the long-nosed ape
(*Nasalis larvatus*), a large species with reddish fur, and of most singular
and ridiculous aspect.   It is, with the exception of the rare and little
known *Rhinopithecus* of Mupin, the only monkey which possesses a
prominent nose, a peculiarity which has struck the fancy of the
Malays, who have given it the nickname of orang blanda, or Dutch-
man (Fig. 10).   A very young specimen which I kept alive was the

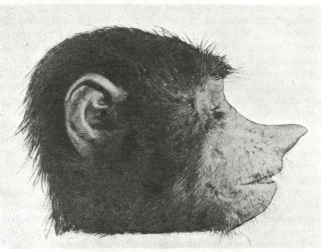

Fig. 10.—HEAD OF PROBOSCIS MONKEY, *Nasalis larvatus*.

funniest of comic creatures, with a long nose as pink as that of a
child, but bigger in proportion than that of a full-grown man.
I had often met with this curious creature on the big trees
along the river near the town, feeding on the fruits of the " *Kayu
peddada*," botanically, *Sonneratia lanceolata*, for which they have a
special predilection, and which, indeed, form their principal food.
During the daytime they keep to the shelter of the jungle, but towards evening they usually approach the river, where they find an
abundance of their favourite food, and usually prefer to pass the
night.
     Why amongst all apes, with the sole exception above mentioned,
this one should alone be provided with a long, prominent, and fleshy

[1] " Utan " in Malay means " wood ;" thus " Orang-utan " means " man
of the woods," or " wild man."

nose, somewhat hooked at its extremity, it is, indeed, difficult to say. According to the Darwinian theory, it might possibly be attributed to sexual selection. If such were the case, we might, perhaps, congratulate this monkey on its good taste. The nose is, no doubt, an important feature in mankind, and furnishes important racial characters as well as individual distinctions ; but as far as I am aware no one has hitherto sought for an explanation of the very various shapes which it assumes. As it can scarcely be admitted that mere sexual selection has influenced the shape and length of the nose, we must suppose that its modification can only be due to use. But it is not easy to determine what external stimuli can have caused such modifications of the organ. Defence of the respiratory passages against the introduction of foreign particles may be one cause ; i.e., the phagocytic action against pathogenic microorganisms floating in the air. Again, special sensorial stimuli may have come into play tending to the extension of the sensorial surface. Analogous causes (i.e., the direction in which such sensorial functions are brought into action) may have influenced the position of the opening of the nostrils. As a case in point it is worthy of note that races of men who have lived from time immemorial in open countries, for instance the Semitic people, are furnished with prominent noses having narrow nostrils directed downwards ; whilst Negroes and Malays, for the most part dwellers in the forest, have snub noses with wide nostrils turned upwards, such as characterise most monkeys. It may be further noted that in the human race nasal development has progressed from the equator towards Central Asia, where it appears to have reached its maximum of development.

Considering the very large number of species of birds which live in the Bornean forests, it was remarkable how few were brought to us alive. The " burong siúl " (*Rollulus rouloul*)—" burong " means bird in Malay—was one of the few we got. It thrives easily in captivity, and is a handsome species about the size of a partridge, of fine dark coloration, a deep sheeny green and chestnut brown predominating ; the cock has a curious crest of purplish brown feathers. But the best cage-bird is undoubtedly the mynah (*Gracula javanensis*), a general favourite, which easily learns entire phrases, imitating the human voice far better than parrots do. Doria and I brought back from Sarawak some 800 bird-skins, representing 226 species. This collection has formed the basis of a book by Count T. Salvadori on the avifauna of Borneo, being vol. ii. of the *Annali del Museo Civico di Genova*. In this work no less than 392 species are described, but the learned author writes to me that the known species of birds of this great island are now double the number of those enumerated in 1874, when his work was published. It is, however, a strange but true fact that the Bornean avifauna has few forms which are peculiar to it and which give it a marked physi-

ognomy, as do the Paradiseidæ to New Guinea. Most of the Bornean
birds, even permanent residents, are found in the neighbouring
islands (especially in Sumatra), or in the Malay Peninsula ; whilst
several of those not found elsewhere only differ in minor characters
from allied species living on neighbouring islands.

Not unfrequently our hunters and collectors would bring us
snakes, mostly living, and suspended by a slip-knot to a stick.
These usually met their fate in a jar of spirits, but some of them
were sufficiently large to render the operation a little embarrassing.
One day a Malay brought me a " chinchin mas " [1] (*Dipsas dendrophila*
of zoologists), an entirely black species, with yellow rings ; it was a
fine specimen, about six feet in length. This species frequents
trees by the riverside, or the mangroves, and it is not uncommon for
specimens to drop into a passing sampan, for it has a habit of resting half-twisted on overhanging branches, easily shaken by a passing
boat. The natives assert that it is poisonous. When I handle
snakes, whether poisonous or not, I always hold them by the neck
between the thumb and index finger of the right hand, for thus held
they cannot possibly bite. When putting them in spirits I take
care to have a jar with a wide mouth of adequate size ready, and
introduce the snake, held as I have stated, tail foremost. In the left
hand I hold the stopper of the jar, and when the body of the snake
is well in I drop the head, and with a rapid movement close the jar.
In performing this operation on the above-mentioned " chinchin
mas "—a very lively specimen—the moment I let go the head I
distinctly saw it emit with some force two fine jets of liquid from
the mouth, just as a poisonous snake might do. On another occasion I had quite a struggle with an " ular sawa," a species of python,
small of its kind but exceedingly vigorous. I had it as usual by the
nape and was going to pot it, when it twisted itself with such
force round my arm that I was obliged to call one of my men to my
assistance to free myself from its coils. We kept several pythons
alive, and one escaped and remained hidden for some weeks in a
neighbouring house, where I found it. When not too big these
snakes are quite harmless, and may even be considered useful, for
they are kept in houses, where they do excellent service in destroying
rats. One day I caught one of these big snakes in a singular manner.
Our cook was in the habit of keeping a few live fowls in a cage in a
corner of the kitchen, a small separate hut a few yards from the
bungalow and level with the ground. On going to fetch a fowl he
was surprised to find in its stead a large python, which, having entered
the cage through the bars, had swallowed the fowl and coiled itself
up on the spot for quiet digestion. Even had it wished to leave
the cage it could no longer have done so, having considerably increased in girth. A similar tale is told of a bigger python, which,

[1] Anglice, " gold ring."

having got through the bars of a pigstye, swallowed the pig and could no longer get out. The Malays assert that the biggest of these snakes are capable of swallowing a deer, after having well reduced it in size by crushing it in their coils, and lubricated it with abundant saliva. The horns may for some days remain projecting from the mouth of the serpent, but even these eventually manage to pass. Pythons of ordinary dimensions are very plentiful in Sarawak, and account for many domestic fowls and their eggs ; in this, however, they have a competitor in the " biawak," a big lizard (*Monitor bivittatus*), which is very common, and often exceeds a yard in length. On one occasion whilst at Singapore I saw the remains of a gigantic python : a Chinaman passed by the verandah where I was, carrying in two big baskets the transverse sections of the animal's body, some of them quite equal in diameter to a man's thigh. The Tuan Muda spoke of a python which he caught, measuring just 19 feet in length, which had a monkey in its stomach ; and St. John mentions another killed at Bruni, which was over twenty-nine feet (8 mètres, 91 centim.) long. The Malays talk of specimens 7 "*depa*"[1] in length, which would be about 38 ft. 6 in., but I do not believe that in Sarawak well-authenticated cases of pythons exceeding 20 feet have ever been recorded.

Amongst the snakes I often kept alive I may mention the " ular bunga," or flower-snake (*Tragops prasinus*), a long, slender, elegant creature of a brilliant green, which is said to be tameable. Another species which was common in the meadows around our residence was *Dendrophis prasinus*, which is rarely more than three feet in length and as thick as one's finger. It frequents swampy places and feeds on frogs, which it catches by fascinating them. I once witnessed an instance of this myself. Being on our verandah one day, I was attracted by a persistent and strange croaking emitted by some frogs in a small streamlet a few paces from where I stood. I went to see what was the cause, and found a frog, of a species common around Kuching, which was uttering most lamentable sounds. Hardly a hand's breadth from it was a snake with erected head, staring at it and quite motionless. The frog was also quite still, poised upright on its hind legs, the front legs being extended, and with one jump it might have escaped, but it remained as if hypnotised, and fell an immediate prey to its enemy. But I avenged the poor victim immediately after, killing the snake with a smart blow from a thin stick across its back. This is an excellent method of capturing small snakes without danger, and without spoiling them as specimens. I found that a shot in the head with a small charge of dust-shot was the best way of dealing with large snakes.

Some of the Bornean reptiles produce singular sounds. The com-

[1] A " *depa* " is about 5 ft. 6 in., and is the distance between the tips of the fingers, holding the arms extended.

monest amongst them is a gecko, the " chichak," which name imitates
perfectly the cry it produces ; and at Government House they could
be heard and seen every evening chasing moths attracted by the
lights on the ceiling of the dining room. Some fell on the table, nearly
always at the expense of their very fragile tail.   A much louder and
more characteristic cry is that of *Goniocephalus borneensis*, a large
lizard which lives on trees and has a high and serrated crest down
its back.   The Malays call this lizard " kog-go," an imitation of
its call-note, which is frequently repeated. The cry of this species,
like that of the wa-wa, is so singular that one can hardly believe
that it is not produced by some bird ; and it is one of those,
with others even more frequent of the cicadas and hornbills, that
most impress the traveller who is not yet accustomed to their daily
occurrence.

   Several poisonous snakes are found in Borneo, amongst others
the *Trigonocephalus wagleri*, of which the Malays assert that the
potency of its poison is such, that when a person is bitten by it he
has not even time to take off his jacket before falling dead.   In
Kuching the cobra (*Naja tripudians*) is found, but it is not common.
As a matter of fact, during my whole stay in Borneo I never once
heard of a death caused by snake-bite.[1]

   Amongst the various small reptiles which we were able to collect
in our neighbourhood the most singular were the flying lizards (*Draco*),
the " belalang sumbak " of the Malays.   These surprising little
creatures can be seen at any moment during the hot hours of the
day flying through the air from one palm tree to another by the aid
of the membranous expansion with which the sides of their bodies
are provided.   When they take their spring they start with the
head downwards ; when they reach their destination they alight
with the head upwards. We used to get these flying lizards with
the " sumpitan " or blow-tube, of which I shall speak further on,
but instead of darts we used clay bullets.

   In Borneo there are not only flying lizards, but also flying squirrels,
flying foxes, flying frogs, and, could we believe the Malays, flying
snakes. Of the latter I have seen none, nor do I know of any such
mentioned in any scientific work.   It is not impossible, however,
that in the unexplored parts of Borneo, yet unknown to naturalists,
a tree-snake may exist capable of spreading out the skin of its sides

---

[1] The collection of reptiles formed by Doria and myself in Borneo contained eighty-eight species, of which nineteen were new to science.   They
were described by Peters and Doria in a paper published in the *Annali del
Museo Civico di Genova*, vol. iii., p. 27, pl. ii.–iv. *Genoa*, 1872.   A general list
of the Reptilia and Batrachia Anura of Borneo has been published by M. F.
Moquard in *Nouvelles Archives du Musée d'Histoire Naturelle*, 3ᵉ série,
vol. xii., p. 115. *Paris*, 1890.   The species enumerated are 204 ; of which
three are crocodiles, forty-nine lizards, 103 snakes and forty-nine frogs.

to such an extent as to form a parachute enabling it to float from one tree to another. It is well known that the cobras (*Naja*) can spread out the side skin of the fore part of the body, and could they do this lower down they would be exactly like the flying lizards, in which the skin-folds of the flanks are spread on free and lengthened ribs. I may add that not only do the Malays and Dyaks believe in the existence of flying snakes, but they have a name for them, and call them " ular teddong-kumbang." [1] It should also be mentioned that the Malays are most excellent observers of nature, and are well acquainted with all forms of forest life. I can assert on my own experience that I have never found their information in such matters without foundation.

The flying frog of Borneo (*Rhacophorus reinwardtii*) is described and figured by Wallace in his well-known book on the Malay Archipelago ; but it must be rare in that part of Borneo I visited, for I never had the good fortune to meet with it.

Besides bats and flying foxes (*Pteropus*), other flying mammals can be seen any day in Sarawak. The commonest are the flying squirrels (*Pteromys*), which I have already mentioned. But the strange *Galeopithecus volans* is also abundant, and can easily be kept in captivity. The skin expansions of this curious creature are more developed than those of *Pteromys*, and not only do they make an efficacious parachute, but afford an ample cloak for the animal to envelope itself during the daytime, when it sleeps. Flight in these animals, in whom aerial locomotion was not a primitive condition to which the entire organism has been co-ordinated, affords ample ground for philosophical speculations. Considerations of safety, and the necessity of being able to pass rapidly from one tree to another may have supplied the needed stimulus, in a given species, to endeavour to add to its powers of locomotion by adopting flight. In other members of the same class, special powers in jumping or in running may have a similar explanation. I have always thought that there must have been a formative epoch, in which every creature had the power of special adaptation to its own needs—nay, even to its own wishes or caprice. In this epoch of " plasmation," if I may so term it, when the so-called force of heredity—which tends to reproduction according to the type of the progenitor—had but little power, the world being still young, the organism must have been far more susceptible of modification by external forces, and the limbs more ready to adapt themselves to special usage. Considering the very great number of animals that can fly, and how varied they are, it is plausible to suppose that in the higher organisms the desire to press upwards and skywards, whether to escape danger, seek food, or to enjoy the heat and light, must have been general. This desire,

[1] In the *Sarawak Gazette* of January 4, 1886, flying snakes are mentioned and it is added that there are two species of them.

which manifests itself often in man in dreams, and which in dreams he often realises, is not easy to explain, or to connect with physiological phenomena depending on innervation or circulation ; but it is conceivable, during the epoch in which the entire organism of every living being was more easily adaptable to external conditions, and could be modified in form according to the stimuli felt, that certain organs, in animals influenced by desire or necessity to leave the ground, may have been so far modified as to become adapted to aerial locomotion, as a consequence of phenomena analogous in their nature to those which come into play with us when we dream that we are flying.

As animals provided with organs of flight which were not originally destined to that manner of locomotion are relatively numerous in Borneo, it must be presumed that some peculiarity in the nature of the country they inhabit must have contributed towards this very special kind of modification. Such a peculiarity appears to me to lie in the fact that Borneo, like all countries with an analogous fauna, is a densely tree-clad region, and was formerly, without doubt, one unbroken primeval forest from the sea coasts to the summits of its highest mountains. The only bare ground at that period was the narrow wave-washed strip of its coast-line. This explains how in Borneo and Malaysia generally land animals, in the restricted sense of the term, could hardly prosper and multiply as would those of arboreal habit. If the Malayan mammals be compared, for example, with those of Africa, the difference is enormous. In Africa most of the Mammalia are adapted to move and live on extensive plains, and most of them are swift of foot. In Malaysia, on the other hand, arboreal animals far outnumber the others, and hence, when it comes to rapid movement, the most suitable method of attaining it is by flight.

In illustration of the above remarks we may now glance for a moment at the most important of the Bornean mammals.

All the species of apes and monkeys inhabiting Borneo, fifteen or sixteen in number, live on trees in the forest ; many, probably, never come down to the ground, while others descend only occasionally. Even the Carnivora are mostly arboreal. The tiger, the biggest terrestrial carnivore of Southern Asia, is wanting, and its place is taken by the peculiar tree-leopard (*Felis nebulosa*)—the " rimau dahan " of the Malays. There are different kinds of Viverridae and wild cats which come to the ground by night in search of prey, but all retreat to the trees and remain hidden during the day.

The binturong (*Arctictis binturong*) is so essentially arboreal in its habits that it has acquired a prehensile tail, and though the " bruan," or Malayan bear (*Helarctos malayanus*), does occasionally come to the ground to ravage the nests of ants or termites, it generally keeps up trees, and has a predilection for the honey of the wild bees which it gets there.

The Bornean Carnivora which are not arboreal are aquatic or semi-aquatic ; such are some otters and the rare *Cynogale bennetti*[1]. A singular exception is the " anjin utan," a kind of wild dog (*Cyon rutilans*), which I have never seen. All the squirrels, and they are many, are arboreal ; and so are the insectivorous tupaias, of which several species are known.

Various species of rats and mice, and some insectivores found in Borneo, are, no doubt, terrestrial in their habits, and live in burrows in the ground or in the hollows of tree-trunks ; they are thus hardly to be considered cursorial mammals, and are of small size. Among true terrestrial mammals are several Ungulates ; but of these the rhinoceros (*R. sumatrensis*) and the tapir (*T. indicus*), although adapted for existence in unwooded regions, are also perfectly organised to wander amid dense vegetation, where their weight and size ensures an easy passage. For these, however, swiftness is not a necessity, for they have no enemies they need be afraid of. On the other hand, the wild pigs, of which, according to Everett,[1] there are no less than six species on the island, are perfectly fitted for rapid movement through the forest undergrowth.

The " banteng " of the Malays (*Bos sondaicus*) is a noble creature, the largest ruminant in Borneo. It is not so scarce and keeps to the jungle, and especially to the forest of second growth, in the interior. The diminutive plandok, or chevrotain (*Tragulus*), appears to be a true forest animal, as also the " kidjan " (*Cervulus muntjac*), another small deer with non-branching horns. The " rusa," a true stag, is found mostly in clearings, in old rice-fields, or on hills covered with lalang grass. It appears, I might say, as an alien amongst the forest fauna of the country, and, as a matter of fact, one may suspect that it has been introduced by man. The Malays distinguish the " rusa balum," with doubly branched horns, and the " rusa lalang," smaller and with bifurcated horns. A third species is also said by some to exist in Borneo.

We find then, in the island, a bare dozen of Ungulates adapted to run and roam on plains, but already modified for forest life, against over 150 species of mammals belonging to other Orders, of which two-thirds are strictly arboreal when not aerial (*Chiroptera*). This shows to what an extent the primeval forest has impeded the evolution or perpetuation of terrestrial mammals (in the sense of dwellers on the ground), and especially of those which are fleet of foot.

Deer and pigs are the chief large game to be had in Sarawak. The former, however, are not found in the immediate vicinity of

[1] *P.Z.S.*, 1889.

Kuching, but must be sought in the clearings on the territories of the Singhi or Serambo Dyaks, some miles away. Wild pigs are common everywhere, and often do much damage to plantations. At Kuching I shot and preserved the entire skeleton of a boar which was of unusual size, measuring 4 ft. 9 in. from the root of the tail to the end of the snout, with a diameter of over 16 in. at its widest girth. It was remarkable for the extreme length of the head, which was prolonged into a narrow and sharply-pointed snout.

CHAPTER IV

Missions—Bishop MacDougall—Up the Batang-Lupar—The Bore—
Banteng—Christianised Dyaks—Nepenthes bicalcarata—Simanggan—Undup—The Sea-Dyaks

THE head of the Protestant mission in North Borneo was then
the Right Rev. F. T. MacDougall, Bishop of Labuan and
Sarawak. He was a highly distinguished man, but judging from
appearances one would scarcely have supposed him to be a dignitary
of the Church. He was a skilful surgeon and at the same time a
brave warrior, and had distinguished himself in the latter capacity
in various expeditions for the suppression of piracy. His birth-
place was Malta, and as he spoke Italian fairly our intimacy grew
apace. His hospitable house was ever open to us, and we often
were his welcome guests. And, as I write, a feeling of gratitude for
the memory of our friendship arises in my heart.

The Sarawak mission had various stations in localities widely
separated and distant from the capital. It was possessed, however,
of a good cutter, which the worthy bishop, who was also an excellent
sailor, used to navigate himself when he visited his flock in those
distant stations. He invited me to go with him on one of these
tours : an inspection of the missions on the Batang-Lupar.[1] It was
an excellent opportunity of seeing a different part of the country,
and of visiting the Sea-Dyaks in their own domain, of whom I had,
until then, only seen a few in the bazaars at Kuching.

On September 1st we left our moorings and descended the river to
the Maratabas (perhaps more correctly *Muara tabas*) mouth, where
we anchored for the night.

The next morning was fine, and, aided by the land-breeze and
with the tide in our favour, for the breeze soon slackened, we soon
passed Pulo Burong, and eventually cast anchor for the night at
the mouth of the Batang-Lupar. The river is at this point about
three miles wide, but it has a bar with shallow water (about ten feet
at low tide) which only permits small vessels to enter. At certain
periods of the month, navigation on the Batang-Lupar is dangerous,
even for small vessels, on account of the "bore," caused by high tides
meeting the descending waters of the river and forming a wave, or a

---

[1] " Batang " in Malay means " the trunk of a tree," but it also signifies
the principal part of the course of a big river.

succession of big waves, which advance with extraordinary velocity up the river, carrying all before them. This phenomenon is most marked when the tide is strongest; thus during full moon and new moon the bore is at its maximum, and at such times woe betide those who are unfortunate enough to be caught by it on the river. The bore-wave, which is about six feet high, advances with a foaming crest across the entire width of the river with a velocity of several miles per hour. It is felt about ten miles inside the mouth of the river, and penetrates also the Lingga, which is the first affluent of the Batang-Lupar, continuing up the main stream for about thirty miles, a loud roar announcing its advent. The singular width of the first part of the Batang-Lupar, quite out of proportion to the length of the stream, is, perhaps, an effect of the bore, which has carried away the banks and thus widened the bed of the river.

For the safe navigation of the river, exact information regarding the season of the stronger tides and the time at which they flow is essential. It is also necessary to take a local pilot who knows the places uninfluenced by the bore, or so protected that a boat can safely wait until it has passed. But, notwithstanding these precautions, fatal accidents frequently occur.

On the morning of September 3rd we ascended the river as far as the mouth of the Lingga, an affluent on the left bank at about twenty miles from the sea. We entered the latter and proceeded up stream for about ten miles, when we sighted Banteng, a hill which looks as if it blocked up the river. On its summit we could make out the mission house, the residence of the missionary, Mr. Chambers. The villages of the Balu—for such is the name of this tribe of Sea-Dyaks—are clustered around on the hill at its feet, and on the river bank.

The mission house is a wooden structure, very comfortable, and in a lovely position. Shaded by gigantic durian trees, its verandah overlooks the river, for on that side the hill is steep-to. The view over the distant plain and the winding stream, with a high isolated mountain, Gunong Lingga, rising in the foreground, is magnificent. The summit of the Banteng hill is flat and somewhat extended; along it is a kind of avenue formed by huge durians and other fruit-bearing trees, at the end of which is the mission church. Most of the day passed in religious services, the church being crowded with converted Dyaks and catechumens. The converts dress differently from the other Dyaks, wearing trousers and shirt, but I cannot say that it improved them in looks. The native costume shows to singular advantage their statuesque and well-modelled figures, and though scant, is much more healthy in a climate where dress is a superfluity. The exaggerated sense of shame which leads to the clothing of every part of the body is a product of the inclement North, and is a result of the real need of defence against cold; and thus we find that the sentiment is one which diminishes in proportion as we advance from the temperate to the tropical zone.

On the morning of September 4th, we descended the Lingga, and re-entering the Batang-Lupar made our way up-stream to Simang-gan. The country which we traversed was by no means interesting, for the river runs through a plain where the primeval forest has been destroyed nearly entirely, and its place taken here and there by rice fields.

At one period some of the boldest piratical tribes in Borneo had their stronghold in this river, and with those of the Seribas were long the terror of the coast. They were reduced to order by Rajah Brooke and Admiral Keppel, who destroyed Pamotus, their principal stronghold.

Simanggan is one of the most populous centres of the Sea-Dyaks. A fort, built on a slight eminence on he tleft bank, commands the river, which is at this place about one hundred yards wide. The fort is built entirely of timber, square in shape, with a small tower at each corner. It mounted some guns, and the Rajah has garrisoned it with a strong detachment of native soldiers.

We spent the night at this place, and early next morning proceeded along a good pathway inland to Undup, a large and populous Dyak village and also a mission station. The path crossed an untouched primeval forest, which had probably been allowed to stand because it covered low, marshy, ground, which could hardly be brought under cultivation. Such places in our climate would be mere marshes, but here they are covered with tall forest trees. True aquatic and marsh plants are uncommon in Borneo, but a large number of trees in that island, palms, aroids, etc., may be almost considered as such, for their roots are always wet. On this occasion, I was able to do but little for my botanical collections, but I was glad of the opportunity of getting an idea of this portion of the country, as I intended later to return for a long stay. I was fortunate enough, however, to meet with some specimens of *Nepenthes bical-carata*, which is certainly one of the most curious of all the Bornean pitcher-plants. Our excursion only lasted a few days, and on September 13th we were back in Kuching.

This little trip with Bishop MacDougall gives me an opportunity of saying a word or two on the Sea-Dyaks. The Land-Dyaks I prefer to leave for the present, until I come to speak of my doings in the country in which they live.

The villages of the Sea-Dyaks are situated in the territory between the Sadong and Rejang rivers. The more warlike and enterprising tribes at sea have been those of the Seribas and of the Sakarrang, one of the branches of the Batang-Lupar river. Some tribes of the Rejang, the Kanowit, and especially the Ketibas, were at the period of which I write not yet quite subject to the government of the

Fig. 11.—SEA-DYAKS OF THE SERIBAS.
(Armed with Sumpitan and Parang Ilang.)

Rajah, and had not given up head-hunting. The Sibuyo Sea-Dyaks live on the Lundu river, near the westernmost point of Borneo. This tribe is said to have migrated from the lake region on the frontier of Sarawak, between the Batang-Lupar and the Kapuas river.[1]

The Sea-Dyaks are usually of middle height or rather small; the taller men rarely exceed 5 ft. 5 in., and 5 ft. 3 in. may be considered their average stature. They are stoutly built, with broad chests and well-proportioned limbs, although not usually showing any great muscular development (Fig. 11). The skin is brown and often a shade lighter than in the Malays; the face broad, with very prominent cheek-bones; but the lower jaw is weak and the chin pointed. Their expression, however, is calm and resolute. The eyes are straight and not sunken; the nose is always snub, but not depressed, often straight, but with very wide alæ. They have no hair on the face; that on the head, black and smooth, is worn tied up into a knot or else very long and loose behind, but cut more or less in front.

The women are always smaller than the men, and have the nose somewhat more flattened, and the forehead narrower. Even when quite young, they are less elegantly shaped than the men, and always rather clumsy in their gait; they are, however, often well formed and have a pleasing face, but very Mongoloid in its character (Fig. 13). They usually wear the *bedang*, a kind of short petticoat, wrapped tightly round the waist, and hardly reaching the knees; it consists merely of a piece of dark-coloured cotton cloth of their own make. At times they also wear a jacket or baju. The strangest part of the dress of the Dyak women is the collection of rings of thick brass wire, for which rings of rotangs (rattans) are substituted in the poorer classes. These are worn in great profusion round the waist, and besides fixing the bedang, effectually cover the abdomen.[2] The head is usually uncovered, but on festive occasions special head-dresses are to be seen, such as the highly characteristic " *sisir* " of silver worn by the Seribas girls (Fig. 12). Often necklaces of glass beads and bracelets of silver are worn, but more commonly the forearm up to the elbow is covered with a spiral of close-fitting rings of thick brass wire.

The usual dress of the men consists merely of the " *jawat*," a piece of cloth passed between the legs and secured round the waist, hanging with the ends in front and behind. This cloth is at the present day usually of European manufacture, but many still wear

[1] Low. *Sarawak*, p. 167.
[2] A similar costume is worn by the Kachin women in Burma, and the Karin, who have so many traits in common with the Dyaks, cover the body and limbs with big spirals of brass wire. (FEA, *Quattri anni fra i Birmani*, pp. 204, 465, 466, figs. 152, 153. *Milano*, 1896.)

Fig. 12.—GIRL OF THE SERIBAS DYAKS WEARING
THE SILVER *Sisir*.

the original native article, made by beating the bark of different trees, or else woven in cotton, and similar to that used for the bedang of the women. On the head the men wear a piece of cotton cloth, elegantly folded, or else a piece of bark cloth dyed yellow, and not infrequently ornamented with the black and white feathers of the hornbill, or of other large birds, which contribute greatly to the elegance of such a head-dress. The most characteristic ornament of certain tribes of the Seribas and Sakarrang Dyaks consists of the huge brass rings they wear in their ears. Through the biggest rings the fist can easily pass, and these hang below; above are smaller ones, gradually diminishing, and surrounding the entire margin of the ear, which is for this purpose bored with holes all round. Around the neck they wear necklaces of glass beads or teeth, the latter sometimes human. On the upper arm a thick ring of white shell is very frequently worn, and the forearm is covered with a spiral of brass wire reaching the elbow. Similar spirals are worn on the legs, below the knee. The ornaments worn on the head, neck, arms, legs, etc., etc., and many other minor peculiarities in dress, are far from being of a uniform type, and often are distinctive and characteristic of each tribe.

The favourite weapons of the Sea-Dyaks are spears and the " sumpitan," usually combined ; but most characteristic is the peculiar long knife or kris called the " parang-ilang." In addition to these they have a kind of sword. For defence they use big shields of a light wood, and padded jackets, an efficient protection against the small poisoned darts blown through the sumpitan. Of these, and also of the parang-ilang, I shall speak at greater length further on. The sumpitan darts are carried in a small bamboo quiver, about fourteen inches in length and three inches in diameter, worn on the side and secured by a hook to the waist-cloth. The Dyaks are poor hands at throwing the spear, and very inferior in this respect to the Papuans and other primitive tribes. They excel, however, in the use of the parang, both in war and for sundry domestic purposes.

The use in warfare of the *arme blanche*, which can only be wielded effectually at close quarters, ought to prove great personal courage in those who use it. But although I do not wish to deny a certain amount of this quality to the Dyaks, yet it must nevertheless be confessed that their warfare consists always in sudden assaults on people who cannot defend themselves. Their war expeditions, indeed, do not deserve such a name, for they hardly ever consist in a battle between armed parties, but in sudden attacks and treacherous surprises, though often the exploits of Dyak warriors are strictly personal.

The expeditions of the Sea-Dyaks are less for the sake of glory or of booty than for the purpose of procuring heads. It does not matter whether these be taken from defenceless or unsuspecting victims, man or woman, or from harmless villagers, surprised in their sleep. The prowess and bravery of the warrior is secure in the eyes of his fellow tribesmen and neighbours if he be only in possession of the coveted trophy. It has been said, and the assertion is quite true, that the title-deeds of nobility amongst the Dyaks consist of the number of heads a man and his ancestors have collected. Not infrequently a Dyak starts on a head-hunting expedition by himself, as a relaxation or to wear off the effects of a domestic squabble, just as with us a man might go out rabbit-shooting to get over an attack of ill-humour. To obtain a head is for these savages the acme of glory, and the rejoicings and festivities held on such occasions are considered by them harbingers of happiness and plenty, bringing fine weather and good crops of rice and fruits, abundance of fish and game, no less than health, and fertility in women. For a Dyak it is on given occasions an absolute duty to get a head; as, for example, to gain the affection of their lady-love by a palpable proof of their prowess, or to enable them to go out of mourning for the death of a relative.

The *bangkong* or war canoes of the Dyaks (Fig. 14) are specially constructed and quite different from the Malay sampan. Some are quite eighty feet in length, and are light and very fast. They can be taken to pieces, being constructed of planks bound together by ligatures of rotang. When a party of Sea-Dyaks on one of their war expeditions found themselves surprised by an enemy of greater strength, they would run ashore, take their canoes to pieces, and disperse with the planks in the forest, where it was impossible to follow them.

During my stay in Sarawak no warlike expeditions of the Sea-Dyaks occurred, but it is not so very long ago, as St. John tells us, that the Sakarrang and Seribas Dyaks used to put to sea with as many as 200 war canoes, extending their head-hunting expeditions as far as the Natunas and Pontianak. The same author narrates that sometimes when overtaken at sea by bad weather these Dyaks would jump overboard to lighten their canoe, holding on or swimming alongside, and if there were sharks about they took the precaution to tow astern a bundle of roots of " tuba " (used for stupefying and catching fish), to keep them off.

It is said of the Sakarrang and Seribas Dyaks that within the memory of man they were peaceable and inoffensive, although they did take a few heads from inland tribes ; but afterwards the Malays and Lanuns took advantage of their skill as warriors, and joined them in piratical expeditions along the coast, for the Dyaks were content with the heads alone, and left the booty to their associates.

When a small party consisting of two or three Sea-Dyaks start on a head-hunting expedition, they only take salt with them as provisions, feeding entirely on leaves, the young shoots of palms or bamboos, and the wild fruit they find in the forest. They do not object to any kind of food, and are very fond of hunting wild pigs, which are considered a great delicacy; but almost every animal is eaten by them. Whilst at home their staple food is rice; they also cultivate bananas, sweet potatoes, and sugar-cane, as well as tobacco and cotton.

On the religion, superstitions, and legends of the Dyaks much has been published, both in English and in Dutch. But I made no particular attempt to gather further materials on so interesting a subject, to do which a thorough knowledge of the language, which I could not claim to be possessed of, is necessary. Moreover, during my wanderings I generally kept away from the Dyak villages, around which the primeval forest was either absent or greatly modified, and afforded me little of interest.

According to St. John [1] the Sea-Dyaks believe in the following deities :—

(1) In a Supreme Being called " Batara."
(2) In " Stampandei," who presides over generation.
(3) In " Pulang Gana," who gives fertility to the soil.
(4) In " Singalang Burong," the god of war.
(5) In " Nattiang," [2] who inhabits the tops of mountains and is apparently a good spirit.
(6) In " Apei Sabit Berkait," a spirit hostile to Nattiang, and of opposite nature.

The Sea-Dyaks are great lovers of festivities, and appear to know how to enjoy themselves. On such occasions they go through endless ceremonies with music and singing, and partake of interminable banquets with a huge profusion of food of all kinds, during which they drink abundantly of their native toddy or palm-wine, or of arak. The first is obtained from the fermentation of the saccharine juice which flows from the incised inflorescence of the *Arenga saccharifera*; the arak is made from fermented rice, by a process which the Dyaks probably learnt from the Chinese. By a similar process they also make an arak from the fruits of the *Tampue*, botanically, *Hedycarpus malayanus*, Jack.

The principal feasts of the Dyaks are celebrated for the planting of rice, and to commemorate a death, especially if during an expedition on which heads have been obtained. On the latter occasions an ancient song in praise of Singalang Burong, the Dyak Mars, is sung. This, which is called " Mengap," has been handed down from generation to generation, and is in a dialect which is almost

[1] *Op. cit.* I., p. 60.
[2] This corresponds, perhaps, to " *Nat* " of the Burmese. (Cf. FEA, *Op. cit.* pp. 158, 159, 385.)

Fig. 13.—WOMAN OF THE SERIBAS DYAKS WEAVING.

unintelligible even to those well acquainted with the Dyak language.[1]

Head-hunting is not, indeed, restricted to the Dyaks of Borneo, but is found amongst many peoples of the Indian Archipelago from Sumatra to New Guinea and beyond. In past ages it was probably practised in many other countries where civilisation has now caused it to become obsolete. The custom must, however, be looked upon neither as an expression of savage brutality, nor as a sort of collector's mania for accumulating the proofs of acts of bravery, as a sportsman keeps the trophies of the big game he has killed. The psychological motive which from generation to generation has influenced, and in a certain way consecrated, such a barbarous custom, is probably analogous to that which maintains —or used to maintain—amongst some tribes the custom of human sacrifices. The ardent desire in a Dyak for the possession of a head is always the outcome of a superstitious sentiment, of a duty to be performed, to propitiate or to earn the favour of a spirit, or to serve and benefit the soul of a dead relative or chief.

The Sea-Dyaks have not a special " head-house," such as the Land-Dyaks have, which is that in which the unmarried men live. They suspend the heads they have collected over the fireplace, in the middle part of the verandah of the common dwelling-house.

A Dyak house is an assemblage of apartments, inhabited by various families ; the quarters of each being partitioned off. Each division is called a " pintu," which means, literally, " a door." These long houses, in which many families congregate, must have originated in an insecure country to facilitate defence in case of an attack by a hostile tribe.

The Sea-Dyaks enjoy a free and easy kind of life. There is no parish clerk to register every birth and death in the community. They have solved the problem of conjugal and family life in the simplest manner. It is not rare to find amongst them men and women who have been married seven or eight times before meeting the mate with whom they could end their days in peace. A girl of sixteen or seventeen years of age may have already had two or three husbands, and is not for that reason less respected. The causes of divorce are many, and often absurd or capricious, but this never causes serious inconvenience. Our vaunted civilisation, the cumulative product of centuries of ignorant prejudices and foolish customs, finds insurmountable difficulties where they would not exist, if, in lieu of moral convention, the simple laws of Nature and hygiene were but followed.

The Dyaks are very superstitious and are always in a state of anxious pre-occupation regarding the spirits, or " Antu," which they

[1] This song has been transcribed and printed by the Rev. J. Perham in the *Sarawak Gazette*, No. 130, April, 1877.

Fig. 14.—LANDING-PLACE OF THE SEA-DYAKS, WITH OFFERINGS
TO THE SPIRITS, AND A "BANGKONG."

fancy they see everywhere and recognise in any strange or un-usual sound. They believe that these "Antu" wander in the forests, hiding in the hollow trunks of trees, or else among rocks or on the tops of hills, their sole business being the care of the affairs of mankind. To find out the intentions of the spirits regarding them, especially in times of trouble or danger, the Dyaks endeavour to draw omens from the heart of a sacrificed pig, or from the flight and appearance of certain birds. Everything which appears to them as supernatural, especially cases of sickness, is attributed to evil spirits, and they have "medicine-men" or shamans, whom they call "Manang," who are consulted on these occasions. These "doctors," among other peculiarities, go about dressed as women and charge themselves with the duty of exorcising the evil spirits producing the disease. The same result is supposed to be attained by depositing offerings in diminutive huts built on purpose at the landing-places or near the village.

The Sea-Dyaks inter their dead, but to this rule there appear to be exceptions. Thus certain shamans or priests called "Mulana," are placed after death on a raised platform : a custom practised elsewhere in the Eastern Archipelago, especially among the Papuans, but which in this case might suggest that followed by the Parsees, who, as is well known, place their dead on towers built for that purpose.

It can hardly be doubted that certain beliefs amongst the Dyaks are derived from more highly-civilised people or from wandering apostles of various creeds and religions coming from the Asiatic continent. To such contacts must be traced their tradition re-garding the Deluge, which is very like the Biblical one ; [1] and the belief in Paradise and in Hell, called by them "Sabayana," and supposed to be divided into seven different stories. [2]

[1] Cf. R. J. PERHAM, *A Sea-Dyak Tradition of the Deluge*, in the *Sarawak Gazette*, No. 133, July, 1877.
[2] Cf. St. JOHN, *Op. cit.* I., p. 65.

CHAPTER V

W E had been more than four months in Sarawak and as yet
we knew nothing of the Land-Dyaks, although from our
verandah we could see the hills on which they lived.

The desire to visit some of their villages was thus most natural ;
and acting upon it, on the night of November 1st, when the tide was
in our favour, we took our sampan with our own men and sufficient
provisions, and started for a week on the Serambo hill, where the
Rajah had a wooden bungalow used as a country villa and sanatorium. The tide carried us as far as Lida-tana (i.e., " Tongue of
Land "), about fourteen miles above Kuching, where the Sarawak
river divides into two branches. We took the one on our right,
which turns abruptly to the west. The current was now against
us, for the tide has no effect beyond Lida-tana, except at certain
seasons ; whilst, on the other hand, during the great rains when the
river is swollen—" Ayer bawa," as the Malays express it—the tide is
only felt as far up as Kuching. It was daylight when we reached
Bilida, about seven miles above Lida-tana, and here we landed on
the left bank of the river, opposite the Serambo hill.

Blida, Bellida, or Bilida, for it is thus variously rendered, is a
small wooden fort, constructed at a time when the opposite bank
was crowned by the big Chinese village of Sinyawan, which was
destroyed during the mutiny to which I have already alluded. The
fort stands on a slight eminence on the river bank, and was considered by the Malays a strategic point, and used as such during
wars, even before Rajah Brooke came to Sarawak. It is now
deserted, and only used occasionally as a hunting lodge by Europeans from Kuching, for deer are abundant in the neighbourhood,
and there are plenty of marsh-loving birds such as snipe and plover.
We found large flocks of wild pigeons on the trees growing around,
the " *punai* " of the Malays (*Treron vernans*), and shot many of

them as we awaited the Dyaks from the hill, whom we had sent for to take our luggage.

These porters did not keep us waiting long, and cheerfully picked up our traps and provisions. The pathway led at first across low swampy grounds, once paddy or rice-fields, but now overgrown with sedges and long lank grass such as *Scleria* and " lalang," and ferns. The hill is very steep, and we more than once scrambled up perpendicular faces of rock by the aid of wooden ladders. After climbing up about 300 feet or so, we reached the first village. Here the " Orang Kaya,"[1] or head man, invited us to rest in the " Panga " (Fig. 15). This is the house set apart for the residence of young unmarried men, in which the trophy-heads are kept, and here also all ceremonial receptions take place. It consists of a great hall of circular shape, raised above the ground on high stout piles. The roof is conical and pointed, and covered with a thatch of sago and Nipa palm leaves. All round are window-like apertures which can be closed with shutters, hung on so as to be capable of being lifted or lowered when desired. Inside, a low bench runs round the entire hall : it is the general sleeping couch at night and a divan by day. In the centre is the fireplace. The entrance is an aperture in the floor, which is reached by a notched pole.

In the " Panga " of Serambo were suspended all round a large number of skulls and dried heads, just like those I had seen in the houses of the Sea-Dyaks. Most of these had been taken from the Chinese during the mutiny of 1857. The common dwelling-houses, raised on piles several feet above the ground, were spread over the hill most picturesquely in the midst of great masses of rock, and were embowered in palms, bananas, and other fruit trees.

We did not remain long in the village, wishing to reach our destination, Pininjau, another 300 feet higher up, without further delay. When we got there we found that the carriers had already arrived with our luggage. The small bungalow which was to be our temporary abode was not situated on the actual summit of the hill, but just below it, in a charming position. It was surrounded by different sorts of fruit trees, especially durians and coconut palms, but not so densely as to impede the view. Pininjau means a place which has an extensive view, and it is well named, for we commanded a great extent of country, and could get a comprehensive idea of the entire basin of the Sarawak river. Only the mountains in which it arises were hidden from us by the summit of Pininjau, the remainder of the horizon being open.

Towards the north the view extended to the sea, and the intervening plain below us was like an immense carpet of verdure, broken only by the river, which cleaves it in undulating curves, and can be

---

[1] " Kaya " signifies " rich " in Malay.

Fig. 15.—HEAD-HOUSE OR "PANGA" OF THE LAND-DYAKS OF MUNGO BABI.

traced to its mouth, which is well marked by the isolated Santubong hill. Farther to the west Singhi, the Mattang group, and in the far distance Gunong Poe are visible. Due west no mountain chains exist, but on the other side of the Sarawak river, and at no great distance, the Staat hill can be made out, and a curious isolated pillar-like rock about 200 feet high, which, I was told, is called Gunong Bulu. Between this pillar-like rock and Gunong Gumbang the country is flat, and across it lies the best and shortest road leading from the territory of Sarawak into that of Sambas. Not only is it entirely without mountains, which are, nevertheless, marked here in almost all the maps of this part of Borneo, but not even slight elevations are to be seen. The Dyaks have a legend that in olden times the sea covered these lowlands, and assert that canoes could cross from Sambas into Sarawak, which was an island completely detached from Borneo.[1] The view is closed by Gunong Bunga, whose irregular and pointed peaks are extremely picturesque. Besides the mountains mentioned, which form, as it were, the frame of the picture, there are other elevations which can scarcely be called either mountains or hills, but rather isolated crags. These are of limestone formation, and in some of them veins of antimony are found ; whilst the alluvial soil all round affords gold washings, in which a large number of Chinese are employed.

A few steps from Pininjau bungalow is a cave out of which flows a stream of deliciously cool water, which is one of the most attractive features of the place. On the Serambo hill are three Dyak villages : Pininjau, Bombok, and Serambo, all situated below the bungalow. The hill does not form part of any mountainous chain, but rises abruptly from the plain, like the calcareous rocks above mentioned ; but it differs from these in its formation, consisting of crystalline rocks of a porphyritic nature. To this formation, too, belongs Singhi, and also probably some of the adjoining hills, whose geological structure I was not able to examine closely.

Round about Pininjau bungalow numbers of a small swift were continually flying. We secured specimens for preservation, and found that it was *Collocalia linchii*, Horsf. & Moore. This is a species often confused with the other producing the gelatinous nests so highly esteemed by the Chinese. The Dyaks brought us its nests, which we found to be made mostly of moss glued together by a small quantity of the prized gelatinous substance. The nests of good quality are, however, formed entirely of this white and trans-

---

[1] Cf. regarding this legend, W. DENISON, *On Land-Dyaks*, in *Sarawak Gazette*, No. 125, November 1876, who writes : " In old days they say ships and boats came right across from what is now the Sambas coast, past the Sibungo range to Sarawak. A small columnar mountain midway between Gumbang and Gading, called " Ji-mas," was then only just above water, and praus used to touch there for ballast and big stones for anchors."

lucent material, with little or no admixture of feathers and other impurities. The swifts producing the valuable edible nests (*Collocalia nidifica*) inhabit the caves in the limestone hills near Serambo, and are a source of considerable revenue to the Dyaks of the village.

Wallace had lived for some time at this very Pininjau bungalow, and made some memorable captures of nocturnal lepidoptera. They were singularly successful, but we were not so fortunate, although many were the species which used to fly about the verandah, attracted by our lights.

One day I started to visit one of the limestone crags in our neighbourhood, and got some Dyaks to guide me to Gunong Skunyet, a small isolated eminence which rises abruptly from the plain to the north. The route we took led us through a part which was once cultivated, and no traces of the primeval forest remained ; in point of fact there is no such forest around Pininjau. The ground is varied and undulated, forming ridges and depressions ; some of the former are covered with lalang grass, but the vegetation is mostly that which always grows where the old forest has been cleared, and is composed mainly of species which have a wide geographical distribution, and are in no way specially representative of the endemic flora of the island. But amongst them was an exception, a shrub belonging to the Scrophulariaceæ, which turned out to be the type of a new genus, described by Bentham under the name of *Brookea dasyantha*.

Most of the plants grew as bushes or large shrubs, and were species of the genera *Eurya, Adinandra, Ficus, Vernonia* (an arboreal composite), *Mappia*, etc., etc., all characteristic of the forest of secondary growth.

In the low-lying parts the path was very bad, and we sank in mud and water to our knees, whilst elsewhere it was most difficult to keep one's footing on the slippery argillaceous soil. When such paths are recently made, and lead to a new plantation of the Dyaks, they are fairly practicable, the worst spots being improved by laying down small tree-trunks ; but these rot in a very short time, and then only make matters worse, for they are apt to snap suddenly and precipitate the traveller with scant ceremony into the mire.

In the small valleys between the hills the grasses grow tall, and form the habitual feeding grounds of deer ; but we met with none on that occasion. It took us fully four hours to reach Gunong Skunyet, an enormous limestone crag which rises abruptly into peaks, is quite isolated, and most difficult of ascent. I got up to a sort of cave or fissure which penetrated the cliff, but I did not even attempt to climb to the summit.

In limestone cliffs such as these the rock is full of holes, erosions, fissures, and caves ; and the configuration often most fantastic, and so sharply pointed and jagged that climbing was a painful business, wearing, as I did, thin-soled cloth shoes, wet and sodden into the bargain by the previous wading through mud and water. I thus gave up the attempt to get to the top, which could only have been done by means of the creepers and roots, which, not unlike gigantic serpents, hung from the perpendicular face of the rock. This was so precipitous as to be in many places quite bare—a rare case in Borneo—whilst along the summit of the cliff the vegetation grew like a huge crest.

The erosions in the limestone are no doubt due to the atmospheric agency taking effect in those places where the rocky mass presents inequalities of composition. But the big fissures and the caves, so frequent in rocks of this kind, must be a consequence of their origin. If, as I believe, these peculiar limestone crags are of madreporic origin, they are the result of an accumulation of inorganic matter deposited by polyps in the sea. Everyone who has had occasion to examine living corals or madreporic rocks in situ, and has noted how the polyps multiply, can easily understand how caverns may form in the rocks they give rise to. In a coral rock in process of formation, the polyps at work very rarely grow in a uniform manner, and never form compact masses—interspaces and hollows frequently occurring between one colony and another. When such interspaces are extensive, as in the case of colonies growing separately and coming into contact later in the progress of their growth, fissures or caverns necessarily result, which are not less marked in the rock when it has emerged from the sea than in its former submarine condition.

The non-calcareous hills and mountains in Borneo, however precipitous, may always be distinguished by their smooth and rounded outline, which is partly due also to the vegetation which contrives to take root even in the smallest crannies. And this vegetation does not consist only of grasses, mosses, or small bushes, but of large shrubs, climbers and trees, which cover every inch available.

I had only brought as provisions some cooked rice and a box of sardines, but on the road we had found an addition to my dinner in the shape of some cucumbers which the Dyaks had sowed in their paddy-fields. Though rather bitter, these were very refreshing. We returned by a route only slightly different from that we had come by, but we were under the disadvantage of walking during the hottest hours of the day, over ground which, being covered by forest of secondary growth, offered but a poor protection against the sun's rays. I was therefore very thankful when we reached the foot of the Serambo hill, and entered a fine grove of durian trees, under whose welcome shade we halted to rest. I brought down some of the big fruits with a shot or two from my gun. They were not yet quite ripe, but the pulp covering the seeds was already well

Fig. 16.—FRUIT OF THE DURIAN, *Durio Zibetinus*
(about ½ nat. size).

developed, and in this state I found it even more palatable than when completely ripe. The durian is the favourite fruit of the Dyaks, and the rich buttery pulp which surrounds the seeds is considered most delicious by those Europeans who have been able to overcome the strong smell of rotten garlic which it gives forth. (Fig. 16).[1]

A delicious bathe in the cool and limpid spring entirely took away the effects of the heat and the long tramp, and I was able to sit down to dinner with a splendid appetite.

On November 7th we discovered to our dismay that our provisions were running out, that our ammunition was expended, and that the paper for preparing botanical specimens was also exhausted. A return to Kuching became imperative, and with great regret we were obliged to put an end to our delightful visit at Pininjau, and to say good-bye to the good Dyaks of Serambo.

The Land-Dyaks, concerning whom I will now say a word or two, are limited to that portion of Western Borneo which is included between the Sadong and Pontianak rivers. A large portion, therefore, of these people live on Dutch territory, whence it is believed that the Sarawak tribes also originally came.

These Dyaks have not the bold and arrogant look which distinguishes the Sea-Dyaks. They are quieter and milder in their habits, and more modest in their dress. They are undoubtedly Malayan like their sea brethren, but differ from the latter in many respects. They are in general smaller and uglier. Some grow scanty moustaches and a slight beard on the chin (Fig. 17). They are often affected by a skin disease known in Borneo as " kurap," which is produced by a minute acarus which penetrates beneath the epidermis, and is very similar, if not actually identical, to that producing the itch. I at least recognized this amongst the Papuans and in the Molucca Islands, where the same disease is very common and is known by the Portuguese term of " cascado." [2]

[1] I have written at some length on the durian, and on the wild species of this fruit which grow in Borneo, in my work entitled *"Malesia"* (Vol. III. p. 230). The durian, as I have already remarked, is unknown in the wild state ; but considering that various wild species very nearly akin grow in the Malay Peninsula and in Borneo, it must belong to the flora of these regions. We are thus obliged to suppose that the durian in its present form must have grown in the past in land then existing between Borneo and the Peninsula ; or else that in the wild condition it has been exterminated by man in the Bornean and Malayan forests. But we are also free to suppose that the fruit owes the extraordinary development which it has attained to cultivation, or, better still, to the indirect protection afforded it by primitive man. For a durian left to its own resources has scant chances of being able to reproduce itself, for its fruits are gathered on the trees by monkeys and other arboreal animals, while on the ground wild boars, attracted by the powerful smell, soon come and devour them.

[2] Cf. MALESIA, Vol. I., p. 94. Probably the acari found by the author

The honesty, and I may add the genuine goodness, of the Land-Dyaks is remarkable, and they are at the same time noted for their ingenuousness and simplicity. The Malays often take advantage of this to impose on them. They nickname them " Bodo," i.e., " Stupids," and make fun of their spirits and religious ceremonies. In past years the Land-Dyaks suffered greatly from the head-hunting expeditions of the Sakarrang and Seribas Dyaks, by whom they were often decimated. The Malays, too, used to victimise them, and before the advent of Sir James Brooke forced them to work in the antimony mines at a ridiculous rate of pay, such as a few beads or rings of brass wire. They are now fairly prosperous. The Rajah's government does not require of them, nor of any of its other native subjects, any kind of obligatory labour; and each head of a family merely has to pay a small tax.

They grow a sufficiency of rice for their own use, with a surplus to sell; they possess an abundance of fruit both cultivated and wild, while the forest gives them in addition a variety of products for their own use and for trade. They do not, like the Sea-Dyaks, eat all kinds of food. Thus the ox—which, however, they rarely see—is regarded as sacred, and they would not dream of eating beef. Nor do they eat the buffalo or the goat; and some tribes, e.g., the Singhi, will not eat the flesh of the deer. In some cases they even refrain from poultry. Pork, however, is regarded as a great luxury, and wild pigs are hunted with dogs, but oftener taken in traps called " petti," which consist of a horizontal bamboo stake (*jerunkan*), driven by a strong spring, which is released on the animals touching a string which is placed across the path. These traps are very dangerous for human beings who wander incautiously where they are set, generally producing a frightful wound in the knee, that being the height at which the bamboo stake or arrow is placed to transfix the pig.

The Land-Dyaks usually cremate their dead, an unusual thing amongst primitive peoples. They make no idols or images representing the souls of the departed. It is said, however, that on certain occasions some tribes pay a sort of worship to wooden figures representing birds. They have plants which they consider sacred, such as the " bulu gading," or ivory bamboo; the " bunga si kudip " (*Eurycles ambonensis*), mentioned by Low, which, however, I have not myself met with in Borneo; and *Dracæna terminalis*, which latter appears to have followed human migration from Southern India as far as New Guinea.

were accidental merely, for the disease known as "cascado," so prevalent in Malaysia and the Pacific Islands, is due to a vegetable parasite (*Trichophyton*), and has gained its scientific name, Tinea circinata or imbricata, from the circular and overlapping patterns it produces on the body.—ED.

The Land-Dyaks are very superstitious, as are their fellow-countrymen the Sea-Dyaks, and fancy that they see spirits, or "*Antu*," as they call them, everywhere, floating in the air, and wandering in the forest, or on the summits of the mountains. According to Low the chief of these is "Tuppa" in the case of some tribes, "Jeroang" in others. "Jewata" is also known, but is

Fig. 17.—LAND-DYAK, WEARING COLLAR OF BOAR'S TUSKS.

probably not a native divinity, the name being evidently derived from the Indian "Dewata." "Tuppa" and "Jeroang" are superior and kindly disposed divinities, who have belonging to them certain secondary spirits called "Pertjia." The bad genii they call "Jim" (evidently the "Jin" of the Arabs); these frequent the lower strata of the atmosphere, the other spirits keeping to the upper regions. The "Triu" and "Kamang" are mountain and forest spirits; the first good, the latter maleficent, and both of bellicose tendencies.

The Land-Dyaks, like other primitive peoples, have a super-stitious awe of mountain tops, whither they can with difficulty be induced to accompany travellers. They fear the spirits which they firmly believe to be always prowling about such places. The Dyaks imagine the " Kamang " as having bodies covered with reddish hair like the orang utan. It is for this reason that hairiness in man is not only considered unclean, but also uncanny : a feeling of repulsion which may possibly have originated generations ago amongst the ancestors of these people, in consequence of a hostile invasion of a hairy race. An instinctive abhorrence to red hair was felt also by the ancient Romans.

It may be hardly possible to trace the origin of the Dyak divinities, although the origin of gods is doubtless subject to fixed rules. I have no doubt that, if the Land-Dyaks were for the future to be completely isolated from civilisation, the memory of Sir James Brooke would be transmitted to their descendants in the shape of a new deity. Low, in fact, asserts that in addition to " Tuppa," "Jeroang," the sun, the moon, and the stars, the Land-Dyaks worship Rajah Brooke, the elder.

What especially strikes all who have studied the ways and habits of these people are the patent and abundant traces of Hinduism which they retain, and which may be looked upon as the remnants of a former Hindu-Javanese domination in Borneo. I do not, however, believe, as some do, that the Land-Dyaks are derived from the Javanese colony of the epoch corresponding to the great Indo-Javanese dominion, when Hindu civilisation flourished in that island. That hypothesis is based on the discovery of ruins of Brahmanistic buildings in Sarawak, which doubtless are referable to that period. The manners and customs of a people do not, any more than their religion, necessarily show their origin. Just as there are at present in Borneo missionaries of different religions, Mussulman and Christian, so it was probably in olden times ; and the apostles of Hinduism may have left scant traces of their presence in the shape of descendants modifying the physical characters of the people amongst whom they lived, but may have been completely successful in substituting their own for the original belief of the natives.[1]

The houses of the Land-Dyaks are built much in the same way as those of the Sea-Dyaks, but have a lesser number of " *pintu* " or apartments. A Land-Dyak village, instead of consisting, as is often the case with those of the Sea-Dyaks, of one huge long house,

[1] It may be suggested with some certainty that, if the Dyaks came originally to Borneo from over the sea, they must have had the same ancestors as the savage tribes who can still be traced on the islands off the West Coast of Sumatra. The remarkable similarities which exist between the customs of the Land-Dyaks and those of the natives of Nias, so well described by Elio Modigliani, almost suffice to prove this. Most important of these is the constructing of a special house in which bachelors sleep and the trophy-heads are hung.

in which many families live, is composed of separate houses with only a few families in each. The houses are rather scattered, taking advantage of the local conditions, and mostly built in places not easily accessible.

The principal article of dress amongst the Land-Dyaks is the " *jawat,*" already described, once generally made of bark-cloth, but now that they have grown richer often of foreign manufacture, or else of a strong cotton cloth with variously coloured designs, woven

Fig. 18.—GIRL OF THE LAND-DYAKS.

by the women on a very primitive loom (Fig. 13). They also use a cotton head-cloth, or one of bark-cloth of a yellow colour, but they do not wear it with the nattiness and elegance of the Sea-Dyaks. The women have the same kind of clothing and ornaments as their sisters among the Sea-Dyaks—a short petticoat and similar ornaments of brass and shell on the arms and legs (Fig. 18). In many villages they wear a broad belt of bark-cloth called " saladan," which is worn tight round the abdomen in a way which seems uncomfortable enough. In other villages this is replaced by a belt formed of several hoops of rotang. They usually go bare-headed, but on certain festive occasions they wear a cap and a long skirt, and put round their necks all they possess in the way of necklaces, formed of most heterogeneous materials, to which are hung various amulets and charms.

The weapons of the Land-Dyaks are the plain spear and the parang, which is very like the Malay sword termed "parang battok." The blade is about twenty inches in length, widest near the extremity and gradually narrowing towards the hilt, which is bent at an obtuse angle to the blade. In the Malay weapon the hilt is of wood, in the Dyak parang it is of iron, continuous with the blade and usually provided with a small bar placed crosswise which serves as a guard, and terminated with a tuft of hair. The Land-Dyaks do not use the sumpitan.

Another article invariably carried by these Dyaks is a small bag of woven rotang strips, in which they keep the siri ingredients and fire-lighting apparatus, as well as a small knife for cutting the areca nuts, and splitting rotangs, of which they make much use.

CHAPTER VI

EXCURSION TO MOUNT MATTANG—MALAY ADZES—CYNOGALE BENNETTI—
IN SEARCH OF A ROAD TO THE SUMMIT—SOME METHODS OF SEED
DISPERSION—DIFFICULTIES IN GETTING BOTANICAL SPECIMENS—HOW
A FOREST CAN BE EXPLORED—MY REASONS FOR CLIMBING
MATTANG—THE " UMBUT "—DWARF PALMS—THIN ROTANGS—A
LANKO—SUDDEN STORMS—IMPRESSIONS IN THE MATTANG FOREST—
PHOSPHORESCENCE AND FIREFLIES—INSECTS, FLOWERS, AND LIGHT—
QUOP—FLYING-FOXES.

AFTER my first attempt to reach the Mattang mountain by
crossing the forest of Kuching, the Tuan Muda had kindly
ordered the Singhi Dyaks to cut a path from Siul to the mountain.
In October this pathway was completed, and I decided to use it at
once and endeavour to reach the summit. It was arranged that
Tuan-ku Yassim was to be my companion.

I left Kuching at eight o'clock on the morning of November 13th,
with four men and provisions for a week, consisting principally of rice,
which is the basis of daily food for Malays and Dyaks ; the remainder
was to be got with our guns in the forest. Each Malay, besides the
inseparable parang, had taken a " bilion," with him—the instrument
always used by them for cutting down trees. The bilion is an iron
adze, made on the principle of the stone one to this day in use among
various tribes of New Guinea and Polynesia, and in prehistoric times
amongst Europeans. It has a wedge-shaped blade which comes to
a point at the butt-end ; this is ingeniously fastened by rotangs to a
knee-like handle in such a way that it can be turned at various in-
clinations and easily taken out, which enables the implement to be
used in different ways, and also like an axe. The handle is named
" perda," and is made with a soft but tough wood, " kayu plai."
In the hands of a Malay the bilion is far more efficacious than
the best European axe, to which he greatly prefers it.

As I was anxious to travel quickly my personal luggage was
reduced to the smallest dimensions, and one man took both his own
things and mine in his " tambuk," a light but strong basket made
of thin slips of rotang and carried like a knapsack on the back. I
took no botanical paper, and restricted myself to a jar filled with
spirits for preserving zoological specimens, the indispensable
taxidermic instruments, a thermometer, an aneroid, and a few
medicines, especially quinine, chlorodyne, and laudanum ; fever and

dysentery being the two principal maladies to be guarded against in this country.

We got on pretty fast as far as Siul, where the Tuan-ku was to join us. He was not ready when we passed his house, but he caught us up, accompanied by another native, at the little stream which had barred my way when I first attempted to reach Mattang. Over this we found a tree-trunk, or " batang," had been thrown, by which we crossed. As we were proceeding, a small dog, which had accompanied the Tuan-ku, started two animals which looked much like otters. I fired at one, but my gun had got damp with the rain which had been falling fast for the last hour, and did not go off. The Tuan-ku having fired at the other and wounded it, the dog gave chase, and we ultimately secured it.

The forest was at this point very marshy, the ground covered with surface-roots, which formed alternate lumps and awkward water-holes, and it was no easy matter to get along. I sank several times up to the knees in soft black slush, but where undisturbed, the water was limpid and drinkable, though of the colour of strong tea. The trees here were not of large size, but grew thickly together ; the number of species was large, and had I been able to stay and collect I should no doubt have got some interesting novelties. But for the present I had to content myself with the fact that I had secured a good specimen of *Cynogale bennetti*, a rare and curious animal with the habits and appearance of an otter, but belonging to the family of Viverridæ.

We continued along the pathway made by the Dyaks, which improved as soon as we got out of the low marshy tract. On nearing the mountain the ground got quite dry, and the forest less choked up with underwood, bushes, etc., so that we were able to travel faster. Towards three o'clock in the afternoon we reached a small gambir plantation recently made by some Chinese.[1] In the midst of the clearing was a hut built by them, and here we halted for the night.

As the rice was being cooked I skinned the *Cynogale*, making a present of the carcase to our hosts. I had just finished the operation, and was still holding the skin, when one of the Chinamen who was looking on suddenly snatched it out of my hands, and, before I could prevent him, pulled out some of the long moustache-like hairs from the creature's muzzle. He had evidently been watching his opportunity, but what on earth he wanted with the hairs I was unable to learn. I got them back soon enough, however, and gave him, as may be imagined, a good talking to.

---

[1] The *Uncaria gambir* is a shrub from which a dark astringent substance, a kind of catechu, or terra japonica, is extracted ; it is now much used in commerce both by dyers and tanners.

The hut was small, and the four or five Chinese to whom it belonged, after finishing their meal—which was more ample than ours, by reason of my contribution to their larder—and their pipe of opium, went to sleep. We made the best of the accommodation afforded us, and slept more or less badly till morning.

The next day, November 14th, I wished to get off before sunrise, but I had to give up the idea. Early starts were always a difficulty with the Malays, for whom the morning slumber has special charms. The Chinamen's hut was at the foot of the mountain, near a deep, narrow ravine which appeared to descend abruptly from the summit. To reach the latter from this side appeared difficult. We therefore decided to go round the base of the mountain in search of a better place for the ascent. Our way led us through a part where the forest was of extraordinary beauty, the variety of the trees being almost unlimited. But I had at that moment to be content with admiring all these treasures, for had I attempted to collect even a portion of what I handled we should never have reached our destination. Besides, this was the place where I intended to explore the forest exhaustively later on, the principal object of the present excursion being to find a spot on the mountain on which a hut could be built. This was to be the centre of future explorations, and it was my intention to remain several months in it, with my men and all the requisites for collecting.

In merely crossing the forest, as we did, little indeed can be collected by the naturalist. It is true that on the way many plants are met with within easy reach of the hand, such as small palms, aroids, gingers, grasses, etc., or dwarf shrubs and bushes from which specimens may be got with a few strokes of the parang. But the bulk of the vegetation in Borneo consists of forest trees which are inaccessible to the passer-by, and for that very reason less known and more interesting.

A Bornean primeval forest is not formed like our European woods by one or at most a few kinds of trees, but of an incredible number of species. I have never counted the number of trees growing on a measured area in a Bornean forest ; but the number is certainly very large, both in individuals and in species. Naturally, it would vary in different localities ; thus on the slopes of mountains the number of individuals of a given species is greater than in the valleys or on the plain ; whilst on these the variety of species is larger, for it is here that fruits and seeds carried by the streams and spread by frequent inundations accumulate in large quantities. I believe that such indeed is the most efficacious of the many ways of dispersion of seeds of forest trees on the plains, the more so as the rainy season corresponds with that of the ripening of their fruits. It must not, however, be forgotten that there are quite a number of plants for whose seeds no such means of dispersal are available.

In these seed distribution is ensured by means of the wind, by birds, or by other animals.   In this group undoubtedly come all epiphytes, so abundant amongst the high branches of the great forest trees, and so tantalising to the botanist who cannot collect them when circumstances oblige him to travel hastily through the forest.   The same may be said of climbing plants, for although in many cases their flowers may actually grow along the stem, their foliage usually twists and climbs high up amongst the trees, rendering it often impossible for the passing collector to get specimens.   For these and other reasons a complete investigation of the forest flora is not possible during cursory excursions.   One way of overcoming such difficulties is to get information of spots where clearings for industrial or agricultural purposes are being made in the forest ; one can then easily superintend the operations of tree-felling and select such specimens as may prove interesting, taking advantage, naturally, of the flowering season.   Another way—the one which I usually adopted—is to go into the forest with a party of natives, good climbers and wood-cutters, and direct the collection of such specimens as are wanted ; but for such work plenty of time is required, and it cannot be got through hurriedly.   For these reasons, then, I resolved to build a hut on Mattang, where I could remain sufficiently long for a thorough investigation of the local flora.

Our route round the base of the mountain was a varied one.   In the dips and valleys the vegetation was unusually thick and matted on account of the great number of rotangs.   In places where water accumulated the number of species was greater than elsewhere, and the shade was of the densest.   Not the slenderest sun-ray penetrated the mass of vegetation.   Here shrubs with long slender stems were frequent, literally covered with mosses, Hepaticæ, and small ferns, chiefly *Hymenophyllaceæ*.   But one peculiarity which could not fail to strike the botanist in the kind of forest which I have attempted to describe, is the quantity of cryptogamic growths living on the green and growing leaves of the shrubs and bushes forming the undergrowth.   Almost every leaf, even those of herbaceous plants, is covered with minute Hepaticæ, lichens, mosses, and fungi.

Near a small stream we met with several specimens of a very tall palm, a species of " nibong " (*Oncosperma horrida*, Griff.) usually known in Sarawak by the name of "lammakor."   It has amidst its central fronds a " cabbage," which is excellent eating. The Malays call this part, which is also edible in other palms, " umbut."   As we were rather short of provisions anything of the kind we could procure in the jungle was very welcome, and we cut down the tree to utilise its cabbage.   It was 118 ft. in height, and the stem alone from the ground-level to the insertion of the first frond was 102 ft.

Wandering on without finding a suitable place to commence the ascent of the mountain, we reached a part of the forest where the trees were of enormous height and size, the ground beneath being quite bare and devoid of undergrowth. I found by examining the dead leaves, which formed a soft, brown carpet over which it was pleasant to walk, that these trees were of species belonging to the genera *Shorea*, *Hopea*, and *Dipterocarpus*, members of the family which bears the latter name. Game was scarce, and except a few " pergams," huge pigeons of the genus *Carpophaga*, which were perched high up in the trees beyond range, no animals were met with.

After a very long tramp we found that we were going round a projecting spur, which would have led us away from, rather than towards the mountain. This induced us to try the ascent, although the place was very steep; but the vegetation was so dense and there were so many roots to hold on by and obtain a footing, that we managed to reach a sort of terrace which extended on a level for a considerable distance. This led us, though at a higher elevation, back towards the spot where we had been turned aside by the mountain spur. Here I found a diminutive pinang very abundant, with a stem hardly as thick as one's little finger, and growing to about a man's height (*Areca minuta*, Schaff.) We also met with a small species of *Licuala* with undivided and nearly circular leaves, of the shape of a Chinese fan (*L. orbicularis*, Becc.). The Dyaks use these leaves, which they call " daun nisang," for making thatch and hats, and especially for wrapping up " nassi " (cooked rice), tobacco, etc., etc.

After a couple of hours or so of hard climbing and a rest for some food, we at length gained the summit, or rather what we imagined to be so. Even here it was forest-clad, and I was obliged to cut down some trees to get a view. These were neither very tall nor very stout here, but their wood was singularly tough. When they were cleared away we found that we could overlook the country as far as Kuching. From this elevation the plain looked like an immense expanse of verdure extending to the far horizon, formed by the upper surface of the dense forest. In some places large blotches of another tint were conspicuous ; these were mostly white, and were caused by forest trees in full blossom. Some, however, were of a bright red, a colour which I found later to be due to the flowers of a giant liana(*Bauhinia Burbidgii*), which displays its brilliant colouring by climbing over the tops of the biggest trees. Having found a small bit of level ground, we all set to work to clear it in order to build a " lanko," or temporary hut, wherein to pass the night. In case no water was to be found on the summit, I had had sections of bamboo filled at the spring where we took our last meal.

While the men were busy setting up our lanko and lighting

the fire to cook rice, the Tuan-ku and I followed the crest of the mountain to see whether we could get higher. We found a pathway evidently traced by wild animals. The Singhi Dyaks occasionally, though rarely, ascend the mountain in search of very slender rotangs which grow nowhere else in these parts, and which they apply to various uses. We also found them abundant here, and collected a quantity; the Malays call them "rotang rawat," i.e. brass-wire rotangs, or "rotang tikus," i.e. mouse rotangs, to denote their diminutive size. Some of them when cleaned are hardly more than one-fifteenth of an inch in diameter, the stoutest being one-fifth of an inch. They belong to a variety of *Calamus javensis*, or a very closely allied species.

After walking for about half an hour we reached another peak; but through the trees we could make out that we were not, even then, on the highest point of Mattang. I did not collect any plants, but noted that the most abundant tree about the summit was a *Casuarina* which is very like one which grows also in the plain. But it was getting late, so we returned to where we had left our men working at the lanko. We took back with us a good bundle of rotangs, the best existing binding material the forest affords.

The "lanko" or "langko" are temporary huts which the Dyaks put up in the forest when required. In a country like Borneo, where the necessary materials abound, this is easily done. Such huts are a necessity to those obliged to pass a night in the forest in a climate so damp and rainy, where it would be impossible to sleep on the ground *sub Jove*, if only on account of the innumerable insect pests. To construct a lanko two small tree-trunks of requisite length are cut down and placed parallel to each other on the ground at a distance which varies with the size of the hut required. The use of these trunks is to raise the flooring from the ground. This flooring is formed by laying a number of sticks transversely across the two trunks. Over this a slanting roof is constructed formed by a frame of forked branches stuck in the ground and cross poles, over which leaves, preferably those of a palm, are placed to form a covering.

Our lanko was soon ready; and as the weather was fine and it did not look like rain, we merely covered it with leafy branches, having no better material handy; while to render our bed less hard we spread over the stick flooring some sheets of smooth bark. There are many trees in these forests with smooth and even bark which can be detached with ease and forms excellent flooring. The night was less cool than I should have expected, but I have lost the note I made of the minimum temperature we experienced. Towards dawn it was, however, considerably less than that to which my men were accustomed, and had the effect of making them rise before the sun. We were therefore able to begin the descent in good time.

As I have previously remarked, my principal object in this excursion up the Mattang mountain was not to reach its summit so much as to find a suitable locality for building myself a house. After some exploration, I decided that the most convenient spot for my future headquarters was that where we had halted for lunch on the previous morning during our ascent, on a sort of terrace about 1,000 feet above sea-level, between two ravines, from one of which water could easily be led to the place where I intended to build my hut.

My men, under the direction of the Tuan-ku, set to work to construct a large and commodious lanko, as a shelter during the building of the house. In this locality palms abound, and the roof of the temporary hut was made entirely of their fronds, and was quite impervious to rain. The trees were felled all round, and a big one was cut so as to fall across and bridge the nearest ravine. It was an enormous trunk, about 100 feet in length and three feet in diameter; it fell just as we wished, and formed a solid bridge some sixty feet above the bottom of the gorge.

My house was to be of the Malay type, raised on piles; and by a fortunate chance, on the very site I had chosen, there grew three thin trees about nine inches in diameter, and situated so as to form exactly the three corners of a square at a distance of some thirty feet apart. These were chosen as the corner pillars of the house to be built. One of them was flowering, and I preserved specimens from it. It was a *Canarium* (?) as yet undescribed by botanists, and evidently fully grown. The other two were young specimens of large forest trees, and from their foliage I recognised them as belonging to two distinct genera of Dipterocarpeæ, and in all probability of undescribed species. This may help to give an idea of the richness of the flora of Gunong Mattang, that three trees selected by mere chance, only thirty feet apart from each other, should belong to three distinct genera and to species probably peculiar to Borneo and new to science. Their trunks were cut at thirteen feet from the ground, for the flooring was to be of such a height as to permit anyone to walk beneath it. All the other trees for a good space around were felled or rooted up, especially in front of the future house, not only to get a clear view, but to allow the sun's rays to dry the ground and generally to neutralise the dampness, which otherwise would have rendered the drying of botanical specimens a difficulty.

From the bigger trees the bark was detached to be used for the lanko and later for the house. A search was made for long, slender stems suitable for the framework, and these were solidly planted in the ground; the tranverse poles were tied on with rotangs, of which also there was no lack. Another excellent material for tying was furnished by the *Nepenthes*, whose stalks, about a quarter of an inch in diameter and twenty feet or more in length, are as strong as rotangs. In the whole building not a single nail was used.

The house was to have a verandah in front and another behind, and was to be divided off inside into three rooms : the central one serving as a hall, one of the side ones to be my bedroom and study, and the other the sleeping room of my men. The kitchen was on the ground beneath. In three days the principal portion of the framework was set up. The Tuan-ku not only superintended the work, but took the most active part in it, never resting for a moment. At night we all slept in the lanko, where we were sometimes obliged to seek refuge from sudden and heavy showers in the daytime. The rain-bringing north-east monsoon had already begun, but for the present its effects showed only in occasional afternoon showers.

From the small clearing we had made in the forest, we could follow the big grey clouds passing rapidly overhead, hiding the sun which had warmed our clearing but a few moments before, and darkening the plain. Thunder growled and incessant lightning streaked the lowering sky ; the rain descended in torrents, producing a singular sound as it beat on the dense foliage of the trees. On the ground in the forest the deluge does not fall with uniform regularity. The rain loses its impetus on the aerial vegetation and reaches the ground as it can, now in huge drops, now in streamlets down the tree-trunks ; but in the end the water penetrates the forest just as it does the open. After such a downpour a slight mist rises from the soil, and the hot reeking dampness transfuses a powerful influx of new life and energy into the vegetation.

Who will ever be able to form an adequate conception of the amount of organic labour silently performed in the depths of the forest under such conditions ? Who can even in imagination realise the untold myriads of living, palpitating cells that are struggling for existence in the tranquil gloom of a primeval tropical forest ?

Our habitual conception of life is that we see exemplified in animals, and few reflect that every tree-trunk and stem, every leaf and flower, is composed of innumerable microscopic cells, most of which contain an organised protoplasm, soft, extensile, contractile, capable of sensation, of reacting to stimuli—of fulfilling, in short, essentially at least, the functions we generally associate with superior beings. How immense a field lies open to the meditations of the philosopher and naturalist in the primeval forest now that the veil which hid the mysteries of plant life is beginning to be lifted !

Up to a quite recent period vegetable physiology was believed to be based on purely chemical and mechanical processes, and nobody thought of the possibility of an individual entity (*anima*) presiding over the entire organism. A plant was considered not as a living thing, but as a composite mechanism in which the cells acted much as the parts of a machine. But we now know that the particles of protoplasm enclosed in an involucrum of cellulose, i.e., living cells, of which plants are formed, are endowed, at least at times, with a vitality which is perfectly comparable to that of animal cells. To those who have not followed carefully the results of recent investigation such an assertion will appear absurd, for in plants outward manifestations of any such vitality are wanting, and they cannot move. But the common notion regarding the want of movement in plants is a fallacy. In the living, or, as one may term it, the animated parts of plants, protoplasm moves and can change its place ; indeed, in some, if not in all, in certain parts and at certain moments, the protoplasm circulates continually, being sensible to the stimuli of light, heat, and even touch ; therefore it might with some approach to accuracy be argued that plants can even see and feel.

Living cells which react to stimuli may be looked upon as nerve cells, and plants are provided with such cells in almost every part of their organism. Darwin has compared the ends of roots in plants to the brain of animals ; but I think that the comparison can be extended even further, for it appears to me that many of the living cells of plants have a great analogy to nerve cells. Few indeed are aware of the activity and sensibility of certain plant cells. And yet all the roots, the internal layers of the bark, the nervures of the leaves, and the flowers abound in such. The so-called soft-bark or phloema (perhaps the most important portion of the entire vegetable organism) is made up of cells which are extremely excitable and very much alive. Indeed, we have every reason to believe that these cells are in direct communication with each other, and with the entire vegetable organism to which they belong, by means of very slender filaments, analogous to those of nerve cells. In the protoplasm of plants, as in that of animals, are included all those mysterious forces which represent the vital patrimony of the past, and which have to be transmitted to the future, a fact which is amply shown in the phenomena which accompany sexual reproduction in the beings belonging to both the vegetable and the animal kingdom. This alone would be quite sufficient to show the uniformity of the laws which rule matter throughout the entire organic world.

What numberless obscure vital phenomena run their course, motionless and in silence, under the shadow of these ancient trees, and to what an infinity of microscopic beings does not the death of one of these giants give birth ? How can one picture the vast hosts of these creatures peopling the soil and air, the roots, trunks, flowers, and fruits, and realise their metamorphoses, their habits, and the relations in which they stand towards the plants amongst which, or on which, they live ?   In short, how can we ever come to know the biology of this vast living world, which even the profoundest philosopher fails to grasp as a whole ?

The first nights passed in the primeval forest can never be forgotten ; their charm is indescribable ! I was as yet unaccustomed to jungle life, and could sleep but poorly on the hard sheets of bark and uneven flooring of the lanko.   In my moments of wakefulness I saw the forest under a new aspect hardly less beautiful than that it presented during daylight.   In these dense woods the nights were extraordinarily still ; not the lightest breath of air stirred a leaf ; the temperature was delightful.   The profound and solemn silence was only interrupted at long intervals by the harsh and penetrating cry of the Argus pheasant.   Through the gaps left by the trees we had felled the sky could here and there be seen, but the blue was not so intense as that of Italy, and the stars did not seem to shine so brightly as at home.   The intense darkness was lit up from time to time by brilliant intermittent flashes—the love-lights of enormous fireflies.[1]

On the surface of the ground the darkness of night unveils a world which the light of the sun only hides by day.   Every dead leaf, every branch or twig in a decaying condition, was luminous, showing a pale glow through the slight mist which rose from the humus of the forest soil.   The rain of the preceding day had apparently set alight the whole network of mycelium thread which, invading the ruins of the giant vegetation, slowly disorganised and consumed them.   A huge rotten tree-trunk a few feet from where I lay emitted a brilliant phosphorescent light, emanating from certain white fungi belonging to the genus *Agaricus*.   A single one of these enabled me easily to read a newspaper when placed upon it, so strong was the white and very beautiful light it gave off.[2] The temperature at the time was 80° Fahr.

[1] The firefly which was so abundant at Mattang, and of which I procured several examples, has only recently (1895) received the name of *Pyrocælia opaca* (E. Olivier).   Hitherto it has remained undescribed among the large collection of insects in the Museo Civico of Genoa.   It measures 21 by 9 mm. In Sarawak we found five other species of firefly (*Lampyridiæ*) and among them one still larger, *Lamprophorus nitens*, which measures 22 mm. in length. (v. *Ann. del Mus. Civ. di Genova*, Ser. 2a., Vol. II., p. 345.)   I here gladly avail myself of the opportunity of expressing my heartiest thanks to my friend, Professor Raphael Gestro, Vice-Director of the Museo Civico at Genoa, and one of the most distinguished of entomologists, who has always afforded me his valuable aid when I have required information on the collections made during my travels.

[2] This *Agaricus* was entirely white, with a dimidiate and lobate pileus, exceedingly short lateral stipe, decurrent lamellæ, scanty and nearly dry flesh.

The luminosity of the ground in the forest and the phosphorescent insects flying about tempt to long digressions, the subject being a highly suggestive one. So far as regards their biological relations with other beings, luminous mushrooms probably do not derive any advantage from the light-emitting property they possess. It is merely the manifestation of a chemico-vital phenomenon, which accidentally becomes so marked as to be visible.

The case is very different with the fireflies, for in them the phosphorescence ensures the meeting of the two sexes, and evidently the phenomenon takes place under the stimulus of the reproductive cells. That sentiment which is expressed by the word " love " impelled the dark and invisible progenitors of the firefly to render themselves as dazzling as the moon and the stars, the only luminous objects with which their nocturnal habits made them acquainted. It is well known how nocturnal insects are fascinated, one might even say hypnotised, by light. And such must have been the case also, and perhaps to a greater extent, in the remotest plasmative epoch, when living beings, through processes as yet mysterious to us, assumed the forms they now have. In this connection, according to an hypothesis which I have long ago expressed in a different form, I incline to the belief that the luminous organ of fireflies, placed in the terminal abdominal segments of the body, is the result of a kind of reproduction of luminous impressions received through the eyes, and may thus be regarded as a special form of mimicry.

In the same way, I do not think it impossible that the attraction for luminous and glittering objects may have been the *prima causa* of the production of luminous spots and metallic or iridescent colours in many beetles and butterflies. Thus, the golden green of *Buprestis* reproduces, possibly, the shiny surfaces of leaves in strong light, on which they love to rest ; and the mother-of-pearl spots on the wings of some butterflies might find an explanation in the fascination which reflected sunlight on a pool of water has for them. Phosphorescence and mimetic luminosity would thus in insects have been derived from a common cause ; but in nocturnal insects, in whom the colour of the external portion of the body cannot have originated any ambitious sentiment, the physiological process which has rendered luminous phenomena possible has shown its effects internally ; whilst in the others its manifestation is on the external surface of the body.

Whilst my men worked at the construction of the house I wandered about in the forest, or searched for insects amidst the branches of the trees we had felled, which retained their freshness for several days on account of the great dampness. Where a ray of sun lighted their shining foliage I was sure to find some kind of brilliant beetle with resplendent elytra. But on the ground, except on dead tree-trunks or under their bark, I found little to collect. It could scarcely be otherwise. In the forests the last stage of the life of most insects, and especially those with vivid colours, is passed amidst that portion of the vegetation which receives the direct rays of the sun, and this is, naturally, hardly within reach of the collector. To make a good collection it would be necessary to lower the crowns of the gigantic trees, or else to be able to skim over them.

Nearly every flying insect is attracted by light or else by flowers. Now these in Borneo are comparatively few and rare near the ground, though of almost infinite number and variety far above our heads. Here, too, blossom not only the big trees, but the epiphytes, parasitical plants, and lianas. These, whose weak stems would seem to condemn them to a miserable existence in the shade of their stronger rivals, manage to force their way up among the trunks and branches of the largest trees and eventually to outgrow them, and expand their flowers above their tops to the life-giving rays of the sun.

In this struggle of plants towards light, the final victory often rests with those apparently weakest. For in Borneo many of the plants with large, brightly coloured, and odorous flowers are lianas, and these are the most attractive to insects. Again, it is high up in the trees amongst the epiphytes and parasites that the most conspicuous flowers are found, such as those of the *Loranthus*, orchids, *Fagræa*, etc. The higher they are the more conspicuous these flowers become ; the brilliance of their colour is greater ; the expansion of their corollas larger. These strange shapes and powerful odours are all means which the coquetry of flowers, if I may render it thus, employs to attract insects, the unconscious pronubæ of their love-making. Singular, indeed, are the morals of flowers, and far from affording examples to be imitated by us. For in this respect to ensure success Nature uses every possible artifice, every sort of deceit, every kind of cruelty ; and flowers offer innumerable instances of what might well be termed the most vicious propensities.

During this first excursion to the mountains I only collected two species of birds, but both were new to Borneo ; the first was a small thrush (*Ixidia squamata*), which I shot at the highest point reached, the other a fine hornbill (*Rhytidocerus obscurus*), of which I secured two specimens.[1] On November 19th our provision of rice was exhausted, and we were obliged to return to the plain.

Later in the month I went with Bishop MacDougall on a visit to the mission of Quop, not far from Kuching, but my collections there were poor.

[1] Cf. Salvadori, *Uccelli di Borneo*, pp. 210, 90. *Genova*, 1869.

I was obliged to postpone my return to Mattang to complete the construction of my house on account of the rainy season, which was now (December) at its height with the prevailing N.E. monsoon. This is also the fruit season ; and the bazaar at Kuching, well provided with durians, exhaled a fearful stench of rotten onions, which, though delicious to the natives, did not commend itself by any means to us. At this season immense numbers of flying-foxes (*Pteropus*) passed over Kuching every evening, flying at a great height, and quite out of range, but when night closed in they congregated in search of food on the fruit-bearing trees, and then I was able to secure specimens, especially along the river, on the " P'dada " trees (*Sonneratia acida*), the fruit of which they devoured with avidity.

CHAPTER VII

NEW Year's Day was passed merrily at Kuching. The Tuan Muda held a levée in the Rajah's name at Government House, receiving the European residents and the native notabilities. There were games and amusements of various kinds, amongst others a regatta on the river, which came off most successfully, and was especially interesting to us on account of local peculiarities. It was now time to think about finishing my house on Mattang, which I had been obliged to leave as it was, owing to the incessant rains of the previous month. The framework was practically completed, but it had to be filled in and roofed. As I wanted to have a solidly built house in which I could live several months, it was necessary that I should get " ataps " carried up. This is the name of the thatching generally used for houses in Borneo and other parts of Malaysia. It consists either of nipa or sago-palm leaves, according to the locality. At Kuching ataps are usually made of nipa leaves, and last two or three years ; those made with sago-palm leaves are more durable. The ataps in both cases are made with the leaflets or lateral strips, about a yard long and a couple of inches in width, on either side of the midrib of the fronds of the palms in question. An atap is made with a certain number of these leaflets folded across a stick about a yard and a half in length, each leaflet placed so to overlap its neighbour, and the whole held or sewn together with rotang threads.[1] The result is a series of enormous but very light vegetable tiles, which, arranged so as to overlap some four or five inches, form an excellent roof, which is proof against all rain and sun. Moreover, and this is no small advantage in such

---

[1] From a woodcut on p. 466 of Fea's previously quoted] book on Burma, it is evident that in that country " ataps " are made precisely as in Malaysia.

a climate, the ataps are bad conductors of heat, so that houses roofed with them are much cooler than those covered with ordinary tiles or with wooden boards. I had learnt by experience that in Sarawak it is not always easy to get what one wants, and especially at the time one wants it, so I resolved to get my own men to make the ataps I needed.

After my first excursion to Mattang I had heard from the Chinese that, in addition to the track across the forest by Siul, there was a far easier route by water leading to the very foot of the mountain. Several rivulets find their way down the north side of Mattang, and, widening on the plain, form an intricate system of canals which are under the influence of the tide. I was told that, following at high-tide a small water-passage, or " trusan," it was easy to travel by boat from the Sarawak river to the foot of the mountain without having to go round by sea.

Accordingly, in the beginning of January, I started up this trusan with my men, and entered the Mattang channels. We stayed here for about ten days, at a place called Salak, where nipa palms grew in abundance, so that my men had every facility for making the ataps I required. During the excursions I made all round I had ample opportunities of investigating the peculiar vegetation along the streams and estuaries which are influenced by the tide.

Descending the Sarawak river, just below Kuching, the " kayu p'dada," or " peddada " of the Malays (*Sonneratia lanceolata*, Bl.), abounds, a mere variety of *S. acida*, which is not, however, strictly an estuarine plant, for it thrives also in places where sea and fresh water do not mix.[1] Together with the *Sonneratia*, but usually farther away from the water, the predominant trees on the lower Sarawak are *Heritiera litoralis* and three species of *Brownlowia*.[2] On the banks of the river *Acanthus ilicifolius*, with glossy and spinose leaves, is about the only herbaceous plant which grows. The true ligneous salt-water plants on the Sarawak river are about ten species; amongst these are *Skyphiphora hydrophyllacea*,

[1] In Celebes, at Kandari, on the banks of the Lepo Lepo river, where *Sonneratia acida*, or a nearly allied variety, is common, I have observed that during heavy rain the leaves change their position. and from the usual horizontal take a vertical direction. The flowers are nocturnal, but are open morning and evening, and are then frequented by various sunbirds (Nectariniidæ).

[2] These are *Brownlowia sarawakensis*, Pierre ; *B. Beccarii*, Pierre ; and a third species yet unnamed. All these have the under surface of their leaves silvery, such as botanists call " lepidote," i.e., covered with minute scales. *Heritiera litoralis* has similar leaves, whilst in *Avicennia* the under surface of the leaves is covered with a thick white woolly coat. Considering the small number of trees which grow along the river near the sea, to find amongst them five species with lepidote leaves suggests the idea that local biological circumstances render this peculiarity advantageous.

Lumnitzera coccinea, Excœcaria agallocha, Ægiceras major, and *Sonneratia alba;* all shrubs, which grow in the foremost ranks. True mangroves, or *Rhizophorœ,* are represented by three species : *Brughiera gymnorhiza, B. cylindrica,* and *Randelia Rheedei,* and mixed with these, two trees are always found—*Carapa moluccensis* and *Avicennia officinalis.*

Two of the most characteristic plants on the banks of the Sarawak river, near the sea, are the nibong, already mentioned, and the nipa. The first is an invaluable palm to the natives, who generally use its straight and tough stems in house building, especially as piles. Splitting the stems longitudinally, they obtain long, slender slips, which, tied neatly together side by side with rotang, form " lanté," a light, strong flooring which is excellent for houses and boats.

The nipa palm (*Nipa fruticans*) forms usually a dense hedge in front of the masses of arboreal vegetation as far as salt water extends. It evidently requires a swampy ground, on which it spreads its big stems, which resemble both in aspect and dimensions those of a coconut palm lying on the ground, while like the latter they show the big cicatrices left by detached leaves. But the nipa stems are flattened, and from their lower side, in contact with the ground, a number of rootlets grow. The head of the palm, too, is never raised any height from the soil. The fronds of the nipa, which may exceed thirty feet or more in length, resemble those of the coco (Fig. 19).

The uses of the nipa are innumerable, and from it are produced sugar, wine, vinegar, and salt. The fruits grow close together, forming a great ball a foot across, and each fruit, when immature, contains, like the coconut, a watery liquid and the soft edible albumen of the seed. Of the young white leaves bags are made, and mats called " kajang," very serviceable for covering boats or making partitions in houses. From the same leaves, taking away the harder part and leaving the epidermis, cigarette papers are obtained, and the " rokos," or cigarettes, which Malays continually smoke with great zest, are all thus rolled. The nipa serves many other purposes, and the natives, practised in the art and craft of backwoodsmanship, know how to avail themselves of it under a variety of circumstances.

Boating along the Sarawak river at low tide below Kuching, an infinite number of living creatures can be observed on the exposed mud-banks. Small amphibious fish with prominent eyes, which look as if they were being forced out of their orbits (*Periophthalmus Kolreuteri*), flop about with extraordinary agility ; whilst quaint blue crabs move backwards and sideways in all directions. Here and there singular straight elongated bodies resembling horns, conical in shape, and from one to two feet in length, may be seen

Fig. 19.—NIPA PALMS, *Nipa fruticans.*

rising vertically out of the slush. At first they might be taken for young plants shooting up, but they show no trace of leaves. They are really organs produced mostly by the roots of the *Sonneratia*, and are always to be found where this tree grows. It appears, moreover, that all plants growing in estuaries influenced by the tide produce analogous root-appendages. *Avicennia* and *Carapa* have root-horns which are shorter, broader, and less pointed than those of *Sonneratia*, but are otherwise identical.[1]

Entering the trusan of Mattang, the arboreal vegetation is found to consist exclusively of mangroves, belonging to the species already mentioned. Only from good photographs can one realise the curious mode of growth of these trees and the intricate system of roots they exhibit. From the trunk, as well as from the larger branches, innumerable roots as large as a stout walking-stick are produced, which arch over to plunge into the water or mud below. From these larger roots smaller ones arise, and everywhere are produced in such abundance that the whole forest to a height of some ten or twelve feet is densely packed with them. From the obstacle that these roots and the mud present, a mangrove swamp is one of the most difficult and fatiguing things in the world to traverse. To live in it would be the most abominable of existences, if only for the myriads of mosquitoes that swarm in it. Its aspect is singularly monotonous, weird, and desolate. All over the world within the tropics it is the same. It must, however, be admitted that the epiphytal vegetation in a mangrove swamp is often varied and interesting. Some of the most beautiful orchids and the most singular ferns are found attached to mangroves, on which in Sarawak I found also *Rhododendron Brookeanum*, a lovely plant with large yellow flowers.

Parasitical life on mangroves is favoured by the great and constant dampness of the atmosphere, caused by the continual evaporation under the action of a tropical sun. To this cause is also to be attributed another strange peculiarity of the *Rhizophoræ*, which is that the seeds contained in their fruits germinate whilst yet attached to the parent plant, and before falling to the ground ; there being no interruption between the acts of flowering, formation and ripening of the fruit, and germination of the seed. From the centre of the glossy leaves at the extremity of the smaller branches in all *Rhizophoræ* hang green fusiform appendages, varying in length from two to eighteen inches in the different

---

[1] Recently these organs have been diligently studied by Karsten and Goebel, who consider them to be normal roots which grow upwards in search of air instead of penetrating downwards into the soil. Their special function would seem to be that of procuring oxygen for the plant to which they belong, in order to supplement the small quantity of that gas obtained by the ordinary roots in the mud. They have, therefore, been termed respiratory roots.

species. These are simply the roots of the seeds, which having germinated whilst yet adherent to the involucra of the flower, as I have stated, sprout out, lengthen, grow, and enlarge in the air till at the right moment the future plant gets detached. On account of its weight and vertical position, it sticks in the soil on falling, where it at once begins to grow, developing leaves from the apex. Thus in a very short time the transformation is accomplished, and a new treelet is coming up. The *Rhizophoræ* may thus be considered viviparous plants.

Whilst my men were engaged in constructing the ataps, I went again to Salak, where there is a small hill which rises in the estuary of Mattang, and is partly washed by the sea. It was of special interest to me, for its geological formation, in a small area, is more varied than I have seen anywhere else in Borneo. The central mass is granite, overlaid on the one side by metamorphic silicious rocks, and on the other by sandstone. Near the landing-place at the foot of the hill, I found two other kinds of rock, both apparently ferruginous, but one stratified, and the other honeycombed and somewhat similar, apparently, to what is called laterite, so abundant at Singapore. Unhappily the samples I collected were lost and thus their determination is uncertain.

On the top of Salak grow in abundance huge trees of "mengkabang (or engkabang) pinang," a Dipterocarp (*Shorea falcifera*, Dyer), noted for the excellence of its timber, and useful besides, as are other trees of the same genus, for the oil which is extracted from its seeds. This oil, "*mignak mengkabang*," is solid at the usual local temperature, and is highly prized for cooking purposes. I was unable to ascertain whether these trees were remains of the forest or whether they were planted by man, like others of the same kind which I had observed near Malay houses in Kuching. On Salak I saw another gigantic tree, which grew isolated in a plantation at the foot of the hill ; it was a " minuang " of immense proportions (*Octomeles sumatrana*, Miq.), with enormous root expansions. The gigantic trunk, straight, with white smooth bark, rose without branches to a great height, and supported a huge crown of foliage. The "minuang" is one of those trees adapted for isolated growth, and I have never met with it in the primeval forest. Its wood is very light, and it must grow rapidly. I did not measure this specimen, but it was certainly over 200 feet high.

As the ataps were finished I returned to Mattang and thence to Singhi, to get the Dyaks to come and help carry them up the mountain. But the Dyaks showed themselves unwilling to move, and I was obliged to ask the Tuan Muda to order them out. They obeyed, and by the beginning of February all the materials had been conveyed up the mountain, and my house, which I had named " Vallombrosa," was soon finished. I had hoped to have gone directly after to live there with Doria, but the latter's health had been failing, and a delay was necessary.

Whilst on Mattang superintending the finishing of my house I determined to climb to its highest point. I started on January 22nd, at 10 a.m., and in an hour had reached the spot where we passed our first night on the mountain, at an elevation of 1,827 ft. I did not stay, but continued to ascend, and following the ridge at a point some 2,400 ft. above sea-level, I found in great abundance a palm which I have since named *Eugeissonia insignis*. It has the aspect of a sago-palm, but its stem is only twelve or fifteen feet in height. Its inflorescence, which issues from the crown of leaves, measures about ten feet, whilst the leaves, which have spiny stalks, are from twenty to twenty-five feet in length.

About an hour after noon I at last reached the true summit, formed by two points of equal elevation close together. The elevation I made to be 3,071 ft., but in the *Sarawak Gazette* of January 1, 1889, the height is given as 3,130 ft. Here there were no big trees, merely bushes, only a few feet in height, and with very small leaves. All were out of blossom. Of special interest was an undescribed rhododendron with willow-like leaves and large yellow flowers (*R. salicifolium*, Becc.), but not then in bloom. I also remarked a quantity of *Sphagnum*, which is always found on mountain tops in Borneo.

As Doria's health showed no signs of improvement, his return to Europe became necessary, and at the beginning of March he left Sarawak. I accompanied him to Singapore, where we remained together nearly to the end of the month.

Of our stay at Singapore I shall merely recall a week passed at " Woodlands," in a small wooden bungalow which our Consul, Mr. Leveson, had built on the Johore Straits, and which he kindly lent to us. The house stood on a slight elevation overlooking the sea, and was most picturesquely placed, with a view across the water of the southern extremity of the Malacca Peninsula and the capital of the State of Johore. It was surrounded by the then untouched primeval forest. On the sea, always as smooth as glass, a delicious bathing place had been constructed, shut off by a palisade, a necessary precaution against sharks and crocodiles.

The shallow parts of the Straits were covered with a marine plant (*Enhalus acoroides*), which has the aspect of our *Vallisneria*, and produces similar flowers, but of larger size. The female flowers of the *Enhalus* are not, as in *Vallisneria*, at the extremities of spirally twisted stalks, but nevertheless they rise to the surface of the water at low tide and can thus come in contact with the male flowers. These, at first enclosed in a sort of small bag under water near the roots, get detached when mature and float on the surface of the sea, forming large patches of white powder.

The Malay servants who were with me at "Woodlands" used to follow me, being afraid to remain alone even for a short time, as they knew that tigers were abundant in the neighbourhood. But when they heard that, a few days before, a tiger had been seen entering the kitchen (a small hut a few feet from the bungalow), they insisted on sleeping in my own bedroom.

For several evenings I lay in wait for the tiger until overcome by sleep; but nothing occurred to disturb the peaceful quiet of my pleasant stay at this place, where I should have been glad to stay still longer, for the forest was a constant source of manifold interest. But the day approached on which the steamer for Europe was to leave, and I naturally wished to see as much as I could of Doria before he started.

The parting with my friend was a great disappointment to me, for it left me alone to carry out the programme of exploration which we had planned together, and to the fulfilment of which I had so ardently looked forward. After he had gone, I left in the *Rainbow* for Kuching, getting there at the beginning of April. I very soon started to take up my abode in the house on Mattang, where I intended remaining some time. On this occasion I went there by water, as being more convenient for the transport of my provisions to the foot of the mountain.

Just near the starting point on the river was one of the Chinese social-houses which they call "kunsi" or "kongsi." Like all Chinese houses, it was built on a dry levelled site, not raised on piles. It was divided into three parts, the central one being open in front; and here, at the end opposite the entrance, was an altar with the image of "Tai-pek-kong," the god of riches, at the side of which hung tablets covered with large gold characters. One of the lateral rooms was a dwelling place, the other a store. The wife of the head Chinaman was a Chinese girl, very young and very small, not a beauty, but with hair such as I had never seen before: it was of an intense black, very abundant, and hung loose down her back, reaching quite to her heels. She was evidently proud of this natural ornament, and could often be seen, to the admiration of lookers-on, combing it in the central hall, which was also used as an assembly room.

The Chinese are extremely superstitious, and never undertake anything without previously seeking to propitiate by certain ceremonies the spirits which they believe may prove malevolent. On one occasion I got to the kunsi just as they were performing the ceremonies considered necessary to ensure success to a new gambir plantation. The small Chinese colony, consisting of eight or ten persons, were congregated in the central hall; on the altar were a number of porcelain cups containing eatables, and many lighted tapers of red wax. Joss-sticks, too, were burning in profusion, made of the perfumed wood of *Aquilariaa gallocha*. Suddenly the door leading to the store on the left of the entrance was opened, and a man rushed out dressed in a sort of surplice of rich material not unlike that worn by Roman Catholic priests in saying mass. Staggering and shaking with a violent convulsive movement, he placed himself in front of the altar, turning his back on the spectators. He continued trembling like one possessed for some time, but the convulsions gradually passed off, and when he was quite calm he turned round towards the audience. He then took two big needles, or rather skewers, about eight inches in length and spatulate at one end, and thrust them, one on each side, into his upper lip from above downwards. By violent contortions of the lip these were kept rolling about, and imparted, with the hanging lip, a singularly horrible expression to the face. But this was only the prelude to a still more repulsive spectacle. Opening his mouth as wide as possible and holding in his right hand one of those small triangular razors used by the Chinese, he made a deep longitudinal cut down the middle of his tongue. At the same time an assistant handed him a porcelain cup in which he collected the blood which flowed abundantly from the wound. With this the wizard traced with the tips of his fingers various cabalistic signs on bits of red paper, which were successively burnt by his attendant. After this he retired to the room he had come from. All was done with singular imperturbability and indifference.

I do not believe there was any trickery in what I saw, for during the whole ceremony I stood quite close to the altar and could have touched the performer. It is, however, quite possible that he may previously have worked himself into a superexcited condition, such as to make him insensible to pain.

On reaching Mattang I found my house just as I had left it. I at once set to work to finish it, and fit it up so as to render it as comfortable as possible. In the hall I fixed a large table, in my sleeping room a bedstead, while opposite the window, which opened towards the east, I had a small work-table placed. All these were what house-furnishers would term " fitments," were strongly though simply made, and of a practical kind. The legs of these articles of furniture were fixed in the floor and strengthened with cross-bars tied with rotangs. The flooring was of lanté of nibong, over which I had had spread squared sheets of bark with the smooth side upwards.

My large dining-table was more useful to me for preparing botanical specimens than for taking my frugal meals. The bedstead, after laying over it a thin mattress covered with a fine pandanus mat from the Natunas, was comfort itself. My small work-table opposite the window witnessed many happy hours during the months I lived at my Bornean " Vallombrosa," for on it I took my notes and drew the more interesting plants which I from time to time discovered.

With some big bamboos, which I found in the neighbourhood, I made an aqueduct, by means of which cool and limpid water was conveyed to the house. This I tapped sufficiently far up stream to enable me to stand upright beneath what I may call the supply-pipe at the house, and there twice a day I took a delicious and invigorating shower-bath. Nothing could be better for the health under the circumstances, and such a bath after the tiring work of collecting in the forest was not only most invigorating and enjoyable, but it gave me besides an excellent appetite. The kitchen was on the ground beneath the house, and just over its fireplace I had a small room made, which I used for drying my botanical specimens, an operation which I should hardly have been able to perform otherwise, on account of the great and constant dampness of the atmosphere and the enormous number of specimens which I collected and prepared each day. This happy contrivance was suggested by my remembering the system adopted by our Tuscan mountaineers in drying chestnuts. In the small room I am speaking of a simple lanté mat acted as a grating above the hearth, and was sufficiently high to prevent too much heat reaching the plants. These latter dried so quickly and thoroughly that I was able to change them twice a day, and the specimens thus obtained were excellent.

The temperature on Mattang was mild, and pretty nearly equal night and day. The maximum never rose above 82° Fahr. in the afternoon, and the minimum at sunrise was on the average 73°. In such climatic conditions it is not necessary to wear much clothing. My dress was simple enough, consisting only of trousers, a light linen jacket, and a Chinese bamboo hat. I usually went bare-footed, having begun to do so at Kuching, on account of the badly healing sores caused by leeches, but I wore cloth shoes, generally without socks, on undertaking long excursions.

My servants at " Vallombrosa " were a Chinese cook and four Malays. One of these, a native of Java, was an extraordinary hand at climbing trees ; the others were good wood-cutters, and felled the trees I wanted which could not be climbed.

The forest trees of Borneo are usually provided with great laminar expansions at the base of their trunks, known as *banner* in Sarawak,[1] a species of stay or buttress, whose use is to augment the stability of the tree. Now in such cases, if a tree were to be cut through close to the ground, the labour of felling would be enormous. To get over this difficulty, a sort of scaffolding, called

---

[1] Gaudichaud writes that in the French colonies these laminar expansions are termed " accabas."

" parà-parà," is built round the trunk a few feet from the ground, so that the woodcutters can work on the cylindrical portions of it.

I took careful measurements of some of the ordinary trees of medium size felled around my house. A species of *Hopea* was 121 ft. high ; a tree of an undetermined species measured in the cylindrical portion of the trunk, bare of branches, 79 ft., and " over all " 145 ft. The bare trunk of a *Shorea* was 65 ft. in length, the entire growth being 138 ft. Such measurements only give an idea of the medium height of the forest trees halfway up Mattang. On the plain below, many trees I felled reached or surpassed 160 ft. in height, and in favourable conditions in the mountain gorges, and where the soil is rich, some trees in Borneo attain very much larger dimensions.

As regards girth, one of the largest—and it was very common near " Vallombrosa "—was the bilian (*Eusideroxylon Zwageri*). I measured a trunk of one of these trees which was 33 ft. in circumference at a height of 4 ft. from the ground. The bilian produces what is, perhaps, the most valuable timber in Borneo. No insects attack it, not even the white ant, and it does not rot in water nor deteriorate by exposure. It is asserted that even under the worst conditions it can last over 200 years, and it is, therefore, much used in the construction of houses.

In my earlier journeys to Mattang I had had ample opportunities of noting the immense variety and richness of its flora, but my expectations were greatly surpassed by the reality. Every morning I used to go into the forest with my men, and I always returned with loads of specimens. I used carefully to search the ground for indications of blossoming trees of which it was worth securing specimens, for most have inconspicuous flowers not easily seen from below. Thus, only a careful examination of the soil beneath can lead, by the detection of fallen flowers, to the knowledge of the right time of collecting. But in many cases it was not easy to trace the tree which produced the flowers found on the ground ; and more than once I was obliged to cut down two, three, and even four trees before getting the right one, and this although I had acquired some experience in distinguishing the principal families of trees by the bark, and especially by the nature of the sap, i.e., if milky, watery, resinous, etc.

The flowering of trees in Sarawak is nearly continuous, or, rather, trees are found in blossom at all seasons of the year. But when seasonal abnormalities occur, which is by no means rare, the flowering also varies somewhat, and may repeat itself more than once during the year. Many of the Bornean species, however, come into blossom at regular periods, and often all the species of a genus develop their flowers at the same time. Thus, there was a period for the genus *Diospyros*, then came the turn of the *Sapotaceæ*, and then of the *Dipterocarpeæ*.

Fig. 20.—LEAVES AND FLOWERS OF PALAQUIUM OPTIMUM
(about natural size).

The *Sapotaceæ* blossom principally in July. Amongst the numerous species of the family which I collected during this month, I one day at last secured a specimen of "niatto durian," a tree I had long sought for as being in Sarawak the most esteemed producer of gutta-percha. I had often met with felled trunks of this species on the slopes of Mattang, and in the forest between it and Kuching, cut down by the natives to extract the gutta; but I had never before managed to find a specimen in blossom or with fruit, although my men had often pointed out young or sterile trees. On account of the great demand for its product, good yielding trees had become scarce around Kuching, and the native collectors had to search far and wide in the forest. The specimen whose flowers I had secured was apparently an undescribed species, to which, on account of the excellence of its product, I gave the name of *Palaquium optimum* (Fig. 20, 21).

The *Dipterocarpeæ* were in blossom during most of September, and in December their fruits were ripe. During those two months my principal occupation consisted in quartering the forest in search of them. Their presence was revealed by the quantity of flowers or fruit on the ground beneath the tree from which they had fallen. And huge giants, often, were the trees which I was obliged to fell or climb, in order to detach from the higher branches the necessary specimens for my herbarium. Great, indeed, was the labour such deforestation caused me; and more than once to obtain the spoil from a single species of *Dipterocarpus* or of *Shorea* I had to work with three or four men for a whole day to fell the forest giant. I nevertheless managed to obtain not less than fifty species of Dipterocarps in the two above-mentioned months, within the radius of a mile from my hut. Amongst these fifty species were seven *Dipterocarpus*, thirteen *Hopea*, fifteen *Shorea*, four *Balanocarpus*, two *Cotylelobium*, two *Dryobalanops*, and two *Vatica*, most of which were at the time new to science, only a few having been previously met with on the islands of Bangka and Blitong, whose flora has strong affinities with that of Borneo.

Some of these Dipterocarpeæ have certainly a marked resemblance to species which grow in Sumatra and on the Malay Peninsula, but they are, at least at present, unknown from other localities, although most undoubtedly they must have a greater diffusion than the contour of Mount Mattang. It is, however, I think, well worthy of note that here the Dipterocarpeæ are represented by several allied genera, including a considerable number of species, which, often presenting amongst themselves intermediate characters, may be supposed to be derived one from the other. This is, I opine, one of the essential features of a truly endemic flora, and very strongly contrasts with the character of an adventitious immigrant flora, in which the genera and species are an assemblage of forms of wide geographical distribution, coming from diverse regions and with little or no affinity with each other.

The fruits of most of the Dipterocarps have wings, which at first sight might be considered most efficacious in carrying them far from the parent plant ; but in point of fact this is not so, for the seed is usually too large and too heavy to allow the flying apparatus to act properly.[1]

Having found in so limited an area so large an agglomeration of allied species belonging to the same genus, and so many representatives of various genera belonging to the same family, I am led to

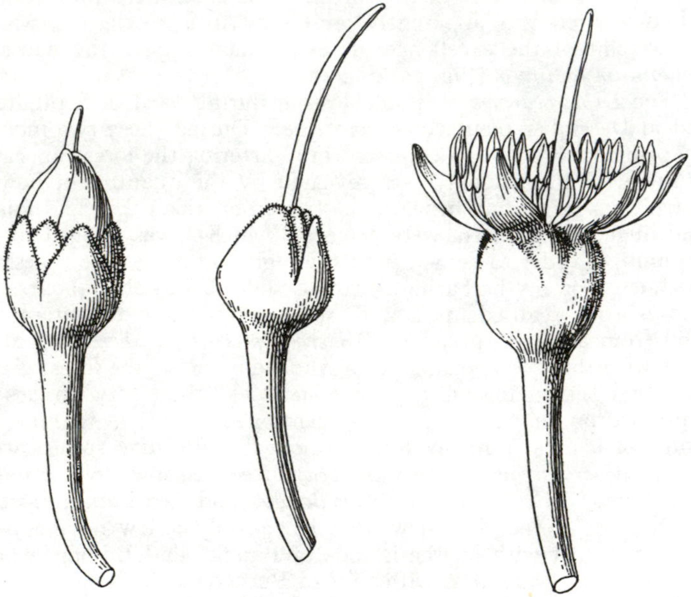

Fig. 21.—FLOWERS OF *Palaquium optimum* (enlarged).

the conclusion that the part of Borneo where all these Dipterocarpeæ are assembled has been a creative centre in the formation of species, and that these have remained on the very spot where they were first formed. It appears to me presumable that a flora must be the richer in endemic elements the more the land on which

---

[1] If some of the Bornean Dipterocarpeæ have a relatively wide geographical distribution, they are species which live near water (*Isoptera Borneensis*, Scheff., *Dipterocarpus oblongifolius*, Bl.), in which the wings may possibly serve as navigating organs.

it grows has remained geologically at rest. I therefore believe that when a flora is rich, it must be on land which has long remained emerged and unchanged, at least from the middle of the Tertiary period, which means from a time in which the formation of new specific forms had not yet ceased. If it be possible to imagine a spot where the forest has remained untouched and unchanged since remote geological epochs, and where the vegetation has continued to flourish uninterruptedly for hundreds of centuries since the period when that land first emerged from the ocean, and if any such localities exist on the surface of the earth, the forest of Mattang and that in the vicinity of Kuching ought to be among their number.

It remains to be seen whether all the forms belonging to the above-mentioned genera of Dipterocarpeæ, found in so restricted an area, are in reality forms due to the gradual evolution of a few archetypes, or if they be not rather the result of hybridism amongst the latter. I have not a blind faith in the slow and gradual progressive evolution of organisms, and in the formation of species as a result of continuous but insensible variation from pre-existing forms. I am more inclined to admit the sudden appearing of some principal adaptation forms, and I believe that originally hybrids between such prototypes have been the reason of the concatenation of all organisms and of the apparent descent of one from the other. I hold that hybridism has had a large share in the formation of existing species; and it seems to me possible that, in the creative or plasmative period, even widely differing types could cross and produce offspring, owing, as I have previously said, to the very imperfect influence of the force of heredity at the period when the world was young.

CHAPTER VIII

DURING the rainy season, when the north-east monsoon blows, it is so rough off the northern coast of Borneo that it is difficult and often dangerous to go out to sea in the flat-bottomed river boats, though in fine weather these are well adapted for coasting. I had, therefore, delayed investigating the littoral flora of Sarawak. Now, however, with the arrival of June, this could safely be done, for the weather was favourable. Being obliged for the time being to leave Mattang in order to provide dried fish for my men and fowls for myself, I decided instead of going to Kuching to make a little tour along the coast, where I could get from the fishermen what I wanted in the way of provisions. It gave me the opportunity, at the same time, of gaining some idea of the nature of the littoral vegetation.

I therefore proceeded to Sibu,[1] a small hamlet beyond Salak to the west. The sea-shore is sandy, and clothed pretty nearly to the water's edge with tall Casuarinas of the common species, the forest behind being mostly very thick and nearly impenetrable. Trees of species widely distributed on tropical sea-shores abounded, but amongst them were some restricted to Borneo. I found large pandani, with gigantic arm-like branches supported by thick air-roots, and numerous creepers, particularly frequent being those of the genus *Gnetum*. Calami of a great variety of species also abounded, rendering progress through the jungle extremely difficult, though they compensate for this by their many useful qualities. Where the sandy shore was free of trees a fairly extensive flora of herbaceous plants of wide range had established itself. Besides various Cyperaceæ and grasses, species of the following genera—*Crotalaria*, *Indigofera*, *Phaseolus*, *Vigna*, *Tephrosia*, all widely distributed, were growing. The big violet corollas of two convolvuli reminded me of the *C. Soldanella* of our Mediterranean shores.

In July I again left Mattang for the purpose of exploring the

[1] Not to be confounded with Sibu on the Rejang river.

94

conical hill of Santubong (2,974 ft.), which I climbed on the 20th
of that month.

Without a guide it would have been no easy matter to find a
passage up the precipitous rocky cliff which bars the way at the
very outset ; but I happily found one in one of the huts at the base
of the precipice, and we managed to get up somehow, holding on
to the roots of the trees, though I found it pretty hard climbing.
When we had got over this difficulty we came to a sort of terrace
leading up the least precipitous side of the peak—that facing the
sea. By this we were able without much difficulty to reach the
summit, which I found to consist of a small area of level ground.

To set foot on the top of a mountain is always a pleasant sensation, which various causes doubtless combine to evoke. To the
mere climber—whose sole aim is to reach the summit apart from
the desire of rest — the attaining of the wished-for goal is perhaps in itself the chief source of joy : the sensation of exultation
at having reached the upper dominating regions of the
atmosphere, and vanquished Nature which has tied man
down to the earth. Or it may be that our gratification is
merely the outcome of those ambitious feelings which spur on so
many to endeavour to rise above their fellows. But to the naturalist
the attainment of the summit of an unexplored mountain is a
genuine source of delight, from the hope he ever has of finding
species yet unknown which may afford him new data for discoveries
in the field of geographical biology. Nearly always, on the summits
of mountains or isolated peaks in Borneo, as in other parts of
Malaysia and New Guinea, are to be found species belonging to
genera of plants existent in very distant regions, as if such spots
were the last refuge of the remains of an extinct flora. Such
mountain tops, arguing from these facts, are, perhaps, the last
fragments of an older world of former continents now broken up
and in great part destroyed.

On the top of Santubong, as I had observed on the summit of
Mattang, shrubs with small coriaceous leaves abounded. They
were without flowers, but I could see that several belonged to
Myrtaceæ of an Australian type, usually found on the mountains
of Malaysia, but at much greater elevations than that of Santubong.
This leads me to suppose that neither the elevation nor the low
temperature explains their presence in such localities, but other
circumstances as yet little known, and perhaps, in the first place,
their being able to hold their ground against the invading species
of the lower regions. On the higher elevations of the mountains
in Malaysia light seeds of many plants are doubtless carried by
the wind, such as *Nepenthes*, *Rhododendron*, orchids, etc., which, had
they fallen in the forests of the plain, would have perished ; whilst
in more open and better-lighted localities they find bare spots where

they can grow and develop. The same may be said, no doubt, of plants which multiply by spores ; and thus on the top of Santubong I collected two beautiful large ferns—*Matonia pectinata* and *Polypodium dipteris*, which may be said to be inseparable, and, indeed, are found also associated on other mountains far from Borneo, e.g., on Mt. Ophir in the Malay Peninsula.

Amongst the many other interesting plants which I met with on the top of Santubong, I shall only mention two new species of *Didymocarpus*,[1] two *Rhododendron*, and the striking *Nepenthes Veitchii* (Fig. 22), which grows as an epiphyte on the larger branches of the trees among the mosses and detritus of all kinds which easily accumulate in such situations. This is one of the finest and rarest of pitcher-plants ; the pitchers or *ascidia* it produces are bag-shaped, rather wide, and blotched with blood-red patches. Some of the specimens I got measured quite ten inches in length. The mouth of the pitcher in this species is certainly its most conspicuous and remarkable part by reason of its rich orange colour and its vertical position. It is also a perfect trap to entice insects into its interior. attracting them from a distance by its bright colours. Sir Joseph Hooker compares the mouth of the pitchers of *N. Veitchii* to the gills of a fish, to which, indeed, with their narrow lamellæ converging to the centre, they bear considerable resemblance.

In all the species of *Nepenthes* I have observed, the young pitchers, even before their lid opens, contain a certain quantity of liquid, produced by the plant itself ; but the water which is found in full-grown pitchers is evidently due in great measure to the rain. In the pitchers of *N. Veitchii* from the summit of Santubong, in addition to the usual drowned insects, most of them more or less putrid, I once found quite a mass of frog-spawn. It would be extremely interesting to know whether some casual frog, having by chance discovered this receptacle full of water, deposited her eggs in it, or whether some particular species may not perhaps exist which makes a practice of so doing.

On July 23rd I visited the neighbouring island of Satang.

---

[1] These two species of *Didymocarpus* are small herbaceous plants, mere rosettes of small leaves, from the midst of which thin stalks shoot up, supporting lovely violet flowers. One, *D. rufescens* (C. B. Clarke), is one of the very few Bornean plants with leaves thickly coated on both sides with an abundant growth of silvery hairs ; though leaves of this type are frequent in plants that grow in arid and dry places, especially on rocks on the seashore and in Alpine regions. The other, *D. bullata* (C. B. Clarke), is also a singular and elegant little plant, with leaves of a dark purplish green, velvety on the upper side and with fairly regular transverse folds. These two *Didymocarpus*, which I have not met with elsewhere, have the type of numerous Gesneraceæ peculiar to China, and their presence on Santubong is perhaps explained by the open-air position they have been able to secure amongst the fissures in the rocks where no arboreal vegetation could get a footing.

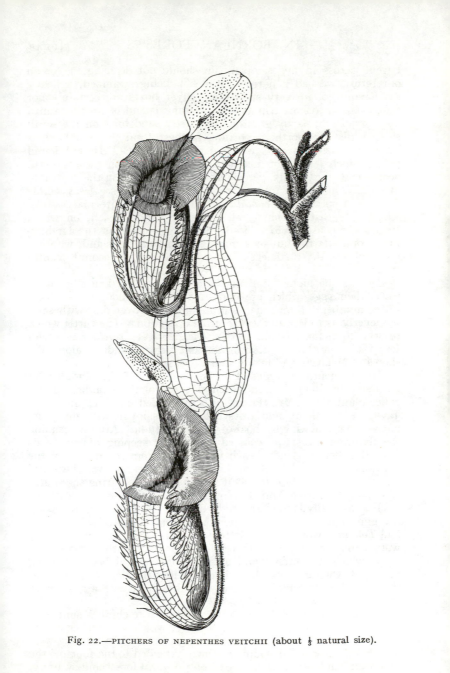

Fig. 22.—PITCHERS OF NEPENTHES VEITCHII (about ⅛ natural size).

I went across in my sampan, but should not do it again, for on our return we had a narrow escape of being swamped, a heavy sea having got up very suddenly. River boats are certainly not safe, even for a short trip at sea. Satang Island is mostly formed by a small hill, partly granitic and partly sandstone, on the south side, whilst its northern portion, farthest from the mainland, is limestone, rising in cliffs which overhang the sea. Here I found plants which I had not met with elsewhere, but on the southern, nearer end the plants were identical with those on the sea-shore at Sibu. On the calcareous rocks overhanging the sea I saw edible nests of a species of *Collocalia*, but they were quite inaccessible. Along the eastern side is an extensive sandy beach, on which turtles come ashore to deposit their eggs. Here is the landing-place, opposite the hut of a man in charge of the island, who not only collects the turtle-eggs, but takes care of a coconut planta-tion.

During the night I remained on Satang several turtles landed to lay their eggs, which are deposited in a hole about $2\frac{1}{2}$ feet deep, to the number of from 100 to 180, and are then covered up with sand so cleverly as to leave no trace of the operation. The turtle which resorts to Satang Island is the *Thalassochelys caretta*, a species found also in the Mediterranean, and very abundant along the shores of Malaysia and in the Indian Ocean.

In the month of August I accompanied the Tuan Muda on an excursion to Mount Poe, in search of a site for the establishing of a coffee-plantation. Mr. Martin, an experienced coffee-planter from Java, went with us, and I started in my sampan with my usual native crew, following the boat of the Tuan Muda. After descending the Sarawak river, we coasted westwards, keeping a few yards from the shore, a sandy beach which runs from the mouth of the Sarawak river to that of the Lundu. The weather was beautiful and the sea perfectly calm, as it nearly always is during the south-west monsoon, from April to November.

I occasionally landed and walked along the sandy beach, taking my gun, and getting a shot now and then at shore-birds (*Tringa* and *Totanus*), which ran along by the water's edge feeding on small worms and crustaceans. We reached thus the mouth of the Lundu river, which we entered and ascended for several hours, landing at a spot whence an excellent road, leading through a magnificent forest, took us to Sadomak, a large Dyak village with a missionary station, where we slept.

On the morning of August 14th we started to climb Mount Poe. A number of Dyaks carried our luggage, which was rather bulky, as we intended to camp for several days in the forest. Our road led at first over a flat country, which extended to the foot of the mountain, and was mostly cleared of primeval forest and swampy.

In the wilder tracts *Eugeissonia minor* abounded—a palm of the same genus as that I had found on the summit of Mattang, but much smaller, with a short stem raised from the ground, pandanus-fashion, by a great number of slender roots, about three feet in length and not thicker than the finger. These roots are largely exported to Europe, where they are known as " rajah-canes," and are used for making umbrella handles and walking sticks.

After a long and fatiguing tramp we came to a temporary hut or shed of the Sadomak Dyaks on the banks of the Burangan torrent, and here we thought it best to camp for the night, although several hours of daylight still remained.

Next morning we began to ascend the mountain, and found it an easy task, for the gradients are slight. We walked on a layer of fallen leaves in a forest of big trees with very scanty undergrowth. Few of the trees were in blossom, but on examining the leaves I detected the presence of several *Dipterocarpeæ*, and of at least five or six species of oak.

We noted not a few spots where the slopes were slight and the thick stratum of vegetable earth was very well adapted for plantations ; but, strangely enough, there was no water on the mountain side. The rain has hardly fallen ere it is absorbed, disappearing between the masses of granite, of which the bulk of the mountain is composed, without forming anything like a brook or stream.

After a climb of several hours we reached an elevation of about 4,300 ft., and camped in a kind of grotto between two huge blocks of granite, which met above our heads and formed a good natural shelter from the rain. The forest here is truly beautiful, but the trees do not appear particularly varied. Over a considerable area the ground is nearly level, and forms small valleys dotted with blocks of granite, hidden under a soft green mantle of mosses. The forest has thus a very different aspect from that of the plain, and to this the presence of conifers, so rare in Borneo, contributes in no small degree. Amongst the latter the most important is *Phyllocladus hypophylla*, which Sir Joseph Hooker has described from specimens collected by Low on the great mountain Kina Balu. This plant represents an exotic element in the flora of Borneo, for the only other two known species of the genus are found, one in Tasmania and the other in New Zealand. Moreover, the frequence on the upper slopes of Mount Poe of two or three species of *Podocarpus* and of a *Dammara* or *Agathis* (*A Beccarii*, Warb.), give a botanist the impression of being in an austral forest. From the trunk and branches of the above-mentioned *Dammara* exudes a resin, which collects at the foot of the tree, and forms stone-like masses. One of these, now in the Botanical Museum at Florence, is as big as a man's head and weighs eleven pounds. This resin is called " Dammar-daghin," i.e. " Flesh-resin," on account of its colour, and is one of the best commercial kinds.[1]

Amongst other plants of great interest to the botanist, I found on the higher parts of the mountain a new type of vegetable parasite, or perhaps a saprophyte,[2] which I afterwards described and named *Petrosavia stellaris*, in honour of my former master, Professor Pietro Savi, of the University of Pisa.

Very little animal life was to be seen in the forest on Mount Poe, and I did not get a single mammal or bird. Even butterflies and other insects were very scarce.

We passed the night comfortably enough in the grotto or rock shelter. At dawn, on August 16th, the thermometer stood at 64° Fahr., and the barometer at 667.74 mm. With these data I calculated the elevation of this spot to be 4,238 ft. above sea-level. Taking a few Dyaks as guides with me, I started at once, accompanied also by my Malays. No pathway existed, but it was easy to find the way to the summit by following the ridge on which we were. The slope was not at all steep, and the forest, always beautiful, was easy to traverse. As we proceeded the trees diminished in height and got more and more covered with mosses. We reached the summit without trouble, where one of the first objects which caught my eye was a new conifer (*Dacrydium Beccarii*, Parl.), a small but very elegant tree, with the aspect of an *Araucaria* ; its branches bent upwards and forming a large umbrella-shaped crown. This was the sixth conifer which I found on Gunong Poe's heights ; a remarkable fact, which I think cannot be wholly accounted for by the facility with which the seeds of such plants are dispersed. It is more likely that on the top of Mount Poe we have the remains of a very ancient flora, which, once owning widely-diffused types, has transmitted a few to the present epoch in such localities as have been least affected by telluric disturbances, which in remote times have certainly wrought vast changes in the configuration of the Indian and Polynesian Archipelagoes.

The summit of Poe is nearly always wrapped in dense mist, and the all-pervading dampness has caused a thick carpet of sphagnum to cover the ground, and a coating of other mosses, especially

---

[1] In the forest on the plain near Kuching I found another Dammara (*Agathis Borneensis*, Warb.), which produces no resin. Both, however, appear to me to be mere varieties of *Dammara alba*.

[2] It is very difficult, amidst the dense masses of intertwined roots which struggle for mastery in the arena of a tropical forest, to isolate such small plants with the necessary precautions, and to ascertain beyond doubt that they really are saprophytes, viz., independent and living on elements taken from the humus, and not parasites, and adherent to some root of another species. It is still more difficult to discover whether such organisms have not had a primitive parasitical stage, becoming later independent or saprophytic.

Hepaticæ, to clothe the stems and branches of the shrubs.   Of
the latter I collected a large quantity, of which not a few were new
to science and of great interest.[1]   Amongst the more noteworthy
plants I collected were three species of *Nepenthes* (not, however,
amongst the finer ones), and two orchids, viz., a *Renanthera* with
large orange flowers, and a *Spathoglottis*, also with very large flowers
of a yellow colour.

At noon in the shady and cooler spots on the summit the thermometer marked 70° Fahr., and my aneroid 639.31 mm., which
would give for Mount Poe an altitude of 5,520 ft.[2]   It is thus the
highest mountain of Sarawak and of all the western part of Borneo.
It marks the frontier with the province of Sambas, of which a large
portion can be seen from the top as a uniformly undulating stretch
of woodland.   On the side looking towards Sarawak the trees,
although only of medium height, impeded my view.

I had heard that a species of *Rafflesia* was to be found on Mount
Poe, one of those extraordinary parasitical plants whose huge and
startlingly conspicuous flowers spring from the ground like gigantic
mushrooms.   I had accordingly hunted everywhere for it, but till
then in vain.   I spoke about it to the Dyaks of our party, and one
of them assured me that he knew the plant, and offered to take me
to a spot where he had seen it; so I put myself under his guidance
and left my companions, followed by some of the younger and more
active Dyaks.   I may here remark, incidentally, that I was on this
occasion not a little impressed by the advantage I had over them
in the descent, which we took at a run, for I wore shoes and they
were obliged to be constantly on the look-out not to wound their
naked feet.

When we got to the foot of the mountain, we turned off for about
half an hour from the path we had followed in the ascent, penetrating into the heart of a magnificent jungle, which reeked with
damp from the density of the shade and the many streamlets which
bubbled up everywhere, winding about amidst the blocks of granite
which had rolled down from the mountain.   I had been told that
close to the *Rafflesia* a gigantic tree grew, which had been climbed
a few days before by my guide in order to get the honey of some
wild bees.   We soon came across the very tree, which from its
fallen leaves I discovered to be a *Shorea*.   It was bigger than any
of these giants of the forests that I had previously seen, and the
cylindrical portion of its trunk was about 6½ feet in diameter.   I
was not able to measure its height, but I do not think I exaggerate
in asserting that it must have been over 230 feet.   Later, I saw

---

[1] Cf. DE NOTARIS. *Epatiche di Borneo raccolte dal Dr. O. Beccari*, in " *Atti
R. Accad. di Torino*," series ii., vol. xxviii.
[2] In calculating heights with my aneroid I have followed the directions
and used the formulæ of Comm. Felice Giordano.

in the vicinity other specimens of the same tree, quite as gigantic. Searching for the *Rafflesia* as we walked along, I came across several fungi, especially agarics, amongst them one which appeared to be identical with our own poisonous *Amanita phalloides*, whilst in another I recognised the common and edible *Cantharellus cibarius*. From the dead leaves and fruits which formed a thick layer on the ground, I was able to ascertain that the forest was chiefly composed of *Bombaceæ*, *Artocarpeæ*, *Myristica*, *Sterculia*, *Diospyros*, *Quercus*, *Dipterocarpus*, etc. Here, perhaps, as much as in any place in Borneo that I examined, was the oldest primeval forest, the most free from shrubby or herbaceous undergrowth. On the ground, however, many stems of creepers and rotangs contorted and intertwined in every direction, and trailed like huge serpents ere raising themselves upwards to the light and air by aid of the great tree-trunks.

We were now on the spot where the *Rafflesia* grew, but the irregularities of the ground as yet hid it from us. A minute and careful search, however, had its reward, and I at length caught sight of the long sought-for botanical treasure—an open flower level with the ground, inserted on the rampant stem of a climber of the genus *Cissus*. The newly expanded flower measured rather over 22 inches in diameter (Fig. 23).

In *Rafflesia* the flower alone is actually all there is to be seen of the plant, for the growing portion is buried in its host, and is so intimately connected with the tissues of the plant on which it is parasitic, that it is not only impossible to separate them, but is also very difficult to distinguish them by careful microscopic examination. The flower is very fleshy, of a deep vinaceous colour, and it gives off a most offensive stench much like that of putrid flesh, or, to be botanically exact, like that of the spadix of *Arum dracunculus*, and of certain kinds of *Amorphophallus*. It makes its first appearance as a tumour on the stem of its host, and grows before expanding quite to the size of a child's head. I found a specimen in this stage of development, covered with brown scales, which reminded me, except for its colour, of a well-grown cabbage. The globe on expanding shows five almost circular petals inserted round a great central cup, in which are the reproductive organs.

The Lundu and Sadomak Dyaks call this *Rafflesia* " bua pakma " (pakma fruit) ; evidently a corruption of " patma " or " padma," the sacred lotus (*Nelumbium speciosum*) of the Hindus, which is not a native of Borneo. This is, no doubt, one of the many traces of the ancient faith once professed by the Dyaks, who have preserved the memory of the emblematic flower, transferring its name to that of another plant conspicuous for its size and singular appearance. In Java, as well as in Sumatra, the *Rafflesia* is known as " patma " ; but there the fact is not surprising, for the prevalence of Hinduism in those islands is a matter of not very remote history.

Fig. 23.—RAFFLESIA TUAN-MUDÆ, BECC. (flower 22 inches in diameter).

As no one had described the *Rafflesia* of Mount Poe, I named it *R. Tuan-Mudæ*, in honour of the present Rajah of Sarawak, Sir Charles Brooke.[1]

Before my party rejoined me, I had brought to the Dyaks' house my precious find, taken the requisite notes on the fresh specimens, and made drawings of the entire plant and of its more important parts. Not being able to preserve the flower entire, I had to content myself with such portions as might be useful for further study, and these I put into a jar with spirits.

We then returned to Sadomak, from which place on the following days we made an excursion to Gunong Gading, also a granitic mountain. We passed the night of August 22nd under a lanko, at an altitude of about 1,700 feet, and on the following morning climbed the summit nearest the sea, which proved to be 3,209 ft. high, the thermometer standing at 70° Fahr., and the aneroid at 685 mm. I found nothing of any particular interest on this mountain top.

From Gunong Gading issues a stream which forms a fine water-fall, plunging into a deep and limpid basin beneath. On these rocks, always wet with falling spray, I discovered a singular Aroid (*Rhynchopile elongata*, Engl.), with shiny spadix of a cherry-red. I got besides several other interesting plants, amongst them a new Anonacea (*Goniothalamus suaveolens*, Becc., *P.B.* N. 2,327 [2]). It is a shrub with large, fleshy, greenish flowers inserted on the slender trunk and exhaling a most delicious perfume, very similar to that of the pompadour or allspice (*Calycanthus floridus*).

At Sadomak, on the rocks in the stream near the Dyak houses, I discovered two singular algæ, both of which were new. One of them, of a red colour, which turned out to be a *Delesseria*, and was later named *D. Beccarii*, Zan., is of great botanic interest, for it belongs to a genus of which all the previously known species are marine. It covered the rocks with a red coating. The other, which has been named *Thorea flagelliformis*, Zan., is one of the most beautiful of freshwater algæ, being composed of tufts of long plumose filaments, some four inches in length, of a lovely violet colour.

I returned to Kuching well pleased with my botanic harvest,

---

[1] Fuller details of this plant are given in the work of Count H. von Solms-Laubach on the *Rafflesia*, published in the *Annales du Jardin Botanique de Buitenzorg*, vol. ix. p. 185.

[2] To every plant I collected in Borneo I attached a number corresponding to a catalogue, kept regularly, to which I added notes from time to time. These numbers are attached to all the samples of Bornean plants in my herbarium, or which have been distributed to the herbaria of Kew, Paris, St. Petersburg, Vienna, and others. It is for this reason that here, in mentioning a plant, I also give its number with the initials *P.B.* (*Plantæ Beccarianæ*).

only regretting that I was unable to prolong my stay on Mount Poe. As to the selection of a suitable ground for the proposed coffee-plantations, which had been the main motive of the trip, it was afterwards found more convenient to give the preference to Mattang.

CHAPTER IX

ON my return from Mount Poe I went back to Mattang, where I remained all September and a portion of October. The collections I formed during this period were very important, for the trees then in blossom were numberless. The honey-bees had also taken advantage of the season, and flew in countless myriads from flower to flower amongst the higher branches in search of nectar. The flowers of the Dipterocarpeæ appeared to be their especial favourites.

In Borneo there are two species of honey-bee; one fairly large, the other small. The first, *Apis dorsata*, is the *lanyeh* of the natives, and is found in Central and Southern India, and throughout the entire Malay Archipelago.[1] The small species, *Apis nigrocincta*, is known in Sarawak by the name of *nuang*. It occurs in Celebes, and even in China.

The nuang produces a small amount of wax and a large quantity of honey, not of the best, perhaps, but nevertheless highly relished by the Dyaks, who, in order to be able to indulge their taste for it, rear these bees near their houses, just as we do our common species. The large Bornean bee, on the other hand, produces a small quantity of excellent honey, and immense combs of wax, which can often be seen hanging from the larger branches of giant trees known as "tapang," which tower above the other denizens of the forest, offering a safe and isolated refuge to the bees, who have many enemies. Amongst these the most dangerous is the little Malayan bear (*Helarctos malayanus*), who is a very glutton for honey aud cares nothing for stings.

---

[1] In the *Sarawak Gazette*, May 2, 1881, it is stated that at Singapore a swarm of bees settled on the mast of a steamer starting for Kuching and returned with the same vessel to Singapore, leaving it afterwards for a tree near the docks.

The Dyaks are clever at climbing tapangs, constructing a sort of ladder with pegs fixed in the trunk of the tree and connected with longitudinal poles. The large bee is not, however, so very particular in choosing the site of its colonies, high cliffs and also ordinary trees being at times selected, as is shown by the following incident of painful memory, of which I was the victim.

One day in the forest I had had a tree felled, amongst several others of like size, not being aware that it had a bees' nest hidden amongst its branches. This was naturally broken in the fall, and the affrighted bees, swarming out in a highly irritated state, massed together and attacked one of my men, Laksa by name, who was dressed only in a pair of short trousers. Being at a certain distance when the tree fell, I might have escaped scot free, but poor Laksa in his agony rushed up to where I stood, imploring me to free him from the infuriated insects, which covered his head and chest. Without giving the matter a thought, I took off my jacket, remaining about as much dressed as my man, whom I began to beat with the jacket, in the hope that I might free him from the bees. But crushed bees appear to give out an odour which serves only to irritate their living brethren still more, and they now all turned upon me. In vain I strove to free myself. I tried to escape by running, attempting to get back to the house as quickly as I could, but this I found impossible, for I was bare-footed, and had to cross a clearing full of prostrate trunks, and the thorny rotangs tore my feet fearfully. On the way I came to a deep water-hole, and in despair plunged into it, hoping that the bees would leave me. But the relief was only momentary, for, as soon as I put my head above the surface to breathe, an infuriated swarm dashed down upon it, immense numbers having collected above me while I was under water. There was nothing for it but to rush out of the water and once more make for the forest, which I did, and here, fortunately, I was met by my men, who, called by Laksa, had come to the rescue, armed with lighted torches of green wood, which gave out plenty of smoke, and this at last drove off my enemies. The Dyaks always make use of these to get at the honeycombs without being stung.

I was in a sad condition, and my face so swollen that I could hardly see. Happily, I had some ammonia with me, and used it freely ; this soothed the pain and caused the swelling to diminish. Laksa, who would not use my remedy, was in a bad state for two days. The number of stings in my skin was prodigious, especially on my back, and for a good hour and more my men were occupied in extracting them with tweezers.

As is well known, a bee after stinging cannot draw out its sting, and, losing it, dies. Nature, which rarely—if, indeed, ever—is quite perfect in her work, makes these insects pay a very high price for the weapon with which she has provided them. That in the brain of an irritated bee the idea of a weapon of defence for itself, its home, and its progeny may have arisen, is possible ; but the manner in which Nature has gratified such a wish by providing the sting and the venom is inexplicable, or at the least in the highest degree wonderful.

The clearing which I mentioned above had been made for the coffee plantation, for which Mattang had been finally selected as the best adapted site, after the rejection of Mts. Poe and Gading, as stated in the preceding chapter. For this reason, the Tuan Muda and Mr. Martin came to stay with me during September

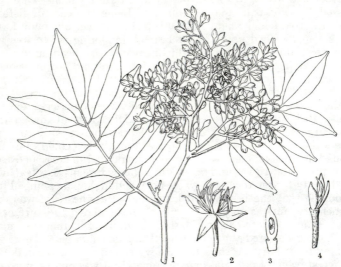

Fig. 24.—(1) FLOWERING BRANCH OF THE TAPANG, *Abauria excelsa*, the largest tree in Borneo, (about ⅔ natural size). (2) A FLOWER ENLARGED. (3) SECTION OF OVARY, ditto. (4) OVARY WITH ONE STAMEN, A PETAL AND A SEPAL *in situ*. (Figs. 2–4 enlarged about ¾.)

at " Vallombrosa," in order to superintend about a hundred Dyaks who were engaged to fell the forest. It had been decided to leave at intervals some of the bigger trees, that they might protect with their shade the young coffee-plants, a practice which I think is not without its drawbacks. It was useful to me, however, to have all this tree-felling going on, for I was able to collect specimens of a large number of trees not yet represented in my herbarium. Unhappily, many of the felled trees were not in blossom.

I have already mentioned the tapangs. A very big one grew not far from my house in the neighbouring ravine, a majestic giant of incredible height. My desire to obtain specimens of the flowers and fruits of this tree, which I believed to be as yet unknown to botanists, had hitherto been unsatisfied, but one morning I was delighted to find on the ground beneath it a few small branches bearing flowers, which had been broken off by a violent gust of wind during the night. The flowers were very small and greenish.

I have named this extraordinary species, which belongs to the Leguminosæ, *Abauria excelsa*, dedicating the new genus to my friend and fellow-traveller, the Marquis Giacomo Doria.[1] I shall have an opportunity further on in my narrative of again mentioning this tree, which is probably the largest and most majestic in Borneo, and, indeed, must take rank among the giant trees of the world (Fig. 24). I may here mention that the term "tapang" is often applied to any tree of exceptional dimensions, usually selected by bees for their nests. But the tapang *par excellence*, which is noted also for its splendid and valuable timber, is the *Abauria*.

From "Vallombrosa" I used to make excursions in all directions, but for miles and miles around I found nothing but the unbroken primeval forest, with the insignificant exception of small clearings made by Chinese at the foot of the mountain.

My nearest village was Singhi, about the same distance from the house as Kuching. Leading towards the former was a sort of pathway made by wild pigs, to catch which the Singhi Dyaks used to lay the traps already described, which they call "petti"; but these had been providentially removed by order of the Tuan Muda when I went to live on the Mattang.

Why the slopes of the mountain should have remained uninhabited was a puzzle to me. When I was there, there was not a single hut on it. It may be that the attempts at cultivation were unsuccessful, and were therefore abandoned. The whole mountain appears to be formed of sandstone of very coarse grain, over which is a goodly layer of vegetable earth, which, even had it not been originally of the best quality, could not fail to become so through the vast accumulation of vegetable detritus in the forest. But, from what I can judge, the Singhi Dyaks do not like to fell the primeval forest, which gives them so many valuable products. It may be also that they find it too much trouble to fell the big trees, and prefer to make their clearings in the forest of secondary growth, where the trees are smaller and mostly soft-wooded.

The word "Mattang" means a sacred place, the abode of spirits; and it is not improbable that the name of the mountain explains why its primeval forest has remained untouched to this day. If

---

[1] Cf. *Malesia*, vol. i. p. 169. *Firenze*, 1877. "Abauria" is the ancient mode of spelling the name of the Doria family. Recently *Abauria* has been replaced by Taubert in the genus *Koompassia*, from which, however, it is most distinct; amongst other differences the fruit of *Abauria* does not appear to be winged.

it be true that the Land-Dyaks are the descendants of old Javanese or Sumatran colonists, the fear inspired by the mountain might be explained by its resemblance to a volcanic cone and by old reminiscences of terrible eruptions, so frequent in the islands whence they came, confusedly transmitted by the memory of the immigrants. The flames, smoke, vapours, boiling water, mud, ashes, and lapilli ejected at intervals by volcanoes, the subterranean rumblings in their interior, the violent earthquakes, etc., in short, all the concomitants of eruptions, are phenomena which must have produced a deep and lasting impression on a primitive, ignorant, and superstitious people. It is thus not strange that the Dyaks should consider mountain tops with feelings of awe and terror, and believe them to be the residence of those supernatural beings termed by them "*Kamang*," which it is neither right nor prudent to disturb.

Although I can have no doubt as to the primeval condition of the Mattang forest, yet on the spot where I had built my house were indications that at some time it may have been the abode of man. I was led to think this by the large bamboos I found growing there. Cultivated bamboos do not grow and multiply spontaneously in the primeval forests of Borneo. They are reproduced by division of the root, and perhaps sometimes by cuttings, but they rarely blossom and still more rarely produce seed. For these reasons I came to the conclusion that the isolated clump of bamboos which had furnished me with pipes to convey the water to my house could not have spontaneously sprung up on that spot, but had much more probably originated from bits of the cane left there by Dyaks who had come to the tapang growing near, in search of honey. Another vestige of the presence of man was possibly the *Alocasia macrorhiza*, one of the cultivated "kaladi," with feculent tubers, which grew and multiplied naturally, attaining colossal proportions (the leaves measured 5 ft. in length), down towards the lower part of the brook, near the place where this reached the plain.

At this spot there was quite an accumulation of beautiful plants, no doubt brought about by the many seeds and fruits carried thither from all parts of the mountain by the waters of the stream. Amongst them I may mention a new and magnificent palm (*Arenga brevipes*), and several singular Anonaceæ, as *Sphærothalamus insignis*. Hook, and *Marcuccia grandiflora*, Becc.[1] In the same locality, attracted by the sweet and delicious scent exhaled by some fallen fruits, I discovered one of the most exquisite wild durians of Borneo, *Durio dulcis*, Becc.[2]

The question of the age of the great forest trees was one

[1] *Nuovo Giornale Botanico Italiano*, iii. p. 181. *Firenze*, 1871.
[2] *Malesia*, iii. p. 243.

which often came in my thoughts during my solitary wanderings in and around Mattang, and I ultimately came to the
conclusion that the great majority can hardly be long-lived ; for
they grow very rapidly and continuously all the year round on
account of the warmth and equability of the climate. As no
periodical rest in vegetation occurs in Borneo, the trees which
grow there do not show in a transverse section of their trunks
those regular concentric rings or zones which elsewhere allow an
approximate evaluation of the age of the individual. But it is
presumable that the age of Bornean trees is never very great, and
cannot be reckoned at many centuries. An argument in favour of
this supposition is the great facility with which even arboreal
vegetation appears to renew itself in that country, as the many
dead and rotten tree-trunks found lying on the ground in the forest
amply prove. I found on one occasion a large tree with a trunk
about three feet in diameter, almost completely decayed, yet standing upright, its roots still in the ground in the position they had when
living, covering completely and surrounding the trunk of another
tree of about the same size as the first, which was lying prostrate and
rotten. Now, evidently the time required by the yet standing tree
to grow, die, and rot had not been sufficient to decompose entirely
the fallen one, which was dead and prostrate when the other grew up.
Considering the rapidity with which even the most durable
timbers decay in the tropics, I cannot believe that the dead and
prostrate trunk could have been there a very long while, as I should
certainly have believed had I found in my own country the trunk
of an oak of similar size in like condition.

Again, the abundance of tree-trunks lying dead in the forest
shows that the life of forest trees is relatively brief in the tropics, and
proves that there arboreal plants are being continually replaced and
renewed. The accumulation of vegetable detritus produces the
humus which is found in all densely wooded areas, where water
cannot wash it away. In tropical forests the humus accumulates
in an extraordinary degree, and it can be asserted that in Borneo,
and in countries under analogous climatic conditions, the richness
and nature of the plants which cover the ground is a direct effect of
its depth and quantity.

Amongst the flowering plants whose existence depends on the
humus are certain saprophytes, diminutive plants which possess
the means of absorbing the substance required for their nutrition
directly from the humus, without the necessity of leaves or of
chlorophyll. Of this group, leading an existence very similar to
that of the fungi, which they not infrequently resemble in aspect,
Mattang possessed a goodly series. Several turned out to be new
and of great interest to the botanist ; and sundry forms of slender
and transparent *Thismias*, filamentous *Triurideæ*, and various

Burmannias [1] were the reward of my patient and careful search in places where the forest was thickest, the shade densest, and the stratum of humus richest (Fig. 25).

Under like conditions I was pretty certain to come across those small ground orchids (*Anœctochilus*, *Goodyera*, etc.), with variegated leaves, spotted and striped with gold and silver and showing metallic sheens, which form the joy of orchid lovers, and are undoubtedly amongst the most charming and marvellous products of

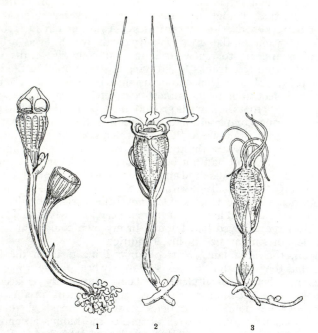

Fig. 25.—BURMANNIACEÆ OF THE MATTANG FOREST (natural size). (I) GEOMITRA EPISCOPALIS, BECC. (2) THISMIA NEPTUNIS, BECC. (3) THISMIA OPHIURIS, BECC.

the vegetable kingdom. The slender and wax-like saprophytes just mentioned have very minute seeds, which cannot possibly be raised from the damp soil of the dense forest on which they fall so as to attain the higher currents of the atmosphere, and it is rather difficult to see how such plants succeed in widening their geographical range. The fact remains, however, that some of them are to be met with on almost all the Malay islands, from the Malay Peninsula to New Guinea. I have endeavoured (*Malesia*, vol. iii. p. 325) to explain the matter through the agency of earthworms

[1] *Malesia*, vol. i. p. 240, and vol. iii. p. 318.

which, living in the humus, swallow, together with inorganic particles, the seeds which may be mixed with them ; and, in their turn,
being devoured by birds, the undigested seeds may pass through the
latter's intestines and be evacuated intact in localities such as those
whence they originated.   The mysterious dissemination of certain
fungi of hypogeous growth—of truffles, for example—may be
similarly explained, for their spores, like the above-mentioned seeds,
can pass from the intestines of earthworms to those of birds, and
thus be spread far and wide.

Mycetes and fleshy fungi were also not uncommon in the vicinity
of my house, and I often came across *Mytremyces, Hymenophallus,
Mutinus, Clathrus*, etc., the joy of whose discovery only the
mycologist can appreciate fully.   One day it was our common
edible mushroom (*Boletus edulis*) which gave me a happy surprise,
taking me back to our Italian woods.   And here, too, I met with
several other European forms of *Boletus* and *Agaricus* which had
been long familiar to me.

It is a general belief that fungi are not abundant within the
tropics, but this belief must be greatly modified.   One day in
September I made a note of the species of fungi I could collect in
an hour in the immediate vicinity of my house, and the result was :
Myxogastri, three species ; *Agaricus*, fourteen species ; *Polyporei*,
ten species ; *Auricularinei*, six species ; *Pezizeæ*, three species ;
Phacidieæ, three species ; *Sphæriacei*, ten species ; total, forty-nine
species.   On another occasion (June 14) I found in the forest, in the
vicinity of the house of the Chinese, eleven species of *Agaricus* and
five or six of *Boletus*.   Moreover, from my arrival in Borneo to
September, 1866, I find that I observed no less than ninety different
species of *Agaricus*.

From my hermitage at " Vallombrosa " I often went down to
the Chinese settlement near the river to renew my provisions, and
especially to procure rice, which I kept in large tin boxes.   These
I also used for stowing away my collections in, when the plants were
perfectly dry.   During one of these visits to the Chinese I had occasion to note that several foreign plants had invaded the grounds
around the " kunsi " ; amongst them were two in great abundance
which were in no way tropical—*Amaranthus mangostanus*, L., and
the plantain, *Plantago major*, L., both eaten by the Chinese.

Following the stream on which was the landing-place, and penetrating the forest, I came to a small and perfectly level valley extending for nearly a mile, where Nature showed herself in her wildest
aspect.   In the thick layer of rich humus which the floods of years had
deposited there, the vegetation throve in an extraordinary manner,
and the trees had attained enormous dimensions.   I was pleasantly
surprised at the large number of palms which I found here.   In
the rank soil the spiny *Zalacca* abounded.   Here, too, I collected

specimens of the largest known Calamus, and of the diminutive *Iguanura palmuncula,* which is probably the smallest of known palms. Its four or five fronds, which constitute the entire plant, and are about the size of a man's hand, are borne at the summit of a stem a few inches high and of the thickness of a goose-quill. In this same locality I collected at least twenty species of rotangs (*Calamus*), and hence I named it the "Rotang Valley." Many a time I lacerated my skin and tore my clothes in making herbarium specimens of these plants, some of which have stems as thick as the wrist and a couple of hundred feet in length, and are defended by a formidable array of thorns.[1]

On account of the difficulty in collecting and in preserving these plants botanists usually content themselves with very imperfect specimens, and do not keep the long filaments armed with hooked spines which enable these rampant climbers to ascend and hold on to trees ; nor do they preserve the leaf-sheaths which envelop the stem and are the parts most covered with these thorns. Yet these are precisely the parts which it is most essential to have and to study, for they present the characters on which specific distinctions are principally based, and by which the species of the genus *Calamus* can be distinguished.

It may be laid down as a general rule that when plants are provided with spines or thorns they possess nutritive qualities, and are sought after by animals. The Calami, and other thorny palms, have a central bud or "cabbage" (*umbut*)—a most delicate morsel, much relished by many animals, monkeys amongst others ; and if this most essential portion of the plant were not well defended, it would be easily damaged or destroyed.

In Borneo, except certain palms, the pandani, and some forest Cyperaceæ (*Dapania* and *Scirpodendron*), which are also obliged to defend their central buds, thorny plants are comparatively rare, whilst they abound in those countries where ruminants are frequent. There are, however, several kinds of spinous fruits in Borneo, such as those of the durian and other *Bombaceæ,* the species of which are so numerous on this great island. These fruits contain seeds which are edible or surrounded by a pulp of agreeable flavour, and are hence much sought after by various animals.

It is, perhaps, not so easy to explain the relations which exist between the nutrient qualities of an organ or a tissue in a plant and the defensive thorns which are developed on it. My own opinion is that these latter owe their first origin to the stimuli caused by animals, especially by bites, punctures, and other lesions. In the

---

[1] Some authors have asserted that rotangs attain a length of 200 mètres (656 feet), but I cannot believe this possible. Loureiro, in his *Flora of Cochin China,* describes his *Calamus rudentum* as having a stem " 500 et lutra pedes longus ! "

remote epoch of the plasmation of organisms, an animal in gnawing a plant shortened its branches, and these, under favourable climatic conditions, were reproduced shorter or acuminated. Likewise, fruits, leaves, or other parts of plants being bitten, pricked, or torn by animals, the cicatrising tissue may have given rise to swellings, projections, spines or other hyperplasia, which on repetition may have become hereditary.

I have been speaking in the present tense; but it is not in the present period that such effects can have been produced. What can now be observed in Nature, or be produced artificially as an experiment, can only reproduce in infinitesimal measure what must have taken place in the primordial epoch of life, and this because one cannot suppress the influence now exerted on all living beings by the interminable phalanx of their progenitors. It is this inherited influence which prevents the living beings of to-day from adapting themselves to the circumstances which surround them, and obliges them to reproduce and transmit the characters inherited from their ancestors, even when such characters in the changed conditions of existence have become useless or even pernicious.

I used to visit the "Valley of Rotangs," not only for its plants, but also in search of animals. Dead tree-trunks, either standing or prostrate, were an inexhaustible field for the entomologist, and on the fungi, especially *Polyporus*, which grew in great numbers on such trunks, I always made large captures of Coleoptera, mostly dark in colour with yellow spots, belonging to the *Erotylidæ* and *Endomychidæ*. Under a large and ancient tree-trunk, fallen across the torrent, so as nearly to form a bridge, I had, on one occasion, the rare good fortune to capture a *Mormolyce*, one of the wonders of the insect world. It is a Carab of large dimensions, measuring about three inches in length, and of extraordinary shape, for its body is laminar, with elytræ greatly extended at the sides, and the head is strangely elongated. It is difficult to see what is the use of the singular conformation of this insect, which, on account of its flattened body and dull coloration, would appear to be adapted to live under the bark of trees, where, however, it has never been found. Later I found a *Mormolyce* in Sumatra, and on this occasion also it was on the surface of the inferior portion of a dead tree-trunk, slightly raised from the ground and in the densest part of the forest.

It was also in the "Valley of Rotangs" that on September 12th I came across a small flock, some five or six specimens, of a beautiful bird which I had not previously seen. Having shot one of them, the others showed no fright, and I was thus able to secure four specimens one after the other. I was not long in recognising them to be *Pityriasis gymnocephala*, one of the few birds restricted to Borneo and characteristic of its avifauna, and for this reason, long sought for by me. I was thus delighted at having secured it.

This bird is about the size of a thrush, with a large stout bill. With the exception of a wide collar of brilliant scarlet, the plumage is entirely of a glossy black. The crown of the head is bright yolk-yellow, denuded of feathers and covered with small and thickly set conical fleshy papillæ, while the space round the eyes is also bare, with the skin coloured bright red.[1]

Pityriasis can boast of a prerogative rare amongst birds—the females are more brightly coloured than the males. The difference in the plumage between the sexes is not great, but in the females the flanks are spotted with red, whilst in the males they are of a uniform black. The bird feeds on insects, and the stomachs of those I shot contained the remains of Coleoptera, especially *Brenthidæ*. This explains the presence of the birds in the neighbourhood of a recent clearing, where, on the felled trunks, such insects abound. This was the only occasion on which I met with *Pityriasis* during my three-years' stay in Borneo.

In mentioning *Pityriasis* I remarked incidentally that Borneo possessed few peculiar species of birds, i.e. such as are not found in the neighbouring regions. And this is quite true; for although Borneo supports such a rich and varied series of organic products, strange to say it is not, proportionally to other insular regions, rich in endemic types giving a marked character to its fauna, as the birds of paradise in New Guinea.

Both the fauna and flora of Borneo belong to the forest type which extends over the Malay Peninsula, Sumatra, and, in a lesser degree, Java. It is, however, with the Malay Peninsula, perhaps, more than with Sumatra, that the organic products of Borneo show closest affinities, so much so as to cause surprise that these two regions are now separated by a wide tract of sea ; indeed, the resemblance could not be greater were they united. So much is this the case in regard to the fauna, that it can be safely asserted that the mammals, birds, and reptiles of Borneo are either absolutely identical, or else represented by closely allied species on the Malay Peninsula.

The same may be said in a general way of the flora, though Borneo has a larger share of peculiar species. But, notwithstanding this, it forms one and the same botanical region with the Malay Peninsula. A notable exception is, however, caused by Mount Kina Balu, whose very elevated summit, with a special climate, has enabled strange heterogeneous forms, derived from different distant regions, to exist amid the insular flora.

---

[1] In the coloured plate of this species published in the fifth volume of the *Annali del Museo Civico di Genova*, the circumocular region is made rose colour. Such may have been the case when the specimens, which I had preserved in spirits, were taken out to be mounted. But my notes taken at once from the freshly killed specimens are very precise on this point.

On Mattang there was a great scarcity of birds, not only as
regards species, but individuals. The Great Hornbill (*Buceros
rhinoceros*) was one of the few common kinds to be seen. Hardly
a day passed whilst I was there without my coming across a couple
of these strange birds, whose presence is made very evident by the
tremendous noise they make when on the wing, a noise which recalls
that of an approaching railway train. When flying in pairs, moreover, these hornbills utter a loud and peculiar call, which can be
heard at a great distance—" *N'gam-gok, N'gam-gok*," repeated
several times in succession, a peculiarity which has earned for the
bird the name of *burong n'gam* among the Malays. It is in every
respect a singular creature, with its enormous bill surmounted by
a curious red helmet, the object and utility of which is a mystery.
This strange bill is in great request as a head and ear ornament
amongst the Dyaks ; the Chinese also prize it, and pay as much as
a dollar for a single head. The hornbill is probably quite as proud
of its enormous bill and red helmet as the Dyak is when he adorns
himself with the cumbrous eardrops which he makes with it. The
birds can hardly feel comfortable with this huge appendage, and
yet, as most ladies do, they submit, or rather have submitted, to
the tyranny of fashion, in order to attain that special ideal of beauty
during a determined psychological moment.

The monstrous bill of *B. rhinoceros*, besides being very much in the
way, appears also badly adapted to the sort of food preferred by
these birds, which consists mostly of the fruits of various species of
Ficus. These the hornbill easily plucks with its bill, but it is then
obliged to throw each fruit high up in the air, and catch it with
open mandibles and a clever jerk. Birds of this species live easily
in captivity, always taking their food in the peculiar way just
described.

Of the few mammals found on Mattang I only obtained a porcupine, which my men discovered one day in a hollow trunk lying on
the ground. We pushed the creature out with a long pole, and
secured it with a blow on the head when it emerged. Except a
few *tupaias* and squirrels, I hardly ever met with a mammal during
my wanderings in the forest. Even monkeys were scarce there.

Night after night I used to hear the call of the " burong ruei "
of the Malays, the beautiful Argus pheasant. It is extremely
difficult to shoot this bird, and it is usually caught with nooses
carefully set in the forest. But on Mattang none of my men were
proficient in this art of bird catching. Only once in the forest did
I get a glimpse of an Argus ; but I frequently found its broad wing-
feathers, so wonderful for the row of eyes, the dots, and the vermi-
culations, produced in infinite shadings of brown, which adorn it.

The Bornean Argus (*Argusianus grayi*) is considered distinct
from the one found in Sumatra and on the Malay Peninsula (*A.*

Argus). It is a bird of nocturnal habits, and it is during the night only that the cock utters its love cry. But even if its nocturnal habits were not well known, I believe that they might have been more than suspected by a look at the coloration of its feathers, a character which is usually connected with the manner of life the bearer leads. I may take this opportunity of mentioning the singular analogy to be found between the coloration of birds and that of Lepidoptera. In both cases tho general colour is in numerous instances so similar to that of their usual surroundings that the two are practically identical, and the bird or butterfly is invisible to its enemies. In other instances it would seem as if they had selected from their surroundings the most brilliant and brightly coloured object as a pattern for their adornment. The Argus suggests to me a case in point, its ocellated feathers resembling in a remarkable manner the tints and distribution of colours in our largest moth (*Saturnia pyri*). The ocelli on the wings of this moth, as on those of the Argus, are so close an imitation of the eyes of an animal that even the reflection of light is reproduced in them. I take it that these ocelli represent false eyes, and were originally the product of impressions received from real ones : in short, that the pigment granules of the scales of the moth and those of the bird's feathers have grouped and arranged themselves in certain points so as to reproduce exactly the luminous impression received. There must, therefore, be some sort of correlation between the nervous system and the blood-vessels to have reproduced the image of the eyes ; and we can thus compare the feathers of birds and the scales on the wings of Lepidoptera—or rather the pigment which gives them colour—to sensitive photographic plates acted upon by the image formed on the retina of the eye.

The life I led in my retreat at " Vallombrosa " was in every way agreeable to me. I found pleasant occupation for each hour of the day, and was so thoroughly happy and contented that I felt no wish for change. But it was not so with my men ; and one day towards the end of September they came to me in a body, complaining of the cold, and saying that they wished to return to Kuching. I felt that I could hardly refuse them their request. My Chinese boy, who acted as cook, alone did not express any desire to leave me ; but then he was hardly sufficient for the work at a time when a great number of new trees were successively coming into blossom, and specimens of them had to be collected. I therefore sent him also to Kuching along with my Malays, with instructions to find and engage new men. But several days passed and no one came, so that I was quite alone.

The solitary life of a hermit in that grand forest was to me far from unpleasant ; I may even confess to a certain satisfaction at having to depend upon no one but myself. My health was perfect, and I had nothing to fear from man or beast. My provision of rice was sufficient, and my hencoop was well stocked. Here, however, a small cloud arose. The greater solitude and quiet of the place emboldened certain four-footed marauders, perhaps some of the *Viverridæ*, and every night my stock of poultry diminished This made me resolve to eat them myself as fast as I could, rather than let them furnish food to the thieves, of whom I was never able to catch a sight. More than once during the night I was awakened by a cry of distress coming from my poultry yard : the old cock always gave the alarm, fought courageously, and was thrice wounded, but I never succeeded in reaching the scene of the battle in time.

Of course, among my daily occupations was now that of preparing and cooking my dinner : wringing the neck of my daily fowl, plucking it, and putting it into the pot with the rice, which completed my menu. This was occasionally varied by a pigeon or a hornbill, which took the place of the fowl in the pot, unless I preferred to grill it over the grating where I usually dried my plants. One of my chief anxieties was that of keeping my fire alight from day to day. Being unprovided with matches it was only with the greatest difficulty that I managed to re-light it, if it once went out, by means of a flint and steel which I had. The difficulty, however, was not to get my tinder to ignite, but to obtain a blaze, for the weather was rainy and every object was saturated with moisture. Thus I took the greatest precautions to keep the fire constantly alight. But one morning what I feared came to pass, and on going to the fireplace not a spark could I find under the ashes. A fire was necessary and had to be lit ; but for fully an hour my efforts with the flint and steel were ineffectual, until at length I remembered that I had my gunpowder, and when once the tinder was alight I had no longer any difficulty in starting my fire.

But the weather now kept getting steadily worse. The north-east monsoon was making itself felt, and frequent and sudden storms threatened to level my hermitage with the ground. In this solitary clearing in the continuous forest the wind had good play, and several trees threatened to fall. One of them, indeed, did do so, and fell on my house, knocking in one of the corners ; but this fortunately happened during the day time.

Another hurricane, on a night as dark as Erebus, almost made me think the end of the world had come. The furious blasts shrieked through the tops of the giant trees and tore off branches in all directions ; while every now and again the roar of the fall of some monarch of the forest was heard above the storm. The rain fell in torrential downpours, accompanied by a hail of sticks and branches. I was afraid that one of the latter might kill me as I lay, even if my house escaped destruction by the fall of one of the big trees surrounding it. At last the storm died down and I was able to get some sleep. The next morning I found that the house had been badly damaged and required repairs. It was the twelfth day that I had been left by myself, and now, if I wished to stay on, men would be required for repairing the house, as well as for other necessary work. I therefore made up my mind to return to Kuching, and did so on the following day.

At Kuching I found that my Chinese boy had not only never attempted to get fresh men for me, but had actually left the country. It is certainly wonderful how easily servants desert you in Sarawak, but as a compensation it is quite as easy to get new ones ; and this I at once did.

Having collected my new servants, I went, as a first excursion, for a shooting trip to Buntal, at the mouth of one of the smaller branches of the Sarawak river, where I had been told that shore birds abounded, and some good shooting was to be had at that season. We started early on the tenth of October, and when I arrived at the place I found that my information was correct, and the sea-shore was literally alive with birds. I cannot remember how many I shot, but I exhausted all my ammunition, and preserved specimens of eight species as yet unrepresented in my ornithological collection.[1]

During the latter half of October and the beginning of November I was engaged in packing up the collection I had already made. I also collected from the natives every kind of vegetable product I was able to hear of. Towards the middle of November I started on an excursion to the upper waters and sources of the Sarawak river, but I must leave the account of this to the next chapter.

---

[1] The species got at Buntal were the following : *Ægialitis peronii, Æ. mongolicus, Æ. geoffroyi, Strepsilas interpres, Pelidna subarquata, Actidromas albescens, Terekia cinerea, Numenius phæopus* (cf. SALVADORI, *Uccelli di Borneo*).

CHAPTER X

WITH the flowing tide, at half-past three o'clock in the morning of the 15th November, I started from my head-
quarters at Kuching to ascend the southern branch of the Sarawak
river, into which flow the waters collected on the slopes of Mount
Pennerrissen. Beyond Lida Tana we lost the help of the tide and
had to take to our paddles, continuing thus till'noon. After a rest to
cook and eat our rice, we resumed our row up the river, but as the
current was getting stronger and stronger we were obliged to have
recourse to poling. As the river was shallow, we progressed thus pretty
rapidly. We passed the small affluent of Sunta, where we found
a few Malays engaged in washing for diamonds. At three o'clock
in the afternoon we reached the village of Koom. Here, in addition
to a number of Malays, I met an Englishman who, commissioned
by the "Borneo Company," was trying his luck with diamonds,
using a big boat provided with a curious spoon-shaped dredge, with
which sand and pebbles from the bottom were brought up and
carefully sifted and searched for diamonds.

The Malays wash for diamonds in the same way as for gold,
using circular wooden trays (*dulang*) with a wide conical concavity
and measuring some two feet in diameter. The earth and fine
gravel or sand is placed in the tray, to which a slight rotating
movement is given as it is dipped from time to time in the running
water. In this manner the dirt and lighter particles are washed
away, and the heavier ones, such as particles of metal, or precious
stones, remain at the bottom in the central conical depression.
The diamonds found at Koom and elsewhere on the Sarawak river
are rarely of very pure water, and are mostly tinged with yellow.
Some that I saw had a decided reddish tint, a variety much appreciated in the country when the gem is not too small. The
diamonds I saw were of very variable shapes: some were perfect

octahedrons; others had three and six facets on each of the faces of the octahedron; and there were also hemihedral or bisected forms. The diamond-yielding alluvium also contains gold, but in small quantities.

A Malay showed me the results he had obtained in three months' work, consisting solely of four small diamonds, which together could hardly have weighed half a carat. Another in a month's work had found nothing except a few minute flakes of gold of the value of perhaps a couple of shillings. He told me that he had spent four dollars in provisions and in travelling to the spot, and he had besides paid one dollar to the Government for his licence to wash. The more sanguine and hard workers are buoyed up by the hope of finding some stone worth, say, 100–150 dollars, which would recompense them for the labour and expense incurred during the preceding fruitless months.

The Malays use certain seeds called "*Bua saga*" for weighing diamonds. These are of the size of a large pea, and weigh about a carat. They are slightly depressed, of a somewhat irregular lenticular shape, very hard, and with a highly polished bright red surface. They are a product of a leguminous tree, *Adenanthera pavonina*, which is of Indian origin, but is sometimes to be met with planted near huts and houses, even at Sarawak.

I was desirous of ascertaining how nearly these seeds approximated to the weight they were supposed to represent, and was surprised to find that they vary very slightly indeed, corresponding almost precisely in weight to the English carat of 205 centigrammes. Of five such seeds taken at random I found three weighing exactly a carat; the other two were one centigramme under weight.

The profession of diamond washer is well adapted to the Malays, who are born gamblers. They love to tempt fortune, and the hope of one day securing a big prize makes them forget that steady work would prove far more profitable. The Chinese prefer washing for gold, which gives a smaller but more certain gain.

During my stay in Borneo I did not hear of any big diamond being found in the Sarawak river, but it is not in the Malay character to talk much about any such stroke of fortune; and if any were found it is not improbable that they were quietly smuggled out of the country. Perhaps the fear of attracting other prospectors, or making the Government augment the licence tax may also contribute to this. Later, however, I heard that stones of 16, 18, and even one of 72 carats had been got at Koom.

The same evening I and my English friend aforesaid proceeded farther up the river for an hour and a half, using a small boat on account of the shallows and frequent rapids. The banks become more and more picturesque, being formed of lime-stone rocks of strange shapes through which the river winds. These rocks, eroded by the action of the water, are very ragged and irregular. They contain various fossils, such as shells and echinoderms of sorts, and amongst the former some looked like *Terebratulæ*.[1] Here and there the rocks were dotted with rounded masses or tubercles the size of one's fist, and even larger, formed by silicious concretions. The Malays call these "*batu tikus*," i.e. "mouse stones," from their shape and dark grey colour. The trees we met were all different from those which grow on the banks lower down the river. It was quite dark and raining heavily when we got back to Koom. Having arranged to ascend the river towards its source, we once more started on the 16th November. Our party consisted of twenty-five persons in four boats, two large and two small. We got off at 8 a.m., and halted at noon on a small island in the river to cook our dinner. In the neighbourhood, on the sites of former plantations, we found growing abundantly a wild banana (*Musa campestris*, Becc., *P.B.* No. 2,722). At three o'clock in the afternoon we reached S'bungo, a Dyak village, where we decided to pass the night. On examining the pebbles in the river, we found amongst them bits of a substance which had the appearance of graphite, and we proposed next day to search along the banks to find it *in situ*.

The next morning at half-past eight we were again on our way. The rocks of the country we were passing through varied : now limestone, now schists, and now sandstone, while a species of conglomerate was also common. Some of the limestone masses formed vertical peaks rising from 350 ft. to 500 ft. in height, and had plants on them which were unknown to me ; but to get at them was no easy matter on such inaccessible cliffs. We came at length to a bifurcation of the river, and followed the branch to the left, which is the one which penetrates farthest into the interior. Several rapids—or *riam* as the natives call them—were passed successfully. My sampan was rather heavy for this part of the river, but we managed to carry it even beyond the Riam Lidong, the last and most dangerous of them all, dragging it with rotangs over the big rocks between which the water tears and foams, rushing by with tremendous velocity. This last part of the river is picturesque beyond description, the trees clinging to the rocks, and spreading their serpent-like roots in all directions, whilst their branches overhung the water and gave us a shade which was not a little appreciated.

One of the commonest trees here was a species of fig (afterwards described from my specimens by Sir George King under the name of *Ficus acidula*), which bears on its large branches bunches of fine red fruits, very like our own figs, of an acidulated and not

[1] This is from my notes. The specimens which I collected have been unfortunately lost, and cannot, therefore, be determined accurately.

unpleasant flavour. Acid juices are unusual in the genus *Ficus*, and this is the only species to my knowledge which presents such a peculiarity. Amongst the notable trees in the vicinity I must not forget to mention the handsome *Dillenia indica* and a Dipterocarp, the "mengkabang chankie" of the Malays (*Isoptera Borneensis*, Scheff, *P.B.* No. 2,795). This tree produces an immense quantity of small fruits similar to hazel nuts, surrounded by a calyx with five rounded lobes. These fruits ripen in the rainy season, and falling in large quantities into the water are carried by the current down to Kuching, where they are collected by women and children, being highly prized, for the best quality of mengkabang oil is obtained from their seed. A short distance beyond Riam Lidong the river bifurcates again. The left branch (for those who ascend) leads to Senna. On the right one, houses at once come into view. These belong partly to Chinamen, who have gardens here, partly to Malays, small traders, or diamond washers. This place, which we had taken five hours to reach from S'bungo, is named Pangkalan Ampat, which means the landing-place (*pangkalan*) for four (*ampat*) villages, and several Dyak tribes come here for trade.

Having asked the Malays at Pangkalan Ampat if coal or "*Batu aran*" (charcoal-stone) as they term it, existed in the neighbourhood, they asserted that it was to be found on the banks of a small stream which ran into the river just below the nearest rapid. Several hours of daylight were still available, and we decided to go there at once and see how far the assertion was true. Taking a small boat and two men well accustomed to descending the Riam Lidong, an operation much more dangerous than the ascent, we reached in a few minutes a place named Batu Ujong, where on the left bank a small stream enters the river. Ascending this streamlet for five or six hundred yards we came upon the so-called coal deposit. It was merely a seam about three feet thick of a carboniferous-looking schist having in certain places the aspect of graphite, interposed between the sandstone and the limestone. Our informants told us also that diamonds had been got in this stream. I picked up fragments of silicified wood, which was apparently that of a species of *Cycadoxylon*.

On November 18th my companion was obliged to return to Kuching; but I remained, awaiting the Senna Dyaks, whom I had sent for to fetch my luggage, and to guide me to Mount Pennerrissen, of which I wished to attempt the ascent. But as they did not turn up, I pursuaded two other Dyaks, who had come down to Pengkalan Ampat from Tappo Kakas to buy salt, to accompany me to their village and carry my luggage, which I had naturally reduced to the smallest possible dimensions. They willingly accepted, and we started at 11 a.m., together with my Malays. After crossing several Chinese orchards we soon found ourselves at the foot of a hill, whence two pathways led to the village of my guides—one crossing over the hill, and the other going round its base. The latter follows the course of the river, here called Sungei T'bia, in whose waters it was necessary to wade most of the way. Fearing that my botanical paper might get wetted if I followed this path, I took the other one, but soon found that, instead of one hill, we had to go up and down several, and, in addition, cross a torrent many times, which was in some places deep and rapid. Indeed, I more than once felt almost carried off my legs by the force of the current, and should certainly have been had not the two Dyaks taken me between them and supported me. They, with their naked feet, could get a good grip of the stones in the river bed, and thus had the advantage over me in my European shoes.

In various places we crossed over deep ravines on bare bamboos ingeniously bound to the trees on each side, and forming a most elegant suspension bridge (Fig. 26), but much pleasanter, however, to look at than to cross.

It was nearly dark when we reached the village of Tappo Kakas, On the road I met with a large specimen of that most beautiful of Bornean orchids, *Vanda (Renanthera) Lowi*, in full bloom. In hothouses at home this plant produces a profusion of flowers, perhaps even more than in its native land ; but the manner in which it in cultivated, placed erect in a pot, cannot convey any idea of it in its native forests, where, adhering by its roots to the limb of some big branch or to its bifurcation, its leaves shoot upwards, whilst its grand racemes of large flowers, sometimes quite ten feet in length, hang pendulous below.

The ground here is very steep and broken, but appears to be of a better quality than the soil near Kuching ; it is abundantly supplied with water, which wells out in every direction, and collects clear and sparkling in the numerous streamlets and torrents.

At Tappo Kakas I was lodged in a house at the end of the village, which for the time being was deserted, most of the inhabitants being away in the fields clearing the rice of weeds. It was my intention to start from this place, which has an elevation of about 1,150 feet, for the summit of Gunong Pennerrissen, or as I have also heard it pronounced, " Mengrissen." This has been considered one of the highest mountains in Sarawak, but it is certainly inferior to Gunong Poe. Seen from a distance, Mount Pennerrissen does not seem to have any very striking summit, nor to tower much above its neighbours.

The Dyaks of Tappo Kakas, for some special motive of their own, showed no wish to guide me up the mountain. On the contrary, they did their best to dissuade me from attempting the ascent, and declared that unheard-of difficulties would beset me on my road to the summit. Most certainly from the village in which I was the way to Mount Pennerrissen was neither short nor easy, as I could see for myself. Besides, I had brought with me only a small quantity of provisions. So making a virtue of necessity, I contented myself with the ascent of Gunong Wa, an easy undertaking from Tappo Kakas. On November 19th, accordingly, I started with four or five Dyaks accompanying me as guides. The side of the mountain was far from steep, and after a couple of hours very easy climb up an excellent pathway, we reached the summit, which is a kind of plateau, the mountain having no real culminating prominence. For this reason there was no view, it being impeded on all sides by the forest trees, and I was in consequence somewhat disappointed with my excursion.

The formation is sandstone, as I believe it to be in all the hills of the group I had crossed, of coarse elements, containing pebbles of quartz and other silicious minerals, and easily disintegrated. It might almost be called a quartzose conglomerate. Having examined the *karangan*, or gravel beds, in which diamonds are found at Sunta, and all along the Sarawak river, it appears to me highly probable that the gems originate from the disintegration of the rocky mass of the Pennerrissen group. If this be true, they ought to be found *in situ* in the rocks of which these mountains are composed.

Up to an elevation of about 2,000 feet the slopes of the mountain either were then, or had some time or other been, under rice cultivation, and the primeval forest had therefore disappeared. In most of the abandoned plantations a gigantic bamboo grew with great luxuriance, forming huge clumps, which recalled to my mind those I had admired along the Mahawelliganga in the Botanic Gardens at Peradeniya, in Ceylon. It was, no doubt, a *Dendrocalamus*. The internodes of its young shoots contained a large quantity of limpid cool water which flowed out as from a tap if an incision was made in them. I am not aware if this peculiarity is constant in this species of bamboo, or whether it occurs in others when growing in localities provided with a superabundance of water in the soil, as was undoubtedly the case here.[1] I have stated in a previous chapter that cultivated bamboos in Borneo rarely run to seed, and are never met with in the true primeval forest, except in localities once under cultivation or near

---

[1] Recently here, in Florence, after abundant rain, I found the young shoots of a bamboo (*Bambusa viridi-glaucescens*) with their internodes full of water. But this abnormal absorption soon caused them to turn yellow and perish, the internodes becoming detached one from the other.

Fig. 26.—A BAMBOO BRIDGE ON THE UPPER SARAWAK.

habitations. The gigantic bamboo mentioned above may therefore have been introduced from Java, probably with other cultivated plants, at the period when the benefits of the Hindu-Javanese civilisation was extended also to the people of Borneo.

On Gunong Wa I noticed an ingenious way of utilising bamboos in the construction of huts or temporary shelters in the jungle. The big stems split in halves were not only used for the sides of the house, but a very efficient roof was made by laying them alternately with the convex and with the concave side upwards, with the edges over-lapping.[1] Our tiled roofs have the same arrangement. Is it possible that they have originated from similar constructions in bamboo used by our remote ancestors ?

On the top of Gunong Wa I was not able to collect many plants ; most were trees and out of blossom. I noted, however, several species of *Quercus*, and some very large specimens of *Podocarpus cupressina*, R.B., and the *Eugeissonia*, which I had already found on Mattang ; it appears to love sandstone hills. But the best find I made on this excursion was a new *Joinvillea* (*J. Borneensis*, Becc.), a plant which possesses the attributes both of the grasses and of the palms, with a stem of the size of a slender reed six or eight feet high, and with elongated and folded leaves. Of the genus *Joinvillea* only two others are known besides this species, one from the Sandwich Islands, the other from Fiji. All three are very similar, but the Bornean one is more akin to that from Fiji, from which it only differs in minute characters of the flower. The discovery of this plant on Gunong Wa is very singular on account of the enormous distance which separates it from the allied species. It is not unlikely that the *Joinvilleas* were formerly plants of far wider diffusion, and that some special cause has destroyed them in intermediate localities.

One of the more important additions to my collection on this occasion was also a new species of parasitical plant, a *Balanophora*, with the aspect of a mushroom, which I have named *B. reflexa*.

I had decided to go back to Pankalan Ampat on November 20th, but the Orang Kaya (headman of the village) invited me to stay, for on that day one of the great annual fêtes of the Dyaks was to be solemnised in the village.

From early dawn preparations for a grand banquet had been going on on the platform which projected from the covered part of one of the biggest houses. On one side of this platform about a dozen gongs hung from a horizontal pole. This was the orchestra, whose harmony was to enliven the banquet. On large banana leaves, which acted as tablecloths, were placed the dishes, consist-

---

[1] The roofs of the huts of the Kachin in Tenasserim are made in precisely the same way (cf. *Fed, Op. cit.*, p. 382).

ing of boiled rice and small pieces of boiled pork and fowl, with dried and salted fish. But the favourite condiment was a horrible paste made by mixing well-rotted minced pork and squashed durian pulp. I need not describe the appalling exhalations of that paste, the greatest delicacy of the Land-Dyaks! From noon till dusk the gongs and drums beat unceasingly, and eating went on. All who came were welcome guests, and invited to partake of the food abundantly supplied.

Wishing to utilise my time, I got the Dyaks to bring me samples of all the species of fruit which they cultivated around the village.

Fig. 27.—LAND-DYAK GIRLS.

Besides those I was already acquainted with, which are to be found near all the Land-Dyaks' villages, I found here that of the *Elateriospermum Tapos*, Bl., which they call *bua ruppi*. The tree which bears it is a handsome Euphorbia, and its fruit divides into three segments, each of which contains a big feculous seed about one and a half inches long. The ruppi is cultivated, but I was told it is to be met with in a wild state in the neighbouring forest; its seeds are edible only after having been for some time macerated in water. But the most remarkable fruits at Tappo Kakas were five species of

Nephelium, similar to the common rambutan (*Nephelium lappaceum*), but yet distinct.   At the time of my visit they were as yet unknown to science, but they have since been described by Professor Radlkofer, of Munich, from the specimens then obtained by me.

These fruits differ slightly in external appearance, but are similar in the flavour of the pulp which envelops the seeds.   Are they forest species, brought and planted round the houses, or are they hybrids between wild species and the cultivated *Nephelium lappaceum*? I am unable to answer these queries, which naturally arise in the mind of a botanist.   It is certainly an unusual thing to find cultivated in one village five congeneric species of excellent fruits as yet unknown to science.

From Tappo Kakas various roads, or rather pathways, lead into Dutch territory, and as it was my intention later to cross the border, I collected all available information about them.   Descending Gunong Wa on the side opposite to that which I had gone up, one comes to the upper part of the course of the Sambas river, and from here a track leads south, which is probably the easiest way from Upper Sarawak into the Dutch possessions.   Slightly to the eastward, between Gunong Wa and Gunong Sikkom, is a pathway which leads to the headwaters of the Landak river.   A third route, still farther east, passes between Gunong Badji and Gunong Pennerrissen, leading to the village of Sango, near which flows the Sikayan or Karangan, an affluent of the Kapuas.

From Senna, also, one can get into the basin of the Kapuas. The road leaves Mount Pennerrissen to the west, crosses the Sodos hill, from which the Sadong takes its source, and reaches Senankan, near the sources of the river of this name.   The first part, from Senna, can be got over in a day and a half.   From Senankan, five or six hours' march, without any notable hill climbs, takes one to Sempio, and thence to Mrao and Sintas, all villages on the Karangan river.

The Pennerrissen group is an isolated elevation which is not connected with any extensive mountain range, and lies between the territory of Sarawak and that of Sambas and Pontianak.   From its northern slopes flow the waters of the eastern arm of the Sarawak river, and those of the Sadong ; while from the southern slopes rise the Sambas, Landak, and Sikayan rivers, the latter, as I have said before, an affluent of the Kapuas.

On November 21st I was back at Pankalan Ampat, where I remained the following day to collect the many interesting plants I had noticed passing through.   Amongst them was a wild mangosteen—known to the natives as *bua kandon*—(*Garcinia Beccarii*, Pierre), which I had noticed elsewhere on the banks of this branch of the Sarawak river.   It is a small tree producing fruits similar in size and in shape to small wild apples, with a rosy yellowish rind.

The few seeds are surrounded by an acidulated pulp of extremely pleasant flavour, which recalls that of the mangosteen. The fruit of the Garcinia is, perhaps, the best of those of the wild species of this genus (known in various parts of Malaysia by the name of *bua kandis*) which are often pleasant enough in flavour, but always too acid. In addition to the excellence of its fruit, *Garcinia Beccarii* is also worthy of note for a species of gamboge which exudes from the trunk.

On the 23rd I went to Senna, an easy journey by river, the stream flowing shallow and clear over a level bed of gravel. As the water was so low we had to pole along, and I had a good opportunity of seeing how skilfully the Dyaks of this district, both men and women, handle the " *swar*."

Senna is one of the largest villages of the Land-Dyaks, and numerous houses occupy both sides of the river, built on fine level ground, shaded with splendid durians, rambutans, coconut and areca palms, and other fruit-trees.

In one of the larger rambutans, amidst its big branches, I noticed a hut, in which were living, isolated from the rest of their fellow creatures, a few miserable beings afflicted with a loathsome disease, probably leprosy, which the Dyaks recognise to be contagious. More than twenty years before, Low had observed the same system of isolation at Senna, and it is not improbable that the hut I saw was on the same tree. At Senna fruit-trees thrive splendidly, and evidently the soil is most favourable to them. Some were new to me, as the *bua paya* (*Flacourtia acida*), *bua sintol* (*Sandoricum Maingayi*), and *bua lagnier*, better known to the Dyaks under the name of *bua mignarin*. The tree of the latter is small ; I could find none in blossom and cannot say to what genus, or even to what family it belongs. The fruit is yellowish green, perfectly spherical and smooth, of the size of a small orange, but not of much value for eating, the white pulp which envelops the seed being very sweet but rather nauseous. It is, however, much used by Malays as a sort of soap wherewith to wash their heads.

The Senna Dyaks cultivate various tuberous plants, amongst them a *Tacca* and a *Dioscorea*. To the latter genus—at least to the best of my belief—belongs a plant known as *gadong*, of which I was only shown the leaves. It was stated to produce tubers of such enormous size that two men are required to carry one.

The rice fields at this time of the year are overrun with weeds, and the women were very busy rooting them up. It is hardly necessary to say that they all belong to species of wide distribution. Amongst the most abundant were some *Cyperaceæ* (*Cyperus compressus*, L.; *Mariscus umbellatus*, Vahl., and others).

Next day I visited a thermal spring, which flows from the bank of a streamlet at about an hour's walk from the village of Senna. The water was clear and left no appreciable deposit, even when allowed to stand for a time in a glass tumbler. It had a sulphurous smell. A thermometer I placed in the spring reached the high temperature of 163° Fahr.

On the 24th I returned to Penkalan Ampat, and the next day found me on my journey back to Kuching. On the way I stopped at Sabungo to ascend Gunong Braam, a limestone hill in the vicinity, where I got some interesting botanical novelties. In Borneo the plants which have a predilection for calcareous soil do not appear to be frequent; on the contrary, the greater number dislike it, leaving the epiphytes out of the question. All herbaceous forest plants, as well as ligneous ones, live in the humus and extend their roots in the superficial stratum formed of vegetable detritus. This is no doubt the reason why most tropical plants cultivated in hothouses require a compost rich in humus, and must have water that is free from lime. I passed the night of the 26th at Koom, and the next day reached my house at Kuching.

In December I returned to Mattang, where I found plenty to do in collecting specimens of the fruit of those trees of which I had previously collected the blossom. The *Dipterocarpeæ* formed the special object of my search.

The greater part of January was employed in constant excursions around Kuching, where I remained during the whole of February chiefly occupied in arranging and packing my collections. During March I made an excursion to Lobang Angin, one of the caves in the limestone hills along the western branch of the Sarawak river. We started from Kuching on the morning of the 2nd, in my sampan with its usual crew. Close to the banks of the river, a little above the town, I was struck by the very peculiar colour of a herbaceous plant, which caught the eye at once among the rest of the vegetation, and was called by my men *daun balik angin*, i.e. " the leaf that changes with the wind "—a name probably derived from the very different coloration of the leaves, which are green at the lower part of the plant, and of a brilliant salmon red at the upper part, where the flowering takes place. The plant is a *Clerodendron*, which I have distinguished as *C. discolor* (Becc., P.B. No. 35 and 3,584). I passed the night at Busso, and the next day we continued to ascend the river. On a tree on the bank I noticed two squirrels, one brown, the other perfectly white; they were probably male and female, and this is the only albino mammal which I saw in Borneo. We also met with a crocodile sleeping on the bank, belonging to the species called by the natives " *buaya katak*." I snatched up my rifle, but it was too quick for me, and disappeared under water before I could fire.

We next passed under Gunong Tundong, a small limestone

Fig. 28.—LOBANG ANGIN, UPPER SARAWAK.

mountain, steep-to, as are all such on this and the other branch of the Sarawak river, and after some hours travelling we reached the cave. This has several openings, but one of the chief of them practically debouches on the river. It has received the name it bears with the Malays, which means Cave (*lobang*) of the Winds (*angin*), because at certain times a strong current of air issues from its aperture. Just within the entrance we found a bank of deposit, which, at the time of our visit, was a good deal above the level of the river. Beneath it the floor of the cave had been much hollowed out by the river, which, during floods, must enter this mouth and striking against the farther wall, make a sort of whirlpool, wearing away the wall on one side, and forming deposits on the other. The soil thus formed was yellow and argillaceous, and was in some parts covered with stalagmite, in others bare. The height of the deposit, evidently greater than could possibly be accounted for by the highest floods, led to the conclusion that considerable changes of level must have taken place.

I had not brought with me any spades or other implements for digging, but I managed to do a little with a pointed stick, and was so far successful that I got some pieces of human bones, an entire human lower-jaw, various fragments of earthenware vessels, and a small perforated disc, probably part of a necklace. I also found bits of charcoal, which was very abundant in some places, together with fragments of marine and freshwater shells—the relics of native repasts of no very ancient date.

The cave penetrates deeply into the mountain, but being then without a proper guide I did not attempt its exploration. Bats were hanging from the roof in numbers, and the small swift which I had seen with Doria at Pininjau (*Collocalia linchii*) was abundant. I shot several as they flew in and out of the cave ; their edible nests are of a very inferior kind.

Coming up the river I had shot various birds, amongst them a hawk, a kingfisher, and a remarkable barbet with a big and brilliantly coloured bill, the *Cymborhynchus macrorhynchus*. This bird also possesses the most beautiful eye I have ever seen. The iris is a brilliant emerald green, with metallic changing dots, like a piece of Venetian glass—so far as I know, a unique instance of the kind in the bird world.

I continued to ascend the river in the hope of finding some one who could act as guide to me in exploring the cave. That evening we reached Bidi. Along this portion of the Sarawak river there is no primitive forest, and the plains stretch away from the banks entirely covered with lalang grass, and only broken here and there by the usual abrupt isolated hills of limestone rock. At Bidi I found the man I wanted in the person of a Dyak, who was bought over by a *bijit* monkey I had shot on the way ; in exchange for which coveted morsel he consented to be my guide to the Lobang Angin.

The Dyak led me to another entrance of the cave, on the land side, also wide, but not so easy of access as that on the river, for we had to climb a steep rock, very rough and beset with sharp points, in order to reach it.   On this side, as on the other, the cave presented a spacious hall which extended deep into the mountain in a winding manner, branching off into lateral corridors leading to various outlets.   Nearly in the centre of the large hall-like portion, in a deep fissure of the vault, is the breeding place of the true edible-nest swift (*Collocalia nidifica*), its gelatinous nests being attached to the nearly vertical rock.   There were none now, for the Dyak who was with me as guide had been there on the very day previous for the purpose of taking them.   From him I learnt that a small mouse-like animal inhabits the cave, in holes in the ground. I saw a goodly number of these holes, but nothing of the animal itself.   I searched in vain, too, for blind Coleoptera, and any other special cave creatures.   A good deal of loose earthy soil, undoubtedly carried in by water, is to be found in this part of the cave, as in the other, which would be further evidence of a general elevation of the hill at a period not very remote.

Whilst descending the river on my way back I found a specimen of the lovely *Dendrobium superbum*, with large lilac-rose flowers, growing on the trunk of a tree.   It is, I think, one of the most beautiful orchids in Borneo, and is found also in the Philippines. At Bau I stayed awhile to have a look at the gold washings, which are worked by a considerable number of Chinamen.   At this place, and not in the above described cave, as has been asserted, fossil teeth of rhinoceros have been found.

I passed the night at Busso, and the next day went on to Blida, where, crossing the river, I shot a small crocodile, the only one amongst the many I fired at which I was able to secure.   In the Sarawak river the common species of crocodile (*Crocodilus biporcatus*) is abundant, even in the vicinity of Kuching ; and there have been instances of persons carried off by these voracious reptiles, even from the bazaar quay.   A premium of one rupee was given per foot (in length) for every crocodile caught.

That evening I remained at Blida, where I was able to secure several species of birds which abounded on that portion of the banks of the Sarawak river.   A beautiful pink and green bee-eater (*Nyctiornis amicta*) was particularly abundant.   I also got some plovers, which made an agreeable addition to my ordinary meals of curry and rice.   On March 6th I again ascended the Pininjau, partly for the sake of its splendid view, and partly to get specimens of the small swift which is so abundant there, and which Doria had asked me to collect for him, for at that time our knowledge of the edible-nest swifts (*Collocalia*) and their allies left much to be desired. The temperature on the top of the hill was delicious : at 11 a.m., when I reached the Rajah's bungalow, the thermometer was at 77° Fahr. ; at 2 p.m. it had only risen to about 80°. In the evening I was back at Blida, where I always stayed with pleasure on account of the excellent shooting to be had. Next day I returned once more to Kuching.

CHAPTER XI

DURING the two years I had been wandering among the forests of Borneo, I had not yet met with a single Orang-utan ; but up to that period botanical collections had so occupied my time, and the country I had explored had given me such rich results, that I had not cared to stray far from Kuching, where the great anthropoid ape is very rare, and to go in search of it on the Sadong or on the Batang Lupar, where it abounds.

On the Sadong Wallace had long resided and collected ; I therefore chose the Batang Lupar, whence I could easily pass into the Dutch territory of Kapuas, and visit the lakes which exist along the upper portion of the course of that great river.

In March, 1867, the Tuan Muda, having occasion to send his gunboat, the *Heartsease*, to Lingga, kindly allowed me to take this opportunity of going there with the larger portion of my provisions, while at the same time my men were to take the sampan which was to convey me during the remainder of the journey.

At 8 a.m., on March 17th, the *Heartsease* left her moorings, steamed down the Sarawak river, and reached the sea by the Maratabas channel. The weather was splendid ; the sea like a mirror. We turned eastwards, making straight for the mouth of the Batang Lupar. Behind us rose the dark bold outline of Tanjong Po, slowly emerging from the thin morning mist ; and on our right the low coast line revealed itself with its monotonous fringe of verdure, consisting of mangroves where the shore is muddy, and of casuarinas where sand prevails. Behind this belt of interminable forest rises Gunong Lessong, remarkable for its truncated form and its wide base.[1] Passing quite close to Pulo Burong, I could see that

---

[1] *Lessong* is the name given by the Malays to the large wooden mortar for husking rice. For this operation they use a long thick pestle, which is not unlike our grape piler. Gunong Lessong owes its name to its resemblance to one of these mortars turned topsy-turvy.

this little rocky island was completely clothed, especially on its upper portion, by a handsome palm, whose enormous racemes loaded with flowers and fruits looked like small Cypress trees protruding from the midst of crowns of sago-palm fronds. It is undoubtedly a species of *Eugeissonia*, which, although I was unable to examine it more closely, I consider identical with one I subsequently found on the banks of the Rejang and at Brunei. As it is a useful plant from which good feculum can be extracted, I should not be surprised if orginally its seeds had been brought to the island by Dyaks. Borneo, forming the very centre of the area of their past piratical expeditions, may have been used by them as a victualling station. A little before sunset we passed the small island which stands in the middle of the mouth of the Batang Lupar. When the sun dipped below the horizon, darkness came on very suddenly ; but the night was clear, and our captain being well acquainted with the soundings, we continued our way up stream. At 9 p.m. we had reached our goal, the old fort of Lingga, once the residence of the Tuan Muda, and now completely abandoned. It is placed on the right bank, near the mouth of the Lingga river, the first affluent to be met with on the right, ascending the main stream. As my boat had not yet arrived, I had my luggage taken into the fort—a low wooden building, hidden amidst coconuts and fruit trees. All around the soil was swampy and honeycombed by hosts of crustaceans, which make myriads of little hillocks with the earth extracted from the burrows in which they live.

The next day, my boat still not having arrived, I took my gun and explored the neighbourhood. I was able to shoot several species of birds which I had not met with before ; amongst them was *Lalage terat*, Cass., a bird which, in flight and size, is somewhat like a swallow. It has the habit of taking a few rapid turns in the air and then perching on the extremity of a bare branch of one of the trees growing on the banks of the river.

On the opposite side of the Lingga river the land is low, and was in former times occupied by rice fields, but at the period of my visit was overrun with a large kind of grass, a species of *Ischæmum*, which forms immense meadows, pleasant to see at a distance, but in which walking would be impossible, for it reaches a height of some eight or ten feet. Moreover, the soil underneath is a morass, and one would sink up to the knees in mud and slush. The mosquitoes thrive by the legion, and render life intolerable.

On the nineteenth of March I left Lingga fort before the tide flowed, but awaited the tidal wave at the mouth of the Sungei Batu, another affluent of the Batang Lupar, where, in a safe position, I was able to observe the curious effect that this produces in the shallower parts, where, instead of the ordinary bore, the water appears violently agitated in disordered movements, and seems as if it were boiling tumultuously.   At 4 p.m. I reached Fort Simanggan without notable incidents.

The next day, about four o'clock in the afternoon, having ascertained that the tidal current had reached the fort, we continued our ascent of the river with its aid.   Soon afterwards we passed the Undup, an affluent on the right bank, and later on the Sakarrang, on the left.   Higher up, the main stream, which still retains the name of Batang Lupar, grows much narrower.   Up to this point the country could hardly be less attractive, with its low banks, bare and monotonous, or with at the most a few scattered trees. But these are the signs of a densely populous region, and of soil adapted to the cultivation of rice.   The shrubs scattered over the country are the remains of forest species not entirely destroyed by fire during the clearings, and appear as strangers amidst the vegetation of the plains.   We passed the night at Balassan, a Dyak village of nine families.

Early on the 21st we started paddling, aided by a slight tide for a short distance, but this was very soon overcome by the current of the river.   I shot here a burong bubut (*Centrococcyx eurycercus*, Cab. and Hein.), a large species of cuckoo, which keeps to open plains and abandoned rice fields, flying from bush to bush.   Its loud and oft repeated cry—" bubu-bubu "—is heard for hours in monotonous regularity on these plains, and its native Malay name is derived from this peculiarity.

I saw here for the first time that singular fish (*Toxodes jaculator*) which has received from the natives the name of " *Ikan sumpit*," literally " blowpipe-fish."   It is neither remarkable in shape nor coloration, but it has the strange power, on coming to the surface, of being able to squirt a jet of water from its mouth.   This it uses with unerring aim against insects, such as grasshoppers, flies, and even spiders, resting on plants near the water's edge, causing them to fall into the water, where they become an easy prey to the clever marksman.   The ikan sumpit has thus a special advantage over other fishes also preying on insects.   The annexed vignette (Fig. 29) shows a scene on a Bornean river, and an ikan sumpit squirting water at a larval Orthoptera ; but the artist has drawn the fish with colossal proportions, whilst in reality it scarcely attains the size of one of our common domestic goldfish.

Primitive Man managed to obtain possession of living animals in motion by virtue of the admirable structure of his hand, which enabled him to grasp a stone or other missile, and to hurl it at the animal he wished to capture.   Such must have been the origin of the first suggestion of implements of the chase.   In Man's case the sentiment which caused the action was desire, followed by an act of volition.   But it is indeed singular that a fish, intellectually so greatly man's inferior, should exhibit reasoning capacity similar to that of a human being under like conditions. The remote ancestor of the ikan sumpit must have beheld objects which it desired to possess, but which were beyond its means of capture, and, destitute of both prehensile organ or missile, may have tried to spit (if I may so express it) at the insect which, settled on a blade of grass overhanging the water had tempted its avidity. The fish thus utilised

Fig. 29.—"IKAN SUMPIT," OR SUMPITAN FISH.

the only means in its power towards an attempt to throw something at the desired prey. The conclusion is that acts of volition have induced the ancestor of the ikan sumpit to endeavour to perform certain movements in its buccal apparatus towards the attaining of an end for which originally its organism was not morphologically adapted. The modifications, therefore, which finally caused so perfect a water-ejecting apparatus to develop can only have had their origin in the stimulus I have indicated, namely, a voluntary act of the fish and the desire to get possession of an object which was useful to it.

The manner in which the ikan sumpit captures insects has much analogy to the methods of the chameleon. In both cases we have special adaptations in certain organs whose modification can only have been caused through impulses of the will. It must have been the wish to capture prey, and this only, that has rendered possible those morphological adaptations by means of which the desire could be attained.[1]

It is, however, singular that, among the numerous series of its more stupid brethren, this little fish should alone have had, one far remote day, at the dawn of its specific existence, the spark of genius which led it to discover that spitting at a fly sitting beyond its reach would cause it to fall into the water and become an easy prey. It would thus appear that even in beings at present least gifted by intelligence, this latter can at one time have existed anterior to instinct, which in final analysis is merely an inherited form of intelligence.

We passed Bansi, a Dyak village-house containing nineteen families. The river banks continued bare and monotonous, but the mountains of Marop came into view. The only interesting plant I met with was a Loranthus (*Beccarina xiphostachya*, v. Tieghem), a magnificent species, parasitic upon a small tree hanging over the water, and covered with beautiful rose-coloured flowers five inches in length very similar to those of some of its congeners of the Andes, in which, however, the flowers are even more remarkable, attaining the extraordinary length of seven or more inches.

After a short rest at Unggan to cook our rice, we continued our ascent of the river, passing several Dyak villages. This is one of the more densely populated districts of Sarawak, and at the same time more cultivated, thus affording little to interest the botanist. The rocks I saw, and they were but few, were invariably sandstone. Towards three o'clock in the afternoon we reached the landing place for Marop. I disembarked my luggage at once, and stayed in the house of a Chinaman—there being quite a little Chinese village here. The following day, March 22nd, I found without difficulty Chinese and Dyak bearers to convey my luggage to Marop. The former did so by suspending the load, divided in two portions, at

---

[1] The rather bold hypothesis that the will may have had a strong influence in causing the assumption in animals of certain characters, has already been expressed by me in a paper bearing the title, " *Le Capanne ed i Giardini dell' Amblyornis inornata*," published in the *Annali del Museo Civico di Genova*, vol. ix. 1876–77.

the ends of a bamboo pole resting on the shoulders ; the latter carried their loads on their backs, secured with bands of bark passing under the package and over the head of the bearer.

The road from the landing place on the river to the village of Marop—about an hour distant—is one of the best I came across in Sarawak. One might even drive a light buggy or dog-cart over it, were such a conveyance known in these parts. I was delighted to see on the way that the primeval forest had not been all cleared away, and that there were places where it was evidently intact. It had, indeed, not a very vigorous aspect, but it looked different from that I was already acquainted with, which made me look forward to the possibility of finding some novelties. Meanwhile I came across a *Dipodium* (P. B. No. 3,256), a ground orchid, with fair-sized, slightly perfumed flowers of a milk-white colour, covered with vinaceous blotches.

Marop is a Chinese village, placed in a small valley surrounded by low hills. The stream from which it takes its name runs through it, supplying an abundance of cool limpid water, and giving off a minor torrent which dashes merrily amidst the houses. The village was very clean ; most of the houses were made with mats or palm leaves, but the big house, or residence of the Kunsi, the headman of the Chinese, in which I took up my quarters, was almost entirely built of wood. My lodgings were on a spacious platform forming a kind of first floor, where I made myself fairly comfortable, having ample room for my big and cumbrous cases.

I was impatient to explore the country ; and as soon as I had seen my luggage safely housed, I made an excursion up the nearest hill, where I at once fell in with a troop of red-haired monkeys (*Semnopithecus rubicundus*), a fine species I had not met with before, as, like the orang-utan, it is not found in the neighbourhood of Kuching. In the afternoon I went up the Batu Lanko, the highest hill in the neighbourhood, though it hardly reaches the elevation of 300 feet. It owes its name to an enormous block of granite raised on other similar masses, so as to form a sort of cave or shelter (" batu "=stone, " lanko " =hut). On the slopes of this granite hill I found layers of clay, evidently alluvial, with traces of gold. The spot was then abandoned, but from the disturbed condition of the surface over a large area it was plain that very active gold washing had gone on there not long before. The system followed is the usual one—that of washing the auriferous deposit in a stream of running water canalised so as to lead into successive flat pans or basins at decreasing levels, where the gold particles, on account of their greater specific gravity, remain, whilst the earthy and other lighter materials are washed away by the running water.

I extended my walk to Ruma Ajjit, a Dyak village, situated on the crest of a steep hill. Ajjit—for such was the name of the headman, or Orang-kaya, of the village—as soon as I approached him, took my right hand in his, and passed twice over my head a fowl which he held in his left hand. After this he presented me with the fowl, inviting me very civilly to sit near him by the hearth-stone. This was the place of honour, over which hung several smoked human heads, precious trophies of his past acts of bravery. He gave me siri and betel, according to the established custom amongst Dyaks as well as Malays, the first act of hospitality towards a welcome guest ; and after some conversation, having asked him to send me fowls which would be well paid for, and to get his people to collect animals for me, I took leave of my worthy Dyak chieftain and returned to my quarters in the Kunsi's house.

At Ruma Ajjit I saw an albino girl. She had a good figure, and in Europe might easily have been mistaken for a German or Swiss maid, with her fair hair, blue eyes, and full rosy face, but the latter was somewhat disfigured by scurfy spots and freckles.

On the twenty-third of March, with several Dyaks as guides, I again ascended Batu Lanko hill, where I had been told that orang-utans, or " Mayas," as they are called here, had been seen. I did not meet with any, but found, and was able for the first time to study, their nests or shelters. The term nest is rightly applied to the beds or resting-places which these animals construct on trees wherever they remain for a time. They are formed of branches detached from the tree on which they are made, and heaped together, usually at a big bifurcation of the trunk. There is no attempt at anything like an arrangement, nor is there any roofing, and they merely form a platform which serves for the creature to lie down on.

The orang-utan nests I saw were evidently each for a single animal ; possibly a united couple may build for themselves a more commodious couch, but I was unable to find out more of the domestic habits of these primates. As I have said, what I saw were merely beds or couches for lying down on ; but I think it very possible that on cold nights, or during rain, these creatures may also use branches and fronds as a shelter or to cover themselves with. It is well known that in captivity the orangs like to wrap themselves up in a cloth or blanket.

The forest in the vicinity of the village being deprived of most of its attractions, I directed my steps next day towards the low ground in search of plants, and was by no means unsuccessful. That evening all the sick and invalids of the village assembled at my house, for my fame as a doctor had spread far and wide. My system of cure was the simplest, and, thanks to my good fortune, gave splendid results. To those affected with fever I gave quinine ; to those who suffered with dysentery, chlorodyne ; to the others, fresh water, coloured with a little Worcestershire sauce. Sometimes I added a little arack; but I soon had to careful with the latter remedy, for the number of my patients increased instead of diminishing.

My out-patients having all been attended to, I went to sit up for deer by moonlight in a " lanko " which commanded a small plain surrounded by bushes, where the grass was very long and thick. The deer ought to have come here to feed, but the only thing that did come was clouds of mosquitoes, which, had I had any desire to sleep, would have effectually rendered it impossible, while, if they were not sufficient, the floor, formed as it was of large stakes, placed side by side, was not of such a nature as to tempt to drowsiness.

On the 25th I again went in search of plants towards the plain. From the hill I had noted all the localities where clumps of trees still stood, and each day I proposed visiting one.

Towards evening a Chinese hunter brought me the first orang-utan, but it was so mauled and covered with parang cuts that I did not skin it. Mayas were apparently far from being scarce in the neighbourhood of Marop, and I felt certain that I should soon be able to get better specimens. This one was a female of the kind named " Mayas Kassa " by the Dyaks, who distinguish several varieties or kinds of the orang-utan. The hair on the body was red, the skin beneath was of a deep copper colour; the face was much darker—a blackish-olive.

Next day I went into the jungle in search of Mayas with the Chinaman who had brought me the one above mentioned. Nevertheless, I was not favoured by fortune, and we wandered for four hours in the forest without seeing a single animal of the kind. When I got back I found another Chinaman waiting for me with a second Mayas, very similar to the first, but rather smaller. It was also a female of the Kassa variety, and it had still attached to it its little baby son, which had remained clinging to the mother when she fell wounded. In the fall the poor little creature had broken its left humerus. I prepared the skin of the mother, who had received a single bullet in the head, and had broken the bones of both arms in falling.[1] None of my men were proficient in taxidermy, and I was thus obliged to do nearly all the work myself, to tell the truth, not too willingly. I had decided, however, to devote a whole month to orang-utans, and to preserve a complete series of these most interesting animals, both skins and skeletons, so I set to work at once without more ado. As I was eating my supper in the evening, the

---

[1] The following were the dimensions of this specimen :—

From the vertex of head to the end of the coccyx . .	0·70	m.
From the vertex to the soles of the feet . . .	1·08	,,
Across the outstretched arms	1·86	,,
Circumference of thorax at bottom of sternum . .	0·71	,,

" Tukan mas," or goldsmith of the village, came to tell me that he had killed a Mayas, but the hour being late had left it in the jungle. Three other Chinamen who were with him had remained on the spot, partly to guard it, and partly in the hope of shooting other specimens.

The Chinese at Marop were big and strong, and excellent walkers ; they had come from Sambas, and were as well acclimatised as the Dyaks themselves. In the evening they used to gather round me and talk for an hour or two, asking me all sorts of questions on Europe and the Europeans, while some of their queries were, perhaps, somewhat less ingenuous than those of the Dyaks.

Next morning, March 27th, I finished preparing the skin of the Mayas which had been brought to me on the previous day. At noon they arrived with the one shot by the Tukan mas. It would have made an excellent specimen had it not been spoiled by the Chinaman who killed it, and who, in taking out the viscera, had badly split with his parang both the sternum and the pelvis. It was a male of the Mayas Kassa kind, and offered no appreciable differences from the female I had prepared already. I measured it carefully, with the following results :—

Total height (vertex to soles of feet)	1·17	m
Across the outstretched arms	2·10	,,
Trunk from vertex to coccyx	0·73	,,
Circumference of thorax below sternum (the viscera having been removed)	0·81	,,

I may here state that I always took the measurement of the height by stretching the animal on the ground and measuring the distance between the crown of the head or vertex to the under surface of the heel. The exaggerated dimensions of the height of orangs, given, nevertheless, by conscientious and trustworthy persons, depend on having extended the latter measurement to the tips of the toes. In other cases the body and limbs have been measured along the curves instead of straight from point to point, which naturally has increased the general dimensions.

The Mayas Kassa, which is the more common species of orang-utan here, was now becoming well known to me, for I had in my possession a male and two females quite adult, besides a young one. The male, as I have remarked before, differs very slightly from the female. I only noticed a small difference in the teeth, which may possibly have been accidental. The male has a very small gap between the canines and incisors, but in the female this space is more marked.

I had heard of two other kinds of orang-utan, one called Mayas Rambei, the other Mayas Tjaping. The first appeared to be only slightly different from the Mayas Kassa, being described as smaller, but with longer hair. The Mayas Tjaping, however, was very remarkable on account of its great size and the strange expansions which widen its face. It appeared also to be much scarcer than the Mayas Kassa, and I offered a reward of six dollars for every specimen brought to me in good condition. I also gave special instructions to the village hunters as to eviscerating the animal, and removing the larger muscular masses in order to lessen the weight and prevent decomposition, so rapid in this climate ; and this without injuring the skin.

This morning one of my Malays escaped to Simanggan, for some reason unknown to me ; but the Malays are a strange people, and even their ideas appear to be nomadic, just like the life they best like. I at once engaged a Dyak in his stead, a youth named Pagni, who proved also useful in aiding me to compile a small Sea-Dyak dictionary for my own use—a language much more distinct from the Malay than is that of the Land-Dyaks.

The Dyaks of this part of the country are now quiet, and their devotion to the Tuan Muda may be said to be unbounded. They are at present also on good terms with the Chinese, but I believe not from any love for them, and were it not for fear of the Rajah, many a Chinaman's head would even now be added to the grim trophies hanging over the fireplaces of the Dyak houses. More than once, jokingly of course, when on a visit to me at the Kunsi's house, they asked my permission to cut off the heads of the Chinamen, but I am pretty sure that the joke concealed a covert hope that I might grant them leave.

I had no reason to complain of the Chinese, but they had been grumbling and expressing the wish that I should cease preparing Mayas skins in their house. And, indeed, I must confess that they were not entirely without excuse, for the odour of the skins and skeletons, done in the rough, was not too pleasing, although I sprinkled them abundantly with carbolic acid. The Chinese soon learnt to appreciate the antiseptic virtue of the latter, and every morning one or the other would come and beg me to dress some sore or old wound with carbolic solution.

My orang skins caused me much trouble and anxiety, for the damp, combined with the heat, made it most difficult to dry them properly, and to prevent the cuticle from peeling off and the hair from falling. To add to these difficulties the specimens were all very fat, and it was indeed by no means an easy task to clean the skins thoroughly.

Marop is an excellent station for a zoologist, but a poor one for a botanist. Wherever the Dyaks had not made rice fields, the forest had been long devastated in search of rotangs, bark, and timber for building houses, etc. ; and this had rendered the more useful natural products scarce. I can easily understand how edible wild fruits or plants of economic value can disappear, with

the native system of cutting down every tree of such a nature.
Nearly the whole extent of country I could see around Marop from
the hills was in this condition ; or else covered with secondary
jungle, which had grown where the primeval forest had been
destroyed.   This is usually invaded by a large fern (*Pteris arachnoidea*, Kauff.) called rassam by the Malays, which produces long
tough stalks, and, being also semi-scandent, so binds together the
underwood as to render it practically impenetrable, and where it
abounds one is obliged to cut a passage through the jungle with the
parang.   Large areas of the country are also covered with the common lalang grass, and with thickets of " onkodok " (the common
Melastoma).   Such are in Borneo the " bad lands " for the botanist.

The bits of primeval forest which I had noticed on my way up
to Marop from the landing place on the river had evidently never
been turned into rice fields on account of their sterility, the soil
being entirely formed of white crystalline sand.   The trees there
were small and somewhat stunted, but many species I found to be
peculiar and not growing in other places in the neighbourhood.
Although formed by different species, I believe that the areas
covered by this kind of forest correspond to those of the *mattang*
mentioned in previous chapters, and I am disposed to regard them
as ancient islands, as it were, left high and dry, on which the vegetation has continued unchanged since the time when they were surrounded by the sea.   This hypothesis would account for the special
character of the forest in such localities, so different from that of
the country all round.[1]

On returning one day from my daily morning excursion
to the forest in search of new plants for my herbarium, I
had sat down to skin the baby Mayas brought to me with the
first one I had prepared.   I had tried to keep it alive, but it had a
broken arm, and had been badly shaken, so that my care was of no
avail, and it died.   Whilst I was thus engaged, Atzon, my best
Chinese hunter, came in with a magnificent specimen of the Mayas
Tjaping tied to a pole and carried by two men, who, however,
had been obliged to get help on the way from the Dyaks, the weight
being too much for them.   Entire, I do not believe that the creature
weighed less than 16 stone.   Following my directions, the
viscera had been properly extracted without damaging either skin
or bone ; a large part of the bigger muscles had also been removed,
and it was thus in excellent condition.   It was also quite fresh,
having been killed in the gloaming of the previous evening whilst
asleep with its head on its hand on a big branch.   It showed only

---

[1] The " mattangs " appear to me to have a certain analogy with the
" campos " of Brazil, which might also be considered ancient islands which
have been surrounded with alluvial lands of recent formation.

one wound, near the coccyx, the bullet having penetrated all the viscera without touching a single bone.

It was a fully adult male, but the more experienced hunters maintained that it had not by any means attained its full dimensions. Atzon assured me that he had once killed a much bigger one, very old, with hair nearly white, having lost its canine teeth through age. Before skinning the animal my measurements, taken with the precautions already mentioned, gave the following results :—[1]

Total height from crown to sole of the feet (Some little addition should be made to this measurement, for the body was stiff and the legs much bent) . . . . 1·260 m.

Width of the extended arms			2·430 ,,
Length of trunk, crown to coccyx . . .			0·915 ,,
Circumference of thorax, just below sternum . .			1·090 ,,
,, of neck			0·700 ,,
,, of forearm			0·350 ,,
,, of arm			0·330 ,,
,, of thigh			0·470 ,,
,, of leg			0·300 ,,
Width of the face			0·323 ,,
Length of the face			0·310 ,,

The face is, beyond doubt, the most singular feature in this animal. Certainly, considering that it is one of the anthropoids, the resemblance to that of Man is very much hidden, I may well

[1] Recently two living specimens of the " Mayas Tjaping " reached Europe, and were kept alive for some time in the *Jardin d'Acclimatation* at Paris (cf. *L'Illustration*, 13 janvier, 1894). Both were males, and had the expansions on the face strongly developed ; in one, indeed, which must have reached the fullest possible growth, they were extraordinarily so. This specimen, fully confirming the assertions of my hunter, had white hairs on the lips, perhaps also a sign of great age. Its height from crown to sole was 1·40 m. or 14 centim. more than the specimen shot by Atzon, but it should be stated that the Paris specimen, besides the lateral face expansions, had a large fleshy or fatty protuberance on the crown of the head, which must have added somewhat to its stature. The width of its extended arms was 19 centim. more than in my specimen (8ft. 7¼ in.) ; but even on this point it must be noted that in orang-utans the fingers can never be fully extended, and this may cause some difference in such measurements. On comparing the figure of the head of the oldest of the two Mayas Tjaping which lived in Paris (published in an excellent memoir in the *Nouvelles Archives du Musée*, 3ᵉ serie, vol. vii. 1895) with that of my biggest specimen, now mounted in the Museo Civico at Genoa, which was modelled on the drawings and measurements which I took in the flesh, I note that the Paris specimen presents a greater accentuation of the features, owing probably to age, as may be often seen in aged individuals of the human species. Thus the superciliary ridges are much more prominent, the eyes more sunk, the fatty expansions thinner and more laminated than in the specimen at Genoa, which was, I imagine, killed at the florid epoch of middle age.

say, masked; and it is certainly less human than that of the Mayas
Kassa. The flat circular face of the Mayas Tjaping is very much
like that of the moon as given in popular almanacks. The eyes
are on a level with the skin, somewhat like those of a Chinese,
small, and with a chestnut-brown iris, while the very small amount
of sclerotic which is exposed at the corners of the eye is very dark
in colour.

The singular shape of the face of the Mayas Tjaping [1] is
due to the expansions of the cheeks, caused by an accumulation of
fat just over the masseter muscles in front of the ears, which are
thus hidden from view when the animal is looked at from in front.
These expansions are compressed and laminar, about an inch and a
half thick, and not rounded as they are reproduced in badly mounted
museum specimens. The skin over them is tense and smooth.
Except as regard their position, they may be compared to the protuberances on the face of *Sus verrucosus*, or to the hump on the
back of Indian cattle. The colour of the naked portions of the face
is nearly black, or, rather, blackish olive. The body is covered
with very long hair of a deep fulvous red.

The skin was very thick and tough, and the operation of taking
it off extremely arduous and unpleasant, for I had to work on the
ground without proper tools, tormented all the time by ants, flies,
horse-flies, and mosquitoes, not to mention the excessive heat and
the unpleasant emanations. A Chinaman and my Dyak boy Pagni
helped me pretty well to get off the fat and clean the skin, and
afterwards to take the flesh off the bones.

Whilst I was thus hard at work another Mayas Kassa was
brought in, but it had been so badly mauled that neither the skin nor
the skeleton were worth preserving, even had I had time to attend
to it. It was pregnant, I learnt, but unfortunately the fœtus
had been taken out and thrown away with the viscera. I
had put the skin of the already mentioned baby orang-utan
with a broken arm into spirits, for the huge Mayas Tjaping took
up all my time; in fact, I worked at its preparation all that day,
all the next, and part of the third. I was obliged to incise longitudinally each of the fingers and toes to clean them thoroughly;
even the terminal phalanges were taken out, so that both
skin and skeleton should be complete.[2] I dressed the bones

[1] *Tjaping*, in Malay, is the term applied to a small, nearly triangular or
heart-shaped piece of silver which is hung in front of baby girls as a fig-leaf,
and is, in the early years of their lives, the only bit of clothing they wear. Flat,
triangular, hemihedric diamonds are called *Intang tjaping* because they;
have the same shape as the silver *Tjaping*; and for the same reason, I believe,
the term has been applied to the broad-faced orang-utan.

[2] This specimen, perhaps one of the best in existence, is in the Museo
Civico at Genoa.

well with arsenical soap, which prevented putrefaction, and kept them from the ravages of animals, and, tying them up together in a bundle, I hung them under the roof of a hut which was occasionally used as a blacksmith's shed, where they could dry without giving me further trouble. But the task of preserving the skin was another affair altogether, for the season was rainy and the dampness excessive. I therefore covered it on both sides with arsenical soap, wherever the hair did not prevent it, and, placing it on a bamboo grating, where it lay flat, I hoisted it up under the roof in the middle of the hut, so that it might dry well with plenty of air all round. If necessary, I might have lighted a fire in the hut to dry the air—not to attempt to dry the skin by such means, which would have been a great mistake. Skins of animals collected in tropical climates where the air is damp should never be dried over a fire or exposed to the sun's rays, for by so doing they undergo a sort of cooking, and either get excessively brittle, or else remain liable to absorb damp, so that it is difficult to mount them afterwards as museum specimens, for if they do not fall to pieces they lose both cuticle and hair.

The consequence of this hard work on big mammal skins and skeletons with inefficient tools was that my hands and fingers were more or less cut, and the arsenic getting into the wounds and under the nails caused painful sores, which suppurated.

On the first of April fine weather returned, and we had a bright sun and a pleasant breeze. This was good for my skins, whose preservation was causing me no little anxiety. I had not only to fight against the pernicious effects of the climate, but against ants, rats, and, above all, dogs. Of the latter no less than seven were kept in the Kunsi's house, and fattened to be eaten on grand occasions. Notwithstanding my constant attention, and although I placed the skins in positions which I fancied to be quite secure, I discovered that the heel of one of them, which was nearly dry, had been gnawed. A dog had done the damage, and had got at the skin by climbing up a pole, just like a cat. Certainly, up to that date I had no idea that Chinese dogs were capable of climbing.

For several days I had been aware that the Kunsi was not pleased at my being in his house, and would have been glad to see me go elsewhere. He said that the orang-utans stank and spoilt his meals. This may have been true, although a horror of bad smells is scarcely what one would expect in a Chinaman, but I believe the real fact was that he attributed a malevolent influence to my work, fearing, perhaps, that the irate spirits of the big apes might wander near their mortal remains and clamour for vengeance. I was very nearly obliged to employ violence whilst skinning the big Mayas Tjaping, for the Kunsi wanted it carried out of the

house.   The Dyaks present grinned, and whispered to me not to
bother, and that if I only said the word they would soon have the
heads of all those Chinese pigs.

From what I could make out the diabolic influence of my deeds
was considered already to be at work, having prostrated an old
Chinaman by severe illness ; but I believe that the poor fellow was

Fig. 30.—ADULT MALE MAYAS TJAPING.

already ailing, and suffering from an attack of typhoid fever when I
arrived at Marop.   The Chinamen, however, had got it into their
heads that my orangs had reduced him to a dying condition.   I
witnessed the singular treatment to which they subjected the poor
sufferer.   They made him swallow two pills as big as cherries,
of a composition unknown to me, poking them down his throat
with their fingers.   He was then obliged to smoke opium several

times, walking up and down the room, and when he could no longer move through sheer weakness, they put him to bed, taking thither the opium-smoking apparatus. To get him away, I believe, from the evil influences of which I was the cause, they carried him to another house. But as he was in a high fever, they soon after took him down to the stream, and kept him immersed in the water for a quarter of an hour. Apparently the use of a bath to keep down fever has been practised in China long before it was known to us. After the bath they made him swallow two bananas, and then obliged him to smoke opium repeatedly. The next morning the poor old man was dead, which was not surprising. And yet they believed that my Mayas had killed him !

On the 3rd April the weather was again damp and rainy, and I became anxious about my orang skins. I accordingly had a fire lighted in the smithy to endeavour to keep the air in the hut as dry as possible. After breakfast I was told that a Mayas had been seen in the vicinity, so I sallied forth with my gun and followed my guides. In less than twenty minutes they showed me a big tree, about 150 feet high, on which, sure enough, I saw the animal, still in the same place where it had been first seen. It was partially hidden amidst the branches, and would not move, although we made plenty of noise. From where I stood at the foot of the tree it was a difficult shot, for I had to aim nearly vertically upwards I fired first one and then a second shot, but could not make out whether I had hit him or not , he then slowly moved, but did not leave the tree. This was growing at the bottom of a deep ravine, so I climbed up one of the slopes, and was then able to see the creature well ; it was looking down, and was evidently badly wounded. I got a good position, and, after a careful aim, fired again. This time the Mayas fell crashing through the branches, which happily somewhat broke its fall, or, from the immense height of its perch, it would have reached the ground a bag of broken bones. When I got to it, it was quite dead. My last bullet had gone clean through its heart and had passed out at the nape of the neck, splitting the occipital bone. I noticed that as soon as it fell it gave off a peculiar odour of venison. It proved to be a half-grown male, and the girth of the thorax, just below the sternum, was 62 centim. I preserved the skin of this specimen in spirits, and on my return presented it to my former teacher in zoology, Professor Paolo Savi, of the University of Pisa, where it is now mounted in the Zoological Museum.

CHAPTER XII

AT last, with the first days of April, we had a spell of fine weather.
With the sunshine beautiful butterflies made their appearance, and amongst them the gorgeous *Ornithoptera Brookeana*, with
its great velvet wings ; an insect which Nature has adorned with
few but indescribably brilliant colours. These splendid creatures
flew through the village of Marop, but their flight was so rapid that
I did not succeed in capturing any. I was, however, more fortunate
in getting several other fine species. Finding the season favourable I continued collecting insects, especially Coleoptera, which
came out from their hiding places in unusual numbers, attracted,
no doubt, by the bright sunshine after so many dull and rainy days.

On the 5th April a Chinese fête occurred, and at the Kunsi's
house a big dinner was given, to which I had been invited. A
fine clean mat had been laid in the central hall, where, in all such
houses, the altar of the tutelary deities is placed, and all guests are
entertained. A number of bowls containing food were placed in
the centre of the mat. The larger ones contained rice, boiled in water
and well dried, while smaller porcelain bowls held the tit-bits—
small pieces of neatly cut boiled fowl and pork, some in sauces,
some with gelatinous substances of dubious aspect, and by no
means appetising. Other dishes contained beans and vegetables,
cooked in different ways. I had an idea, too, that one or more of
the Kunsi's fat dogs had been laid under contribution for the occasion. The guests, and I amongst them, all squatted in a wide circle
around the mat, which served as dining table. Each had a big
deep bowl before him, which was first filled with rice, this being the
basis of the daily meal both for the Chinese and the Malays. Both
place the dishes with food in their midst ; but the Malays help
themselves with their fingers, whilst the more refined Chinaman

uses his chopsticks. I preferred to have my knife and fork and spoon brought, and did my best to do honour to my hosts, though at the same time I took good care to choose only the least suspicious of the dishes.

On this occasion I was able to note the complete democracy that obtains in these Chinese societies. Even the head-man is elected by a majority of votes; he may be a mere workman, but he must have proved himself to be a keen and able business man. But in the case of my friend the Kunsi at Marop, however, I did not remark that he was the most laborious of the community, though he certainly smoked the most opium. This, nevertheless, did not deprive him of the requisite qualities for holding his post. He looked intelligent, and was certainly treated with respect by all his dependants, who, however, were on a footing of the most perfect equality.

Apart from all that is undoubtedly true regarding the use, or rather abuse, of opium, I have observed generally throughout my wanderings that the principal Chinese merchants, the richest, most influential, and most successful in business, are all great smokers of opium. The vice appears to show its pernicious effects more on the physique than on the intelligence. The state of torpidity it induces may, I think, be compared to a kind of somnambulism attended with fantastic visions, during which ideas manifest themselves in multiform aspects, and disconnected, as it were, from the material world. It might truly be said, quoting our great poet, that during that peculiar lethargic condition caused by opium—

> . . . la mente nostra pellegrina
> Men dalla carne, e più dai pensier presa
> Nelle sue vision quasi è divina.

I never personally experimented on the effects of opium smoking, but a rich Bugis at Makassar used to tell me that he appreciated the habit because it " exalted his intelligence "—" naik kira-kira", as he expressed it.

To me it does not appear utterly impossible that the nerve stimulants which have been used by Man in a remote past may have exercised an important influence on the development of his intelligence. I do not, therefore, think it unlikely that opium, just as wine, may have contributed to the evolution of new and original ideas in those ancient inhabitants of Central Asia, and that some of the many useful inventions which have come to us from the Far East may have had their first rudiments of existence in the dreamy visions of some opium eater.

For several days I had no more specimens of Mayas, and I suspect that the Kunsi had forbidden the Chinese hunters to get me any more, hoping thus to induce me to leave. But if that was his intention he was doomed to disappointment, for on the 11th April some Dyaks brought me a young Mayas, only just weaned and nearly dead. The colour of the body was a fleshy or slightly rosy brown, as were the lips and eyelids. Such is the colour of the bare parts in the young animals; but as they get older the skin darkens, until it assumes the blackish olive tint which it has in adults. Of this young Mayas I only preserved the head in a strong solution of spirits and salt. Some Chinamen from Macao took the body and cooked it, and told me afterwards that it made excellent eating.

On the following day I started with a party of Dyaks for Tiang Laju, an isolated peak a few miles from Marop, from which, on a clear day, all the Batang Lupar country as far as the Kapuas lakes can be seen. I wanted especially to get an idea of the situation of these lakes, for it was my intention to visit them as soon as I could. In an hour and a half's brisk walking we reached Ruma Pranghi, a Dyak village which lies at the foot of the hill, but we could get no farther that day owing to the incessant deluges of rain. Next morning was bright and fine, and as soon as the sun rose we began to climb the hill. At an elevation of about 1,600 feet I left my luggage and part of my men with orders to construct a lanko to shelter us that night. On the way up a Dyak, with his expert eye, sighted one of the most venomous snakes in Borneo, the " ular unkudi " (*Trigonocephalus Wagleri*) [1], which was coiled on a shrub on one side of the path we were cutting out with our parangs. It could hardly be distinguished from the foliage on account of its green coloration. It is extremely sluggish and slow in its movements, and does not, as a rule, attempt to bite man, but the Dyaks are, nevertheless, very much afraid of it.

We continued to ascend through a very fine forest, where few impediments retarded our progress. There were few shrubs in the way, and the ground covered with fallen leaves made walking pleasant, had it not been for the innumerable land leeches which attached themselves to our feet, causing the blood to flow freely. On the top the mountain is reduced to a very narrow ridge, which explains the sharp aspect of the peak as viewed from Marop. Here we came to a pathway which would have frightened the timid, had not the vegetation on each side afforded support. This little track, like others which I had observed on the way up, was, according to my guides, the work of the *babi blida*, or hill pigs. These I had not met with, but they were described to me as being much higher on the leg than the common wild pig. We were now on a level with the clouds, or, I should say, above them; for at times we got glimpses of clear sky and the sun shining overhead, whilst, except at rare moments, all beneath us was shrouded in driving mist.

[1] This snake, according to Low, bears also the native name " Ular ledong."

The mountain is entirely formed of sandstone. As we progressed upwards we found the trees growing smaller. On the summit they were reduced to mere bushes by the action of the winds, and on account of the thin layer of soil for their roots. But mosses and *Jungermannias* flourished, and covered the ground, stones, and tree-trunks alike with a soft damp carpet. I did not, however, find any sphagnum, which I had seen on the other mountains I had climbed. Many beautiful butterflies passed over my head, fluttering above the abyss, which looked more awe-inspiring from the mist

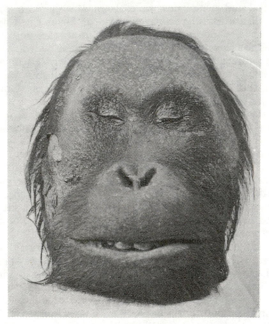

Fig. 31.—HEAD OF SUPPOSED FEMALE OF MAYAS TJAPING.

which hid its depths. There were only a few plants in blossom, but I succeeded in finding three species of rhododendron, and one little orchid, a *Corysanthes*, a true mountain gem, was abundant amongst the mosses. It is only a few inches high, but its relatively large solitary flowers, of a lovely violet, were like amethysts strewn on a bed of emeralds.

The flora of Tiang Laju appeared to me to be less rich than that of other mountains nearer the sea. I recognised by the foliage several species which, it is true, I had not met elsewhere, but I had decided never to collect any specimens that were not in a condition to be identified, and only rarely did I preserve plants that had not their flowers or their fruits. I noticed, however, the absence of many species which I had always met with in the forest near the coast. Thus I only saw two Dipterocarps and a single *Quercus*, plants easily recognisable by their leaves.

On the summit the thermometer, in the shade of the bushes, marked 77° Fahr., and my aneroid 686 millim. From these data I made the height of the mountain to be about 3,267 feet. I waited in vain for the mist to clear, but was at length obliged to retrace my steps to the lanko, which I did slowly, collecting plants by the way.

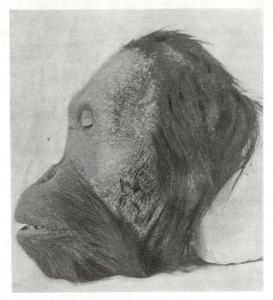

Fig. 32.—PROFILE OF SUPPOSED FEMALE MAYAS TJAPING.

It was near sunset, and the cicadas, here of several species and extraordinarily numerous, simply deafened us with their piercing and discordant stridulations, it being at this hour that they commence their love songs.

We cooked our rice, Dyak fashion, in long internodes of bamboo, and then turned in to get some sleep. It rained the whole night through. In many things I took kindly to the ways and habits of the Dyaks, but on a bed of bark I could not, as they do, find peaceful repose. Stiff and tortured on one side I turned over on the other, and repeated this operation a dozen times before morning, catching snatches of sleep only in the intervals. During my many wakeful moments I had glimpses of the forest all alight with phosphorescence. Every object which lay on the ground was luminous : fallen leaves, rotting branches, and prostrate trunks. The night, nevertheless, appeared interminable, and it seemed to me that daylight would never come. The sun was certainly above the horizon ; but a dim twilight still prevailed, with a thin dense rain, after which the mist rose. The temperature was 68° Fahr. Wishing to climb to the summit again in order to get a view of the surrounding country, I waited till noon, hoping that the weather would clear. Meanwhile I passed the time in listening to the Dyaks, who were relating to each other dreams of the previous night. As I have already remarked, the tops of mountains are for them places of terror, awe, and mystery—the abode of spirits. To dream of a benevolent deity is a most fortunate occurrence, which the Dyaks would often seek by sleeping on the top of mountains ; but this is an act which in their opinion calls for such audacity and cool courage, that few indeed are bold enough to overcome their terrors and attempt it. My guide told me that he once passed three consecutive nights on the top of Tiang Laju, but no good-omened dream came to recompense his bravery.

As the weather showed no signs of improvement, I returned to Ruma Pranghi, and without stopping continued my march to Marop, which I reached in two and a half hours of rapid travelling.

Throughout the latter half of April it continued to rain at Marop, but I did not give up my daily excursions in the forest, and continued to find interesting novelties. During one of these excursions I came across a Upas tree (*Antiaris toxicaria*), which was not wild, but had been planted by Dyaks. This is another forest species utilised by man which will probably in time disappear altogether as a wild tree. At Banting, also, I had noticed several large specimens of the Upas growing amidst fruit trees. The Dyaks here do not extract poison from this tree, but obtain a kind of cloth from its bark, with which they make their clothes for daily use, such as the " jawat," when they cannot buy imported stuffs. Even the blankets with which they cover themselves at night are often made of Upas bark cloth. This is prepared by beating the bark until the woody cortical portion is removed, leaving only the felted, thin, and pliable fibres forming the inner bark or librum. Other plants of the same family to which the Upas tree belongs (*Artocarpeæ*) are similarly utilised for making cloth.

One day, on a hill, I found the ground dug up pretty deeply in several places. Pagni, my Dyak boy, who was with me at the time, said it was certainly the work of a " Bruan," the Malayan bear, searching for ants, of which it is very fond.

Very rarely had I succeeded in finding the nests of birds in the forest, where usually they are placed so high up on the trees or are so well hidden that it is most difficult to get them. I once found the nest of *Pitta granatina*, one of the most beautiful of Bornean birds, the eggs of which had not, I believe, been previously known. The nest was on the ground in a *Maranta* thicket, near a streamlet, in the denser part of the jungle ; it was formed of dry leaves, and only contained two eggs. The bird slipped off when I was close to its nest ; but although I did not obtain it, I am quite sure that I identified the species aright.

The Dyaks used to bring me rare and curious animals, though not as often as I should have expected and wished. One day they brought me a small owl, with which I was greatly delighted, for nocturnal birds are scarce in Borneo. What is the reason of this I wonder ? Another day it was a very fine pheasant (*Euplocamus nobilis*), a hen bird, which is devoid of the brilliant dress of its mate. The eye, however, is magnificent, with rosy carmine iris, and the naked skin around of a clear amethyst.

I also bought a live bear—a youngster, and very tame. It was comic in its habits, and would sit by the hour sucking its paw and grunting, and never seeking to get away, although perfectly free. It took kindly to boiled rice. The Dyaks assert that they are acquainted with two species of bear. The one they had brought me, the commonest, is entirely black, with a yellow semicircular mark on the chest and short hair ; the other, a rarer kind, has long fur, no mark on the chest, and reddish hairs on the sides of the face ; the latter they call " Bruan rambei." [1]   In Sarawak I had also heard of a third species called " Bruan bulan," i.e. " Moon-bear," entirely black, with a light semilunar patch on the head and not on the chest.

I went to collect some wild bananas which I had remarked growing abundantly along a little stream on a hill not far from the Kunsi's house, in cleared spots which had been formerly cultivated. I found three distinct and very characteristic species, but from what I learnt two more, which I have not seen, are known to the Dyaks. A fact of no little interest is this existence of no less than three species of *Musa*, apparently endemic, growing together promiscuously in a restricted area, never found in the primeval forest, nay, actually dependent on its destruction for their own existence. I cannot now explain the series of considerations which have led me to the hypothesis that such species of *Musa* are the product of a retrocession to the wild state of hybrid cultivated forms, believing that it is man who has prepared for them a convenient environment

---

[1] " Rambei " is perhaps derived from *rambut*, hair, and is the adjective by which the Malays distinguish long-haired animals.

for development, and who has contributed largely to their specific formation.[1]

A curious new Zingiberaceous plant deserves special notice among my Marop novelties, *Alpinia crocidocalyx*, recently described and named by K. Schumann from my specimens. It is called *goppak* by the Malays, and produces large, long, compact radical spikes, in which the flowers are hidden by a sort of putrescent slime. It is, indeed, the nastiest flower which I have ever seen ; though it belongs to a genus of plants which includes many species with splendid corollas wrapped in bracts, which are also brightly coloured. In the above-mentioned species the bracts instead have become converted into a pale mucilaginous slime, in which an enormous number of Coleoptera seek refuge. These I easily captured by putting the whole inflorescence in water, and obliging the little creatures to emerge from their retreat. The inner part of the shoots of this plant can be eaten cooked, and I have found it very agreeable but slightly acid in taste. The Dyaks make excellent mats with the very fine fibres they extract from the leaf-stalks of the plant.

One morning, Kisoi, my Chinese cook, who had gone fishing in the adjoining stream, brought home amongst other fish a species called by the Malays " *Ikan tion*." When I saw it, it had been got ready for the pan ; but I noticed quite a number of small ones of the same kind, and these Kisoi told me he had taken living from the mouth of the big one. The Malays, who are so well acquainted with the ways and habits of the animals of their country, assured me that the young of the " Ikan tion" always swim close to the mother, and at the approach of danger, and during the night, seek refuge in her mouth. The fish is, I think, a Siluroid of the genus *Arius*.

On the whole, I was not very fortunate with my entomological collections at Marop. Coleoptera were rather scarce, perhaps because there had not been much recent tree-cutting in the neighbourhood ; decaying wood was consequently not abundant. I had, however, obtained a small series of splendid butterflies. But, alas ! one day, just after my return from Tiang Laju, I discovered that a host of minute ants had got into the box in which I had put them, and had practically destroyed the lot.

Amongst the ants at Marop there were some species which had unusual means of protection. Ants may be animals which are sometimes useful, but it appears that from time immemorial they have had many enemies, which fact has obliged them to make use

---

[1] In the *Sarawak Gazette*, July 16, 1875, it is asserted that wild bananas grow abundantly on the banks of the Baloi after the rice is cut, and that they thrive for five or six years, disappearing when the forest begins to grow up.

of all possible means of protection and defence.[1]   One kind, a very large one, which I found on the ground, when touched covered itself with a white froth which issued in quantities from its sharp-pointed abdomen.   Another, which lived on the leaves of an oak, gave off a very strong odour of pepper.   Yet another species, well known to the natives by the name of " *Sumut samada*," and very abundant at Marop, is possessed of a powerful defence in the shape of a sting like that of a wasp.   It is quite black, of an elongated form, and the stings it inflicts are very painful.   As it lives on the ground and is gregarious, woe betide the unfortunate person who camps in its vicinity ; he must decamp at once !   But the most ferocious of all is the " *Sumut tinggal-'pala* " (" the ant which leaves its head "), so called by the natives on account of the ferocity with which it bites, leaving its head attached to the object it has seized with its jaws sooner than let go.   I once found this species in possession of a *Myrtacea* in blossom in such numbers that none of my men dared to climb the tree, and as I had no axes with me to cut it down, I had to leave it without getting specimens ; so that actually on account of this ant the plant is not represented in my herbarium.

There is, again, the very common " *Sumut kassa*," or red ant (*Œcophylla smaragdina*), found everywhere in the jungle of secondary growth, where it makes huge nests, binding together dead leaves by filaments like strong spiders' web.   These are found at about a man's height from the ground on shrubs and in bushes.   It is one of the greatest pests one meets with in the forest, where it is found, for its bite causes a burning pain—happily not of long duration—on account of the formic acid it instils into the wound. More than once I have inadvertently disturbed one of the nests of this ant, and in a second have had all the inmates running over me, getting down my neck and up my sleeves, and fiercely attacking my naked skin in all directions, so that to free myself from them I have been obliged to strip entirely.

The Dyaks eat this ant, or rather they mix it with their rice as a condiment.   It has a pungent acetic taste and smell which they evidently like.   The Tuan Muda told me that a Mayas he had kept in captivity was very fond of these ants.

The manner in which the *Œcophylla smaragdina* procures the threads which it uses to join the leaves forming its nest is so extra-ordinary, that it would scarcely be thought possible had it not been perfectly verified by the observations of thoroughly credible eye-witnesses (cf. D. SHARP ; *Insects*, pt. ii. p. 147).   The adults of this

---

[1] The ants collected by Doria and myself in Sarawak have all been described by Dr. Mayr in the *Annali del Museo Civico di Genova*, vol. ii. p. 133, 1872 ; but my notes on each species have not been quoted, and therefore I cannot give the scientific names of the species mentioned in the text.

species, which is widely spread in Southern Asia and Malaysia, not possessing any substance that could be used to bind together the leaves required to form their nest, have found the way of utilising for that purpose a kind of silk which their own larvæ secrete for making the small cocoon in which they shut themselves up for undergoing their final metamorphosis. To effect this several adult *Œcophylla* hold in their mandibles one of the larvae, and oblige it to drop from its mouth on the edge of the leaf, kept in the required position by other ants of the same family, the coveted gelatinous thread. Thus the silken filaments which ought to serve the larvæ for making their own cocoons are used by the adults of the colony for tying together the materials for building the house of the community, precisely as we might act ourselves towards a mature silk-worm or spider, holding it between the fingers and obliging it to emit the silky thread wherever we desire it to be. Few examples reveal the high intelligence of the ants more strikingly than this.

At Marop I found several species of honey-producing Hymenoptera (*Trigona*) abundant. They are like very small bees, but unprovided with a sting, and make their nests with a sort of resin underground. Their Malay name is *Clulut*. One day I set patiently to work to dig out one of these nests belonging to *Trigona apicalis*. Its entrance was a small cylindrical canal about the size of my little finger, which penetrated the ground amidst the roots of a dead tree, projecting about three or four inches from the soil.[1] The canal led into a subterranean cavity about six inches in diameter, communicating with several irregular chambers all formed of resin. From the central chamber ramifications extended, supporting a large number of pyriform or spheroidal soft waxy cells, which contained the larvæ. These cells, which filled the entire cavity, were loosely connected together, and attached to the walls of the ramified chambers like the berries in a bunch of grapes. They appeared to me to be of two kinds, some darker than the others. Some only contained sour honey: in others were the larvæ. In this nest the best honey was nearly used up, and I imagine that it must have been stored in big cells of a special kind in the secondary chambers. A few of such cells, in fact, remained. They measured about half an inch in diameter, and were irregularly grouped together, and fixed to the sides of the chamber by a common peduncle. The honey they contained was clear, liquid, and slightly sour. Notwithstanding all my care, the nest broke in digging it out, which prevented a more complete investigation.

The nineteenth of April was a very hot day. The thermometer in the sun rose to 130° Fahr., and on the following day we had incessant rain. On the twenty-eighth of April, Atzon,

---

[1] In some nests this canal, which is a tube entirely formed of resin, is twice as long in its external projecting portion.

the Chinaman who had brought me the big Mayas Tjaping, and with whom my dollars had more power than the
threats of the Kunsi, brought me a magnificent head of an
orang-utan which he assured me was that of a female Mayas
Tjaping, but it differed considerably from that of the male,
having only slight vestiges of the lateral face-expansions which are
so characteristic of the bigger species of these anthropoids. It
was, however, somewhat different from any of the Mayas Kassa I
had yet seen, not only in its much greater size, but also in the large
development of the temporal muscles and their insertion near the
middle line of the skull, which, nevertheless, appeared devoid of any
sagittal crest. I preserved this head with all its soft parts in a
strong solution of spirits and salt. It is one of the most interesting
specimens of the series of orang-utans which I sent to the Museo
Civico at Genoa, where it is still intact (Figs. 31, 32).[1]   The body to
which this head belonged had been left in the jungle, for it was
mauled and spoilt, but had the hour not been so late and the spot
so far distant, I should certainly have gone there to verify the
sex. Next day it would have been useless, for during the night the
wild pigs would certainly have devoured it. I must say that I
had not entire faith in Atzon's assertion regarding the sex of the
specimen, for I had backed my strong recommendations regarding
his getting me a female of the Mayas Tjaping with the offer of
a good reward, and he was thus directly interested in bringing me
one, or a specimen which might pass muster as such. On the very
same day Atzon had come across a very big male Mayas Tjaping,
and had fired several shots at it and wounded it ; but it had sought
refuge on a large tree, where, in a high fork, it had formed a nest
from which Atzon did not succeed in dislodging it. Big Mayas
seldom fall, unless mortally wounded in the first instance by a bullet
in the heart or head. I had, however, given special instructions
not to aim at the head in order not to injure the skull.

Atzon having proposed to take me to a place where, according
to his account, I was sure to meet with Mayas, I started on
April 29th for the projected hunt. I arranged with him and a friend
of his that they should each of them receive one dollar per diem, if
their assertion turned out true, and only two rupees if we saw no
orangs. I took with me rice for four days, a few boxes of sardines,
a notebook, measure, scalpels, quinine, and a few other necessaries,
besides my gun and ammunition. A Dyak carried all my traps,

[1] I wish here to thank Mr. G. B. Traverso, of Genoa, for having kindly
taken for me the photographs reproduced in the Figs. 31 and 32 ; but more
specially do I express my deep gratitude to my old friend, Professor R. Gestro,
for the kind courtesy with which he has always satisfied my queries and
furnished me with information on the animals preserved in the Museo
Civico at Genoa, of which he is the Vice-Director.

and his own into the bargain. I took with me, also, several of my Malay boys.

We left Marop at 7 a.m., and towards half-past eight reached the Dyak village of Ruma N'gon;[1] where I was obliged to stop a few minutes in order not to disoblige the good villagers whose acquaintance I had already made and who called out lustily, "*Dudok-dudok!*" ("Please, come in"). We then began the ascent of the hill to the right of the path I had followed on my way to Tiang Laju. I had decided to hurry on without stopping to look for plants; but I should indeed have been a poor botanist had I not made an exception of two vegetable curiosities which I met on the way. One was a *Cordyceps*, an extraordinary small clavate fungus, of a vivid red, which grew on the head of a big black ant lying dead. The other was that strange fungus-like parasite, *Balanophora reflexa*, which I had already found on Gunong Wa, on the Upper Sarawak river. But here it showed itself under a new aspect, for not only was it parasitically growing on the roots of the shrub it had attacked, but it had invaded the base of the trunk all round for about four inches above the level of the ground, projecting from beneath the bark. The species is deciduous, producing the flowers of each sex on separate individuals; but all those I found on this spot belonged to one sex. It was this very circumstance that led me to suspect the existence of an internal organic connection between separate individuals, so that one of these parasites, having taken root on a host, could produce others around it on the same plant, not by seeds or shoots, but by special ramifications within the tissues of its host.[2]

Leaving Tiang Laju on our left, we got on the ridge formed by a series of hills from which flow the waters which join to form the Undup. We had now been several hours on the road, and had reached the district where, according to my guides, Mayas were to be met with. But although I kept a good look-out none could I see. It was near eleven o'clock when Atzon directed my attention to something moving on a big tree. Looking intently, I at last made out something like red hair amidst the dense foliage. There could be no longer any doubt—it was an orang recumbent on its nest. The creature was evidently aware that it had been discovered, and yet it showed no fear, nor did it attempt to fly. On the contrary, it got up and looked down at us, and then descended lower amidst the branches, as if it wished to get a better view of us, holding on to the ropes of a creeper which hung from the branch on which it was at first squatting. When I moved to take aim with my gun, it hauled itself up again, and got back into its nest, pushing forward its

[1] "Ruma" means "house" in Malay; "N'gon" was the name of the chief who lived there.
[2] Cf. my memoir on the subject in *Nuovo Giornale Botanico Italiano*, vol. i. (1869), p. 65, tav. iii. iv. *Firenze.*

head to look at me as it held on to the branches above with its hands.
It was in this position when I fired. I saw at once that I had wounded
it severely, for it threw itself back into the nest bellowing loudly.
At this moment in the midst of the branches I caught sight of a second
orang on another nest. Although I could not see it well, I fired ; the
explosion frightened it, and it left its nest and climbed towards that
of its wounded companion, whose lamentations were painful to hear.
As soon as it caught sight of it, it fled as if frightened, and hid so
well amongst the branches that I saw it no more. It was a youngster,
possibly the offspring of the one I had shot.

I was thinking of having the tree cut down to get the wounded
orang, when to my surprise it got up, endeavouring to escape, and
a second bullet brought it to the ground. It was an adult female
Mayas Kassa, but was so badly injured in the forehead by my two
shots that it was not worth preserving. The tree on which it had
built its nest was a species of wild mango,[1] on whose as yet unripe
fruits it had evidently been feeding.

This incident with the Mayas had kept us about an hour. We
proceeded on our journey, and in another half hour arrived at
Lanko Labok, a temporary Dyak station where they meet when out
hunting or searching for forest produce. The lanko, or rude hut,
was deserted and in bad condition, but it was in lovely surroundings,
being admirably situated just at the end of the succession of hills
over which we had been travelling all the morning. After a frugal
repast consisting of rice and sardines, and a couple of hours' rest,
I sallied out again with my gun, accompanied by Atzon, and took a
turn in the forest. This was here singularly grand, formed of
colossal trees, among which it would have been delightful to wander
had it not been for the land leeches, which swarmed in myriads
amongst the damp fallen leaves, always ready to attach themselves
to our legs. As it was, when I got back in the evening to the lanko,
I removed some two dozen of these horrible creatures from my feet,
enormously gorged and distended with my blood. Yet I had taken
the precaution before starting to tie the lower end of my trousers
tightly round my shoes, but in vain, for when fasting the leeches are
as thin as needles, and penetrate even cloth. Gaiters are also useless
to keep them out. After having begun so well we hoped for a
continuation of our good luck ; but though we wandered about till
dusk we did not meet a single animal, and were compelled to return
empty-handed to camp. We had our evening meal, as frugal as
the noonday one, and retired to get what rest we could on our bark
couches in the lanko.

---

[1] A *Mangifera* which the Malays have named ": Bua kalamantian," and
the very tree which, according to some authors, has given its native name
to the island of Borneo.

Next morning we were up before daylight, and cooked our rice for the day, wishing to waste no time later on over that operation. At dawn, bellowings had been heard far off in the forest, and Atzon assured me that they were produced by Mayas. We started before sunrise, and descended the hill on the slope towards the Undup, stumbling at every step, for it was not easy to keep looking straight up into the air above one's head, and at the same time note where one had to step. We soon reached a stream called Sungei Pajang. The forest here, to an inexperienced eye, would have had the characters of a primeval one ; but it was largely formed of magnificent durians and other fruit-bearing trees. Had we not known from our guides that in this spot had once stood a village of the Undup Dyaks, we might have thought we had discovered the *Durio zibetinus* growing wild. I also noticed several tall tapangs loaded with nests of the honey bee.

Crossing several low hills, we came to another stream, the Sungei Pakit, which we followed for a while. Even here the forest was not a primeval one, but from its wild aspect must have been for years abandoned. The muddy ground showed everywhere the tracks of wild boar and deer. Traces of the presence of wild oxen (*Bos banteng*) were also to be seen in the mud adherent to some tree trunks at a man's height from the ground, where these animals had rubbed themselves clean. Atzon told me that although for about ten years he had frequently visited this forest, only twice had he met with the banteng. He had, however, shot the wild dog, " Anjin utan " (*Cyon rutilans*), which I had as yet been unable to meet with, living or dead. We had been five hours on the tramp without seeing a single beast. Wishing to return to Lanko Labok by a different route, we went round the hill which we had come down to ascend it on the other side. We soon found ourselves in an old forest in which the Mayas nests abundantly ; some looked, indeed, as if they had just been made. The orangs could not be very far off, yet no sound or movement betrayed their presence. At last, however, I perceived something reddish moving on the top of a big tree. I fired at once almost at random, and, to my surprise, a very small Mayas fell to the ground nearly at my feet. Immediately after, a second one, of much larger size, appeared, and climbed up the very same tree. It was soon hidden amongst the branches, and although I fired twice when I caught glimpses of the creature, yet both shots missed. Presently we saw him higher up on a big branch, looking down at us. This time my bullet took effect, and the animal fell, mortally wounded.

The small orang first killed was a male ; the second, an adult female of medium size, probably its mother. Its hair was longer than in any I had had before, and my Dyaks assured me that it was a Mayas Rambei. I was, therefore, anxious to preserve both specimens, and with the help of Atzon and my boys I soon skinned the two, and roughly cleaned the bones of the larger specimen ; of the small one, besides the skin, I only kept the skull. In two hours' work we had completed our task, so that one man was able to carry all the spoil. The female was pregnant, and I carefully preserved the fœtus. There was no water near, and I was obliged to wash my hands with that I got by cutting through the stems of the creepers, which were very abundant on the spot.

It now began to rain, but happily soon stopped. The road we had intended to take was very steep, and having more to carry we thought it wiser to return by the way we came. We went back, therefore, to the Sungei Pakit, on whose banks we breakfasted with the cooked rice we had brought with us. It did not take long, and we were soon on our way again.

As we were passing again through the big durian trees, we suddenly caught sight of a Mayas quite close to us on some low trees. I aimed at him and pulled the trigger, but both barrels hung fire. My gun was an excellent Westley-Richards, but of the old muzzle-loading kind, and evidently the rain had got under the caps on the nipples. As I renewed the caps my men kept the big ape in view ; but it did not go very far, for orangs are not afraid of man, and when I was ready it was climbing up the trunk of a large durian. My first shot appeared to take effect in its leg; it stopped climbing, and passed on to a smaller durian. Here, when it was well in view, I fired again, bringing it to a standstill. Just as I fired, a small orang appeared, but bolted into the foliage, where I lost sight of it, for my men directed my attention to a huge Mayas on the very top of the highest durian, where it was much hidden by the branches. I fired several shots, if only to drive him out, but could not say that I had hit him. The tree was more that 150 feet high, and I was unfavourably placed at its base, having to fire vertically, with the rain, which had begun to fall again, coming straight into my eyes. As this was going on I perceived another big orang on a branch of the same tree. I got my men to keep the rain off, and reloaded my gun ; but meanwhile both animals got on to their nests, and I could see them no longer. Had I had time I should certainly have got both of them ; but it was getting late, and we had to look after the first one I had wounded, and which had not been seen to move from the small durian. I had the tree cut down, but, to our surprise, we could not find the creature amongst the branches, though I knew that it could not possibly have escaped. My men were grumbling to get away, Atzon had an attack of fever coming on, and the rain was falling in deluges. Yet I was not going to lose my specimen, and made them hack away the branches, with axe and parang, one by one, till at last we found the Mayas, quite dead, huddled up in the very centre of the boughs. The day was waning, and we were still a good distance from the lanko. There was thus no time to skin the ape, and I therefore had to content myself with its head, which I had cut off. The creature was a large male, perfectly adult, with the physiognomy of the Mayas Kassa, but with longer hair ; in shape and proportions it resembled the Mayas Tjaping, but had no cheek-expansions. The head was more like that of the large female which Atzon had brought me a few days before, and which I had preserved in spirits.

We resumed our march once more, not expecting, indeed, to meet with any more orangs, of which we had seen so many. But at a short distance from the lanko we came upon two more. I caught sight of the first quite near on a small tree. I fired twice, but did not succeed in killing it. As I was reloading, the second Mayas suddenly appeared, not twenty paces from where I stood, and only about fifteen feet from the ground. It was moving rapidly, catching the branches in front with one hand as it let go behind those it held with the foot, and alternating thus with hands and feet. The jungle was young and very thick, with dense underwood, so that when I had finished reloading my gun both orangs had disappeared, even the first one, which I felt sure I had hit. But " Kap," a small dog I had with me, had followed the latter, and enabled me to come up with it. As I did so the huge beast turned, and it fell dead to a bullet in the chest. It was a female of large size with very long hair, and I should particularly have liked the skin, but I had to abandon both it and the skeleton, and content myself with the head alone.

It was quite dark when we reached the lanko, loaded with orang-utans, drenched to the skin, completely tired out, and famished.

Wishing to preserve the spoils we had secured, it was quite impossible to continue to hunt for Mayas. So early next morning, May 1st, I returned to Marop, which we reached at noon. Our specimens were happily in good condition, and even the fœtus had not suffered. The better to preserve the latter I had kept it under cool running water near the lanko during the night. As soon as I reached the Kunsi's house I placed it in spirits. The skins and heads were also packed as soon as possible in jars containing a strong solution of salt in alcohol.

The first week in May was employed in finishing the drying process of the Mayas' skins, in arranging and making a catalogue of my collections, and in completing the preparations for my trip to the Kapuas lakes.

CHAPTER XIII

ON the seventh of May I had decided to start at early morn for the Kapuas lake, but the rain came down in torrents. If one wants to travel in Borneo one must not mind rain, but it is unpleasant to make a start under such conditions, and especially for the botanist, who is obliged to carry loads of paper for preserving plants, and, what is more, must keep it dry. About noon the sun came out, and although the weather was far from being settled I made up my mind to be off.

I had with me a party of ten men—two Malays, one Chinaman (the cook), and seven Dyaks to carry the luggage, which was rather heavy owing to the botanical paper. I had not been able to engage any more men at Marop, and accordingly my men had heavy loads, and we got along rather slowly. We had several times to cross the Marop stream, whose waters were now full and deep. Near Kumpang the rain, which had been threatening for some time, began to fall again with the usual tropical violence. I had already been in this neighbourhood, during one of my excursions from Marop, to visit the gold washings, which I had been told the Chinese had renewed. At Kumpang the precious metal is found in the alluvium which forms the low hills on the slopes of Tiang Laju. The surface layer for the thickness of some three feet is clay and earth ; then comes a stratum of big pebbles and rounded boulders, evidently rolled and water-worn, in a matrix of bluish clay. It is in washing this clay that gold is met with, either in the shape of nuggets or in large grains.

We proceeded rapidly, not meeting with anything interesting except a *Nepenthes* belonging to a species which I had not yet got. But I have invariably avoided collecting specimens at the beginning of an excursion—not always a good rule, perhaps, as will be seen in the sequel—and so I merely marked the place, intending to take the plant on our return. Our route obliged us to cross the Selle, an affluent of the Kumpang stream, more than once. In its bed I noticed several limestone pebbles, though all the rocks in the vicinity were sandstone. It is therefore probable that in the neighbourhood there are limestone hills like those along the Sarawak river. We came afterwards to the Kumpang, which we forded not without difficulty, for it was both deep and rapid. We were now close to Ruma Udjan, a Dyak house-village, which we could have reached in a quarter of an hour by crossing the impetuous Kumpang twice more ; but after the experience we had just had I preferred making a long detour to running the risk of wetting the provisions and my botanic paper. The Orang Tua of Udjan did all he could to persuade me to sleep at his house ; but it was too early to think of halting, so I gave orders to proceed. We also passed the village of Plagnet without stopping, and stayed for the night at Benda, farther on.

At Benda I was able to engage three more Dyaks as carriers, and thus to lighten the loads of my men. The weather was fine on the morning of the eighth of May, and we started early. Up to the present we had travelled through recent jungle ; but a short distance from Benda we entered old forest, through which we proceeded for two hours. When the forest ceases one may be sure that villages are not far off ; and in this case we soon reached that of Ruma Lassom, perched on a hill, and a short distance farther on came to Ruma Kuda, followed in succession by Ruma Mrassan, Massam, Mindjor, and Unggam, all close together ; the last mentioned being near the Mullangan, a stream which flows from the mountains forming the watershed between the basin of the Batang Lupar and that of the Pontianak or Kapuas.

My Dyaks wished to camp here for the night, but we had only marched five hours, which seemed to me not enough. I was, however, obliged to accede to their request. They complained that their loads were heavy, and asserted that it would not be possible to reach Kantu that night, the only place where sleeping quarters could be got after Ruma Unggam, and Kantu could easily be reached on the following day.

The true reason of their wishing to stop it needed no great acumen to discover when several good looking and lively girls appeared, and I learnt that my young Dyaks had often been there before. In the end, however, I had reason to be glad that I had granted their wish, for had we proceeded we should certainly have been obliged to sleep in the jungle, and that night there was a tremendous storm, in which a hastily built lanko would indeed have been a poor shelter, and we should have been drenched.

Ruma Unggam, one of the usual big Dyak house-villages, had been recently built and was very clean. As it may be taken as a type of such Dyak dwellings in these parts I may as well describe it.

The building was entirely constructed of rough timber and other forest products, on piles about ten feet high, and not a single nail had been used in it. It was much longer than it was wide, with a span roof of ataps made with palm leaves. It was longitudinally divided into two principal parts. One, the back one, was again subdivided, in the usual Dyak fashion, into chambers or " *pintus*," as they are called. The word *pintu*, both in Malay and Dyak, means a door ; but in this case it signifies an apartment occupied by the head of a family. These pintus do not communicate with each other, but each has a door which opens on to the front compartment of the house, and has a *lessong*, or wooden mortar for shelling rice,

Fig. 33.—INTERIOR OF SEA-DYAK'S HOUSE.

standing close to it. This front half of the house has no sides, but the large projecting roof protects it from the weather. It is subdivided longitudinally into three portions of unequal width ; the first and narrowest is that on which the doors of the pintus open, and may be styled a corridor for these. The second portion is the widest, often taking up one half of the total width of the house ; it is the common hall and workroom for each member of the community. Outside this is the third portion, over which the roof is very low, and here the young unmarried men sleep. Quite outside, unprotected by any roof, is a sort of wide terrace or platform, used for various purposes, but especially for drying rice.

Very few of the inhabitants of Ruma Unggam had seen a white man before, and certainly none of the women and children. On my first appearance these fled; but, hearing the laughter of my carriers, they became ashamed of their fears, and allowed me to approach. Having asked the women the reason of their fright, they answered me at once that it was because I was like a Mayas on account of my long beard, and for a time they continued to eye me with an expression of mingled fear and curiosity. Some of the less timid told me that they could not possibly like me unless I cut off my beard. In addition to the usual questions with which I was accustomed to be assailed, many were asked me here concerning the hairiness of whites. The women were particularly anxious to know whether their European sisters also grew beards.

My carriers were a merry set of youngsters, who came with me on this trip to the lakes by no means unwillingly, for they considered it as a good opportunity for some love adventure. Some of them had, indeed, confided to me their love stratagems, and the art of court-ship among the Dyaks. Certain leaves or flowers tucked in their armlets, or placed amidst the folds of their head-cloth in particular positions; a certain manner of playing the roden or Jew's harp, which the Dyak gallant is never without; are the means of secret understandings between lovers. I very soon perceived that this language of love was easily understood by the interested parties. The girls invariably sleep in their pintus, and shut themselves in. But the amorous swains keep an eye on them; and when they see where they have gone, and have made sure that they are alone, they approach the door under cover of the darkness, and imitate the plaintive mewings of a cat desirous of being let in, and the girl, taking pity on the repeated laments of her lover, eventually opens the door.

During the night rain fell incessantly, and next morning it was still falling. It ceased towards nine o'clock, however, and we then continued our journey. We climbed the hills forming the frontier between Sarawak and the Dutch territory—the water-shed of the basins of the Batang Lupar and the Pontianak. The pass here is only about 1,450 feet in altitude. The path is on nearly level ground, and traverses a fine old forest, where walking is easy, but, as always in such places, swarms with myriads of leeches. I noticed various fallen fruits on the ground belonging to species I had not met with before; but I did not see a single plant in blossom, shrub or herb, that I could reach with the hands.

When we reached the Sungei Kantu, the stream which collects, on the Dutch side, the waters of the hills we had descended, we found it so swollen by the recent rains and so deep and rapid that it was quite impossible to ford it. We were thus obliged to con-struct a bridge, but with a dozen of willing Dyaks this was not a

Fig. 34.—PLATFORM OF SEA-DYAKS' HOUSE.

serious matter. A tree growing in a suitable position and of proper size was selected, and it was soon cut down in such a manner as to fall across the stream. This took us about an hour, and we were soon across, I was going to say, dry shod, but the traveller in Borneo seldoms find himself in this condition. Farther on we had again to cross the Kantu in order to avoid a long round; but here the water was less deep, and by holding on together in a chain we managed to ford it in safety. The current, however, was very rapid, and I certainly should have lost my footing had I not been supported by my Dyaks. After this crossing we followed the right bank of the stream, our path being smooth and well shaded by old forest, which only ceased when we approached the village of Kantu, where we arrived early in the afternoon.

The Dyak house-village of Kantu was the finest which I had yet seen in Borneo; finer than Ruma Unggam, but built in the same style. Its length was 100 paces, it was on very high piles, and the covered front divisions were so lofty that one could walk beneath without having to stoop, as is usually the case in Dyak houses.

The women here were engaged in preparing cotton and to-bacco. The leaves of the latter while still green are laid together in bundles and cut up in very fine shreds previous to being dried in the sun. They undergo no preliminary preparation and are not fermented, so that the Dyak tobacco is very mild and has little fragrance.

The Dyak women separate the cotton from the seed with an apparatus they call " Pennigi." This consists of two wooden cylinders fixed close together in a frame so as to revolve on their own axes, one one way, the other the other, like a laminator. Each is turned by a separate handle. One woman takes a handful of the cotton which is to be cleaned and puts it between the cylinders, at the same time turning one handle, whilst another woman turns the other in the opposite direction. The cotton passes through, but the seeds fall to the ground. The Malays have a somewhat similar apparatus, which they call " Putaran," but it is constructed on a different principle.

After it has been freed from the seeds the Dyak women spin the cotton, the instrument employed being a large wheel which, turned by a handle, sets in rapid motion a very small one, the two being connected by an endless cord. In the centre of the little wheel is fixed a horizontal spindle, on which the cotton is spun and twisted. This form of instrument is found throughout all Asia, from Palestine to Japan, and has probably been the origin of all the modern systems of cotton-spinning.

On the tenth of May, not having been able to get any boats at Kantu, we continued our journey on foot, following the stream down its course, and finding its banks rather thickly populated.

The Dyaks of this region, although they live so far from the sea, are comparatively civilised. Their language differs but slightly from that of the Batang Lupar Dyaks. They work iron, but do not extract it, buying it from Malay merchants at Silimpo, on the Kapuas. Their houses are well constructed, and everything about them denotes a condition of comfort and prosperity. Although living on Dutch territory, they consider themselves independent. Their nearest market is at Simanggan, whither they resort to purchase salt. They treated me coldly, and it was only by showing a certain amount of firmness and energy that I was able to obtain paddles. They refused to sell me fowls, although I saw many about the houses. Notwithstanding this hostile attitude Intika, the Orang Tua, readily consented to act as my guide to the lakes.

At the village of Loben, where we halted, I met some Malo Dyaks, who live on the Kapuas, and were engaged in working finger-rings, earrings, and other brass ornaments, much prized by the women here. For a small consideration these Malo people allowed me the use of their canoe, but this was not big enough to contain all my men, and I had considerable difficulty in obtaining another small one, the Dyaks being afraid that I would not pay the sum agreed upon—one rupee !

An hour after noon we embarked in the two canoes, and began to descend the stream. The banks of this portion of the Kantu resemble those of the western branch of the Sarawak river, both in the look of the country and in the nature of the vegetation. As we paddled along aided by the rapid current, a fine " *ikan dungan* " hooked itself on our trailing line—the " *atja* " of the Dyaks. This has neither plummet nor float, and the bait is a piece of pearl shell a couple of inches long, or a bit of white metal, to which are attached one or two fish-hooks. The shell or metal is shaped somewhat like a small fish, and this and its silvery sheen makes it a killing bait for big fish. The " *atja* " is thrown from the bows of the boat continuously, now on one side, now on the other. I was informed that the dungan cannot be caught in any other way. It is an excellent fish so far as flavour is concerned, as I can myself testify, but I should have preferred preserving it as a zoological specimen, for it looked strange and interesting. It has a heterocercal tail, like that of the sturgeon, which I saw in no other Bornean fish. I was told that it is also to be found in the Sarawak river, but is very rare there.

After a couple of hours of easy and rapid progress we reached Grogo, where I hoped to get another boat to continue the journey. After Grogo, one of the usual Dyak house-villages, the river banks are uninhabited for a long stretch, and as the boats we had were mere canoes, by no means well suited to pass the night in, and the river was swollen and dangerous, I thought it more prudent to stay at Grogo for the night.

As I entered the big communal house the children fled shrieking, catching sight of my beard. To the adults a white man was less strange, for the Kantu Dyaks had frequent dealings with Simanggan.

I saw here very fine mats being made with fibres from the sheaths of the leaves of a Zingiberaceous plant, the same, I believe, as those that I had found at Marop, the "*goppak*" mentioned in a former chapter. The Grogo Dyaks are also renowned for their fishing nets, which they make with a very strong twine constructed from the fibres of wild plants of which I was unable to get precise particulars.

From the verandah of the Dyak house at Grogo, two peaks of singular shape are to be seen rising isolated from the plain, at no great distance. One, to the west, is called Tutop, and is easily recognisable by the steep cliffs crowning its summit, which—a rare case in Borneo—is bare, or, at all events, without visible vegetation, and thus bears no small resemblance to the ruins of an ancient castle. From its appearance I should say that Tutop is formed of the same porphyritic rock which I had noted in similar-looking peaks near the Sarawak river. The other peak, Togak, lies N.W. from Grogo, and is of a regular conical shape, like that of a Chinese hat. It is completely clothed with forest. The houses of Kantu village are really at the foot of this last-mentioned mountain ; but when I passed close to it I did not see it—a thing which often happens in a country where the vegetation is so dense. By a rough guess, I should put the altitude of these two peaks at below 2,500 feet, but in such cases it is easy to make a mistake, for there is nothing to serve as a satisfactory basis for comparison.

During the night it rained in torrents, and next morning, May 11th, the river was so swollen that the water reached the big branches of the trees along the banks. The rain continued, and the river still kept on rising. The flood, I found, had carried away our canoes, my men having stupidly omitted to secure them on the previous evening, and now it seemed likely that we should not be able to replace them.

The rain was so violent that I was obliged to remain indoors. My Malays made use of the time in manufacturing fish-hooks, using for this some of the brass rings which the Dyaks wear in their ears. Employing their parangs as sole implements, they managed to shape the hooks, point them, and make the barb.

The Dyaks must be ignorant of that malady which we call ennui. To them laziness is a pleasure, yet they can be at times exceedingly active. When it rains they are capable of sleeping all day, and are not on that account awake during the night ; or else

they chatter for hours, squatting on their heels near the fire with their
hands stretched out towards the blaze.

I noticed but few fruit trees near the village, and not a single
cultivated palm except a stray betel here and there. Near the house
were only bananas and a little sugar, growing promiscuously. I
have observed that only on hills and in positions not easily accessible
are fruit-trees abundant around native houses. The scarcity of
such trees may be accounted for by the frequency with which
Dyaks change their place of residence, abandoning the house in
which they have lived for a few years, and constructing a new one
in a place they think more convenient. Another reason may be
sought in the constant hostilities between the various tribes, during
which the more accessible villages are captured and destroyed
from time to time, and the fruit-trees growing round them cut
down.

It continued to rain till late in the afternoon. During a cessa-
tion of the downpour I sent men to search for my missing boats,
but without result.

In the house where I awaited the return of decent weather,
there were, for the time being, only women and children. All the
men were away, assembled to witness one of the most singular of
Dyak customs. Two young men were rival aspirants to the hand
of a girl, and a challenge had in consequence been issued. The
victor would be the one who managed to remain longest under
water. This singular kind of duel is not peculiar to the Kantu
Dyaks, but is also practised by the Batang Lupar, Seribas, and
other tribes in Sarawak.

The method of procedure is as follows. Each champion names
his two seconds, and a spot is then chosen in the river where the
water is about three or four feet in depth. Here two poles are fixed
vertically in the stream a little distance apart. At a given signal
the two champions fling themselves together under water, each one
keeping his nostrils closed with one hand, while he holds on to his
pole with the other, keeping it right over his head in order to prevent
himself from rising to the surface. At the first sign one of the two
gives of becoming asphyxiated, the seconds, who are close by, take
both from the water. Usually neither of the two would come to
the surface of his own will, and would drown himself rather than
acknowledge his defeat, it being with them a point of honour not to be
beaten in a proof of this kind. Thus it is always the seconds and
spectators who haul them out when they are half drowned. This
they do *secundum artem*, and, holding them up by the feet, head
downwards, endeavour to make them reject the water they have swallowed. The one who first comes round is declared the victor, and has
the right to demand a recognition of his prowess. This often takes
the shape of one of those ancient vases which are so highly prized

and fetch such enormous prices in Borneo, being considered by the
Dyaks as property of the highest value.

These vases resemble very much the big oil-jars (*orci*) we use
in Italy. They are usually of a dark colour, and glazed inside and out ;
some of them smooth, others with designs in low relief. Sham ones
are now made for purposes of trade, but both these and the genuine
old ones are of Chinese manufacture, and no better proof of the
antiquity of the intercourse between China and Borneo could be

Fig. 35.—TAJAU JARS OF THE DYAKS.

found, for some of these jars have been transmitted from generation
to generation in Dyak families, and must be extremely old. Here,
on the Kantu, the smallest and commonest *tajau* (as these jars are
generically called) are the "Alas" valued at from 20 rupees to 20
dollars. Those worth two "Alas" are called "Russa" ; a "Bennaga" is worth 100 to 150 dollars, or two "Russa." Next come
in order of value the "Linka," the "Betanda," and lastly the
"Gussi," which may be worth as much as 500 to 1,000 dollars. I

was told that there are still more names for these jars, which vary in the different villages, and according to minor peculiarities in size, shape, and ornamentation.

It is not only for disputes like the one mentioned that the Dyaks apply this " Trial by water," which is called by them " S'lam ayer " (i.e. " Plunge in water "). It is resorted to in many instances, and whenever a dispute cannot possibly be settled in any other way. Generally before having recourse to it, a cock-fight is undertaken to settle the question ; but if no satisfactory result is obtained, then the severer test of " S'lam ayer " is appealed to. Even slight differences are often settled in this manner ; indeed, serious disputes are rare amongst the Dyaks. The most frequent cause of ill feeling is jealousy, or other disagreements in which women are concerned. Such duels, next to " head-hunting," are for many the great events of a lifetime ; for to pay off the debts contracted on such occasions years of labour and of savings are often required. For the " S'lam ayer " which took place when I was at Kantu, the loser would have to pay a " Russa," at the utmost a " Bennaga."

On the twelfth of May several of the Dyaks who had witnessed the " S'lam ayer " returned to Grogo. It appeared that the trial had not been decisive, and other solutions were to be tried, possibly ending in bloodshed. I saw the young man who believed himself the winner ; he was much excited, and declared loudly that he would invoke the justice of the Tuan Muda ; as to the Dutch, he would not even allow them to be mentioned.

For some hours the rain had ceased, and the river had gone down considerably. My smaller boat was recovered, some Dyaks having found it caught in the branches of a tree about a mile lower down the river. I had also succeeded, after much bargaining, in getting another boat to replace the one which had been lost, capable of containing five or six persons. When all was ready for our departure it was four o'clock in the afternoon, and, as the two boats were not fit to pass the night in, I put off starting until early next morning.

This same day, before sunrise, I made an extraordinary haul of very small insects, mostly micro-Coleoptera. The torrential rain of the previous day had evidently been a veritable Flood for a whole world of small creatures which the violence of the water had washed off the plants, forcing them to seek safety on every floating fragment. And now the waters of the stream retiring had left high and dry on the banks all this flotsam and jetsam covered with myriads of ship-wrecked creatures, which it was easy work to capture. Some of these extempory rafts, I found, were loaded with heads, abdomens, legs, and other fragments of insects which had been destroyed by the flood. These Coleoptera were all the more easy to catch owing to their being half drowned, or reduced to a condition of torpor owing to the cold of the previous nights. I might have gone on catching them had it not been for the mosquitoes and sandflies, but these came out in myriads, and tormented me so incessantly that I eventually had to bring to a conclusion what had been a most successful morning's hunt.

This was the third night which I passed at Grogo, but I did not wish to prolong my stay. The place was in no way pleasant, for the house was old, and the stench which came up from the ground beneath the "lante" was intolerable. Besides the dirt and refuse of all kinds which naturally accumulate under these pile-built houses, and which are never removed, a host of domestic fowls in large cages were kept beneath this one. The odour of a large poultry-yard, mingled with many others still worse, penetrated through the floor to our sleeping-mats, and was enough to turn the most robust of stomachs. I do not know whether it was the effect of this insanitary condition or not, but in this place I found more people sick with fever and dysentery than anywhere else in Borneo. I gave medicine to several, and this caused my presence to be somewhat more acceptable.

On the 13th, as soon as the welcome call of the "Wa-wa" told us that dawn was nigh, I awoke my men, and for a wonder we actually managed to get off before sunrise.

It was one of those cool delicious mornings which are not infrequent in Borneo after violent rain. Many birds which had kept hidden during the bad weather were now flying from branch to branch. The river was still very full and the current strong, and our descent would have been rapid enough were we not often obliged to stop to remove the tree-trunks with which the flood had barred our way. By and by we came to the boat we had lost, caught in the fork of a tree above our heads and quite undamaged. The white and rosy flowers of a fine tree (*Dipterocarpus oblongifolius*, Bl.) perfumed the air strongly. Plants in blossom of many kinds which I had never seen beyond the hills increased in number as we progressed, taking the place of those which I had been wont to see on the Sarawak river. Often, within reach, we came across tree-trunks or overhanging branches loaded with epiphytes, amongst which the magnificent *Vanda suavis*, one of the most charming orchids of our hothouses, with its splendid racemes of big milky-white odorous flowers, was most conspicuous. Several species of *Ficus*,[1] too, threw a cool shade over the water, attracting many birds who feed on their fruits.

The course of the river was very tortuous and its bed narrow, but the water spread widely in the forest on both sides. The space free of vegetation alone marked out its course, the banks being lost to view beneath the water. We paddled thus for six

[1] *Ficus Miquelii*, King; *F. pisifera*, Wall.; *F. parietalis*, Bl.; *F. consociata*, Bl.; *F. cucurbitina*, King.

hours and my men slackened their work somewhat, being both hungry and tired. We landed at the first place where landing was possible, and cooked our rice. The river hereabouts had lost the aspect of a torrent, the flood of water having found its way through the forest. It was still very deep, however, but the current was less rapid. The trees along the banks no longer met overhead, but formed two high green vertical walls on either side. The light attracts the creepers towards the river, and among them a species of Connaracea (*P.B.* No. 3,384) was especially noticeable, having magnificent bunches of rosy flowers. Bauhinias and several Anonaceæ hung their festoons from tree to tree, giving an aspect of perfect impenetrability to the forest. Even the rotangs spread their great pinnated fronds towards the river, pushing through the dense surrounding foliage. To avoid several big bends and shorten the distance, we left the proper course of the stream from time to time, and cut through the flooded forest. That navigation in the deep shade of the primeval trees is a thing never to be forgotten ! We float amidst gigantic trunks as regular and straight as the columns of some immense basilica. It is high noon, and the powerful sun rays fall vertically on the dense cupola of foliage which, hungry for the light and heat, has fought its way upwards from the shade below. If here and there a straggling ray manages to penetrate the thick mass of leaves, it is reflected back by the black waters beneath.

At three p.m. we reached the Segrat hill, round whose base the river winds. This place is called Ujong Kayu Rattei, and has a Dyak village. The river assumes here the name of Umpanang.

The instinct which induces certain people to select and prefer marshy places for their residence is certainly strange. The Segrat Dyaks ought for this reason to be of Malay origin, for with the Segrat hill within reach they have built their house-village in the water, or at least in a hollow so unfavourably situated that, during the torrential rains that had recently fallen, they were obliged to seek refuge on a big raft made with tree-trunks. The flood had carried away their pigs and poultry, and much of their property as well. In this village not only the children, but the women, young and old, fled as soon as they saw me, and shut themselves up in the pintus.

The river abounds with excellent fish. One of these, which I think is a Siluroid, called " Ikan pajat " [1] by the natives, is of a singularly beautiful violet colour, and is excellent eating. Freshwater fish are usually silvery or of dark colours, or more rarely golden or red. I had never before seen a freshwater fish so richly coloured. It must be a forest species, living in the dark but limpid waters

---

[1] Under this Malay name several brilliantly coloured species are, I believe, included. " Ikan pajat " means " Masked fish," i.e. dressed up for parade or ceremony.

of the treed lagoons, if I may thus describe these places, of which in Europe we have no idea. In our Western lands, when permanent lakes or ponds have the depth of a few inches no trees grow in them ; whilst here extensive and grand forests formed of an extraordinary number of different kinds of trees remain in a state of inundation from year to year. I believe that a certain correlation exists between the "ikan pajat" and the locality in which it lives. When one thinks of the splendour of the sea fish of the tropical reefs, and the modest and plain coloration of those which live on sandy bottoms, one is led to suspect that the special local conditions of the water, and the colours of the surrounding objects in it, must have had a very powerful influence on the colours, in one case vivid, in another dull, which the fish now exhibit.

The "ikan pajat" is not found in the Sarawak river, where, however, as I was told by intelligent Malays, a similar but smaller species does exist.[1]

I did not see many birds. The most conspicuous was a *Tchitrea paradisi*, which made a fine show with the two long white feathers in its tail. I noticed several plants in blossom, however, which were new to me, and which I proposed collecting on my return.

May 14th, the night passed at Segrat, was one of torment. The famished dogs, mosquitoes, and sandflies completely prevented our getting any sleep. I, fortunately, had a mosquito curtain, but my poor men were obliged to light a fire and defend themselves from the voracious insects by keeping in the smoke. This was only adding a new torment to the others, for the night was hotter and closer than any I had experienced before in Borneo.

As the requisite quantity of rice had been cooked the evening before, we were able to make an early start next morning. The Umpanang has next to no current ; its waters are black, though limpid, like that which I had found in the forest near Kuching. A small quantity taken up in a glass looks like weak coffee, is quite transparent, and does not show any visible deposit in suspension, nor does it form any then and there, but I did not try the experiment of letting it stand, or evaporating it. It certainly keeps some time without giving signs of decomposition of any kind. These black waters, as I shall call them, are wholesome to drink, and have a not unpleasant, slightly acidulated taste. Their dark colour is undoubtedly due to the quantity of dead leaves and humus accumulated in the forests through which they flow.[2]

[1] This may be the *Cryptopterus bicirris*, Günth. (Cf. D. VINCIGUERRA. *Appunti ittiologici* ; in *Annali del Museo Civico di Genova*, xvi. p. 168. Genoa, 1880.)

[2] In South America some large affluents of the Orinoco and Amazon have black waters. A study of these waters was undertaken by MM. Muntz and Marcam, and may be consulted in the *Comptes Rendus*, cvii. (1888), pp. 908-9. Paris.

Although rains are torrential and continuous, the waters of the rivers in Borneo rarely get turbid, because the amount of soil not covered with vegetation, or cultivated, whence earthy matter can be carried off, is of small extent. Rain, however violent, is in a country covered by forest obliged to filter through great masses of vegetation, and comes gently to the ground, where, again, it meets a thick layer of dead leaves, rapidly decomposing under the influence of heat and moisture and the development of myriads of micro-organisms. The water, therefore, when it collects in streams is poor in earthy deposits, having been filtered through this vast stratum of decomposing vegetable matter ; and when the waters of these streams rise and inundate the forest, they absorb various new substances. Amongst these, humic acid predominates, and it contributes more than anything else to produce the peculiar dark coloration. It is not everywhere, however, even under the circumstances above mentioned, that the waters retain their black colour. This only happens when they do not contain lime. In South American rivers it has been observed that when the dark waters mingle with white waters they at once lose their colour, through a reaction of the humic acid on the lime. I believe that the same thing takes place in Borneo, but I have no direct observations on the subject.

As we approached the lakes the Umpanang increased in width ; but, strange to say, the trees diminished in height, getting so low as to be not more than from ten to twenty feet above the water. But what surprises one most on entering the lake from the river is the very unusual colour of the great sheet of water before us. Looking straight down into its depths it appears so intensely black as to cause a certain sensation of fear. At times I felt as if the boat must sink in that unfathomable dark abyss ! Our ideas on the specific gravity of water are naturally associated with the coloration which is familiar to us. They might be termed innate ideas ; and even a child shows no surprise that a boat floats. But when waters show a coloration so different from the ordinary, even the notion one possesses instinctively of its specific gravity is shaken. These inky waters certainly do not tempt one to a plunge ; whilst, as all know, the opposite feeling is elicited by limpid and transparent water, the mere sight alone of which is always pleasant and attractive.

The surface of the lake, clear and free from arboreal vegetation, extends only a few miles, but nowhere could we see a trace of dry land. As soon as we issued from the Umpanang, we sighted Lamadan, a village inhabited by Malays, towards which we proceeded. My people called the lake Danau Lamadjan,[1] but I believe that it is better known to the Kapuas people as Danau Seriang.

[1] Danau is the Malay for lake.—Ed.

As soon as the head-man of Lamadjan, Rading Sira (the title indicates a Javanese origin), heard of my arrival, he invited me to go up to his house and offered me *siri*, politely insisting that I should stay in his village. Although this is built on an island, there was then not a foot of dry ground around it. The water was nearly on a level with the flooring of the houses. Every year during the rainy season the water rises a good deal on the lakes, but very rarely as high as its then level. Some trees only showed their tops above water, whilst quite a number of shrubs could be seen beneath the keel of our boat.

The people at Lamadjan assured me that the waters of the lake always have the black colour which had struck me so much, and are never turbid. Intika, my guide, asserted that there are about thirty lakes like that of Lamadjan, and amongst the principal ones he mentioned Danau Malayu (or Malau ?), D. T'kanan, D. Bekuan, D. Pandan, D. Bulumbong, D. Gamali. I have an idea that these lakes are for the most part surrounded not by raised land, but by forest, which I would describe by the term "palustral," the soil of which would be dry only occasionally, in periods of great drought, when the waters are at their very lowest.

The lacustrine region, as a whole, must be of wide extent, but the water surface free from trees is, perhaps, never more than five or six miles in length. The natives of Lamadjan asserted that in very dry seasons some of these lakes dry up, leaving a prodigious quantity of fish exposed or densely packed in small pools, where they can be caught by hand. They also assured me that there is no mud on the bottom, which is not surprising, being a natural consequence of the absence of earthy deposits in the water. If in times of flood such as we experienced the water remained perfectly clear, it is evident that it can never be other than in that condition. It would be highly interesting to examine the bottom of these black-water lakes when dry in order to investigate the nature of the deposits. These, I should think, must be entirely of vegetable origin, without any admixture of earthy elements. It would also be instructive to ascertain the results of thoroughly drying them— to learn, in short, whether the great quantity of substances derived from the humus (rich, it should be remembered, in carbon) and held in solution by the black waters can, through the evaporation of their solvent, contribute to augment the mass of carbonates on the bottom of the lake basins, and also whether any special chemical reaction occurs to aid such augmentation.

Considering the great mass of organic substances in decomposition which continually accumulates in the forest, it is presumable that the flood waters dissolve not only the acids derived from the carbohydrates, but also various other substances which, under certain conditions, may originate insoluble deposits of a black colour, similar to those which can be obtained artificially. By a natural association of ideas this possible manner of accumulation of carbonic elements suggests the hypothesis of an analogous origin in the case of coal in Borneo.

That certain deposits must be formed in the Kapuas lakes can scarcely be doubted, for they are surrounded by forest, and receive rivers and streams. Even admitting that the forest retains the greater part of the floating timber which is swept away by the force of the floods, it is certain that a large quantity of vegetable detritus— besides that resulting from decomposed leaves, which does not visibly alter the clearness of the water—must find its way to the lakes and ultimately sink in their depths.

Even supposing that only a millimetre of carbonic substance were each year deposited, in a thousand years a layer over three feet thick would be the result; and this sufficiently demonstrates how rapidly the carboniferous deposits of Borneo may have been formed, if such be their origin.

That pure coal must have been formed and consolidated in basins where no earthy deposits took place cannot be questioned by any one. For this reason it is evident that it had its origin in forest regions where no extensive process of denudation could take place. The absence of the slightest traces of lime in the coal deposits of Labuan [1] proves that the area occupied by the forests which gave origin to them was not formed of limestone, and leads one to infer that the streams which ran through them, flowing into the deposit basins, contained black water. In Borneo the coal-fields are very extensive, and it is hardly probable that they were all formed contemporaneously. One cannot, therefore, generalize on their origin; but the fact that no traces of marine organisms have been found in Labuan coal (Tenison-Woods, *loc. cit.*) permits the inference that some, at least, are of lacustrine origin. Admitting as valid the foregoing conclusions, and bearing in mind the absence of lime in the Labuan coal, we may well imagine that these coal-fields were formed in black-water lakes analogous to those of the Kapuas. All this is quite apart from any considerations concerning the age of the carboniferous deposit, for I have had no opportunity of examining any organic remains from the Bornean coal-fields. For the rest I quite concur with the conclusions arrived at by Mr. Tenison-Woods in the paper quoted, the perusal of which suggested the theory here expressed.

With regard to the asserted temporary drying up of the Kapuas lakes, I do not believe that Danau Lamadjan can ever become perfectly dry, for I have since learnt that a Dutch steamer visits

---

[1] J. E. TENISON-WOODS. *The Borneo Coal-Fields*; in *Nature*, April 23, 1885, p. 553.

the village every month, coming from Sintang, whence it is easy to ascend the Kapuas.

Having noticed a hill on the side of the lake opposite Lamadjan, and hoping to get an extensive view over the surrounding country from its summit, I decided to pay it a visit. The hill is called Bukit Lampei, and on it were several Dyak houses, where Intika told me that he had friends. The usual landing-place was now covered with water six feet deep, and for some distance we paddled through the forest over the pathway leading up the hill.

From the summit of Bukit Lampei I had an extensive view. Eastwards water extended as far as we could see, intersected by clumps of forest ; to the north, hills were visible in the distance. Most of the country was flat and covered with interminable jungle, amidst which small isolated and scattered eminences were here and there to be seen. The hills which separate the watershed of the Kapuas from that of the Batang Lupar lay to the north-west, quite near and of no great elevation. Here is the shortest and easiest road from the Dutch territory into that of the Rajah of Sarawak. The traveller paddles a day's journey up the Sungei Bunut, and then another day's land march takes him to Lobok Antu on the Batang Lupar. Towards the west the highest point is Bukit Kananpei, or Kananpajang, which hardly looks more than twenty miles off. It hid from my view the hills of the Kumpang, which I crossed to descend to the Kantu.

On the Lampei hill the vegetation was entirely of secondary growth. Of plants worth collecting I only found an *Ixora*, and the "*Kayu silimpo*," a Rubiaceous plant of the genus *Sarcocephalus*. The nearest Malay village on the Kapuas bears the name of this tree.

The Lampei Dyaks, although they live on Dutch territory, do their marketing at Simanggan ; and hearing that I came from there, asked eagerly for news of the Rajah.

It was by the Bunut route that in January, 1852, that adventurous lady traveller, Mme. Ida Pfeiffer, crossed over to this region ; a feat which few ladies would try again, even at the present day, when travel is so much easier. Mme. Pfeiffer tells us that in the midst of the lakes she found a large number of dead trees still standing where they had grown. I can only explain this by supposing that the vegetation of which I have spoken, which appears specially adapted to flourish with its roots in the water, had been left dry during a season of exceptional drought, and thus been killed, and that with the rainy season the waters returned once more to cover the roots of the dead trees whose naked branches had so much struck Mme. Pfeiffer.

"To-day," I find noted in my diary of May 15, 1867, "is the second anniversary of my arrival in Borneo."

In crossing the lake to visit Lampei I had not collected any plants, for I was anxious to deposit my luggage and store of botanical paper under cover in a dry place without delay. Next day, however, I devoted to an investigation of the flora of the lake, although the season was, unfortunately, not too favourable, for many species were not in blossom, and, as I have remarked already, the shrubs and underwood were so entirely covered by water that we passed over them in my boat. I was able, however, to collect about thirty-five species of plants which I had not met with before in Borneo. But altogether the flora of these lakes is not very remarkable, and presented no conspicuous form which attracted my special attention ; nor is it rich, consisting of some fifty odd species only, generally abundant, though I should state that I have not made an accurate examination of the species collected in that locality. Except a few epiphytes, the others are shrubs or small trees which appear to be specially adapted to live in freshwater swamps. In this connexion two *Brackenridgeas* and a *Dichilanthe* deserve to be noticed, being remarkable for the floating apparatus with which their fruits are provided,[1] and also for the geographical distribution of the species belonging to both genera. The *Dichilanthe* of Danau Lamadjan (*D. Borneensis*, Baill.) is a singular Rubiacea, with blue irregular flowers similar to those of a Scrophulariacea, in which the small calyx swells and becomes ventricose on the maturity of the seeds, thus originating the floating apparatus. *Dichilanthe Borneensis* is very similar to *D. Zeylanica*, Thw.:— the type species of the genus, and the only other one known— which is found in the mountains of Ceylon. The *Brackenridgeas* are *Ochnaceæ*, of which, besides the two found by me in the Kapuas lakes (*B. serrulata* and *B. palustris*, Bartelletti), five other species are known. One of these inhabits the Malay Peninsula, one is found in Queensland, another in the Fiji islands, another in the Philippines, and the remaining one at Zanzibar. The seeds of a *Brackenridgea* have also been found floating on the sea off the coast of New Guinea.[2] On the whole, although the flora of the Kapuas lakes is not remarkable for variety and beauty, I consider that it is of special interest on account of some of the peculiar forms of adaptation which it possesses, owing to which the species

---

[1] The fruits of *Brackenridgea* are oval or rounded, only a few millimetres in diameter, of a shiny black, and coated with a thin pulp. They must therefore offer a certain attraction to birds, which probably contribute to their diffusion. But these seeds also possess internal closed cavities containing air, which enable them to float on water. This would explain the wide geographical distribution of this genus. It is, however, not a little strange that, notwithstanding the facilities for dispersion of the seeds, the species are all much localized.

[2] Cf. *Report of the Scientific Results of the Voyage of H.M.S. Challenger.* BOTANY, i. 1. lxiv. E.

are capable of surviving a long immersion during the periodical annual floods. Analogous cases occur in the low regions of the Brazils, about the mouth of the Amazons. Some of the plants of the lakes show perhaps a certain correlation with mangroves in their habitus and manner of growth ; but the water was too deep to allow me to see how their roots behaved. Instead of being seashore or estuarine, they might be described as lake-shore trees. Of true marsh plants the only species I met with at Ruma Segrat was *Limnophila sessiliflora*, Bl. I saw no trace of any *Nympheaceæ*, *Hydrocharids*, pond-weeds, or other really palustrine species, nor any of those plants which in marshes contribute to form peat. Not a Graminacea, not a Cyperacea ; plants, it is true, which, had they grown there, would have been then under water. The nearly total absence in Borneo of floating aquatic plants must be attributed to the facility with which waters flow and circulate, the constant and copious rainfall rendering stagnant pools an impossibility.

I found the Dyak house at Lampei contained more dogs than human beings, and at night it was hard to sleep on account of the noise they made. They were small, famished, miserable creatures, all skin and bone, and were allowed to roam about freely at night. The result was that they played havoc with my already scarce provisions, managing to gnaw through a rotang basket in which I had placed my tinned meats, and although these latter were unopened, they bit through the tins, and tasting the liquid which ran out, carried them off, scattering them all over the house. They even gnawed the cork stoppers of some bottles, and one of them went so far as to adopt my hat as his kennel. When my cook, Kisoi, awoke, and discovered the destruction they had caused, he took his revenge by serving out to them morsels of rice in which he had put doses of the arsenical soap I used for preserving animal skins. We never knew the results of this early breakfast on the poor brutes, for when the sun rose we were well on our way towards the Kantu.

As we again crossed Danau Lamadjan, I noted the paucity of birds. The only marsh-loving species I saw was a white egret perched on the top of a tree. The natives, however, told me that when the waters are low the place is populated with hosts of shore birds which come to breed there. I did not see a single monkey or any other mammal. In these localities a long narrow-snouted crocodile, *Tomistoma Schlegelii*, Müll., ought to be found. It was long thought peculiar, and one of the characteristic reptiles of Borneo, but it has been since found in Sumatra and in the Malay Peninsula. I never had the good fortune to meet with it, but it is not infrequent in Sarawak, especially on the Sadong. Its nearest ally is the well-known garial or gavial of India.[1]

[1] " Garial " in Hindustani means " a fish-eater." It is probable that

As we again entered the Umpanang, I stopped to collect specimens of all the plants in blossom which I could find. The waters
must have been extraordinarily high for a long while, for I found
that the leaves of the submerged trees were covered by a thin coating of algæ, probably Diatomaceæ. In the vicinity of Segrat
I stopped at a mattang, on which grew a species of *Eugeissonia*
(*E. ambigua* [1]). I at first thought that this palm was the same
as one which grows in the Malay Peninsula, but most probably
it must be considered as a distinct species. The mattang on which
it grew was hardly six feet above the actual level of the water ;
it was, indeed, the only dry bit of land for miles around. It was
also marked by the presence of the umbrella casuarina (" *Ru
ronan* " or " *Ru umbon* " of the Malays). I have already stated
that I consider these isolated spots of raised land sticking up from
the surrounding plain to have been ancient islands of the sea.
The one on which I found the *Eugeissonia* is a remarkable and
instructive instance to the point.

We once more passed a night at Segrat, even a more miserable
one than before, with the dogs and the swarms of mosquitoes. It was
insupportably hot. To add to our discomfort the hut was now
hardly habitable, for the streaming rain came through the rotten
old attaps in torrents. All night it fell, and the incessant roar on
the roof, combined with the other local amenities, entirely prevented
me from getting any sleep. I was tormented, too, with the idea
that the waters would rise so as to prevent our being able to ascend
the Kantu on our way back. At dawn next morning, although it
was still raining, I gave the order to start. Even my men were
heartily glad to get away from the place, and they paddled away
with a will, notwithstanding the pouring rain, which fell on their
naked shoulders, while I tried my best to obtain what shelter
I could crouched up under a kadjan mat in the middle of my boat.
At last, when it pleased heaven, the sun peeped out.

On the way we made frequent stoppages, for I wished to secure
specimens of all the flowering plants which I had not collected
elsewhere. Partly on this account, and partly because the current
against us was growing stronger, we hardly succeeded during the
day in getting over half the distance we had managed on our outward, down-stream journey. We halted at Ampar, a small Dyak
village, when the sun was low, and my men completely tired out
The bad weather followed us, and we had hardly got into the
house when the rain, which had ceased awhile, came down again

the *Tomistoma* has the same habits as the former, and is not dangerous
to man. Fossil *Tomistomas*, or allied forms, have been found in miocene
deposits in Malta and Sardinia.
[1] Cf. BECCARI. *Nuovo Giornale Botanico Italiano*, vol. iii. p. 28.

in torrents. The roof of bark under which we were was out of repair, and afforded very poor shelter; but no better was to be had. I was in a state bordering on despair on account of the botanical specimens I had collected during the day; they were already wet, and now when I placed them to dry on the floor of the house they were deluged again by the water which streamed from the roof.

We were now near the foot of Gunong Kananpei, the hill which we had seen from Lampei, but it is not visible from the river, being hidden by the trees on the banks.

The following day we paddled continuously against the current. I only had a halt of a couple of hours to dry my botanical paper at a fire, for the weather was so variable, with sudden rain-storms, that I could not spread it, as usual, in the sun. On the next day, too, the 19th, we paddled for ten hours consecutively, with only slight rests for collecting flowering plants. I saw on the trees many Mayas nests, but none of these creatures them-selves. Other monkeys were numerous, especially the *kra*, which were not at all timid, and came close to our boat. At the request of the Dyaks, who wanted them for their dinner, I shot several. We passed Grogo, where we had been obliged to remain three nights on our way down. We continued paddling up the river until we came to the Kantupa, an insignificant stream, into which we turned aside to leave the boats. There was a house there, but we marched on on foot, and in about an hour, at dusk, reached the house-village of Intika, the Orang Tua who had accom-panied me during the trip, and had proved so useful in many ways.

Intika was a very intelligent man, and I had seen him treated with respect at all the villages we passed through, and to him, no doubt, in great measure was due the success of my excursion. He was also a good diplomatist, and asserted that he wished to be on a good footing both with the Sarawak and the Dutch authorities, though the Kantu Dyaks did not appear to look up to the latter much.

The twentieth of May was a well-earned day of rest for my men, who had paddled for three days from morning to night against the current of the Kantu. I myself was glad of a little respite in Intika's house, one of the cleanest I had yet seen, and I had to sort and dry the plants I had collected.

Next day I awoke my men at 4 a.m., so as to be ready to start at 6 a.m. I wished now to get back at Marop as soon as possible in order to ensure the preservation of my collections, which, on account of the constant bad weather, I had been unable to dry, or even to keep from the rain.

We tramped along briskly for five hours, the carriers having lighter loads now that our provisions were consumed. But it rained all the way. On Bukit Tundon, a hill we had crossed on our way out, I only collected three plants, which I found within reach by the side of the path; they proved to be three herbaceous forest forms, beautiful, interesting, and new to science.[1] We rested an hour to cook and eat our rice, and started off again, and after another four hours' tramp we reached Kumpang in the evening, having accomplished in one day what had required two when we were outward bound to the lakes. I believe that the distance covered must have been about eighteen miles, for we walked briskly for nine hours. Even under the best conditions, and along the best roads, it is difficult in Borneo to travel on foot more than two miles per hour. Before we got to Kumpang we were overtaken by another deluge of rain.

Early next morning, May 22nd, we once more started in the rain. On passing by the spot where I had observed the *Nepenthes* on the way out I found my mark; but, unfortunately, the plants I wanted had vanished. Some Chinamen who had come here for the gold washings had built a hut near the spot, and in searching for rotang or other trailers to use as rope had evidently cut the *Nepenthes*, whose long, thin, tough stems are often used for tying.

We reached Marop a little before midday. We had marched consecutively for six hours; but this time the distance could not have been more than ten miles, for we had to travel along narrow pathways on a clay soil, much trodden by Chinamen, and rendered slippery by the rain. Just as we got to the Kunsi's house, my home in Marop, the rain came down again in torrents. Happily, we were now under good shelter, and my collections were safe.

The species of plants collected during this excursion were about 120, almost all different from those which I had hitherto found in Sarawak. In a country where the greater portion of the vegetation is arboreal it is not in hurried trips that rich collections can be formed. Even if one succeeds in getting some of the more conspicuous species occurring within hand-reach along the path, the more important forms, those of the true forest type—the big trees —still remain to be got; and to collect these, as I have already remarked, a long stay at different localities and during different seasons is required.

Amongst the botanic collections brought back from my excursion to the lakes were very few *Araceæ*, or orchids, which appear to be scarce in the country I crossed. Even palms were rare, for I only got the *Eugeissonia* already mentioned; but I did see a few rotangs. Pandani, which are usually so common in lowlands,

---

[1] *Didymocarpus Beccarii*, C. B. Clarke; *D. Kompsobæa*, C. B. Clarke, two fine Gesneraceæ; and *Allomorphia multinervia* Cogn, a Melastomacea.

gave me but a single species. On the whole, the flora of the lake-region appeared to me much less rich than that of Sarawak.

As a philological curiosity I shall give the names of the Dyaks who went with me on the trip. They were :—Sigu Wat, Ili, Uyu, Munao, Udjal, Unka, Ladjan, and Intika.

I employed May 24th in collecting and preparing some aquatic plants, to which the Chinese, in damming freshwater streams for the operations of gold washing, had furnished the necessary conditions of existence, conditions which seldom or never occur naturally in the country.

It is very difficult to discover how long Chinamen have been settled in the auriferous region of Marop. Probably the gold washings have been taken up and abandoned over and over again. As a consequence of these operations water-holes and small stagnant pools have been formed which are not covered by forest. In these I collected a *Nitella* (the only one I met with in Borneo), a *Utricularia* (*U. exoleta*, R.B.), which I had found in the padi-fields at Singhi, and about ten species of freshwater algæ, which are scarce in Borneo,[1] simply because stagnant waters which are not at once invaded by arboreal vegetation are met with only very exceptionally, and are then generally the result of landslips, or the work of man. Small stagnant pools in which the water is not renewed are only formed during unusual periods of dryness ; but such conditions in Sarawak probably last at the utmost from ten to fifteen days. Here rain is almost of daily occurrence, and the constant changing or washing out of the water of such pools prevents algæ from establishing themselves and developing.

At Marop the Chinese had gardens, in which certain foreign plants which appear to follow man in all his migrations had gained a footing. Amongst these were several grasses, especially a *Digitaria*, called by the Chinese " Isu-mion," which had here extended to and completely infested the rice fields. Another *Digitaria* keeps to orchards and gardens, together with a *Poa* (*P.B.* No. 3,291) called " Gniam-kum-so," *Eleusine indica*, and *Elephantopus scaber*, a composite, the " Chisam-teo " of Chinamen. Near the houses grew *Adenosma* (Pterostigma) *villosum*, a scrophulariaceous plant used medicinally by the Chinese, who call it " Sa-chou-con." *Paspalum conjugatum*, another grass which might be useful if more cultivated as pasture, is also common. The Malays call it " Rumput orang-puti," or " Rumput sapi," which means white man's or cow grass. It makes excellent cattle food, and the Malays assert that it has been introduced by

---

[1] *Tetraspora gelatinosa*, C. Ag. ; *Tolypothrix flexuosa*, Zan. ; *T. distorta*, *Leptothrix punctiformis*, Zan ; *Conferva fontinalis* var. *ochracea*, Zan. ; *Zygnema* sp., *Rhizoclonium* sp., *Batrachospermum Borneense*, Zan.

Europeans, and that before Rajah Brooke's time it was unknown in Sarawak. It is, nevertheless, widely spread throughout the whole of tropical America, Brazil, Mexico, etc.; and now in Borneo it has spread into the interior on cleared lands of a fertile kind, especially along the river banks. It is a plant which cannot escape the notice of anybody who goes about in Borneo, for its small eared seeds get easily detached when ripe, and stick on to the dress and shoes, especially when the grass is damp. This is a very efficient method of distribution, which is obtained neither by viscosities, nor by awns or hooks, as in other widely spread grasses, but simply by the long hairs on the margins of the glumes, which, when wet, adhere to any passing object.

O

CHAPTER XIV

DIFFERENT SPECIES OF ORANG-UTAN—THEIR HABITAT, FOOD, ETC.—
PECULIARITIES AND HABITS—THE SUMATRAN ORANG—AN ORANG
FŒTUS—BORNEO AND THE PRECURSORS OF MAN—ADAPTATION TO
ENVIRONMENT—VARIABILITY OF SPECIES—A NEW THEORY OF EVOLU-
TION—CONDITIONS NECESSARY FOR THE EVOLUTION OF MAN AND THE
ANTHROPOIDS—THE HUMANIZATION OF THE ANTHROPOIDS—THE PLACE
OF ORIGIN OF MAN.

DURING my absence at the lakes Atzon, my skilful Chinese
hunter, had prepared three skeletons of orangs according to
the instructions I had given him; namely, roughly cleaning the bones
of the flesh, leaving them all attached by the ligaments, and drying
them at once at a slow fire. In this way putrefaction and bad
smells are prevented, and the operation can be easily performed
anywhere. Lastly, to insure against insects and other animal
pests who might gnaw the ligaments, the bones are carefully
painted over with a thick layer of arsenical soap. Of the skeletons
thus prepared one was that of a young female; one of a male Mayas
Tjaping, slightly larger than the one whose skin I had previously prepared; and the third was also a specimen of the latter
race, but its sagittal crest was less developed in height, and
shorter, although wider, than in the other specimens I had of its
kind. I should thus have supposed that the last skeleton was that
of a female, but Atzon was positive that it was that of a male,
and one with very long hair.

This was the last specimen of orang-utan which I got at Marop.
All told, I had got either the entire skeletons or portions of twenty-
four individuals. Later, Atzon brought me several other heads
of Mayas Tjaping from the same district. But with all this
I came away from Marop without having been able to solve
the doubts I had regarding the species or races of orang-utan.
Moreover, I was not able to ascertain with certainty whether the
adult female Mayas Tjaping can occasionally develop the
lateral expansions of the cheeks which are so characteristic in the
adult male, or whether she is always without them. But the fact
remained that amongst the many Mayas which I had been able
to examine not a single female presented the slightest trace of such
cheek-expansions. Wallace, too, before me appears to have had

exactly the same experience, and even expresses the conviction that the adipose cheek-expansions are peculiar to adult males.

On the other hand, however, many Dyaks at Marop assured me repeatedly that the female Mayas Tjaping has cheek-expansions like those of the male. This was further confirmed by the testimony of intelligent Malays, and amongst others by the Tuanku Yassim, mentioned in the earlier part of this book. Lastly, the Rev. Mr. Mesney, one of the missionaries whom I had met at Banteng, told me that he had himself shot a female Mayas with cheek expansions, and, moreover, that it had a young one with it, still suckling, which also had these singular lateral appendages to its face.

Later, during subsequent travels, I had several opportunities of examining living specimens of orang-utan, and give here the following extracts from my note-book :—

" 6 xii. 1877. I have seen in the Calcutta Zoological Gardens two orang-utans which had had young. The male showed rudiments of the cheek-expansions ; it was as big as the female, which had none, and looked like a Mayas Kassa, fully grown, or nearly so."

" xii. 1877. I have examined at Buitenzorg two living orangutans in the possession of Mr. Teysmann ; both very young and males, and both provided with very visible cheek-expansions. They were the size of the one I shot at Marop on the 3rd of April, 1867, which is now mounted in the University Zoological Museum at Pisa. About the same time, in the Zoological Gardens at Batavia, I saw another yet smaller specimen of orang-utan ; it also had visible cheek-expansions, but I did not ascertain the sex."

It is, therefore, a well ascertained fact that there are both very young as well as fully adult males provided with adipose lateral cheek-expansions, and others, both young and adult, who have not a trace of them. This has induced Wallace and others to express the opinion that at least two species of orang-utan exist in Borneo.

Summing up from what I have myself observed and from the information collected, we come to the following conclusions :—

1. That there is no well-authenticated case of a female orang with lateral face-expansions. That nevertheless there is some evidence to show that such expansions may be met with, if not constantly, at all events occasionally, in the female.

2. That there are young orangs yet in their milk dentition which have well-developed cheek-expansions. These are thus manifestly not a character of age, as the late A. Milne-Edwards has suggested.

3. That adult individuals are found with the expansions rudimentary.

There is no doubt that the presence or absence of these lateral cheek-expansions makes a very great difference in the physiognomy of these apes. Thus whilst the aspect of an ordinary orang-utan, especially if young, is very human, that of the Mayas Tjaping, with its lateral expansions, is much less so than that of many other monkeys.

I do not think that any zoologist at the sight of two orangs of the same age, one with, and the other without cheek-expansions, would hesitate a moment in considering them distinct species. To my eye the difference is, indeed, greater than that between

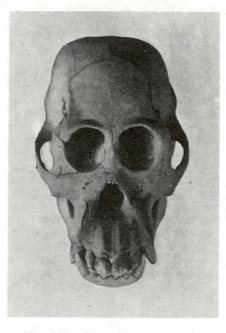

Fig. 36.—SKULL OF MAYAS KASSA ($\frac{1}{3}$).

the Bactrian camel with its two humps and the Arabian animal with one, which are unanimously considered by naturalists as different species. But on the other hand have we not in our own kind the Hottentot women provided with those adipose protuberances which constitute the so-called steatopygia ? Yet this has not caused any competent anthropologist to separate these people, and consider them as specifically distinct from the rest of mankind.

Steatopygia in the human species or in other mammals being merely a local accumulation of fat, corresponds perfectly, except with regard to position, to the adipose cheek-expansions observed in orang-utans, to which the term " Steatoparesis " (fatty cheeks), might be conveniently applied. And the analogy might even be extended to the fatty tail of certain races of sheep, to the hump of the zebu, and perhaps to the facial warts of certain pigs. [1]

In the Mayas, moreover, the steatoparesis bears a definite relation to certain cranial characters. Amongst the skulls of these orangs there are some quite smooth along the vertex, like a human

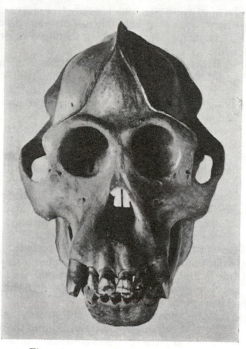

Fig. 37.—SKULL OF MAYAS TJAPING ($\frac{1}{3}$).

skull, others, instead, present a well-marked median sagittal crest, which corresponds to the insertions of the big temporal muscles ; and in addition, at right angles to the latter, a great lambdoidal crest rises across the skull from ear to ear. As a general rule, when cheek-expansions are not present there are no cranial crests, and this is the case also in fully adult and very aged specimens. Thus

---

[1] A beginning of steatoparesis, or fatty thickening of the cheeks between these and the ears, is sometimes apparent in the human species in stout, well-fed persons.

the wider are the "tjapings," or cheek-expansions, the greater is the development of the cranial crest; and we are led to suppose that there is a sort of correlation and that the first character is the cause of the second one. Of course, the augmented weight of the head and consequent development of the cranial muscles may also contribute to the enlargement of these crests which, as a general rule, grow with age in all the Anthropomorpha.[1]

I do not know of any well-authenticated specimen of the skull of a young orang-utan, during the period of the first dentition, with lateral face expansions, and cannot, therefore, say whether in that stage there are or are not signs of any development of the cranial crests. As far as I am aware no skull of a female orang, of any race, is known with crests.

I have observed cases of abnormal dentition even in the series of orang-utan skulls which I collected. Thus that of a female Mayas Kassa had two small fourth molars in the lower jaw, and corresponding supernumerary molars in the upper jaw, still enclosed in their alveoli.

All the orang-utans which I collected—at least all those of which I preserved the skin or the skeleton—were without a nail on the great toe or hallux, or had it reduced to a mere rudiment. Moreover, this peculiarity was associated with the absence of the ungual phalanx in that toe. But specimens of orang-utan are known, both from Borneo and from Sumatra, in which both the nail and the terminal phalanx of the hallux are well developed. Again, it appears that this character is not in any connected with the presence or absence of cheek-expansions, and that there are Mayas Tjaping with, and others without, a nail on their great toes. This has not prevented specific value being given to the character affecting the extremity of the hallux, and the name of *Simia bicolor* has been conferred on those orang-utans which possess a terminal phalanx and a nail on their great toes.

I may remark that the specimens devoid of these two parts offer an example of the extreme effects of disuse and the non-practice of terrestial locomotion; the development of the hallux having diminished in importance to the corresponding advantage of that of the other toes, which, under the conditions of a purely arboreal existence, have assumed functions more similar to those of the fingers.

After all that has been said, what conclusions can we come to regarding the question of a plurality of species amongst the orang-utans? The answer is much more difficult than anyone who is not a zoologist might be led to suppose. For the laity there are big

[1] It is to be remarked that on the skulls of adult gorillas the development of bony crests is very conspicuous, although these anthropoids are devoid of fatty cheek-expansions.

orangs with a wide face and lateral cheek-expansions, and smaller orangs without such expansions; some have short, other have long hair, and thus at least two or three kinds may be distinguished. But for the naturalist the question is a very different one, and is connected with one of the most discussed and disputed points in zoology. However, I shall now venture to give my own opinion on the case, in accordance with the facts I have observed and the materials I have at my command.

From a careful examination of specimens in the flesh, and from the preparation of a number of skeletons with my own hands, I have come to the conclusion that it is rare to meet with two specimens of orang-utan perfectly alike, even when of the same age and sex, and belonging to the same race. Professor Henry Giglioli arrived at a similar conclusion after studying the series of crania which I collected, now in the Museo Civico at Genoa.[1]

There exist, however, as I have more than once stated, two forms of orang especially distinct from the others. One possesses lateral adipose cheek-expansions and highly developed cranial crests: this is the Mayas Tjaping. The second form, even when perfectly adult, has no lateral cheek-expansions, and its skull is devoid of strongly pronounced crests: this is the Mayas Kassa. I do not attach much importance to the third form, distinguished by the natives as Mayas Rambei, on account of its long hair.

It is possible that in a remote past the Mayas Tjaping and the Mayas Kassa were two quite distinct species, perhaps having their origin in separate regions, and only later coming into contact on the same area. The cheek-expansions may possibly have been developed in those individuals living (during the period of specific malleability to which I have before alluded) in localities where there was an abundance of nutritious food, which was devoured immoderately by them, and eventually stored, in the form of fat, in their distended cheeks. On the other hand, the Mayas Kassa at the same evolutive period may have lived in localities where food was equally but sparingly distributed through-out the year, and the need for the storage of fat did not exist. At present, however, it seems hardly likely that the two races should remain distinct, for individuals of each are found promiscuously in the same locality, and even on the same tree.

I am thus inclined to suppose that Mayas Tjaping can give birth to young both with and without cheek expansions, and to any intermediate form, i.e. with rudimentary " tjapings." Nor do I see any impossibility in the theory that from a Mayas Kassa a Mayas Tjaping may be born, just as a human couple

---

[1] E. H. GIGLIOLI. *Studi Craniologici sui Chimpanse*, etc.; in *Annali Museo Civico di Genova*, vol. iii. p. 56. Genoa, 1872.

of dark complexion may have fair children, and vice versâ, according to the influence of dark or fair ancestors in the family tree of the two families. I, therefore, hold that only one species of orang-utan really exists—the *Simia satyrus* ; of which I distinguish two main varieties, retaining for them the native names of " Tjaping " and " Kassa."

Orang-utans are tolerably common in the southern parts of Borneo, especially in the districts of Bandjarmasin, Pontianak, and Sambas. In Sarawak they are common on certain rivers, especially in the districts of the Sadong and the Batang Lupar. On the Sarawak river, as I have said before, they are very rare ; it has even been stated that they are non-existent, but this is not so, and I have heard of an orang-utan killed at Singhin, not far from Kuching. On Gunong Bungo it appears that they are always to be found. I may add that the Dyaks of the Upper Sarawak have special names for the orang-utans, and call the Mayas Kassa " Sekao " and the Mayas Tjaping, " Mara." According to Mr. St. John (*Op. cit.* ii. p. 156), orangs are also found in the Muput country on the Limbang.

The orang-utan inhabits the hills and plains alike ; but does not care to climb very high up the mountains, cold not being at all to its liking. On the Marop hills, at an altitude of from 300 to 500 feet or so, it is very frequent ; but it loves also the lowlands and marshes along the Lingga and Sadong rivers, especially where pandani grow, for it delights in the " cabbages " of these plants, as well as those of various palms.

In captivity, orangs are generally badly kept, being overfed with sweet fruits, especially bananas. In a wild state they feed largely on leaves and buds, and sour, astringent, and, to our taste, wholly unpalatable fruits, very often unripe. They like padi (unhusked rice), and I believe this, with acorns, chestnuts, bread, and potatoes, would be the most wholesome food we can give them in our own climate. The creatures often do great damage to the rice fields, when the rice is ripe. Usually strictly arboreal, they descend at such times to the ground, and, on reaching the padi fields, collect a big sheaf of rice with the heavy ripe ears, and, holding it under the arm, get back to their tree, up which they climb, and enjoy their plunder in peace and comfort on their nests. They do much injury to the fruit-trees, and are especially fond of durians, committing great ravages among them even when unripe. The Dyaks were, therefore, much delighted when we killed them, though the Banteng Dyaks are an exception. They venerate the animal for a singular reason. Once upon a time, the legend runs, enemies came to attack their village, but the orang-utans, moved by curiosity, showed themselves in large numbers, and the enemy, mistaking them for men, were frightened and took to their heels.

Fig. 38.—ORANGS OF THE MAYAS KASSA RACE, ON A DURIAN TREE.

It is not improbable that in many districts in Borneo the orang has been driven away or exterminated by man, especially where the deadly " sumpitan " is used; for it is so large an animal, and so seldom attempts to fly when it is discovered, that it is easily killed.   It is never dangerous, except when wounded; but then its bites are very severe, quite capable of taking off the fingers of a man's hand or inflicting other severe injuries.   There would, too, be small chance for a weaponless man who found himself in the grip of the long and powerful arms.   I have heard the story told of a Dyak who was caught by an orang-utan, and who saved himself by pretending to be dead.   When irritated a Mayas becomes furious; its neck swells out from the distention of its great laryngeal sacs, and it emits fearful howls.

The Mayas has few enemies excepting man, being undoubtedly the strongest animal in the forests of Borneo.   Tales are told of its fights with the bear, the crocodile, and the python, all of which are vanquished by it and killed by its formidable bites.

According to my hunter, Atzon, orang-utans are sometimes attacked by ague, or some similar intermittent fever, and he asserts that he has seen them shivering on their nests when the temperature could not account for this.

I have not ascertained how and when these animals drink.   In a country where rain is so frequent, it is very probable that they do not take the trouble to descend from the trees to drink in a neighbouring stream, but manage to obtain sufficient water from the dripping leaves, using the highly extensible lower lip for this purpose.

It has been stated that, when wounded, a Mayas will endeavour to stay the bleeding by applying its hand to the wound; and some have gone so far as to assert that it dresses the latter with leaves.   My experience does not bear this out; but I have seen a wounded orang examine its wound in a very human manner, and even touch it with its fingers, apparently moved more by curiosity than by anything else.

Even the biggest orang-utans move freely on the branches of trees, but if they have to pass overhead from one tree to another they always try the branches beforehand, to make sure that they can support their weight.   They climb with ease the big trunks of trees, embracing them with their long and powerful arms.   I have, however, noticed that if a creeper is handy they prefer it, and ascend it with great rapidity.   They make better progress, in short, by the lianas than by the tree-trunk, especially if the latter be thick. When they want to get along rapidly they use their arms chiefly, the feet serving more to make their jumps secure than anything else.

In the orang-utan, compared with man, the proportions of the limbs are reversed. The arms take the place of legs, and become the principal organs of locomotion. Their movements in passing from one tree to another are very similar to those of the Wa-wa (*Hylobates*), but much slower. On sloping branches the animal walks on its feet and helps itself on by its hands. On the ground they are very clumsy, for they cannot extend the foot so as to

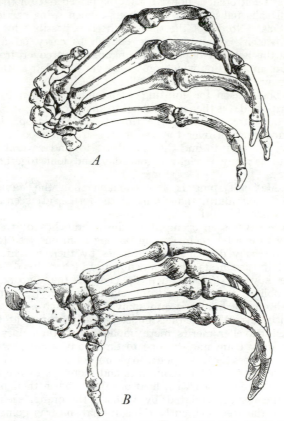

Fig. 39.—A. BONES OF LEFT HAND, AND B. OF LEFT FOOT OF ORANG (⅓).

place the sole on the ground, but walk on the external edge of the foot, which is kept bent. The two hands are applied to the ground by the knuckles, the hand being closed and the fingers bent. This is a well-known character of the Anthropomorpha, although the gorilla approaches man much more nearly in this respect, having feet better adapted for terrestrial progression and capable of being set almost flat on the ground. In the orang-utan the adaptation to an arboreal existence is so far developed that its hands and feet have become very like hooks, and without much muscular exertion the creature can suspend itself by them to the branches. In fact, the phalanges themselves are curved, and it keeps its fingers always naturally bent. The palm of the hand and the sole of the foot can never be stretched, nor can they be placed flat on the ground.

The Dyaks tell many a tale about women being carried off by orang-utans. No doubt the thing in itself is possible, for an adult male Mayas is certainly strong enough to carry off a woman. But that this actually happens, and happens, moreover, from sexual reasons, is an assertion which only deserves to be left as the subject of a romance to some Dyak novelist of the future.

The best season for hunting orang-utans is when the fruit is getting ripe,and it is then not difficult to find five or six, or even more, on the same tree. During the time I was at Marop, the Mayas were wandering all over the forest in search of food, and it was therefore less easy to find them, still less to find several together. Yet I saw as many as eight in one day, and four together on the same tree.

The Mayas Tjaping is less common than the Mayas Kassa; but the Dyaks affirm that many of the former are seen about the villages when the durians are ripe.

I have never seen orang-utans throw branches of trees at the hunter who is after them, but in passing from one tree to another they may easily detach dead branches by their weight, or when wounded in their nests may shake down branches already detached. Wallace, however (*Op. cit.* i. p. 87), tells us that on one occasion he was obliged to get away from under a durian tree on account of the shower of branches and spiny fruits which a female orang-utan with several small ones endeavoured to throw at him. No naturalist traveller merits more implicit faith than does Wallace, and certainly I am not the one to throw any doubt on his state-ment. Nor does the case appear to me improbable ; for it is in accord-ance with the nature of many apes and monkeys to become much excited when disturbed with fruit or other food in their possession, and in the instance related by Wallace, the orang, seeing a man approach the tree, evidently thought that he was going to drive her away, and prevent her from eating the durians, a fruit to which they are extremely partial.

Again, I have never noticed that orangs seek cover behind the branches when a hunter takes aim at them with his gun. On the contrary, I have always seen them lean forward and even get clear of branches to see better when a man approaches, prompted, no doubt, by a sentiment of curiosity to get a better view of a being whom they certainly must perceive bears a considerable resemblance to themselves. It is not easy to imagine what ideas the orang-utans may form of us. I will not, however, deny that in some instances they may have a notion of the effects of a gun, and associate the possibility of being struck by a missile with the presence of man. The experience of these creatures in such a matter may vary in different parts of the country and be strictly individual, as their degree of intelligence may also vary individually. And truly the orang-utans, who are so generally variable, also present, independent of age or sex, a remarkable variation in their cranial capacity ; whence it may be argued that their intellectual development cannot be uniform. Thus Professor Giglioli, in his studies on the orang-utan crania which I collected (*Op. cit.* pp. 138–9), calls attention to the small cerebral capacity of the female Mayas which I shot on April 30, 1867 (that from which I took the fœtus which was preserved). This female may be considered as microcephalous, its cranial capacity not reaching 304 cubic centim. ; whilst that of the young male which I killed at the same time, and which I took to be her offspring, gave a cerebral capacity of 457 cubic centim., i.e. more than the maximum (456 cubic centim.) found by Professor Giglioli in the adult Mayas Kassa. Another male Mayas Kassa of the same age as the one just mentioned, or showing, at all events, the same stage of dental development, had a cranial capacity of 346 cubic centim.

The maximum cerebral capacity found in my series of orang-utan skulls was that of a perfectly adult Mayas Tjaping, which measured 503 cubic centim.

The orang-utan inhabits not only Borneo, but Sumatra, where both the race with cheek expansions and that without them are also found. In Sumatra, however, these animals are certainly much less abundant. During a stay of several months I made there in the province of Padang, in the year 1878, I never even heard them mentioned. It has been met with in the province of Tapannuli at Rambum, and at Siboga on the west coast, near the equator.[1]

In the Zoological Museum at Florence is the skeleton of a young orang-utan, described as coming from Palembang, on the east coast of Sumatra. It is remarkable on account of the extraordinary curvature of the second phalanges of the toes, and for the length of the first, which is much greater than that I have seen in any of the skeletons of specimens from Borneo of a corresponding age. I do not, however, see any reason for separating specifically the Sumatran from the Bornean orang-utan.

The presence of this anthropoid in both islands is certainly one of the best arguments towards proving a past land connexion

[1] Mr. N. Ridley thinks it possible that the orang exists in the Malay Peninsula, where the natives appear to know it by the name of " Mowas," which may, perhaps, be the same as " Mayas " (Cf. *Natural Science,* vi. p. 23).

between them, the orang being a land animal, and devoid of the means of crossing the wide expanse of sea which now divides Sumatra and Borneo.

Of the orang-utan fœtus obtained by me at Marop, and already alluded to, Professor Trinchese, who has published an accurate description of it,[1] writes :—" Its aspect greatly surprises every-one who sees it on account of its extraordinary resemblance to a human fœtus ; a likeness rendered still greater by the nakedness

Fig. 40.—FŒTUS OF ORANG.

of the skin, which a fine down or lanugo is insufficient to conceal." [2] This fœtus is a female, and its development corresponds to a human fœtus between the fifth and sixth month of uterine existence. The forehead is not receding, and the shape of the head has been described as like that of an Eskimo. The neck is short, and the nose does not project. The toes are very long, a character quite

[1] *Annali del Museo Civico di Genova,"* vol. i. p. 9. ; tav. i., ii., iii.
[2] *Loc. cit.*, p. 35.

sufficient by itself to distinguish it from a human fœtus. The arms, hands, thighs, and legs are similar to those of man. Even the foot is formed on the type of the human one up to the base of the toes, but thence differs in the great length of the latter and in the position and proportions of the hallux, which is also devoid of a nail.[1]

From the above Professor Trinchese draws the conclusion that the orang-utan is the more similar to man the younger it is, because the fœtus of the former has a greater resemblance to man than that which exists between the latter and an adult orang.

As Borneo is one of the few places on the globe where anthropoid apes are found, the query naturally arises whether in the past beings may not have existed on this great island more resembling man than the present orang-utans. In other words whether Borneo may not have been the place, or one of the places, where the precursors of man had their origin.

In the absence of any positive evidence on this point, my experience with the orang-utans and my knowledge of the country in which they live is, perhaps, insufficient for me to offer a mere negative or affirmative opinion on this question. I may, however, here express as succinctly as possible some of my views on evolution, and on the causes which may have given origin to the varied and innumerable forms of animal life. To these ideas some allusion has already been made in the foregoing pages; but I shall now ask my reader's leave to dilate upon them somewhat more fully, and to devote the remainder of this chapter to a scientific subject which, I trust, may not be found out of place in this book.

To begin with, I must declare myself an adherent of the theory that the environment, in the widest sense of the word, has been the most powerful and principal agent in causing animals, as well as plants, to assume their present form and structure. That the organized beings now living have been originated through the action exerted on them by the external world, is an old theory which was propounded by a few elect naturalists, who had not much faith in the creation of living beings simply by the action of a supernatural will.

With the appearance of Darwin's memorable book on the Origin of Species, the above-mentioned theory retired to the background, and became, one may say, almost forgotten, so obscured was it by the fascinating theory of natural and sexual selection.

At the present time, however, a tendency to return to the older theory is gaining ground, owing to the grave doubts which have

---

[1] On this point I may quote the following from *Hovelacque et Hervé*, *Précis d'Anthropologie*, p. 177:—" Wyman a reconnu que sur l'embryon humain long d'un pouce environ, le gros orteil, au lieu d'être parallèle aux doigts, forme un angle avec le côté du pied, correspondant ainsi par la position avec l'état permanent de l'orteil chez les Quadrumanes."

arisen on all sides as to the theory that natural selection is the sole means capable of explaining the *raison d'être* of the specific characters of living organisms.

According to the theory of the plasmation of living beings through the action exerted on them by the environment, every species would be the product of the physical forces and stimuli to which its remote ancestors had been subjected.   For this reason every animal and every plant ought to bear in its own structure the traces of its first origin.   Even in familiar talk it is generally

Fig. 41.—FŒTUS OF ORANG, SIDE VIEW.

admitted that each climate has left its mark on the organisms living within its influence.

The varied forms assumed by those groups of individuals called by naturalists species, would be merely the result of a plasmative force exerted by surrounding conditions on primitive beings ; and from a certain point of view it might be said that species represent the impression of which the stimuli, in general, have been the stamp or matrix.

Thus a careful and minute investigation of the structure of any given species ought to lead to the knowledge of the circumstances under the influence of which it has been formed, and reveal the climatic surroundings in which it was plasmated, and consequently the region where it made its first appearance.

A very grave objection, however, apparently arises to oppose the adoption of so fascinating an hypothesis.

Notwithstanding investigations and experiments of all kinds it has been found that species at the present moment are little, if at all, modified by the effects of their surroundings. The stimuli have now but very slight power in the modification of individuals, and adaptation to exceptional or abnormal conditions of existence is not met with in that degree which would be required by my hypothesis. Indeed, we may go still further and assert that living beings vary very slightly or not at all at the present time, and that they perish sooner than adapt themselves to new conditions of life. A sufficient case to the point is that of all tropical plants which are cultivated in hothouses, which would infallibly perish if exposed, even for a single day, to our outside air during winter.

The Darwinian theory of evolution has caused the belief for the time being that accidental variability (sport) exerted an all-important and preponderating influence on the formation of new species, and it has been thought that innate variability, helped by natural and sexual selection, has been sufficient to produce the entire series of organised forms which now exist or have existed. The Darwinian theory does not, however, explain the reason of such an innate tendency towards variation in organisms.

Another argument strongly against the hypothesis that organisms may have been modified by stimuli is found in the absolutely negative results obtained by experiments.

Rabbits have been kept and made to breed entirely in the dark for many generations, and not the slightest trace of impaired or modified vision has been detected in the later offspring. In the same way mice have had their tails amputated, and rabbits their ears clipped short from generation to generation, but never a mouse has been born tailless, or a rabbit without ears.

There are certain well-known mutilations and deformations which have been practised on man himself for thousands of years, and yet no indication of modification of the parts thus treated has been observed.

Moreover, if at the present time isolated individuals assume some peculiar character or modify some organ, whether by use, or as the result of the conditions in which they lived or were experimentally subjected to, the acquired peculiarity or the modified organ is not transmitted to their offspring. Thus the most essential basis is wanting for the support of the theory of the response of the organism to the sensations received, which ought to constitute the basis of the theory of plasmation according to the environment.

If, however, new forms of adaptation are not produced under our own eyes, it must be admitted that, from time to time, accidental varieties, or deviations from the common type, appear in Nature, for we every day see horticulturists obtain new varieties of flowers and fruit, and breeders and fanciers new kinds of cattle, dogs, poultry, and pigeons.

But careful experiments have shown that the supposed variability of species at the present time is more apparent than real. In trying to demonstrate the variability of species by exhibiting the various forms that a given species assumes in Nature, we only prove that it has varied, and thus confound polymorphism with variability.[1]

Experiments and cultivation do not thus confirm the existence in living beings of that extensive variability which many naturalists pretend to believe ; and in any case, such variability is not now of an adaptive kind. Therefore, contrary to the present prevailing tendency to attribute a powerful action to variability during the existing period, and to consider every species as inconstant, I hold the opposite opinion, namely, that at the present time species do not vary in Nature, returning thus to the old idea of the nearly absolute fixity of existing species.[2]

The indisputable fact, however, remains that through cultivation and artificial selection in breeding new forms can be obtained.

The circumstances, however, which at the present time are associated with the production of domestic varieties of animals and plants, are of a very different nature from those which must have brought about variation through adaptation. Thus, for example, if a new variety of *Primula sinensis* makes its appearance with a corolla frilled, jagged, or more divided than in the wild form, this is not because such new characters correspond to any special want or necessity of the plant, or because it is advantageous for it to assume them. In the forms produced or obtained by breeders, or by horticulturists, the first indication which has led to the formation of the new variety or race has in every case cropped out accidentally. without any ascertained cause or reason, and quite independently of any act or wish of the producer. The latter has merely taken advantage of a first tendency or plan of variation which has naturally manifested itself, and, by preserving and causing the individuals who have shown such a tendency to interbreed, has succeeded in increasing and exaggerating the sport. But who can

---

[1] I base this assertion especially on the well-known experiments of Naegeli on *Hieracium*.

[2] I should not consider as an adaptation of recent formation the case of some plants which undergo certain changes if grown in new conditions, as, for instance, that seen in alpine species planted in lowlands. This is merely a latitude in already acquired characters, constant in any given species.

produce this form of intentional selection in Nature? And who has given the first impulse to the " accidental " production of a new variation? I do not deny that even at the present time some form of adaptation can be artificially obtained. Thus horses better adapted to draw than to run, and vice versa, have been produced ; but even in these cases man has merely taken advantage of an innate tendency in the horse, and has selected for interbreeding those animals which, quite independent of any action on his part, were born with one or with the other predisposition.

The means employed by man to obtain varieties consist principally in endeavours to diminish the power and energy of conservative heredity, which obliges descendants to reproduce forms identical with their progenitors. Such means are hybridizing and interbreeding with different species or varieties ; and, above all, a continued interbreeding of blood relations, descendants from the same stock (the principal cause, perhaps, of duplication). Finally, added to this is intentional artificial selection by man—a factor which plays no part in Nature.[1]

The new forms thus obtained by cultivation in no case satisfy a want newly developed in a plant or animal ; they reveal instead merely a tendency towards independence so far as regards the established laws of heredity ; and, indeed, many are probably merely forms which have assumed some of the so-called ancestral or atavic characters, i.e. those which formerly existed in progenitors of the species and now reappear.[2]

I do not, however, entirely exclude the possibility that at the present time some traces of true adaptation may yet be obtained, But what I wish to show is that in all cases *the actual power of adaptation in organisms is at the present day well nigh non-existent as compared with what they must have possessed in the past*. It is sufficient to give one case in point—that of the mangroves, trees which live with their roots constantly submerged in salt water. Would it be possible now to cause any of the innumerable trees which grow in these tropical forests away from the sea to live and flourish in salt water? From time immemorial fruits of all sorts of species have been carried by the rivers to the sea and deposited at their mouths in favourable conditions for germination, yet,

[1] In many garden vegetables in which the hypertrophy of certain parts is the chief feature. as in cabbages, carrots, radishes, etc., it may be suspected that cultivation in a soil rich in nitrogenous compounds has produced the development of micro-organisms, which through some special form of symbiosis may be the cause of such hypertrophy.

[2] As an example I may say that I have obtained specimens of *Cyclamen persicum* with perfectly straight peduncles and erect flowers, with a corolla with open and horizontal petals, just as in a normal primula, and as beyond doubt was the case in the progenitor of the cyclamen.

notwithstanding this, no new estuarine plant has been formed in our times ; thus fully proving the reluctance in existing organisms to abandon the prerogatives with which the past with cumulative effect has endowed them.

Not admitting that at the present day species can vary, or that organisms are capable of an appreciable degree of adaptability to surrounding conditions, and at the same time holding natural and sexual selection as insufficient to explain all the phenomena of evolution, the question arises in what way has evolution taken place ?

The answer appears to me easy and obvious. What does not happen now can nevertheless have happened in the past.[1]

I take it to be a great philosophical error to persist in considering past biological and telluric phenomena as having been produced by forces identical in nature and intensity with those in action at the present day, just as I believe it a mistake to draw too close a parallel between what happened in earlier geological periods with what daily takes place under our own eyes. It would be almost tantamount to arguing that a baby is in every way identical with an old man !

As far as life is concerned, one of the chief differences between the present and the past in my opinion exists in the intensity with which the force known as " conservative heredity " manifests itself, obliging modern organisms to transmit unaltered to their descendants the shape, colours, peculiarities, in short, the entire characters which were transmitted to them by their ancestors. This is the reason why now living beings are, so to speak, fixed and immutable, and cannot assume absolutely new forms. For the very same reason external agents with their stimuli cannot succeed in producing important modifications in the stimulated organs during the lifetime of individuals, and much less can modifications casually obtained in the organism during life be transmitted to its progeny. If, as an instance, we take a monkey which has been trained to stand erect on its legs, and which has also acquired the requisite muscular development for such a gait, it can never transmit to its offspring either the acquired faculty of standing erect, or the muscular development thus obtained. Thus heredity is the obstacle which prevents variation in species now living, or permits it in so small a degree, that even the accumulation of small variations during myriads of years could never have rendered possible the evolution of the organic world, if it has to be thus accounted for.

If, however, one considers that the action of conservative heredity cannot have been always the same, that, necessarily feeble in

---

[1] The first mention of this hypothesis of mine was briefly made in a paper I published in the *Bullettino della R. Società Toscana d'Orticultura*, Anno xiv. (1889), bearing the title " *Fioritura dell'Amorphophallus titanum.*"

the primordial epoch of life (when, as we may say, the organic world was young), it must have grown with time, accumulating and increasing in successive generations, it will be possible to reconcile the theory of the " permanent impressionability " of organisms (i.e. to the stimuli exerted on them by external conditions) with belief in the all but complete immutability of species now living.

That at the present time the power of heredity is such as to put great obstacles in the way of variation is a fact which cannot be denied ; that in the past it had not always the same force cannot be directly proven, but can easily be credited ; and that the further we go back towards the origin of life the less strong it must have been, is only a logical *sequitur* of the admitted strength of the force heredity now exerts.

Thus during the infancy of the organic world, there being then no power to counteract the conservation of new characters acquired by organisms, the latter must have been not only susceptible of considerable morphological malleability during their lifetime, but must have also been capable of transmitting to their descendants any new characters of an advantageous kind they had acquired.

The period of a human lifetime reproduces on a small scale what must have happened in gigantic proportions during the evolution of living beings. No one can deny that infancy has peculiarities which are not possessed by old age. And it is equally true that during the first period of life the force of habit is less powerful than in adult age. In early youth animals can be domesticated or tamed, children learn with facility, and even their limbs are pliable and capable of modification. With age heredity acts more strongly, instincts prevail, and adaptation to new conditions of existence and to new ideas become more difficult ; in a word, it is much less easy to combat hereditary tendencies.

What can have happened at an epoch when heredity did not exist is hard to infer with precision. In the absence of this factor in the evolution of living beings, almost any change or variation in the latter must have been possible. There is even no necessity to suppose that in the remotest past the offspring need have been necessarily similar to its progenitors. Every new generation of organisms might differ from that which preceded it, so that " species," in the sense in which the word is now used, may have been then a term without meaning.

In that epoch, geologically of the remotest antiquity, light, heat, drought, abundant rains, winds, the nature of the soil, colours, the stimuli of insects, *et similia*, may all have contributed to promote modification in the organisms placed under their influence. This would have been the Plasmative Epoch—the epoch of the auto-creation of species.

Thus I attribute to such causes not only the special structures of aquatic, land, desert, and forest plants, but also the infinite number of modifications in floral organs which carry the impression of stimuli exerted by insects. To the action of environment I attribute also the cases of mimicry; and I have extended my theory even further, holding that moral impressions, and especially individual volition, have exercised a great influence in the evolution of organisms.[1]

It is only by admitting a pre-established plan that the existence of certain forms and certain colours in some animals can be accounted for. And this pre-established plan in the case of certain creatures may have had its origin in the desire to attain a given end; a desire often caused by want or necessity, but at times by a love for the beautiful, by pleasure, vanity, fear, or any of the many passions and desires which agitate organized beings. For the genesis of species to have taken place in accordance with the above theory, it is necessary to assume that organisms possessed an inclination to vary, or to allow themselves to be influenced by stimuli, one might say almost without direct need, and in a manner precisely contrary to that which occurs at the present time when individuals and species do not vary, or, rather, cannot adapt themselves to new conditions of existence, even when the need exists.

It is, nevertheless, not impossible that in some instances certain forms may have made their appearance suddenly, and may quite as suddenly have adapted themselves to a new condition of the environment. This is the hypothesis of " Neogenesis," as it has been called by Professor Mantegazza, in favour of which there are fewer facts than for any other hypothesis of the kind. And yet it is the one which has the most attractions for me. If we accept this hypothesis it becomes quite unnecessary to admit a continuous derivation of organisms one from the other by slow modifications; because the connecting links which yet exist, or are revealed by palæontology, would be the result of hybridism between two prototypes of sudden formation, whose reproduction was not impeded because it had no force of heredity to contend with.

The essence of my hypothesis consists in the argument that the power of heredity is so great at the present period as to render variation in living organisms very feeble, if not impossible; that consequently adaptation to surrounding conditions is now all but nil; and that for this reason any modifications which may affect the individual during life are not transmitted to its progeny. On the other hand, in far distant geological times, adaptability to surroundings and sensitiveness in reaction to stimuli must have been greater the further back the epoch during which such influences were active.

---

[1] Cf. BECCARI. " Le Capanne ed i Giardini dell'Amblyornis inornata"; in Annali del Museo Civico di Genova, vol. ix. p. 382 (1877).

For heredity has gone on increasing with the succession of geological epochs, whilst on the other hand the force of plasmation has gradually grown weaker, and ceased entirely at the present day.

Even those who decline to attribute importance to the force of heredity because it cannot be experimentally demonstrated, or, as some express it, because it is merely evoked to interpret phenomena otherwise unexplainable, are compelled to admit that between the reproductive phenomena of organisms in the primordial epoch of the formation of species and those of to-day a difference must exist. It is not within the bounds of credibility that all the reproductive phenomena can have become manifest in the very same mode in the primordial generations as after the lapse of thousands and thousands of generations. In other words, it seems to me a bold thing to assert that no change can have taken place in the effects of fecundation since the first times when the parts forming the nuclei of organisms of opposite sex met, united, and subsequently parted, to give origin to the embryo of a new creature, and now, when the process of fecundation and development has been reproduced for an indefinite period and through an incalculable number of generations. It appears to me that the stability obtained in the phenomena of reproduction, the primary cause of the stability of species, is a consequence of the number of times these phenomena have repeated themselves ; and also that the stability of the morphological characters of individuals must be proportional in any given species to the number of the generations of each, and to the length of time since their specific entity was defined. It cannot be doubted that in the nucleus of the reproductive cell are comprised all the hereditary and physical characteristics of the organisms to which that cell belonged. Now, as it is inferred that every part and every organ of any given living creature must have contributed to the formation of its reproductive cells, into which infinitely minute particles representing each part and each organ must have been carried, it is presumable that in the far remote epochs of specific plasmation, when organisms were assuming the shapes they have since retained, that the transference into the cell nuclei of the infinitely minute particles of protoplasm or micellæ representing the various organs and parts of the living being was partial and incomplete, so that, all the parts of the parental organism not being fully represented, extensive variation became possible ; but as generations succeeded to generations the transference of the protoplasmic micellæ representing the various parts of the parent into the tissue of the reproductive nuclei became more general and complete, and the tendency to variation naturally diminished gradually. At the present time, after an infinite number of generations, the aforesaid transmission must have become so complete that the field is closed to variation, and living organisms are obliged to reproduce themselves with constant and well established characters. It is on this hypothesis that, according to my views, the theory of heredity ought to rest.

Moreover, the continuous and repeated segmentation of the nuclei, and the equal division of their chromatine in the daughter cells, has been the cause, most undoubtedly, of the uniform distribution of the characters of the entire organism in the cells imbued with reproductive power, whether sexual or gemmoidal; consequently, the oftener the segmentation has been repeated, the more perfect will be the reproduction of the organism with constant characters. And this consideration also points to an acceptation of the theory that hereditary force must have gone on increasing with time, in due proportion to the number of generations which a given individual can reckon in its genealogical tree.

As far as plants are concerned, it is not alone in the reproductive cells that the elementary constituents of the entire individual are centred, but also in numerous other cells disseminated in the more vital portion of the plant, that is, in the cambium of every vascular bundle. Each of these cells virtually represents an entire individual, and probably more specially the organ of which it is a portion ; thus to render possible the accumulation of the characteristics of the entire organism in the reproductive cells it would suffice that there should be a transference into these of the micellæ of a limited number of such cells. When presented under this aspect, the theory of pangenesis appears much more simple.

And now let us return to Borneo, and, with facts and deduction to guide us, endeavour to find out whether there is any probability that ancestors of Man have existed on that island.

Admitting species to be dependent on climate, can Man have been evolved in Borneo ? Can the orang-utan be an archaic form of mankind ?

The opinion that the races of Man are climatic productions is a very old one; and that this may originally have been true can hardly be objected to by evolutionists who accept the theory of adaptability to the environment. Only—on account of the intermingling of living races, brought about by various causes—such a belief is now no longer altogether borne out by facts.

But even admitting for the moment that the indications furnished by climate are not sufficient to give us the clue to Man's origin, there are other means of discovering the place of his first appearance. Giving due consideration to the laws which rule the geographical distribution of animals on the surface of the earth, it is difficult not to believe that Man had his origin in the same regions as those in which we find the anthropoid apes. Indeed, according to the Darwinian theory of descent, not only the species, but also the genera of a given group of living beings must be the direct offspring of a common ancestor ; and thus, even when the descendants of the latter are scattered over distant and widely separated regions, their progenitors must originally have occupied the same area.

This is the reason why both geologists and anthropologists have always considered it possible that at some past epoch Borneo was the habitat of an anthropomorph more nearly allied to Man than to the living orang-utan. This idea was mentioned to me by Sir Charles Lyell, when I was in London in 1865, preparing for my expedition to Borneo. The great geologist then urged me to explore the caves in that island, being of opinion that important materials and remains of very great value for the past history of Man might be found in them. He argued that as in Australia, where marsupials predominate, all the fossil mammals yet found belong to that group, so in Borneo, where the orang-utan now lives, one would probably discover the remains of some extinct species belonging to the same order. The exploration of the caves in Borneo has, however, not as yet given the expected results.[1]

In any case, even admitting freely the possibility that anthropomorphs distinct from the orang-utan (and I must add, also, from the gibbons) once lived in Borneo, the question remains whether they could have been the true precursors of Man. To this I answer in the negative. While on the one hand there is nothing to disprove the idea that man may have existed in Borneo from times of the remotest antiquity, there is on the other hand nothing to suggest the probability that the island has been a *fons et origo* of species of the genus *Homo*, though we find there all the requisites for the plasmation of the genus *Simia*.

The theory of adaptability to the environment requires a correlation between the characters acquired by organisms and the stimuli or exciting causes, therefore certain given conditions of existence must have produced corresponding modifications in the living beings which have been under their influence. Now, the more marked differential characters which exist between the morphology of Man and that of the orang-utan are evidently due to different conditions of existence; for the first is modified for a terrestrial, the second for an arboreal life. This divergence in adaptation is the principal, if not the only cause of the generic characters in which *Homo* differs from *Simia*.

To explain why certain creatures have adopted an erect posture and bipedal progression we must assume, *à priori*, that they happened to live where such posture and such manner of

---

[1] Recently in Java the fossil remains of an anthropomorph of the highest scientific interest have been discovered, and the name of *Pithecanthropus erectus* has been given by the discoverer, Dr. Eugène Dubois, to this extinct creature. But the remains as yet found are too few and imperfect to be of much aid to definite conclusions on the history of the primitive evolution of Man.

locomotion was both possible and advantageous. In primitive anthropomorphs, if the necessity of escaping from a foe was experienced in a country covered with forest, the way of escape was manifestly by climbing up trees. If, instead, the ground was bare, safety was sought by flight, and the main efforts must have been directed to getting over the ground by the use of the hind limbs. In these efforts to progress bipedally, the muscles which are attached to the pelvis were certainly those most put in action, and this would account for their greater development, with the result of still further facilitating the erect posture.

As the assumption of an erect posture has more especially differentiated Man from monkeys, it is but natural that the conformation of the pelvis, and the development of the muscles which are attached to it, should constitute one of the principal morphological distinctions between Man and anthropomorphs, because a basin-shaped pelvis and largely developed gluteal muscles are a consequence of the erect posture.

Another most important result derived from the assumption of an erect posture is, I hold, the great development which the brain has been able to acquire from the favourable position which the cranium has thus attained. The brain coming to be in the vertical line, and not outside the centre of gravity, there is nothing to hinder a large increase in the volume and weight of this organ.

Again, the hand being no longer used as a foot (if Man is supposed to be descended from a terrestrial rather than from an arboreal form) has been able to perfect itself in another direction, and to become the executive organ of the brain, placing Man, thus specially endowed, in a position far superior to that of all other animals.[1]

It is obvious that for the erect posture a primitive anthropomorph must have needed a broad foot. Now such a structure and the peculiarities above mentioned can only have been assumed in a country where pedestrian locomotion was easy. For this reason it appears to me very improbable that primitive Man can have originated in the eminently forestal region to which Borneo belongs, a region which could not only never have promoted any aptitude for running or bipedal progression, but also could never have made him feel the need of a terrestrial (as opposed to an arboreal) existence. I therefore believe that neither in Borneo nor in the neigh-

[1] The character which principally distinguishes the human hand from that of anthropoids is the perfect opponability of the thumb to the index. Very singular in this respect is the coincidence of such a conformation, so far as regards its mechanical effects, with the action of the maxilla and mandible of a granivorous bird, in which the bill has undoubtedly attained such a conformation by use, and by the necessity of collecting seeds and grains of plants. Why should not the stimulus caused by the necessity of collecting seeds, small tubers, molluscs, and other small food objects, have caused in man the opponability of the two first digits of the hand ?

bouring forest regions could any anthropoid have attained that kind of perfection which would eventually transform it into Man.

Indeed, I opine that if anthropoids different from the existing ones have lived in a past and remote epoch in Borneo, they must have got there from regions less covered by trees ; and I hold that instead of modifying themselves towards the assumption of an erect gait, they would have deviated towards adaptation to an arboreal existence, unless, indeed, both Borneo and Sumatra once possessed a drier climate and a lesser extent of forest than they do now, as is the case with some African regions—a supposition hardly admissible when we consider the fossils found in the carboniferous formations of both these great islands, which would indicate ancient conditions of vegetation very similar to those of the present day.

According to the ideas I uphold, the passage from a quadrupedal locomotion to a bipedal one is anterior to that which may be styled quadrumanous. The orang-utan in its peculiar structural development has, in a certain sense, surpassed that of Man, being the product of a land in which terrestrial is less advantageous than arboreal locomotion. Thus, if during the period of organic malleability anthropoids who could freely use their hind limbs for progression reached Borneo, where terrestrial locomotion was more difficult than an arboreal one, they would practise the latter more than the former, and their limbs would eventually show a corresponding modification. Thus the orang-utans in Borneo would have diverged from the old anthropoid type instead of approximating to it, and in this case the orang would be, not a progenitor, but a collateral of Man.

To render probable the theory that Man has been derived from an arboreal anthropoid of the type of the orang-utan, it would be necessary to suppose that the feet of the latter, originally adapted to terrestrial progression and converted later into prehensile organs, should once more revert to their primitive terrestrial form. For this reason I have come to the conclusion that neither Borneo nor any portion of the Indo-Malayan forest region can ever have been suitable localities for the " humanization," if I may so term it, of an anthropoid. After this conclusion the reader will naturally ask : " Where, then, do you believe that Man made his first appearance ? " If such a query may be met with an hypothesis, the following is my opinion, based in a large measure on the above-mentioned considerations :—It is certain that Man, who before becoming such must once have belonged to the group of the anthropoids, can only have had his origin in the centre of morphological development of that group. Man must, therefore, have made his first appearance within the tropics, and very probably in a region intermediate between the parts now inhabited by the gorilla, chimpanzee, and orang-utan.

The discovery in Java of the fossil remains of an anthropoid nearer to Man than any of those now living might suggest that island as one of the localities where anthropoids have become humanized ; but I hold many deductions concerning the fauna and flora of a country in past geological epochs which are based on the fossil remains found in its strata to be completely erroneous because the locality where the fossil remains of a plant or of an animal are found is, in most cases, not that in which one or the other formerly lived, but merely the place where their remains were eventually deposited, which may often be far distant from the locality whence they originally came. Thus, that fossil remains of *Pithecanthropus* were found in Java certainly does not prove, according to my views, that that creature lived on the island ; but merely shows that its remains were deposited where Java now is, when that island, during the volcanic disturbances it has experienced, emerged from the sea with its high mountains, and doubtless caused other lands in the adjacent seas to be submerged. My objection to admitting that Java and Borneo may have been centres of humanization rests principally on the difficulties above mentioned, that an exclusively forestal region must necessarily have been ill-suited to an anthropoid's assuming a bipedal means of progression. Considering that tropical Africa produced those big anthropoids which in the structure of their limbs and better adaptation to terrestrial locomotion approach nearest to the human type, considering again that on that continent were evolved the greater number of mammals provided with rapid means of terrestrial locomotion, I am of opinion that tropical Africa—or, rather, perhaps, a land of similar climatic conditions interposed between the African and the Asiatic continents, a land whose existence can alone explain facts otherwise unexplainable in the geographical distribution of plants and animals—must have been the region where Man assumed his erect gait and bipedal progression.

Even the colour of the skin may furnish arguments in favour of the hypothesis that Africa, or an ancient dependency of that continent, may have been the region where anthropomorphs were transformed into man-like creatures ; for Africa is the land where mammals with black skins poorly provided with hair are most frequent, and it may be surmised that the first men were black, because they evolved from anthropomorphs of that colour. The black colour of African Man and his predecessors may be supposed to have been produced during the epoch of morphological malleability by the combined action of the light and heat in the climate of tropical Africa, although at the present time climate hardly has any effect towards changing the colour of the complexion. Again, it may be conjectured that the white complexion may have been acquired by Man in a period when the environment still exerted a certain amount of plasmative force when, wandering northwards towards colder regions, he learnt to seek refuge in caves. The diminution of light may have caused a diminution in the cutaneous pigments ; and the lower temperature causing the blood to accumulate towards the periphery to compensate for the loss of heat on the surface of the body may have communicated the rosy tint to the skin.   This colour is very rare in mammals, and combined with the scarcity of hair is only found, as far as I am aware, in a small and most remarkable hypogeal rodent of the deserts of Somaliland, *Heterocephalus glaber* of Rüppell, and accidentally in the " white " elephants and in certain races of swine in which the black colour of the skin has disappeared, it seems, through breeding in covered styes in a cold climate, and thus under circumstances analogous to those in which the white skin may be conjectured to have appeared in Man.

CHAPTER XV

ON my return from the Batang Lupar I was obliged to stay
some time at Kuching, in order to arrange the considerable
zoological and botanical collections which I had made during my
exploration of that part of Borneo, and to pack them in readiness
to be forwarded to Europe. My sampan, too, stood in considerable need of repair before I could look upon it as in fit condition
for the new excursions which I proposed making.

The sampan is the boat generally used in Sarawak for river
navigation, and also for short trips along the sea coast during fine
weather. It has, I believe, a considerable resemblance to the canoes
used on the great rivers of Cochinchina and Burma. That it has
not had its origin in Borneo is evident from its name, which is
Chinese. Sampans are dug-outs, made from the trunk of a single tree.
The method of construction is very ingenious, because from a tree
whose diameter is, let us say, a couple of feet, a boat may be made of
twice that width. This is done by hollowing out the trunk immediately the tree is felled to the size that its diameter permits, and regula-
ting the shape according to certain rules well known to the Malay
boat-builder, among which is the keeping of the sides of the craft
much higher in the middle than at either end. It is widened by
the application of fire, an easy operation with green, flexible wood,
which yields without splitting under the action of heat. It is
probably because this method of construction gives them a wide
beam that Bornean boats are unprovided with outriggers, which
are, in fact, not necessary. The one exception is in the north, where,
in the Sulu sea, boats have outriggers.

Other people in this part of the world, such as the Papuans and
Polynesians, also use dug-out canoes made from a single tree trunk ;
but, not being widened out by the application of fire, their boats are

too narrow and too round in section, and are thus very crank, out-riggers being an absolute necessity to prevent their being easily upset.

It is hardly likely that the above-mentioned method of making sampans has been invented in Borneo. Like many other industries, it has probably been imported from the Asiatic continent ; indeed, I believe that the same method of widening by fire is used in the manufacture of canoes in Burma and Siam.

The sides of sampans are raised by a high strake or washboard, which is connected to the body of the boat with wooden pegs. The seam is caulked with the soft bark of *Melaleuca leucodendron*, and a resinous mixture made with an oil called " kruing " (the product of *Dipterocarpus Lowii*, Hook.), to which is added resin reduced to a fine powder. With these ingredients a sticky paste is formed, which is used like pitch, and renders the seams perfectly watertight. Sampans have generally a roofing of " kadjan," a sort of matting made with palm or pandanus leaves, under which the men can paddle sheltered from rain or from the sun's rays. Amidships, too, there is usually a kind of cabin, somewhat like that of a Venetian gondola, where one can lie down and sleep in comfort. Sampans are usually propelled by paddles (*pengayu* of the Malays), and have no rudder, being steered by one of the crew with his paddle when necessary, while at other times he paddles with the rest. The Malayan paddle has no peculiarities, and is not ornamented in any way, as are so often those of the Papuans and Polynesians. It is used with the palm of one hand grasping the small transverse portion at the end of the handle, while the tapering part of the latter is gripped with the other hand.[1]

To my sampan I had added a sail, for during the monsoon then prevailing I could even venture out to sea and coast ; a thing which would have been very imprudent in such a craft in any other season.

Everything now being in readiness, I left Kuching at sunset on the thirteenth of June with a crew of five men, bound for Tanjong Datu.

We slept at Santubong, and sailed early next morning, favoured by the land breeze. We were soon at Pulo Sampadien, a small island about thirteen miles west of the mouth of the Sarawak river. We landed to take in a supply of better water than that we had got at a small stream near the village of Santubong. The island is about two miles from the coast, and in the portion I explored is mostly formed of limestone, regularly stratified, and in some places rising many feet out of the water and overhanging it. The limestone is of a dark colour, with conchoidal fracture ; it is more or less schis-

---

[1] I have seen in Italy, on the Lake of Massaciuccoli, near Lucca, a paddle exactly like the Malay one.

tose, and alternates with strata of sandstone containing pebbles of various kinds and nodules of iron pyrites. In some places these pebbles are small or broken up, and cemented into a kind of pudding-stone. Large masses of granite of different kinds are scattered on the beach.

In the sand along the shore I noticed many Foraminifera. Not infrequently during high tide turtles land for the purpose of laying their eggs; but their favourite resort, as I have already mentioned, is the neighbouring island of Satang, nearer to the mouth of the Sarawak river, but farther off the mainland than Sampadien. In the sea, on rocks, I found a few algæ growing, the more common being a species of *Sargassum*.

The Dugongs, or *Duyon*, as the Malays call them (*Halicore australis*), frequent these shores, feeding, I was told, on sea plants, perhaps a species of *Thalassia*. They appear, however, to be very rare in Sarawak, for although I offered a reward of twenty dollars, I was unable to get a specimen.

We passed the night near the mouth of the Lundu. Wishing to take advantage of the inflowing tide, we set sail at 2 a.m. next morning, and, helped by a good breeze, soon reached Samatan. Here we stopped to breakfast, and I shot a species of kingfisher (*Sauropatis chloris*, Bodd.) which I met with for the first time.[1] It was hunting small crabs along the sandy shore, and each time it captured one it perched on some low tree to eat it in comfort.

We soon passed the Talang-Talang Islands, leaving them on our right, and at 3 p.m. came to anchor in a small bay marked on the Admiralty chart as " Sleepy Bay " or " Pirate Bay " ; but the native name is, I believe, Labuan Gadong. On the cliffs around grew specimens of *Cycas circinalis* from twelve to eighteen feet high, some with fruit, others with male flowers like fine cones rising in the midst of the crown of leaves. Here, too, were branching pandani, a *Podocarpus*, feathery casuarinas, nibong palms, and those ever-present rampant climbers, the rotangs, and many other plants. On the beach the *Kayu pennaga* (*Pongamia glabra*, Vent.) was predominant, a common tree on the sea-shore throughout Malaysia. When in blossom it is covered with bunches of lilac flowers which are sweetly fragrant. The place appeared to abound in game, and I saw footprints of plandok, deer, and wild boar, but nothing of the animals themselves.

On the sixteenth of June, after a few hours' paddling, we reached Tanjong Datu, distant about seven miles from our last halting place. I shot a few terns, which were abundant here, and found many of their eggs, which were deposited on the bare

---

[1] *Sauropatis chloris* is a bird of wide distribution, occurring throughout the Philippines, Celebes, the Moluccas, etc.—ED.

rock without any attempt at a nest. We came to anchor near the westernmost extremity of Borneo, in a small cove, which my Malays called Telok Saruban, or Serban.

Here we found a spring of excellent water, and used it at once to cook our rice. After our very frugal breakfast, I started to climb the small mountain which rose at our backs. Naturally, in such out-of-the-way and uninhabited places, there were no paths. The place, and, indeed, the whole coast as far as Santubong, had a bad name for being the habitual resort, during the fair season, of the prahus of the Lanuns and Balagnini, the boldest and most dreaded pirates of the whole archipelago, and Telok Serban was their favourite anchorage.

We commenced our ascent amidst great detached blocks of granite scattered over the slopes of the mountain, which is entirely covered by primeval forest from base to summit. We marked the trees from time to time with parang cuts, and left other signs of our passage on the way, in order to be able to find the path on our return. Before long we were overtaken by a storm with violent rain and wind, but we continued our climb in spite of it, and reached the summit, which, according to the indications of my aneroid, I determined to be at an elevation of 1,640 feet.

Scarcely a plant was in blossom. On the west slope, which is Dutch territory—for the boundary line between Sarawak and the Dutch possessions follows the ridge of the mountain—the trees were scanty and dwarfish, and more or less deprived of leaves, I believe on account of the strong south-west winds which for several months in the year sweep this slope. On the eastern slope—that up which we had come—the trees were thicker and more clothed. On the summit I found nothing to reward me for the fatigue of the climb.

On descending we followed the marks we had left in coming up ; but, at a certain spot, where the colossal masses of granite were heaped up one on the other so as to form caves and grottoes, we lost our direction in following the tortuous path between the masses. We wandered about for nearly an hour and a half without being able to get out of this strange labyrinth, or to find the path leading down to the sea. I was beginning to fear that we should be obliged to pass the night in the jungle, for it was near sunset, and after that complete darkness follows fast, when the happy inspiration occurred to us of retracing our steps up the mountain instead of continuing vainly to search an outlet below. We managed thus to emerge from the labyrinth of granite blocks, and then in another direction, and following Kap, the small Dyak dog I always took with me on excursions, we again directed our steps towards the sea. It was interesting to see how this intelligent beast, constantly turning to look back at us, appeared plainly to wish to show us the right way to be followed. Had it been able to talk it could not have made itself better understood. Certainly, of all animals, the dog is the one which ought to have had the greatest chance of learning how to talk, on account of the instinctive sympathy which, like an electric current, passes between it and Man when it wishes to explain its thoughts or to understand ours. Had Man been associated with the dog during the plasmative epoch, I believe that to the expression of our face and to the sound of our voice there would have been aroused in the dog, owing to the attention with which he listens to us and observes us, analogous movements in its vocal organs, which, instead of expressing themselves by inarticulate sounds, would have enabled it to talk and to learn a language.

The dogs of the Dyaks are small, and have a fox-like aspect, somewhat like that of our Italian " pomer." Their hair is usually of a reddish-dun; their ears are short, erect, and very mobile ; the tail, usually carried high and turned up, and kept in constant motion, terminates in a large brush ; the legs are rather short in proportion to the rest of the body. Not the least of their peculiarities is that they have never learnt to bark. Highly intelligent, they readily attach themselves to the person who takes care of them and treats them kindly ; and they are very plucky and useful in hunting deer or pigs, for which they are especially kept and trained. In Dyak villages they will not let a European approach.

Having spoken of the Dyak dog, it is natural to say something of cats ; and the domestic animal in Borneo deserves a word of mention on account of the singular peculiarity of its tail, which is generally very short, or else marked with a kind of abrupt twist, as if it had been broken, and badly set. I cannot suggest any explanation of this singular character, which is well known and common enough. Perhaps, owing to the perennial dampness of the soil, the tail of cats in Borneo became an impediment. I have noted that animals in confinement with long tails—monkeys for instance— suffer in Borneo when kept on the ground, the tail in such cases easily getting ulcerated. Perhaps this has been the case with the cat, and the shortening and crookedness of its tail is a step towards adaptation to local conditions.

In the small cove at Tanjong Datu, where our boat lay sheltered, the wind at that season being from the south-west, the sea was perfectly smooth. We were only a few hundred yards from the westernmost point of Borneo, where no anchorage exists, even for small vessels, and where the sea is always rough, even during the good season, and very much so during the north-east monsoon.

The weather being fine next morning, I started to round the cape by sea ; but as soon as we got beyond the protection it afforded against the south-west wind, we met with such heavy weather that the sampan began to fill, and to avoid getting swamped I had to turn back. The sea is always more or less heavy here on account of the meeting of two contrary currents off the point. We were soon back in our quiet cove. Near it, as at Satang and Sampadien, there are patches of sandy beach, where turtles land to deposit their eggs. On the overhanging and more inaccessible cliffs *Collocalia nidifica* builds its edible nests ; at least, I believe it to be that species, although I obtained neither specimens of the bird nor of its nest.

It is notable that all along the coast, from Tanjong Datu to Bruni, there are no coral banks, so frequent elsewhere in Malaysia, and their absence causes that of a host of associated marine productions on the entire coast of North Borneo. Tanjong Datu is mostly formed of granite, together with serpentines and other metamorphic rocks.

At low tide I collected seaweeds, and got some very fine species, several new to science.[1] A *Sargassum* was very abundant amongst the rocks, which turned out to be *Sargassum angustifolium*, I. Ag. On no portion of the Bornean coast, however, have I found algæ so varied and abundant as they are on the coasts of the Mediterranean and the Red Sea. The sandy bottom, continually shifted by big waves during the north-east monsoon, and the deposits carried down by the many large rivers, prevent the development of cellular marine plants, and along with them that varied and marvellous world of sea creatures which require clear and tranquil waters for their reproduction.

Beginning my return journey I visited another small cove, where I collected a few plants and some littoral land snails, very abundant in low spots amidst rotting vegetable detritus thrown up and accumulated by the sea.

At 2 a.m. on the 18th, with a favourable tide and splendid moonlight, we paddled for about an hour and came to another small bay, at the head of which we found a little streamlet of beautiful water. Here we anchored again, and as soon as daylight came I collected shells, seaweeds, and other plants. On the rocks in this inlet grew a very fine species of Pandanus ; its straight cylindrical stem, supported on large aerial roots, was about thirty feet high, and was divided above into several horizontal branches, again forking once or twice, and terminating in tufts of rather broad leaves similar in aspect to those of *Crinum giganteum*. It was, perhaps, *Pandanus dubius*, Spreng., or an allied species.

The next day no collections were made. We reached and anchored at Samattang, a village of ten houses, inhabited by Malays and a few Chinamen. Between Tanjong Datu and Samattang are only four insignificant streams, hardly, if at all, navigable, even for small

---

[1] Amongst these, *Dictyota maxima*, Zan., and *D. Beccariana*, Zan., are the most remarkable. (Cf. ZANARDINI. " *Phycearum indicarum pugillus a Cl. Ed. Beccari, etc., collectarum.*" Venezia, 1872.)

boats, and only to be entered at high tide. They are the Samon-saur, nearest to Tanjong Datu; the Bekuching, the Poe, and the Sero.

On the 20th I ascended the Samattang for some hours, but the tree-trunks which had fallen in the river eventually stopped me. The Malays, however, go up it in very small canoes as far as Gunong Poe in search of dammar, which is found there in abundance. Returning nearly to the mouth, I attempted to go up the other branch of the river, which ought to lead to the foot of Gunong Angus, a hill which is said by the natives to be inhabited by *antus*, or spirits of a bad sort, and where one cannot go without great risk of contracting a disease of some kind. This, at least, my men asserted with an air of great conviction, which only made me the more desirous of reaching this abode of the malevolent spirits. The branch of the river I had entered, however, was a perfect labyrinth of canals and small passages between nipa palms and mangroves, quite unknown to my men; and, having no pilot, we found ourselves, after much wandering about, back at the very point we had started from, and were thus obliged to give up the attempt of reaching the enchanted hill, which, in all probability, must have got its name as a specially malarious locality.

I was told that at Gunong Angus many edible nests of the small swift are to be found, but nobody dares to go and collect them.

The Samattang appeared to me very uninteresting, and I found not a single plant or animal that I had not met with before. I was told, however, that along its upper course the " bua pacma "—the *Rafflesia* which I have already described—grew abundantly. In a straight line I do not think that the principal branch of the Samattang river extends for more than ten miles inland. It is very wide at its mouth, and has a very tortuous course; but, after about two hours' paddling up stream, it became so shallow as to be only navigable for small canoes.

On the 21st I resumed my coasting journey towards the Sarawak river. Halting at Tanjong Batu, I found a beautiful specimen of *Cycas circinalis*, L., over thirty feet high, and with a twice bifurcated trunk. We stopped again at Tanjong Plandok to dry the paper of the botanical specimens, where I collected a few good species of seaweeds. The rocks here are of a limestone which is almost black in colour.

We next passed the Belungei river, navigable for some hours by sampans; and the Skambal, a small stream which can only be entered at high tide. It was dark when we reached the mouth of the Lundu, where we anchored for the night.

I had gone to sleep as usual in the sampan, which, with the ebbing tide, became, before long, high and dry. In the middle of the night I was suddenly aroused by the cries of my men, whom, by the feeble light of the stars, I could see rushing out of the boat towards the forest, brandishing their parangs and spears. I could not make out at first what had happened, but soon joined in the laugh when my men returned from the vain chase of a wild boar, which had come sniffing round quite close to the boat, attracted, no doubt, by the odour of our provisions.

On the morning of the 22nd I entered and ascended the Lundu river, which I had already explored, but I wished to pay a visit to my friend Mr. Nelson, then Resident or Government Agent in this district. I reached the Residency just at the time the Dyaks were bringing their annual tribute, which consisted of two dollars for each adult male. At Lundu there were several very big houses, each of which, belonging to a number of families, may be looked upon as a separate village. In one of these houses, which are tolerably common inland, there were living 150 men and an unknown number of women. There was also a church here built of timber, and a substantial house for the missionaries. Above the village the river, which rises behind Mount Mattang, can be ascended for three or four days in small boats. Near its sources the Chinese have found gold, in formations similar to those at Busso and at Bau ; and were at that time asking to be aided by Government to begin working. The Chinese had fine gardens and orchards at Lundu, remarkably well kept, where, amongst other cultivated plants, the mulberry tree was growing. This interested the Tuan Muda a good deal, as he wished to attempt the rearing of silkworms.

The Dyaks mostly cultivate rice on terraced hill fields on the dry system ; but in the plains of Lundu the usual water cultivation is also practised. There, in the abandoned ricefields, already covered with rank high herbage, I found growing a wild species of rice plant called by the Malays " padi pipit," i.e. " sparrow rice," because its grain is much smaller than that of the cultivated plant. I imagine that these must have grown from seeds of the ordinary cultivated rice plant, fallen out of the husk during the harvest, which, in the lack of any cultivation had to submit to a struggle with the weeds, and thus produced smaller grain—a return to the primitive wild form.[1]

Next day I descended the river, and reaching its mouth headed once more for the Sarawak. We passed the night at Sumpa, a small fisherman's hamlet composed of seven or eight huts ; and on the twenty-fourth of June we paddled towards Santubong, where I had a slight attack of malarial fever, the first I had experienced during two years of a nomadic life in the forests of Borneo. I could not at first believe that the uneasiness and the shiverings I

---

[1] This kind of rice has been collected by Zollinger in Java, and distributed under the name of *Oryza sativa* (*L. spontanea*).

felt were caused by fever, the sensation was so new to me ; but later I got quite enough experience of the kind.   At night we reached Santubong.

Between the Lundu and Sarawak rivers are several streams, which, going from west to east, are the following : The Sampadi, Pangerang, Sumpa, Setto, Burungbungan, Sibu, Mersan, and Salak. In the latter and in the Sibu large praus can enter ; in the Sungei Burungbungan only fishing boats ; the others are of insignificant size.

CHAPTER XVI

USUALLY in undertaking an excursion I had in view the collection of some animal, plant, or product which had a particular interest for me, and with which I was as yet unacquainted. Amongst the latter was the rotang which produces the *jernang*, or "dragon's blood," a kind of resin of a bright red colour. Having heard that the plant from which this valuable drug is obtained was common in the densely matted primeval jungle on the north-western slopes of Mount Mattang, I started in search of it at the beginning of July, accompanied by several Singhi Dyaks well acquainted with the locality.

During my residence on Mattang I had visited Singhi more than once, following a pathway through the vast forest. From Kuching, however, the village is reached much more conveniently by going up the Sarawak river to a spot past Bellida, whence a tolerably good path leads in about an hour to the foot of the hill on which the houses are built.

The Singhi Dyaks were old acquaintances and good friends of mine, and I had no difficulty in finding the men I required for the projected excursion. Their houses were scattered over different parts of the hill, all in highly picturesque positions, and always shaded by a grand and luxurious vegetation nearly exclusively formed by cultivated trees, such as durians, coconut palms, pinangs, arengas, langsats, rambutans, and especially bamboos, which acquire colossal dimensions, and form green and spreading clumps of remarkable beauty.

On the Singhi hill I also met with a splendid, and at the same time more or less useful, palm, which is in general allowed to grow near the houses. One might almost imagine it a cultivated species, yet it reproduces itself naturally by seed. I am alluding to the magnificent *Caryota*, which the Singhi Dyaks call "kayuno," and the Malays "baroch." [1] In the rich soil around the houses this palm shows an extremely powerful growth, its stems attaining a height of forty to fifty feet. They are thicker than those of the coconut, perfectly straight, smooth, and marked with many rings, the scars where old fronds were once attached to the stem. These fronds are immense, as much as twenty-five feet or more in length, and differ from the usual type common to most palms in being much divided, with the terminal divisions of a half lozenge or swallow-tailed shape. In enormous bunches hanging from the upper part of the trunk are a prodigious number of fruits of a red colour, and the size of cherries. These are useless, and, indeed, harmful, for when ripe they contain an acrid juice which causes intense irritation if it comes in contact with a delicate part of the skin. The most notable peculiarity of this palm is that its stem swells out in the middle, assuming a fusiform aspect recalling that of *Oreodoxa regia*. The cause of this thickening may, perhaps, be explained by the very rapid growth of the species during the inter-mediate period of its life. Notwithstanding this character—although I was at first inclined to consider the tree as a distinct species, re-stricted to Borneo, and had even described it as such under the name of *Caryota No*—I came later to the conclusion that it must be regarded as a mere variety or local race of *C. Rumphiana*, a widely diffused species in the eastern part of the Malay Archipelago.

The *Kayu No* is by the Singhi Dyaks only used for certain long black fibres, known to them as *talionus*, which they obtain through maceration from the midribs of the leaves, and use for fish-ing lines. These same fibres, woven with strips of the aerial roots of *Eugeissonia*, and of rotangs, are used to make cylindrical baskets called *tambuk*, and for similar kind of work.

I have mentioned the Arenga (*Arenga saccharifera*), another great palm which grows very luxuriantly at Singhi (where it is called *idjok*), and has fronds reaching a length of over thirty feet. In Sarawak this well known palm is appreciated not so much for the wine or toddy and for the sugar which can be extracted from it, as for the black fibre, not unlike horsehair, which is found in large quantities around the bases of the fronds, and clothes the entire trunk. With these fibres rope of all sizes is made, of great strength, nearly ever-lasting in durability, and much used by Malays for the rigging of their praus, and especially for cables. The Dyaks also make an ex-tensive use of ropes of this material ; the finer kinds are preferred to rotang for tying beams and other wooden parts of the framework of native houses throughout Sarawak.

[1] Cf. BECCARI ; in *Nuovo Giornale Botanico Italiano,* vol. iii. p. 12.

Having passed the night in one of the Dyak houses at Singhi, I started at 8 a.m. on July 5, guided by several Dyaks and accompanied by two of my Malays, for the locality where the *rotang jernang* grows. I had brought with me supplies for several days, and everything necessary for camping in the forest, besides a good quantity of paper for drying botanical specimens.

The road at first led up the Singhi hill, where, from time to time, we came upon Dyak houses, passing through perfect woods of fruit trees, mostly durians, and great clumps of bamboos. We descended on the opposite side by a steep and slippery pathway, and, on getting to the plain, found the road even worse, having to cross swampy ground in which we sank up to the knees. Here grew many sago and baroch palms; the latter naturally sown by animals; the sago originally planted. When a stem of sago palm is cut down, new shoots grow out from its stump, which at first run along the ground, and then rise vertically up, producing new stems, without any kind of cultivation.

Having left the swampy tract behind us, we crossed undulating ground covered with secondary forest vegetation, which farther on merges into primeval forest, much easier to get through. We next ascended a spur of Gunong Mattang, about 1,000 feet high, along whose crest we continued for a long while on a sort of plateau. It is a locality where *liran* (*Pholidocarpus majadum*, Becc.), *jattao* (*Eugeissonia insignis*, Becc). *nisang* (*Licuala*), and other smaller palms abound, together with a great variety of rotangs. We next climbed several hills and crossed small valleys, where the vegetation was of a very wild and primitive character. Amongst the more important plants I met with here was a fine Anonacea (*Goniothalamus lateritius*, sp. n. (*P.B.* No., 3610), a small tree which was remarkable, even at a distance, on account of its large flowers of a brick-red colour which cluster in great numbers low down, near the ground, around the warty stem.[1] I also found a small but very graceful species of *Phalænopsis*, with the perianth yellowish-green blotched with blood-red, and the labellum reddish.

After a continuous and rapid march of seven hours, we got to the banks of the Raju torrent, the main branch of the Burungbungan, a small stream I have already mentioned which reaches the sea opposite Pulo Satang, and whose mouth I crossed on my way back from Tanjong Datu. We found there a lanko in fairly good condition, which saved us the trouble of constructing one.

---

[1] This *Goniothalamus* appears to be allied to *G. Riedleyi*, King, which has also large flowers clustered at the base of the stem; but it apparently differs by its glabrous leaves, which are 10 to 12 inches long, with numerous lateral nervures. The flowers of *G. lateritius* are some 2½ to 3 inches across, and are pedunculate, these peduncles being at least as long again as the flower.

Next morning we sallied forth in search of the desired rotang, following up the course of a small torrent, the Skajan, on a hill which bears the same name. After about an hour's walk, we came across quite a number of specimens of the plant I was in search of. Few, however, bore fruits. The *rotang jernang* is a *Dæmonorops*, to which I have given the name of *D. Draconcellus*, having found that it differs somewhat from *D. Draco*, which produces the dragon's blood in Sumatra, as well as from other allied species (*D. micracanthus*, Griff., and *D. propinquus*, Becc.), from which the same drug is extracted in the Malay Peninsula.

Dragon's blood is a resin used as varnish, of the characteristic red colour found on the scales which cover the fruits of rotangs, especially when immature, for in ripe fruits the resinous exudation gets brittle and easily falls off. The drug is only got from the fruits, and not by incisions in the stem, as has been asserted. The gummy sap which exudes from the cut stems is white and milky. The canes or stems of this rotang are of the thickness of the little finger, and of good quality; indeed, amongst the best for the many uses for which the stems of other Calami are employed. But the species is mainly grown for the sake of the fruits, for the dragon's blood which is got from them is a far more valuable product than the canes. Only old specimens which have reached the tops of the trees bear flowers. One which I measured was nearly a hundred feet in length. It is a diœcious species, the male and female flowers being on different individuals.

On the Skajan hill this rotang was abundant, but extremely localized, for I never met with it elsewhere, nor did I see it again during the present excursion. I found two varieties, one with round, the other with oblong fruits. On the same hill grew some very tall *liran* (*Pholidocarpus majadum*, Becc.), one, I reckoned, could hardly have been less than 130 feet in height. This palm, which reminds one of a Livistona, has a stem resembling that of the coconut, but more slender, and its wood is much harder. The leaflets of its fan-shaped fronds are used for making ataps, which are said to resist the effects of weather much better than those made with the leaves of the nipa and sago palms.

In the small ravines along the streams, where rich humus had accumulated for centuries, and where the vegetation was more luxuriant, with the densest shade and reeking dampness perennial, I found some very extraordinary species of Fungi, which, unfortunately, I could not preserve. Amongst others I noticed a fleshy *Polyporus* with the stalk gradually widening into an umbrella about two handsbreadths in diameter, slightly convex above, and of a rusty yellow colour, whilst the under surface (hymenium) had short white tubes. I also found a *Cordyceps*—a kind of mushroom—about eight inches in height, ramified like the antlers of a stag, which grew from the mummified body of a large insect larva. One must be a mycologist to be able to appreciate fully these two marvellous vegetable productions.

Having been successful in attaining the object of my trip, I had now to think of returning to Singhi ; although the locality was one of exceptional interest and richness as a collecting ground, and a longer stay would have given excellent results. Towards evening we were back on the spur which projects from Mount Mattang, and built up a shelter for the night on its ridge under a pelting rain. In a few minutes the Dyaks had collected the requisite timber, the rotangs for tying them together, and the leaves for the roofing. Never before had I found such excellent and handy materials for covering a lanko furnished at the same time by a tree which was both beautiful and rare. This was *Teysmannia altifrons*, a palm with undivided leaves of an elongated lozenge-like shape, quite ten feet in length without the stalk, and three feet in width. If we except bananas, the *Ravenala madagascariensis*, and, perhaps, some of the *Heliconias*, this is the plant which produces the largest undivided leaves anywhere in the Old World. In America, however, there are the *Manicarias*, palms nearly allied to *Teysmannia*, with entire leaves of quite twice the dimensions of those of the latter palm. The *Teysmannia* grows in Sumatra, as well as in Borneo, and has recently been found also in the Malay Peninsula. At Singhi it is called *Sumuruch*, and the Malays of Sarawak give to its fronds the name of *daun-ekor buaya*, i.e. " crocodile-tail leaves."

The Dyaks who were with me were very active and thoroughly at home in the forest. After having erected the lanko they lighted a fire, notwithstanding the ceaseless rain. They are never at a loss to find materials for this, even in the dampest weather, being acquainted with certain plants, I believe of the order *Amyridaceæ*, the wood of which will burn well even when quite green. Of course, to obtain the first sparks they must have a little dry wood, and this they search for inside dead tree-trunks, of which there are always plenty about in the old forest. They are acquainted with the way of getting fire by rubbing two pieces of wood together. For this purpose two small sticks are used, one of hard, the other of soft wood, well dried, the latter having notches cut in it. Holding the first vertically between the two palms, it is rotated rapidly like an egg-whisk, its lower rounded extremity resting in one of the notches of the soft-wood stick. From this small dust-like particles are detached ; these descend into the notch and soon become ignited. Usually, a little tinder is added to facilitate matters. The Dyaks of Singhi know also how to get a spark from a kind of bamboo called *bulu tamian*, on which they strike with a bit of silicious stone or a fragment of Chinese porcelain. The production of fire by pneumatic pressure is also known to them, a little tinder being placed at the bottom of a closed iron tube fitted with a piston. A smart blow on the latter compresses the air and is sufficient to ignite the tinder.[1] But to all these methods they now prefer the usual flint and steel, using as tinder the *lulup*, a soft cottony down which clothes the

Fig. 42.—DYAK METHOD OF OBTAINING FIRE.
(The man here shown is a Malay.)

dilated base of the young fronds in some palms, on the inner part, towards the centre of the bud. The best quality of *lulup* is produced

[1] In Burma a similar pneumatic method is found, the natives using a small instrument like that of the Dyaks, which is described and figured by Signor Fea in his excellent book, *Quattro Anni fra i Birmani*, p. 316, fig. 103. *Milano*, 1896.

by a species of wild Arenga palm (*Arenga undulatifolia* Becc.), but the common Arenga, the Coco, and other palms, also yield it.

When the lanko was finished and the fire lighted the Dyaks went in search of something to eat with their rice. They soon returned with several fish, which they had caught in the brooks in the forest. These were forthwith placed on the embers to roast, after being tied up in palm leaves. They belonged to no less than six species, of which I here give the native names :—

DYAK.					MALAY.	
Ikan	*pappak*	..	..	..	*Ikan*	*blao*
,,	*bokkù*	..	..	..	,,	*kli*
,,	*tekkid*	..	..	..	,,	*tankit*
,,	*siluan*	..	..	..	,,	*siluan*
,,	*pennoghu*	..	..	..	,,	?
,,	*siringin*	..	..	..	,,	?

We passed a pleasant night under the lanko, and I slept better than usual, having taken the precaution to spread branches and leaves over the big sticks which formed the flooring, and over these a pandanus mat which I always carried with me for the purpose. But the Dyaks had no need of such luxuries, and slept like logs on their bed of lumpy and knotted sticks, with no other dress on but their *jawat*. They kept the fire burning throughout the night, however, for, though they do not care for a soft couch, they are extremely sensitive to even the slightest lowering of the temperature.

The morning of July 8th was rainy, but this did not prevent me from going out in search of plants. I found many trees in blossom, of various species new to me ; but it was then quite impossible to collect specimens, either by climbing or by felling the trees, so towards ten o'clock we started on our way back to Singhi, and crossing once more the awful track through the swamp, we reached that village towards 4 p.m.

Next day I returned to Kuching, with a short stoppage at Bellida to get a supply of slender bamboos, called *bulu pretja*, with which I proposed making cane frames for the rearing of silkworms, which the Tuan Muda was anxious to try. I afterwards found that for that purpose the *bulu kassa* is preferable, being still more slender, and very like the reeds we use in Italy.

All bamboos in Borneo are apt to be bored, on drying, by insects, except the *bulu tamian*, which is so hardened by silica that the mandibles of these pests can make no impression on it. It is for this reason used, as I have already said, as a substitute for flint in striking a light. To prevent the bamboos being bored by insects they are macerated for a while in water, or else buried in mud.

Leading the life of a Dyak in the woods one is always learning something new of their ways and customs. Thus on this occasion I was able to find out how they dye their teeth black. They use for this purpose the *bajio*—a slender euphorbiaceous shrub with a stem not thicker than one's little finger, and from four to seven feet high, straight and without any branches, but only a few very large coriaceous leaves at the upper end, in the axillæ of which spikes of insignificant flowers grow.[1] The stems are well dried after the bark has been scraped off, and, when required for use, one of them is lighted at one end and applied against the blade of a knife or parang, or some other smooth iron surface. In burning, a resinous oil appears to exude from these sticks, and is condensed on the metallic surface. To this substance lamp-black (obtained, I believe, by burning dammar resin) is added, forming a black pigment which, applied to the teeth, adheres strongly to their surface. However, to keep them well blacked, the operation must be often repeated.

The Singhi Dyaks, after the fashion of many other primitive people, count on their fingers and pass on to their toes. One of their habitual postures of rest, as with most Dyaks, is that of squatting on their hams, the feet only resting on the ground. The sole of the foot is quite flat in the Dyaks, and often when standing still they keep the foot turned inwards, as if to apply the sole flat against the ground was not natural or habitual to them. This is a pithecoid character, and is seen especially in women and children. It has been suggested that the peculiarity is derived from the habit of climbing trees, and the frequent walking over tree-trunks laid down to form pathways in the forest.

Not only Dyaks, but also many Malays can, and often do, use their feet as supplementary hands. I have seen Javanese labouring in the fields take a stick up between the hallux and the next toe, and plant it upright in the ground. The great toe is always used in a similar manner in climbing up a rope or a liana to reach the top of a tree. And in twisting a cord, or splitting or cleaning a rotang, the great toe is always used to hold down one of the ends. It is also always used to seize a branch or a fruit out of reach of the hand, or to pick up an object on the ground without stooping. A Malay in my service could tear up a sheet of paper, using the two great toes, and holding it by the two opposite ends. The same man could bend outwards and detach his right great toe from the rest for a distance of two and three-sixteenth inches, and the left one two inches, and could spread out all the other toes like a fan, detaching one from the other nearly half an inch, and the little toe from the one next to it more than three quarters of an inch. Malays usually have the second toe much longer than the great toe. In general, their feet

[1] This plant is a new species of the genus *Agrostistachys*, which I have distinguished by the name of *A. Borneensis* (P.B., No. 1,381 and 3,117); it is nearly allied to *A. longifolia*, Benth. I found it also at Johore, in the Malay Peninsula, where its broad leaves are used as thatch on huts in the forest.

are well formed, and very small, and often in women they rival in gracefulness their very elegantly shaped and diminutive hands.

During the month of July I formed a collection of the fish of the Sarawak river. Not a few of the many species found there live both in fresh and in salt or brackish water. However, many of those brought me at Kuching came from Santubong, where the water is nearly quite salt.

The Malays are well acquainted with, and easily distinguish the various species of fish, which, with rice, form their principal article of diet. This is not to be wondered at, if one considers that they are a people who live almost exclusively on the water, whether along the sea coasts, or on the banks of rivers. Their children, almost from the time that they can stand upright, live more in the water than on land, and pass days together in little boats fishing, either with hook and line, or with some other angling apparatus. They thus have a perfect knowledge of the habits of fish, and the ready way in which they distinguish even closely allied species has often surprised naturalists. Just as these do, the Malays assign to species which have a common resemblance a generic name (which often corresponds closely to the scientific one), and distinguish the species with a second specific name, which is usually an adjective, as in the binomial system of Linnæus. Thus " *Bokkut* " is a generic name ; and we have a " bokkut itam " (black bokkut), a "bokkut pasir " (sand bokkut), a " bokkut buta " (blind bokkut, i.e. having very small eyes), and a " bokkut bodo " (foolish bokkut) : four different species of the same genus, distinguished by their most prominent characteristic, precisely in accordance with the rules of scientific nomenclature.

At Kuching, normally, the water is brackish or partly salt, even at low tide, and true freshwater fish are absent ; but during floods some are carried down from the Upper Sarawak. For true freshwater fish one must go to the forest streams, or to the waters of the rivers beyond the tidal influence. There are certain localities which appear to be alternately frequented by freshwater and by brackish or saltwater species, according to the state of the tide. I have myself observed an instance of this in the Mattang river.

According to the natives there are several species of poisonous fish in the Sarawak, of which the most dangerous are the following : " Ikan gurut," " sombilan," " pare," " tukka-tukka," " leppu appi," " leppu benuar." The most poisonous of all is the " ikan sombilan." Less poisonous, but always unwholesome, are the following : " Ikan lundu," " uttit," " jahan," " n'kalang," " quagok," " bahon " ; the last mentioned species lives in clear waters near the sources of rivers and streams. I imagine that most of these fish are considered poisonous on account of their spines and aculei. This is certainly the case with the " ikan pare."

I have only heard of one truly poisonous fish, which cannot be eaten without dangerous and often fatal effects. This is the " ikan buntal pisang " (*Tetrodon sp*.?), which is also notable for the singular sound it produces with its beak-like jaws. I have been told that in this case the eggs are the poisonous part, and if they are removed the fish can be eaten with impunity.

With the exception of the " ikan buntal," the poison in fishes, according to the Malays, is localized in the mucus or slime which covers their bodies, and, getting into the wounds or punctures made by the spines, is the cause of the well-known inflammatory symptoms, often exceedingly painful, but without dangerous consequences. But even here there are, it seems, exceptions, and some of these are several species of " ikan pare," or sting rays (*Trygon*), the large serrated spines of whose tails produce dangerous and sometimes fatal wounds ; for they easily get broken, and by means of the minute barbed spines continue to burrow into the tissues, and if not extracted may eventually cause the death of the patient.

There are various sound-producing, or, as the natives put it, " talking fishes," in the Sarawak. The following were described to me as coming under this head : " Ikan bengot," " gurut," " lundu," " uttit," " bilokan," " jahan," " n'kalang," " quaggok," " bianto," called also " bettot," or " pupput." [1]

Amongst other ichthyological peculiarities there is a fish in Sarawak which is used to detect thieves. It is the " ikan s'luan," and the belief is that if the eyes of a person who has stolen are touched with this fish, he becomes blind, whilst the sight of an innocent person would suffer no harm. In all probability the fish is quite harmless, and the effect it may or may not produce depends on the art or malice of the person applying this singular judicial ordeal, which few persons are, indeed, considered to administer with success. The fishes to be thus used are exhibited for a time to the public, and previously undergo special ceremonies.

In order to complete my collection of fishes, I went down to Santubong between July 27th and 29th, and, making use of *tuba*, endeavoured to capture fish by poisoning the waters of a small stream which flows by the village. The quantity thus caught was not great, but I was able to add several species to my collection. The Malays apply the name of *tuba* to various vegetable substances, fruits, roots, and bark, which are employed to stupify fish by being placed in the water. In our countries the fleshy part of green walnuts and some euphorbias and other plants are used in a similar manner. At

[1] Most of the fishes I collected in Sarawak have been studied by my good friend the able ichthyologist, Dr. Vinciguerra. All were labelled with slips of vellum on which the native name was written ; but, unfortunately, a long sojourn in spirits quite obliterated the writing, and it is now impossible for me to assign to any of them their scientific or Malayan names.

Kuching the long root-like stems of a creeper, *Derris uliginosa*, or some allied species, are usually employed for that purpose ; it is common in the inundated riverside jungles. The fruits of *Sapium indicum* and of *Croton tiglium* are also sometimes used.

The end of July was very rainy, quite an unusual thing at this season. About this time, in addition to frequent attacks of fever, I began to suffer from a malady peculiar to the country known as " *Untut*," which consists of œdema of the limbs, and is considered as a sort of commencement of elephantiasis. In my case the right leg was swelled, especially round the ankle.

Having finished packing all the collections made up to that date, and deposited them in a store of the Borneo Company ready to be shipped to Europe by the first steamer leaving, I was able to avail myself of the long-wished-for opportunity, which now fortunately presented itself, of visiting the Bornean coast as far as Bruni, and after that of undertaking an excursion into the country of the Kayans.

CHAPTER XVII

TAKING advantage of a kind invitation of the Tuan Muda, I
embarked on the morning of August 4th on the *Heartsease* for
Labuan and Bruni. The Tuan Muda was on board, but we were to
leave him a few miles lower down the river, at the *trusan* (channel),
for Mattang, as he was going to inspect his coffee plantation on that
mountain.

The principal object of the gunboat's voyage was to convey to
Bruni the sum of $6,000, which the Rajah of Sarawak at that time
paid annually to the Sultan for the cession made by the latter of his
administrative and political rights over the districts of Muka and
Bintulu. The original territory of Sarawak, that ceded by Rajah
Muda Hassim to Sir James Brooke, extended only from Tanjong
Datu to the Samarahan river, about seventy miles of coast in a
straight line.

I had with me supplies for a journey of four or five months, intending, on the return from Labuan, to get landed at Bintulu, whence
I hoped to penetrate into the interior. I had only two men with
me, expecting to find others at Bintulu. One of my men, named
Sahat, who had been already some time in my service, came from
Miri, a village at the mouth of the Barram river, in the territory of
Bruni, and was well acquainted with the country I wished to explore. In the life of this man there was a mystery. He was at heart
a pirate, if not originally one. His instincts were cruel, and yet he
was honest, plucky, a first rate canoeman, and clever in most things
that natives can do. He spoke fluently several dialects, was a decent
cook, and could act on an emergency both as tailor and hairdresser.
Bakar, my second servant, a pure Sarawak Malay, who might well
have been taken as a type of his race, was seventeen or eighteen years
old, of pleasing aspect and well-built figure. His character
was excellent, his demeanour serious, almost melancholy. He was
far from being stupid, and yet could not be called very intelligent.

He spoke little, and only in the Kuching dialect.   He was a Mussulman inasmuch as he was circumcised and ate no pork, the latter not so much on religious principles as because he did not like the taste of it.   Religious observances he had none, nor did he bother himself in the least about the how and why of things.   For him the past was not worth the trouble of thinking about, and I verily believe that no idea of the future ever flashed across his mind.   Good fortune he accepted as naturally so—a thing which ought to be ; of bad he had had little or no experience, and in any case he did not attribute it to malicious spirits, which he declared he had never seen.   He was timid and courageous at the same time ; and, as he felt himself strong, he never thought of consequences.   Blindly obedient, he always executed my orders without a word, unless some insurmountable obstacle caused him to desist.   His wants were few, and his desires less.   Alone in the forest he would have managed to supply all his necessities.   Excessively abstemious, some rice cooked in water and a little fish were sufficient to content him.   He was scrupulously clean in his person ; and his greatest delight was to come out in a fine new jacket or a pair of new trousers.

The character of this Malay boy of mine is practically that of numbers of his compatriots, but more amongst agriculturists and fisher-folk than in those given to commercial pursuits.   Bakar in my eyes was a perfect philosopher, and the most happy man I have ever known.   He was much attached to me, had been two years in my service, and was the only one of my servants who had accompanied me on nearly all my excursions in Borneo.   Sahat received eight dollars per month ; Bakar, six; and both were fed by me.

Favoured by the tide, the *Heartsease* rapidly dropped down the river.   When we reached the *trusan* for Mattang, the Tuan Muda left us, and we proceeded by the Maratabas channel out to sea.   Outside the weather was fine, and towards sunset we reached the village of Rejang, at the mouth of the river of that name, which is, in point of fact, only the principal branch of the delta of the Baloi, the biggest river of northern Borneo.   The mouth of the Rejang is certainly several miles wide, with a depth of five fathoms, and the river is navigable for 130 miles, even to good-sized vessels.   The delta of the Baloi, or rather of the Rejang, the entire course of the river bearing this name, is of vast area, and is mostly under mud and water, although covered everywhere with the densest forest.   As far as the eye can reach it is quite flat, covered with nipa, nibong, and mangroves.

Mr. Cruickshank, the Resident of the Rejang district, came on board the *Heartsease* here.   His residence was at the fort at Sibu, where the two principal branches of the great delta, the Rejang and the Igan, meet.   Mr. Cruickshank was going with us, for he was delegated to represent the Tuan Muda with the Sultan.

At 10 o'clock that night we left the Rejang, and at 3 p.m. on the following day, August 5th, we anchored about two miles off the mouth of the Muka river. With a fair breeze behind us we soon reached the shore in the ship's launch. The river forms a great bend at its mouth, beyond which is the town ; and to avoid the long way round by water we landed and crossed on foot the narrow neck which intervened between us and the fort.

Muka is the second town of Sarawak, and we found its population composed of Malays and Mellanaos, almost all of whom were occupied in the preparation of sago. The houses are built on piles along the river, in the usual Malay fashion, and the low marshy ground all round is infested with swarms of mosquitoes, rendering life well-nigh insupportable ; while the air reeked with a horrible stench, due to the fermenting feculum of sago, for the manufacture of which the Borneo company had a large establishment. We passed an otherwise pleasant evening with the manager, a gentleman of Dutch extraction, but born at Malacca.

We had, however, to hurry off to the gunboat, which was to sail during the night, and was some distance from the shore. It was already nine o'clock when we started in the launch ; but though the moon was above the horizon it did not give much light, and near the mouth of the river we had the narrowest shave of a capsize, our boat crashing into a *kilong*—one of the wooden frames used to support the huge fish-traps of the Mellanaos. These are enormous bi-conical wicker baskets, open at one end, like our eel-traps, and constructed in such a manner that fish can enter easily, but cannot escape. These *kilongs* are sunk in convenient spots when the tide is rising, with their opening turned towards the current, which leads the fish in. Not only did we lose the best part of our moonlight by delaying our start, but we got out of the river just as the inflowing tide met the descending current, causing a heavy sea on the bar, which was not quite reassuring for some of our party. For a moment we hesitated, some thinking that it was more prudent to turn back. Happily, the exhortations of the more courageous prevailed, and, having got over the flurry of waters about the bar, we found a calmer sea beyond, and were soon safe on board the gunboat. A large barge, however, which was loaded with firewood for the use of the steamer, was unable to get through the surf on the bar, and had to turn back. We took in a supply of fuel at Bintulu next day however, and I left here the men and supplies that were to go with me on my projected excursion inland.

We steamed along in full view of the coast, which got higher and bolder as we proceeded, and was highly picturesque, and at 9 a.m. on August 8th we anchored in Victoria Harbour, Labuan. This island lies about fifteen miles off the mouth of the Bruni river, in a N.N.E. direction, and is nearly triangular in shape, with an area of about forty square miles. It is almost flat, the highest point reaching an elevation of only eighty-six feet above sea level.

Labuan is so intimately connected with the history of Sarawak that I can hardly pass it by without mentioning the more important events which led to its occupation. Sir Edward Belcher, with whom was Captain James Brooke, the future Rajah, landed on Labuan in December, 1844, and the suitability of the island for establishing a station was at once recognized. A few days later Brooke received from the Sultan of Bruni a letter, in which he offered to cede the island to Great Britain. In 1845, Labuan was visited by Admiral Keppel, at that time captain in command of H. B. M.'s ship *Dido*. It was then decided that as a naval station it was preferable to the island of Balambangan, farther north, which had also been thought of for the same purpose. Coal of fairly good quality had meanwhile been discovered at Labuan, and this had no small influence in deciding its occupation ; for what was then wanted was a naval station for supplies, and especially coal, for the men-of-war engaged in the repression of piracy in the China Sea and among the Malayan Islands. Victoria Harbour, as it came to be called, offered, in addition, excellent shelter during the north-east monsoon, which is the bad season in these seas.

The occupation of Labuan was, however, only actually decided upon in 1846. On December 18th in that year Captain Mundy, then commanding H.M.S. *Isis*, got the act of perpetual cession of the island to H.M. the Queen of England and her successors signed by Sultan Omar Ali of Bruni, countersigning it in Her Majesty's name. No pecuniary compensation was, however, paid to the Sultan, as a punishment for his having insulted the British flag. On December 24th, Vice-Admiral Sir Thomas Cochrane and Captain Mundy hoisted the British flag, and formally took possession of the island in the name of Queen Victoria.

The hopes built on Labuan have only partially been realized. The climate is not so healthy as was at first supposed, fever being rather prevalent, and the coal has been the undoing of more than one company for its yield and exportation have fallen considerably short of expectations. When I visited the island, the only Europeans there were the Government officials, those in charge of a penitentiary, and the employés of the company which had the working of the coal mines.

Near the sea and round the harbour were only a few houses, though not badly built, belonging mainly to Chinamen. The bungalows of the Europeans were more inland. The Governor was absent at the time, and Mr. (now Sir Hugh) Low, the Colonial Treasurer, was Acting-Governor. He was most kind and hospitable, and wanted us to go and stay at Government House, where he then had his quarters. Mr. Low had been one of the early com-

Fig. 43.—THE WEST AFRICAN OIL PALM (*Elæis Guiniensis*) GROWING IN LABUAN.

rades of Rajah Brooke, and published an excellent book on Sarawak. Some of the most beautiful of existing plants were discovered by him in Borneo ; and I need only mention the beautiful *Nepenthes* from Kina Balu, and the magnificent *Vanda*, or *Arachnanthe*, which bears his name. Sir Hugh Low was afterwards made resident of Perak, where he did much to promote scientific research. I am glad of this occasion to record the kind aid he gave to a fellow-countryman of mine, the Padre Scortechini, who later fell a victim to his zeal in investigating the flora of the Malay Peninsula.

In addition to many insects, shells, and plants of Labuan, Mr. Low kindly presented me with a singular parasitic plant preserved in spirits, which he had collected during an excursion up the Limbang river. It turned out to be a second species of that most interesting genus *Brugmansia*, belonging to the family of the *Rafflesiaceæ*, which I have since described and named after the generous donor.[1]

Next morning, August 8th, I was up early, Mr. Low having most kindly promised to act as my guide on a little excursion across the island. We first went to his bungalow, then undergoing repairs ; but he wished to show me his plants, for he was passionately fond of horticulture. Round his house the principal fruits of the tropics grew in profusion, the pummeloes, or pamplemousses, and several varieties of orange with delicious fruits being especially remarkable, while mangosteens, lansats, and rambutans abounded. Some beautiful orchids which I had not seen in Sarawak had been collected in the forest, and were growing there, attached to trunks and branches of the trees in the garden. In a streamlet I noted a graceful *Nymphæa*, with light violet flowers, which has now become naturalised on the island, where it had been introduced by Mr. Low, who had collected it on Mount Kina Balu. As I have already remarked, such floating aquatic plants are rare in Borneo, and this fine species was well worthy of notice.

The part of Labuan which I crossed is formed wholly of a friable kind of sandstone, but in some places the soil was nothing but loose white quartzose sand. The very same formation is found in some localities in Sarawak ; as, for example, near Marop, at Sungei Siul, near Kuching, in the neighbourhood of Lundu, at the base of Mount Mattang, and elsewhere. I have already drawn attention to the fact that these localities are characterised by a peculiar vegetation ; by the umbrella Casuarina (*C. Sumatrana* Miq. ?) especially, for instance, and frequently, *Dacrydium elatum*. It was at Labuan, whilst examining this formation, that the idea of considering the above mentioned localities as remains of islands of a now vanished sea first came into my mind.[2]

---

[1] *Brugmansia Lowii*, Becc. ; in *Nuovo Giornale Botanico Italiano*, vol. i. p. 85.

[2] In the sandy spots above mentioned I collected *Rhodomyrtus tomentosa*

The climate of Labuan appears to be much drier than that of the north-west portion of Borneo, and the vegetation is also less luxuriant, partly, no doubt, because of the poor nature of the soil.

The Colonial Surgeon showed me a specimen of *Ptilocercus Lowii*, a singular creature only found in Borneo, which I had been vainly trying to get. It is an arboreal insectivorous mammal allied to the *Tupaia*, and about the size of the common squirrel ; its peculiarity lies in its long tail, which is bare and scaly like that of a rat for about the first half, but has the extremity thickly covered at the sides with long hair, after the manner of the barbs of a feather. The doctor evidently prized his rare specimen, and my praises and insinuations only made him prize it the more. My object in paying him a visit had been that mammal, and I left, alas ! feeling that I had merely lost my time. Mr. Low assured me that the *Ptilocercus* is not rare in Labuan, and that it has also been found in Sarawak ; but I was unable to obtain a single specimen, although I repeatedly showed a picture of it to natives, and offered a good reward to any one who would bring me a specimen.

The following morning we weighed anchor at daybreak, and steamed towards the mouth of the Bruni river. The Bornean coast, as seen from Labuan, is extremely picturesque. The transparency of the atmosphere allowed us to have a distinct view of the grand outline of Kina Balu, more than 100 miles away. This is not only the highest mountain in Borneo, but the highest one on the Asiatic Islands.[1] I watched it with the greatest interest, for the time seemed drawing near when I should tread its summit. This was the dream of my youth, but it was never to be realized ! Yet the marvellous plants which are to be found upon the mountain had, more than anything else, induced me to visit Borneo.

Mr. Low very nearly reached the summit of Kina Balu in 1850, and he made a second ascent of the mountain in 1851, accompanied by Mr. St. John. On these occasions several wonderful forms of *Nepenthes* were discovered, and one of them, afterwards named

(which I had found in Ceylon on the summit of Pedrotallagalla at more than 8,000 feet), a *Leucopogon*, a charming *Burmannia* with violet flowers, a *Salomonia*, a *Utricularia*, two species of *Xyris*, and various kinds of *Juncus* and *Scirpus* ; species which would be thought peculiar to lacustrine regions, but which here grew in dry soil, perhaps because sand easily absorbs and retains moisture from the air. The same thing happens in the case of mosses on mountains, where grow also certain marsh-loving delicate plants, which in Borneo would not find favourable conditions in swampy places on account of the prevalence and great development of plants of ranker growth. I was also pleasantly surprised to find growing here on the sea beach a small fungillus, *Poronia Œdipus*, a very singular species of Spheriacea, first described by Montagne as coming from Martinique, and next found in Italy, near Vercelli, by Baron Cesati, and later again by me in great abundance at the Cascine of Pisa.

[1] Sir Edward Belcher has given its height as 13,698 feet.

N. Rajah, surpasses all other known species for the immense development of its pitchers or ascidia, some of which reach a length of twelve
inches, are six inches across, and can hold seven pints of water.
More recently (1887–8) Kina Balu was explored by the well-known
ornithologist, Mr. G. Whitehead ; and botanically by Dr. G. D.
Haviland, in March and April, 1892.

The coast towards which our course was directed appears but
slightly elevated, and in some places is quite flat near the sea ; but a
few miles inland it rises, forming an elevated mountain chain, whose
higher summits are probably more than 6,000 feet high. Bruni is
thirty-three miles from Labuan in a S.S.W. direction. The entrance
to its river is not easy, and it is not navigable by large ships. On the
bar at low tide there are only six or seven feet of water, which
doubles at high tide. There is, besides, a submerged artificial bar,
constructed in past times as a defence for the city, with a single
outlet, which has to be well known by any vessel wishing to enter.

The Bruni river lies between a double row of hills, which rise on
each side to a height of three or four hundred feet. They were partly
cultivated with rice, and had been cleared of the old forest. I remarked on their crest a handsome palm, which I recognized as a
species of *Eugeissonia,* differing, however, from *E. insignis,* which
I had discovered on the top of Mount Mattang. I was not then able
to preserve specimens, but I believe I am not mistaken in referring
it to a species which I subsequently collected on the banks of the
Rejang (*E. utilis,* Becc.). It is a wild species which produces sago
of good quality, and this explains its abundance in cultivated
localities, for had it been useless it would have been destroyed with
the rest of the forest.

We passed the small chapel of the Roman Catholic Mission,
then abandoned and partly ruined. It was placed on a tongue of
land called Brambanggan, in a charming situation amongst the
hills. From Mr. St. John's book I gather that the Bruni Mission
was founded by Señor Quarteron, in 1857, and that an Italian priest,
Father Ripa, of Lecco, had its direction. Farther on is the house of
the British Consul, and then the city comes in view, which some have
ventured to style the Venice of the East. I admit that Bruni has
its points; but what irony to compare for a moment the city of marble
palaces with this mass of miserable huts, which a single match could
easily reduce to ashes !

The houses at Bruni are almost all built on piles, for which the
stems of nibongs are generally used. They are roofed with "ataps"
made of nipa or sago palm leaves, and the walls are matting, or
sometimes planks. All have a door on the front, against which is
placed a wooden ladder of the usual form, or a tree-trunk merely
notched, which leads down to the water. The piles are sunk on mud
banks in the wide bed of the river, and are always covered with

water, even at low tide, so that always and everywhere the town rises out of the water. Some old chiefs, however, assured us that four generations back the houses of Bruni were all constructed on the river banks.

Following the main canal, we passed right through the middle of the city, and anchored in front of the Sultan's palace, which is scarcely more imposing in appearance than the other houses.

The unexpected arrival of the *Heartsease* caused a great commotion in the town. The men appeared at the doors of their houses, and looked at us passing with the stolid expression usual to Malays ; whilst the women, wishing to satisfy their curiosity without being seen, peeped out of all the holes they could avail themselves of. Groups of boys squatting, *more Malayano*, on the bars of the house-ladders, contemplated our passage ; others jumped into the sampans or into the water, where, astride of a plank or any convenient piece of wood, they congregated around the vessel. The familiarity of Malay boys with water is simply marvellous ! They show plainly enough that they are the descendants of an eminently sea or waterside people. Mr. St. John aptly remarks that Malay children are suckled, smoke, and swim at the same time.

Very soon we were surrounded by a great number of sampans of all sizes. Most of them were loaded with boys, but many were paddled by a single woman, always old and ugly. All had something to sell, generally fruits and eatables of various kinds. Krisses and parangs of different shapes were also offered for sale, but they asked fancy prices, far above their actual value. Bruni was once famous for the manufacture of these weapons, and the Bruni blades were in high repute all over the archipelago, but at present even this art appears to have become obsolete.

As soon as we had cast anchor, we sent a message to the Sultan asking for an audience. The answer, which was not long in coming, was to the effect that at half-past three the Sultan would be pleased to receive us.

The audience hall was not at all unlike the stage of a theatre, and it was quite open on the water side. Along its outer edge were a few bronze cannons of native manufacture. I followed the officers to take part in the reception. There was certainly nothing interesting or remarkable in the room, but I was, nevertheless, very glad to have had the opportunity of seeing it, for it was in this very hall that the cession of Sarawak to James Brooke had been ratified, as well as the treaty of Labuan with Great Britain.

Sultan Omar Ali of Bruni was then a stout old man with an unintelligent face. He complained that his strength was failing, that his legs were getting weak, and that his harem had become useless to him. He was dressed in Malay style, but not over well ; indeed, his *baju* and *sarong*, although of silk and embroidered with gold,

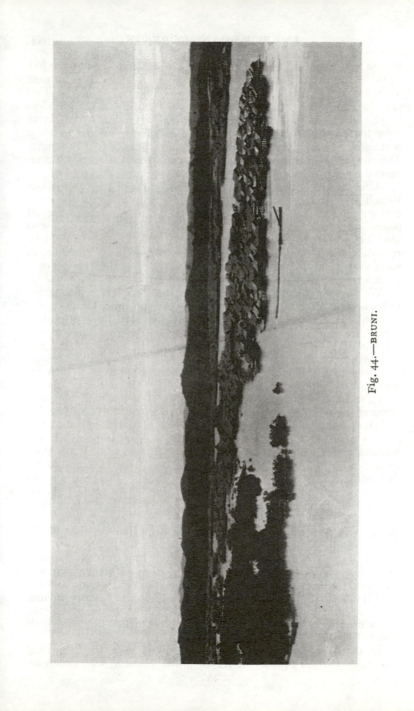

Fig. 44.—BRUNI.

looked as if they had seen long service. He sat at the end of the hall at the extremity of a table, at the side of which were chairs forming a semicircle. We were invited to sit down on his right ; on the other side the Pangerangs, members of the royal family, and the grandees of the kingdom took their seats. Several attendants and slaves squatted on the ground behind us, and *rokos* were offered to us—a sort of giant cigarette, of which some were quite a foot in length. The conversation was not lively ; but then, this was merely a cere-monial visit.

After this reception we visited different parts of the town in our launch, and amongst others the market, certainly one of the most curious on the face of the globe, for the stalls and shops are all boats. The market women were mostly old female slaves, who wore huge hats over two feet in diameter, which, indeed, might be mistaken for umbrellas. In the morning these boats assemble in what may be styled the market-place ; later they disperse all over the town.

We afterwards paid a visit to the British Consulate, where, some years before, Mr. St. John had resided. At the time, however, the large building, mostly of stone, was only tenanted by a caretaker. Whilst the dinner was being prepared in the deserted dining-room, I found time to explore the grounds round the house. I did not find many botanical rarities, nor did I expect to in a place where the old forest had so long been cleared ; but I was able to get a near-at-hand look at the palm which I had noticed on our way up the river, and to collect specimens of a fine *Melastoma* with big rose-coloured flowers (*M. Beccarianum*, Cogn.). Near the Consulate, on the river bank, a fine tree spread a mass of dense foliage. The natives asserted that it belonged to the species from which the Kayans and Dyaks extract the poison with which they tip their sumpitan arrows. It ought, therefore, to be a Upas tree, and under that name it is marked on the Admiralty chart. I did not see any of its flowers, and from an inspection of the leaves alone I should hardly venture on a determination ; but I can without the least hesi-tation assert not only that it is no Upas tree (*Antiaris toxicaria*), but that it does not even belong to the same family, that of the *Artocarpeæ*.

I only saw two merchant praus during our tour through the city : an evident proof of the miserable state of its trade, which was paralysed by the avidity of the Pangerangs, their extortions, and the exorbitant taxation. The natural products of the country inland, such as camphor, rotangs, guttapercha, edible birds' nests, etc., which used to be collected at Bruni for exportation, now find their outlet elsewhere.

In the evening we received on board the visit of Pangerang Mahomet, natural brother of Rajah Muda Hassim, who ceded his rights in Sarawak to Sir James Brooke, and who was assassinated by instigation of the reigning Sultan.

The Malay character, at all events of the aristocratic portion of the population, was well exemplified in this personage. Intriguing, insinuating, and astute, with a mysterious air of self-importance, and employing a curiously figurative language, he endeavoured to make us understand that he was at the head of a popular party who desired European rule. He asserted that his influence over his fellow-citizens was great, and tried to make us believe that the people were tired of the government of the Sultan, and of the pretences of the Panger-angs. Perhaps all he said was true, for the Bruni people could only gain by a change of government. The city showed evident signs of decay, whilst the prosperity of Sarawak and the security all enjoyed there had proved to the people of Bruni that it was far better to be governed by Europeans than by one of their native princes.

There must, undoubtedly, have been a time when all the north-east of Borneo was a dependency of China. According to Mr. St. John,[1] a tradition still lingers at Bruni that North Borneo once belonged to China, and that on the Limbang a Chinese fort once existed. It is well known that at one time a number of Chinese cultivated pepper at Bruni, and on the Limbang river, where people are still living who remember their plantations extending to the Madidit. A story is also told of an Orang Kaya of the Murut who was a direct descendant of a Chinaman from Amoy. Many of the descendants of these old Chinese pepper planters are not now to be distinguished from the natives, having adopted their dress and habits. Some of them, now indistinguishably blended with the Muruts, are, according to St. John, to be found up to 150 miles inland on the Limbang river, and the same author states that some of the people about Kina Balu are very like Chinese. It appears certain that in the past the connexions of North Borneo with China, and also with Cochin-china, were extensive. But who can say how long such connexions had been in existence ? Could the question only be answered we might get some light on the origin of the present population of Borneo. Nowadays the Chinese in Bruni occupy a separate quarter of the town, with shops well provided with the necessities of life, but quite devoid of the products of local industries and manufactures.

We weighed anchor in the afternoon, and with the tide in our favour descended the river ; but when we got to its mouth the water was so low that we ran aground in hardly a fathom, and were obliged to remain within the bar until the next high tide. Whilst in this condition we were approached by several fishing boats, whose crews offered us a singular bivalve, which is eaten like an oyster. It is the

[1] *Op. cit.* ii. p. 313.

Placuna placenta, whose flat, circular valves, which are very smooth, thin, and glassy, and grow to about four inches in diameter, are used by the Chinese as glass for their windows.

In Bruni Bay this mollusc is evidently extremely abundant, for the fishermen who sold them to us had loads of them. I had seen them also at Santubong in Sarawak, and on the neighbouring coast, but only during the north-east monsoon, when the waves probably carry them into depths more accessible to the local fishermen. I have always felt an instinctive dislike to all kinds of shell-fish, and therefore did not taste these, but my companions who ate them found them excellent. After a little time, however, they felt a most troublesome itching sensation in the pharynx, which happily for them did not last long. This unpleasant peculiarity of the *Placuna* was well known to our Malays, who attributed it to a parasitic worm living in the mollusc, which they always take care to extract before eating the latter ; and indeed none of our crew who ate these shell-fish felt the slightest inconvenience. I preserved specimens of the parasite, which resembled a small *Ascaris*, in spirits. I found them in all the *Placunas* I examined.

It is generally believed, and I think with good reason, that the name of Borneo, now used for the island, was originally derived from that of Bruni city. I may remark that the former is quite unknown to most of the natives of the great island. Borneo is without doubt a corruption of Bruni, which I have heard pronounced Brunei and Bornai. An old name of Borneo is " Tana Bruni," for the Malays apply the term " Tana," i.e. " Land," also to big islands, reserving that of " Pulo " for the small ones.

Borneo is known to the natives also by the name of Tana (or Pulo) Kalamantang, on account, it is said, of the fruit so called, a species of wild mango, which abounds in its forests. Whilst on the Upper Rejang I heard the name Gunong Kalamantang applied to the group of mountains in the interior from which the principal rivers in Borneo flow ; they are also called Batu Tabang and Gunong Tilong.[1]

From what I was able to see during my brief visits to Labuan and Bruni, North Borneo differs notably from the more southern parts of the island, not only physically, but also for the political vicissi-

---

[1] In the *Sarawak Gazette*, of June 2, 1890 (p. 74), I find another hypothesis as to the native name of Borneo. Mr. Treacher thinks it possible that the derivation of the name Kalamantang, which he spells Kelemantan, is from " lemantah," the Malay term for raw sago. This hypothesis appears to me to be more probable, for sago is an abundant product on the coasts of Borneo, and has been so from remote times. Even the name Gunong Kalamantang may have a similar origin, on account of the wild sago got from the *Eugeissonia utilis*, a palm which appears to be very abundant in the interior of Borneo.

tudes it has undergone, and the greater contact it has had with more
civilised countries.   The region is also more mountainous, has a
drier climate, and is much more cleared of forests, having evidently
been for a longer period under cultivation, although this has lately
decreased. This is well proved by the herds of buffaloes, oxen, and
even small horses which are found there.

CHAPTER XVIII

EARLY on the twelfth of August we weighed and proceeded towards Bintulu. At sunrise, Kina Balu, which we were leaving behind us, could be distinctly seen through the singularly transparent atmosphere. The outlines of the coast and that of the mountains beyond Bruni were clearly defined, and the eye could follow every feature of the landscape. The peaks far inland have a very different outline from those nearer Bruni; the latter are rounded, and I therefore infer that they must be formed of easily disintegrated materials, perhaps sandstone; whilst the former, among which Gunong Mulu is the most conspicuous, are abrupt and precipitous, and are probably limestone.

On the thirteenth of August we reached Bintulu. The *Heartsease* anchored at some distance from the mouth of the river, which is about 200 yards in width, for a bar with very little water on it renders the entrance impossible to vessels of her size. The fort of Bintulu, which was built entirely of wood, was in a somewhat ruinous condition. It stood nearly on the sea-shore, and just behind it, at the distance of a few paces, the primeval forest commenced. Next day the *Heartsease* left, and I remained at Bintulu as the guest of Mr. Houghton, the new Resident of the district. That night we had a violent storm.

Some Chinamen had settled in the vicinity of the fort and had built a small bazaar; but the village is chiefly formed by the houses of the Mellanaos beyond the Chinese kampong. These Mellanaos used to live farther up the river, but since the construction of the fort, and the installation of an officer of the Rajah near the mouth of the river, they came to settle nearer the sea—a thing which they would never have dared to do in former days for fear of the attacks of the Lanun pirates and the incursions of the Sea-Dyaks. Their houses are built on both sides of the river, always on high piles, and with materials mostly furnished by the nipa and sago palms. They resemble those of the Dyaks, and are also disposed in long rows and divided by planks into many *pintus*. Outside each house, projecting from the main body of the edifice, corresponding to the entrance on the river, is a kind of shed, which is used for domestic purposes and especially for sago-making operations.

I have already stated that the greater portion of the inhabitants of Bintulu are Mellanaos. These are a very singular people, inhabiting the mouths of most of the rivers on the north coast of Borneo, especially those between the Rejang and the Barram. They have also a colony at Santubong, at the mouth of the Sarawak river, where they still speak their own language, which is very different from the Malay tongue. They also differ from the Malays in their customs and habits, and have all the appearance of having always been a peaceful people. Very few have been converted to Islamism ; most are faithful to their old creed, which consists in a belief in good and evil spirits, to which offerings are made to calm their anger or to propitiate their good-will. They possess wooden idols, very rudely carved, but it does not appear that they worship them. They are exposed outside the houses, or have a special place in the village where all can easily see them. Usually, as far as I could judge, the people do not pay much attention to these images, but in times of sickness or other troubles they decorate them in various ways, often using long white slips made with young nipa leaves and plaited in various fashions, very much as is done in Italy with palm leaves on the Sunday before Easter.

The Mellanaos are the principal cultivators of the sago palm on the coast ; and the extraction of the fecula from the trunk of that palm is their chief industry. They also make elegant mats with slips of " bumbang " (*Clinogyne dichotoma*), but where they most excel is as fishermen. During the entire season of the north-east monsoon the shores of this portion of Borneo are nearly inaccessible to the usual Malay—and I may even add European boats—on account of the surf, which is naturally more violent on the river bars, which have not much water on them. Notwithstanding this the Mellanaos go out in almost any weather in their short, but wide-beamed boats, called *barongs*, which are of a peculiar type and very seaworthy.

At Bintulu they also use the same huge fish-traps which I had noticed at Muka, where they had so nearly caused our launch to capsize ; but I was not able to examine one closely. Fishing is an affair of such importance with the Mellanaos, that the women refuse to allow their husbands to enter their houses if they return without having caught anything.

A most singular custom of these people is that of flattening the heads of their girl babies, giving the forehead a sharp slope backward; this malformation is produced by applying a small board to the forehead shortly after birth, and keeping it there for many months.

The Mellanao men at Bintulu dress as Malays; they are never tattooed, nor do they use any kind of personal ornament. The women wear a long shirt or tunic reaching to the feet, made of European cotton cloth of a dark blue or nearly black colour, which is at Bintulu one of the main articles of importation. This woman's dress has very wide sleeves, open on one side with hanging lappets, not unlike the costume of Italian ladies in the fourteenth century. The aperture of the sleeve is ornamented with buttons or bell-shaped pendants, which are often of gold. The Mellanao women also wear costly bracelets.

On the morning after my arrival, I sallied out from the fort shortly after sunrise and walked towards the beach, where I found a lot of women busily engaged in searching amongst the flotsam and jetsam thrown up by the sea. At first it looked as if they were picking up stones; but on approaching nearer I was surprised to find that the object of their search was a species of resin, which occurred in lumps from about the size of a walnut to that of the fist, worn and rounded at the edges just like the river pebbles. This resin is the product of some dipterocarp abounding in the forests of the interior and carried down by floods to the sea, where it acquires the appearance of little rounded stones as above described, and on this account is called dammar batu, or stone dammar, by the Malays.

Besides this resin the sea had washed ashore all sorts of vegetable detritus, amongst them quite a number of fruits, most of which I recognised, though some were new to me. Some distance above the fort a small stream debouched, and after heavy rain I have seen this carry down large quantities of mud, which covered the flotsam and jetsam cast up by the waves. This is highly instructive, for it gives us an undoubted instance of a littoral marine formation which consists nearly entirely of land and freshwater vegetable remains, and in which the pebbles of resin are in surroundings very similar to those in which amber is found.

The rivers of this portion of Borneo, such as the Rejang, Bintulu, and especially the Barram, farther north, must carry down to the sea an immense quantity of débris. According to a statement of Mr. St. John,[1] great accumulations of tree-trunks, floating and covered with seaweed, have been met with out at sea off Barram Point, and have even impeded the course of vessels when the wind was slack. On passing Barram Point I did not notice anything of

[1] Op. cit. i. p. 17.

this kind; but it may easily happen during the bad season after persistent rain, when the swollen rivers carry down to the sea abundant vegetable flotsam, such as tree trunks and even entire trees. From the large quantity of such detritus which I saw myself at Bintulu I have no doubt of the correctness of Mr. St. John's assertion, only the spot where such accumulations take place may vary. Mr. St. John adds that in such places there appears to be a condition of the currents which keeps these floating masses together, and gives them a gyrating movement.[1]

Continuing my excursion, I walked along the beach as far as Tanjong Silei, entering a bay whose north-east extremity, Tanjong Kedurong, at that time marked the boundary between Rajah Brooke's territory and that of the Sultan of Bruni. This bay looks deep and is sheltered by hills from the north-east winds, and ought thus to afford good anchorage during the " Munsim landas," as the north-east monsoon is styled. From Santubong, this is the most elevated part of the coast, which is continuously low, partly swampy and covered by nipa and mangroves, partly sandy and dotted by casuarinas, but always devoid of rocks. On my way back, I diverged and followed for a while the course of a streamlet, the bottom of which was covered by a singular aquatic plant, *Barclaya Motleyi*, a Nymphacea with submerged leaves and small insignificant flowers hidden under water, instead of the large conspicuous ones usually admired in such plants. I had already met with *Barclaya* during one of my first excursions in the forest near Kuching; but there I had found it covered with a thick woolly coating—a very exceptional case in a plants which always lives under water.[2] The specimens I found in the Bintulu streamlet were quite glabrous. Owing to this peculiarity I preserved a certain number of specimens. But the most important botanical booty made on this excursion consisted of three new palms, which grew together on a hillock near the streamlet. Two were dwarf forms with fan-shaped leaves (*Licuala Bintulensis*, Becc., and *L. spathellifera*, Becc.). The third (*Gigliolia insignis*, Becc.) was the most noteworthy one: an extremely elegant palm with a slender stem about an inch and a half in diameter, and some ten feet high, ending in a tuft of large pinnate fronds

---

[1] Small floating islands, often some yards in length, were on several occasions sighted off this part of the Bornean coast during the cruise of the yacht *Marchesa* in these waters.—ED.

[2] In many botanical treatises, even in those of recent date, it is asserted that aquatic plants are never hairy. Amongst floating species, however, this peculiarity is seen in *Pistia stratiotes* and in *Trapa natans*; but, amongst those which are completely submerged, *Barclaya Motleyi* is, perhaps, the only instance. To what physiological necessity hairiness in submerged plants corresponds I cannot imagine; neither can I explain why the same species should be in some cases covered with hairs, and in others glabrus, though in every instance submerged.

of an unusual type. The new genus which I have established for this beautiful palm commemorates the name of Professor Henry H. Giglioli ; and—as I have already stated in my *Malesia* (vol. i. p. 171), where this palm is scientifically described—I was happy thus and with this dedication to discharge a debt of gratitude towards the old friend who has ever followed with much love and cordial interest my various peregrinations. *Gigliolia* is the only generic type amongst palms which is peculiar to Borneo, all the other genera of this family being represented in the neighbouring lands, especially on the Malay Peninsula and in Sumatra.

I had so far been unable to find men for my excursions on the river, or to fell trees of which I wished to secure specimens ; but, thanks to Mr. Houghton's kind aid, I was at last able to engage three Malays, who entered my service with a salary of one *sukku* (eighteen cents) per diem.

On the seventeenth of August it was 72° Fahr. in the night, and I observed the same temperature at 6 a.m. Here, as elsewhere, the minimum temperature in the twenty-four hours is found just before sunrise. The observation of the preceding day was, however, an exception to this rule (which I have almost always found true), for it gave during the night a minimum of 67° Fahr.—the lowest temperature at sea level which I observed during my stay in Borneo, while just previous to sunrise the thermometer stood at 72°.

Next day I went with my men into the adjacent forest, where amongst other interesting plants, I found the " Akar Belangan," a creeper of the genus *Dalbergia* : a leguminous plant, with very spinous stems, the heart of which assumes with age a red coloration, giving origin to the substance which the Malays call "Kayu Lakka." [1] This is much sought after by Chinamen, who use it as they do " Aguila," or " Aquila wood," or " Ankaras," in religious ceremonies, but not as a dye, as the native name might appear to imply, " Lakka " meaning " red dye."

In the Bintulu forest certain creepers belonging to the family of the Apocynaceæ abounded, highly interesting from an industrial point of view, for from some of them indiarubber of a good quality is obtained. Amongst them was a new *Leuconotis*, which I propose to distinguish as *L. elastica*. It is known in Sarawak by the names of " Akar sarapat laki " and " Akar janta-an ular," and I had found it at Kuching ; but it does not appear to be common in any place, and this is a pity, for the milky juice it exudes coagulates at once in elastic filaments, giving an indiarubber

---

[1] The spines which cover the stem of this *Dalbergia*, which appears to be allied to *D. parviflora*, Roxb., are of quite a peculiar nature, and not produced from the epidermis, nor the result of modifications of branches or stipules. Morphologically they appear to me aërial rootlets—a very rare case amongst Dicotyledonous plants, though not uncommon in palms.

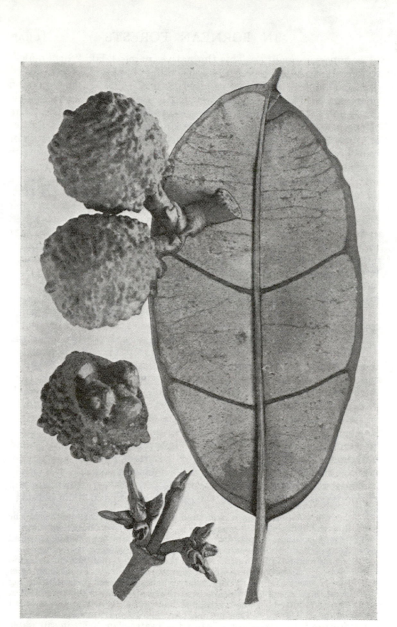

Fig. 45.—*Leuconotis elastica*, Becc.

of a superior quality. This the native name "laki," or "male," would imply, being a term which Malays apply to trees, fruits, or other objects excellent of their kind. The greater portion of indiarubber of good quality, called "Ghetta janta-an sussu," is produced in Sarawak by *Willughbeia firma*, and by *Urnularia oblongifolia*, Stapf. (P.B., No. 2,272), and probably by other species of these two genera, all of which when incised exude an abundant milky juice, though only in a few does it coagulate, giving rise to a product of commercial value.

The eighteenth of August was a fine bright day, of which I took advantage to finish the drying of the plants I had collected, arranging them so that there might be no further danger with regard to their preservation. A large number were already prepared; these I tied up in packages, and hung them up under the roof of the fort, so that they might be safe from rats. Those still damp I also tied up, but not so tightly, doubling the sheets of paper between the specimens. I then hung them up in the Resident's kitchen over the fireplace, but high enough to receive only a moderate heat. On my return I found all of them in an excellent state of preservation.

Towards dusk, on the banks of the Bintulu, I caught some curious crustaceans and a small water snake. It was only after I had been wading about for some time that I discovered that the soft substance under my feet was not mud, but a sheet of vegetation composed of a minute submerged plant hidden by a thin layer of fine slush, so that it was not easily distinguishable at first. I afterwards found that in some places it was uncovered and quite exposed. This plant, which formed patches or small uniform meadows uncovered at low tide, turned out to be an important botanical novelty, *Halophila Beccarii*, Aschers. (in *Nuovo Giorn. Bot. Ital.*, iii. p. 302), belonging to that scarce group of plants which live and blossom in the sea. The flowers of this *Halophila* are very small, composed of three petals of a whitish colour, veined and nearly transparent. When I found them the corollas were open, having evidently taken advantage of the low tide to expand their petals.[1]

[1] This marine Phanerogam suggested to me some further points on the difficulties which beset living organisms in the present epoch in their adaptation to the surrounding medium. It is beyond doubt that the genera and the species of Phanerogams which are now found living on the sea bottom, all belonging to the Hydrocharidæ and to the Najadæ—plants which abound in marshes—are derived from those which grow in fresh water; but the number of the former, compared to that of the latter, is indeed small, notwithstanding that for an immeasurable period of time the seeds of an infinite number of marsh-loving plants must beyond doubt have been carried to the sea and deposited on its bottom. This means that only at one given epoch, and in a very few cases, has the adaptation of a freshwater plant to life in salt water been possible. If it were not so, the sea bottom would now be as well provided with plants and flowers as is the surface of dry land. There are few cases in which so great a power of adaptability is needed as in the one under

During the last few days I had been actively engaged in the necessary preparations for an excursion into the Kayan country by the ascent of the Bintulu river. I had for this purpose procured a boat with a crew of six paddlers; and as the Kayans do not use money, I had bought from the Chinese an assortment of Venetian glass beads or " manet," [1] and a quantity of white, yellow, red, and more especially dark blue cotton cloth, this being one of the more appreciated articles for barter on the Bintulu.

Shortly after sunrise on the nineteenth of August I left the fort, but soon found that our progress was slow; in fact, we had both tide and wind against us ; besides, the boat was both heavy and heavily laden, and as if this were not enough, it leaked. We were fully three hours getting to Spadok, where the piles of the old Mellanao village could still be seen.

A small house which we entered to cook our breakfast was inhabited by a Buketan—a true savage of the interior. He was of athletic proportions and beautifully tattooed, and the lobes of his ears were enormously distended by two heavy brass earrings. I do not know how this " Man of the Woods " happened to be there, where I was told he had been living for some years, but he was the only individual of this peculiar people that I saw whilst in Borneo. I never met him again, and am sorry that I did not sketch his portrait, and take more detailed notes on his characteristics. Amongst my collections, however, is the perfect skull of a Buketan, which was given to me by the Tuan Muda at Simanggan, when I passed through that place on my return journey at the end of October. He had received it from a Dyak, and I do not think there can be any doubt as to its authenticity. It has been carefully described and figured by Professor Arturo Zannetti. [2]

Not much, indeed, can be got from a single skull as to the affinities or diversities of the Buketans with regard to other Bornean tribes. It does not show any remarkable peculiarity, the only character worthy of notice being the strongly developed muscular

consideration, for the strong action of salt water on the cells of the majority of plants is well known. Thus, when the change from a terrestrial or freshwater existence to a marine or estuarine one took place, the capability of plants to adapt themselves to life-conditions different from those to which they were until then accustomed—in a word, to undergo plasmation through their environment—must have been at its apogee, and must have gone on diminishing until it ceased entirely later on.

[1] I have heard or read—I do not now remember where—that the term " manet " is a corruption of the Italian word *moneta* (money), which was used for glass beads at the time when the Venetians were the foremost traders in the world. Admitting this to be true, it must not, however, be forgotten that the Venetians made their glass beads in imitation of the Chinese, who, it appears, had used them from the remotest times in their commercial transactions with the less civilised tribes of Southern Asia and the Malay Islands.

[2] *Archivio per l'Antrop. e la Etnol.* ii. p. 156 ; tav. 2. Firenze, 1872.

attachments on the lower jaw. These might, perhaps, be caused by the abnormal development of the cheek muscles owing to the constant use of the sumpitan or blow-pipe, the favourite weapon of the Buketans.

At 6 p.m., there being no habitation near, we stopped on the bank of the river to cook our supper. Mosquitoes were in abundance. We passed the night in the boat, and had fine rain.

Next morning we were off again at sunrise. Hitherto I had only seen nipa and sago palms on the banks of the river, but now other kinds of trees occurred intermingled with them. I could not then stop to collect plants, intending to do so on my return, and thus I avoided the trouble of preparing them whilst travelling. Nevertheless, I could not resist the temptation of taking a few specimens of the magnificent *Hoya imperialis* ; it was such a joy to be able to handle its charming flowers, which are of a lovely violet, spotted with white at the centre.

At nine o'clock we stopped at a rude hut or lanko of the Punans, a tribe inhabiting some of the affluents of the Bintulu. The Punans, like the Buketans, are true forest nomads, and have no permanent houses, but only temporary shelters or rude huts, which they construct without much trouble in those places where the jungle offers them wild animals to hunt and wild fruits on which they can feed. They naturally undertake no cultivation, except in the case of a few, who, by frequenting the villages of the Mellanaos and Kayans, have learnt the advantage of sowing some rice and planting a few sugar canes and bananas. They hunt wild animals solely with the sumpitan and its small peculiar arrows tipped with upas, and they also use dogs, which they breed in considerable numbers. They make very fine mats ; but this is, I believe, their only art, though they are great collectors of wax, camphor, gutta-percha, rotangs and edible nests. When they have exhausted the produce of a locality they move on to another. My servant, Sahat, assured me that he had once traded a good deal with the Punans, and observed that they are frequently affected by hernia, caused by the constant use of the sumpitan. Besides this weapon they have the parang ilang, and wooden shields for defence similar to those of the Kayans, called " utak " ; but these I shall describe further on.

Physically the Punans differ but slightly from the Kayans ; perhaps their cheek bones are a little more projecting and their lower jaw more heavy. They tattoo slightly on various parts of the body. The operation is performed with the milky secretion of the Bua Rambei, to which they add black pigment obtained by burning dammar. They pierce the lobe of the ears, and insert one or more brass or tin rings, so heavy that the ears get distended to such an extent that the hand may be passed through the perforation of the lobes, which hang down to the shoulders and even reach the

breast. Like the Kayans, they also bore the upper margin of the
ear, inserting the canine tooth of a bear or leopard.

The custom of ornamenting the ears in an exaggerated fashion,
disfiguring them with heavy pendants, appears to have been practised in remote times by the people of India, as may be seen in the
figures on their ancient monuments. Thus nearly all the human
figures of the many hundreds reproduced on the temple at Boro
Budor, in Java, show distinctly this peculiar mutilation, which is
still practised by the more barbarous tribes inhabiting parts of
Burma.

The mode of trading of the Punans and also of the Buketans,
if my information is correct, is peculiar. They never show themselves on such occasions ; but those who know their ways deposit
in certain places the objects they wish to give in exchange for forest
produce. The savages come and take them away, leaving in their
stead what they think is the just equivalent.[1]

The Punans and Buketans are man-hunters ; that is to say, they
consider as their natural and lawful prey any human being with
whom they have no dealings. But they only take the property of
the person they have slain, and do not care to preserve his head as
a war trophy.

Shortly after midday we reached. Pandan, a Mellanao village,
where I saw two remarkable objects. One was a reproduction of
two human figures, one on the top of the other, rudely carved out
of the trunk of a tree, one of the figures holding an " utak " or
wooden shield in his hand. I cannot say whether this curious
artistic reproduction of the Mellanaos was an idol and connected
in any way with religion or superstition, or a sort of monument
commemorating some defunct notability. The other object was
much more elaborate, consisting of a wooden column, about sixteen
feet high, covered with carving, on whose top were two boards
placed horizontally across and at a certain distance, so as to form
a sort of case open at each end. The pillar was thus in shape like
a huge **T**. From the end of each transverse plank hung various
ornaments, among them being young leaves of the nipa, of a white
colour, cut into long slips, some of which were variously plaited,
while numerous strips of white, yellow, and red cotton cloth completed
the decoration. I was able to ascertain that this was really a
monumental grave. The column was hollow, and contained one of
the precious *tajau*, or ancient jars, mentioned on a previous page,
in which were deposited the bones of the deceased. The upper
transverse case contained some of his belongings, whilst others,
such as gongs, pots, dishes, etc., hung outside against the pillar.

[1] This custom has been existent in various savage tribes since the days
of Herodotus, among the dwarfs in Africa, the Veddas in Ceylcn, and the
Kubus of Sumatra.—Ed.

We continued to paddle till 5 p.m., and then rested for the night. At 10 a.m. on the 21st August, after three hours' paddling, we reached Labbang, where we halted for breakfat. The village is built where an affluent of that name enters the Bintulu. It is a deep stream, and can be ascended in boats for five or six days, its waters flowing slowly in a flooded expanse between low banks covered with dense vegetation.

Labbang village consists of three or four houses on piles, like those of every other village on the Bintulu. The floating landing-stage was made of very big tree-trunks, and my men preferred to cook their rice on this to doing so in the houses, which are small, dirty and most uncomfortable. The people here are true Mellanaos, but they have assumed some of the customs of the Kayans, and have the same weapons. The men in the jungle wear merely the *jawat*, but when at home dress as Malays. The women have wide trousers, and a long *baju* or jacket of dark blue cotton cloth, with long open sleeves ornamented with brass buttons or rings, the dress on the whole being very similar to that of the Bintulese. In this part of the country the banks of the Bintulu are cleared only for about a hundred yards from the water's edge—a sign that rice is grown.

At noon we got into the sampan and started again, paddling for five hours. The current was not very strong, but the water was very muddy ; the banks, which rise some six feet above the water, are level and dry. There were said to be many crocodiles here, and that they were dangerous, but we saw little enough in the way of animal life. We passed the night on the bank, as the ground was dry, and sleeping in the boat was very inconvenient on account of the small space available, most of it being taken up by our luggage and provisions. No more villages or even detached huts were to be met with until we reached the Kayan territory.

In the afternoon I had an attack of fever. At 7 p.m. violent rain came on suddenly, with lightning and loud crashes of thunder. It rained the whole night through, and yet this is the height of the dry season ! The Malays slept well, although their bed was far from being a comfortable one ; and I had some difficulty in waking up my men next morning ! The rain had caused the river to rise, but the current was not sufficient to stop our ascent of the stream. The river banks were now very picturesque, no longer level and uniform, but varied with hills, and here and there a projecting precipitous bluff, on which great trees had taken root, spreading huge branches covered with epiphytes over the river. Some giant banyans, too, cast the shadow of their colossal foliage over the stream, and while their myriads of glossy leaves, bathed in shimmering light, seemed to strive upward for still freer contact with the air, the attractions of Mother Earth seemed not less great, for countless filamentous rootlets hung from the branches to the surface of the water, where they assumed the appearance of enormous floating wigs. There was not a trace of the presence of Man, and Nature asserted herself in all her savage beauty and grandeur. These are the spots which I delight in, and which offer the richest harvest to the collector; but I could hardly spare the time to examine the vegetation carefully, for I hoped to reach the Kayan village that evening. Suddenly we heard the distant sound of gongs, which told us that some one was coming down the river, and shortly after, on turning a projecting point, we met Pangerang Rio, a Malay in the Sarawak Government service, on his way back to Bintulu. He had gone up the river by order of the Resident, Mr. Houghton, to acquaint the Tubao Kayans of my coming.

It was half-past four in the afternoon when we left the Bintulu and entered the Tubao. I had wished to reach the Kayan village before nightfall; but even in the Tubao the current was strong—on account of the rain of the preceding day—and after an hour's paddling my men were done, and persuaded me to rest for the night at a small isolated hut which we had come to.

This was a Kayan hut, and, although no one was there, contained the usual furniture and utensils of such habitations. The Kayans are not afraid that their houses will be robbed if left without anyone to guard them, at least, in peaceful times, for they have a plan which effectually prevents this, though it is doubtful whether it would be as successful in our more civilised countries. When the owners of a house are obliged to absent themselves and leave it to take care of itself, they place certain tokens in visible places which cause their property to be respected by any casual visitor of their own nationality. Thus, opposite the house which we now entered, a stone was suspended by a strip of rotang to a pole as a warning to any prospective ill-doer that his head would pay for any object taken away and appropriated by him. Apparently the same signification was to be attributed to a piece of wood cut in the shape of a parang, which was also suspended from a pole near some planks of bilian or iron-wood lying outside the hut.

I believe that it is not so much the fear of material punishment which causes this form of tabu to be so strictly respected as that of the malediction which, on setting up these charms, the proprietor pronounces against the transgressor audacious enough to possess himself of objects placed under *pamali*, or *mattang*, as the Malays term it.

The river here had overflowed its banks and deposited quantities of vegetable detritus around the hut, which I searched through, taking advantage of the remaining daylight. My search was amply rewarded, and I collected quite a number of small land shells and insects, especially micro-Coleoptera, but, unfortunately, all these specimens were afterwards lost. It rained again late at night; but we were this time under a shelter much better than that of the mats or " kadjans " of our narrow sampan.

In the morning it was still raining, but as soon as I had taken my tea we started towards Tubao, as the Kayan village is called, like the river. This latter is tortuous and torrential, and runs between narrow banks covered by vegetation of secondary growth. No forest was in sight, neither did I see any large isolated trees except a few Minuangs. We frequently met with tombs : two were remarkable; but that of Kam-Lassa, a Kayan chief recently deceased, surpassed all the rest in size and decorations. It had the form of a large shed, with a roof surmounted by a carved and perforated ridge of excellent workmanship, and supported by columns of bilian wood. I was told that it was the work of a Bruni artist, and had cost fifty pikuls of bronze objects, especially gongs ; an enormous sum for these countries.[1] Some tombs were merely marked by a board fixed upright, with white, yellow and red streamers stuck around, or even fastened on the branches of the nearest shrubs.

The village of Tubao, where we arrived two hours later, consisted only of four houses ; but they were very large ones and well built, in an elevated position, for the river bank is high. Three of the houses were exceedingly long ; the fourth was much smaller. Each house was, as usual, divided into as many apartments (*pintu*) as the number of the families which lived in the house. The biggest house had twenty-seven *pintus* ; the second, twenty-two ; the third, thirteen, and the smaller one only six.

I took up my quarters in the house with thirteen *pintus*. Like the others, it was built on piles, which raised its platform or flooring about twenty-five feet from the ground, and it was reached by a slender tree-trunk, with deep notches at regular intervals which served as steps ; though it certainly looked much more like a roosting-ladder for poultry than the staircase leading to a human habitation, and required no small acrobatic ability in those who had to climb it. Like Dyak houses the building was span-roofed, and the inside was similarly divided longitudinally into two nearly equal compartments, the front one forming a kind of long common corridor or covered verandah without partitions, where the inhabitants assemble to smoke, work, and chatter ; the back half being divided into apartments or chambers, which appeared to me more spacious and cleaner than those of the Dyaks which I had seen. It must be remarked, however, that this house was of recent construction.

The roof was partly covered with ataps, and partly with flat tiles of bilian wood slightly imbricated, and must thus have been very durable, this wood being all but indestructible. The

[1] The *pikul* is equivalent to 133⅓ pounds avoirdupois, and is divided into 100 kattis.

flooring was much better than that usually met with in such houses, being formed of boards thinned with the adze ; and similar planks were used for the divisions between the *pintus*.

The most valuable things in this house were immense planks of a beautiful wood used for squatting on by chiefs holding councils, and also as beds: They were of a very hard close-grained wood of a deep red colour, taking a beautiful polish, and, to my thinking, finer and superior in quality to the best mahogany. The plank on which I had laid my " tilang " or bedding was over two inches thick, eight feet in length, and six in width. At Sarawak, in the possession of a European, I have seen bigger planks, but I did not note their dimensions.[1] At first I was puzzled by the extraordinary dimensions of these planks, for I could hardly imagine that there were trees with trunks big enough to furnish such sections. But later the manner in which they were obtained was explained to me, and I was also able to see them cut.

The tree from which they are obtained is that king of the forest the tapang (*Abauria excelsa*), whose colossal dimensions I have already described.[2] If one looks at the base of a large tapang it is easy to understand how the above-described huge planks are obtained, for the *Abauria* is one of those trees which produce vast buttresses around their base. These great laminar projections, called by the natives " *banner*," are in some cases of immense size, and at the same time so smooth and thin that by cutting them at their origin from the trunk, and at the ground level, planks like those described can be obtained at but little trouble and expense, and without either cutting down the tree or doing it any injury. I afterwards met with specimens of tapang in the forest which still bore the traces of having thus been operated upon, and which did not seem to have suffered in any way.

In the houses at Tubao we only found three women, all of whom were ailing. The entire population was away preparing the ground for rice sowing. Pangerang Rio had, however, announced my arrival to the chiefs. The Pangerang, a native of Bruni, had managed to become the factotum of Bintulu, and was employed by the Resident in his communications with the inland chiefs. I learnt from the Tubao Kayans that Pangerang Rio had ordered there 2,000 small parcels of siri for the Government, but I am inclined to think that they were a personal compensation for his trip.

In the afternoon one of the Kayan chiefs named Tummusong called on me. He was a tall fine-looking young man of serious expression, who sported a tuft of beard on one side of his chin, the other being completely bare. His hands were tattooed : a distinction

[1] Mr. St. John (*Op. cit.* i. p. 102) mentions a tapang plank 10 ft. 6 in. long, and 6 ft. 6 in. wide, and another 15 ft. by 9 ft.
[2] Cf. *ante*, p. 109.

special to chiefs who have shown courage and killed their man in the wars.

Tummusong and his companions had a good look at me, and next proceeded to examine my things, asking questions and desiring explanations on everything. But what struck their fancy most were the small bottles and glass tubes in which I preserved insects. Having a good assortment, I gave them a few as presents, and saw at once that they were much pleased.

Rain fell nearly all day, and I remained in the houses allaying the curiosity of the Kayans on one side and mine on the other, for I gathered much information on their customs and habits and on their country. I was specially anxious to ascertain where I could find the camphor tree, and the iron ore from which the Kayans extract the metal for their weapons, desiring to go next day in search of both.

It continued to rain during the night; but the morning of the 24th was fine, and at 8 a.m. I started in my sampan up the Tubao after the camphor tree. My Malays had added to their number two natives from the interior of a tribe unknown to me, who had been engaged to serve me as guides by Pangerang Rio. After having paddled for a couple of hours, I found out that these natives were perfect strangers to the country, and were ignorant of even the name of the hills where the camphor trees grew. Moreover, they did not understand a single word of the Bintulu dialect. I therefore turned back to try and find more suitable guides for my work.

On my return to the village I found that other Kayans had arrived. Some came from neighbouring villages on purpose to get medicines from me. They appeared to be quite mad on medicine. Ammonia, as always amongst such people, created a great sensation. The wry faces of those who placed their noses on the bottle containing it were greeted with peals of laughter. All wanted to smell it, and all wanted to have a look inside my medicine chest, and then would load me with questions as to its contents. It seemed as if they were quite sorry not to be ill in order to have an occasion of experiencing the effects of all these remedies on themselves. The fact of possessing the means of healing disease was quite enough to raise me to the dignity of a wizard or sorcerer in their eyes. Indeed, one or two showed me the palm of their hands that I might, from the signs thereon, predict their fortune. To them the physician and the wizard are one and the same, and I contributed to the strengthening of their belief by shooting a bird on the wing. Their surprise became stupor when they saw me handle unharmed an innocent millipede (*Iulus*), which they consider highly poisonous.

In the evening more Kayans arrived, and with them their chief, Kam Nipa, a well-made and active young man about thirty years of age, most civil and intelligent, and owner of the house in which I was staying. He spoke Malay fluently, and did not bother me with continual questions, as most of his fellow tribesmen did. His wife, Henan-Riam, was suffering from ague, and asked me for quinine. She was a fine young woman with a sweet and pleasing expression, and of very light complexion. I was told that the Kayan women were true Amazons, following their husbands on their war expeditions, when they replace the *badang* (petticoat) with the *jawat*, and,

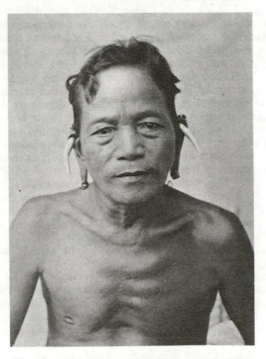

Fig. 46.—ORANG-KAYA TUMANGGONG, KAYAN CHIEF
OF THE BARRAM RIVER.

donning the characteristic coat of goat-skin, arm themselves with the parang-ilang and a spear, and carry a large wooden shield.

Later, the Kayans got up an entertainment for me in the shape of a dance, towards which I contributed the candles. It was very different from the usual Dyak dances, which consist of various contortions and ungraceful movements. The Kayan dance—at least the one I saw—was, instead, a kind of warlike pantomime, with no lack of broad humour, with the *kroré* as orchestral accompaniment.   This is a singular modification of the ubiquitous Pan's pipes, consisting of six slender bamboo tubes, tied together like the pipes of an organ, and inserted in a pear-shaped gourd with a longish neck open at its end.   The mouth is applied to this, and each tube has a finger-hole on one side.   It might also be compared to a bagpipe : the gourd substitutes the bag, and, instead of a single tube with several finger-holes, we have here several tubes each with one hole.   A musical instrument similar to the one now described, but bigger, is used in Siam.

Next day I was able to find a Kayan, named Kam-Uan, who, with two others, undertook to guide me to Gunong Sedaha, the hill on which the camphor tree grows.   I started at 8 a.m., having four of my men in addition to the three Kayans.   I agreed to give each of my Kayan guides four fathoms of red cotton cloth.   We ascended the Tubao for about three hours and reached a lanko, from which the road leading to Gunong Sedaha starts.   The hill was not far off, and after the usual frugal rice dinner we directed our steps towards it without loss of time.   The forest begins about a mile from the river, and extends over the hills, and we had hardly entered it before we came on camphor trees (*Dryobalanops*) of large size, which were quite abundant.   Here, however, as in all Bornean forests, no species of tree predominates so as to influence the aspect of the forest.   The various species are intermingled ; and when I say that the camphor trees were abundant, I mean that perhaps amongst thirty or forty big trees belonging to different families and widely different species, one or two *Dryobalanops* were to be found.   The locality had certainly been often visited, for most of the trunks of the camphor trees bore evident signs of having been tapped.[1]

Wishing to preserve herbarium specimens of the authentic species which produces camphor in the Bintulu region, I had one of the smaller trees cut down, but in its trunk I only found a small quantity of viscid and highly odoriferous yellow oil.

The collecting of camphor is a very uncertain operation, for although a good number of the trees may contain the precious resin in their trunks, few have it in such quantities as to repay the trouble of extraction.   As in the case of most things where luck comes into play, it is connected with many superstitions ; a rule, by the way, which holds good not only with savages, but also with the less educated amongst civilised nations.   I do not think that any one has as yet described the process of collecting camphor in Borneo, and the following notes may therefore be of interest.

When the Kayans decide to start on a camphor-collecting expe-

[1] According to some travellers (Low, *Op. cit.*, p. 45), the camphor tree is found near the Sarawak.   This, however, is not the true tree, but an allied species which produces excellent timber, but no camphor.

dition they hold a meeting, and begin by seeking an omen through birds. This being good they start; and if in the forest one of their number dreams of women, rice, fish, and various other things in accordance with their fancies, they feel sure of good luck. The fortunate one who has dreamt the dream of good omen begins to tap the chosen trunk, notching it deeply just above the foot. But it appears that

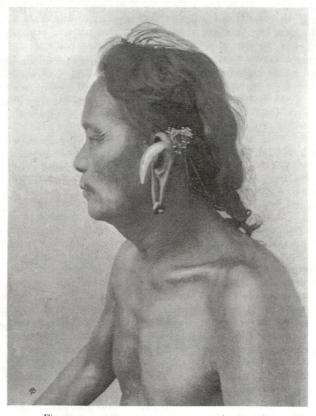

Fig. 47.—ORANG-KAYA TUMANGGONG (PROFILE).

the dreams for camphor successes are very like those for a lucky number in a lottery, for both in the plains and on the hills I met with many a notched camphor tree—a certain proof of negative results.

The first notch is usually cut at about five feet from the ground, and experienced searchers can tell from the smell of the wood if there is or is not any camphor worth the getting. Trees which have been once tried, after a certain time are tried again a little higher up. Sometimes one sees them with three or four of these notches up the trunk. One I saw, which was quite 160 feet high, with the cylindrical portion of its trunk above the butt about three and a half feet in diameter, had three notches partly healed up. Kam-Uan was of opinion that this tree ought to be now rich in camphor, judging by the smell given off by the chips of its wood, and he asserted that he would return to look for it as soon as he had dreamt a favourable dream. In collecting camphor, the Kayans of the Tubao do not fell the tree, but proceed in the following manner. Having ascertained that the tree is productive, they deepen the trial notch and then make another one above it. If this shows camphor they cut a third notch higher still, and so on until no more of the precious secretion is to be seen. Then the trunk is split longitudinally, and all the wood between the notches cut out. It is divided into small pieces, and the resin, which lies in the fissures between the fibres and layers of the wood, is picked and scraped out.

From other sources I learnt that in some other localities in the Bintulu district the tree is felled and cut up into as many portions as there are members of the party, each one extracting the camphor from his own piece. Sometimes, instead of camphor in a solid condition, a soft variety is found, which is whitish and of a mucilaginous nature. Such a find may be the cause of a tragedy, for by a curious association of ideas it is thought to be a proof of infidelity on the part of the wife of the discoverer. I have been told that it has happened in such cases that the unfortunate finder, stung by the jeers of his companions, has rushed home and killed his supposed unfaithful wife without further explanation.

Strange stories are told by the Kayans of transformations of the camphor which is being collected into cigars and siri leaves, but this, no doubt, is the work of some clever light-fingered member of the party. The camphor hunters must only talk of women and erotic subjects; they must wear no article of dress besides the *jawat*. The *priok*—the vessel for cooking rice—must not be used; and they must not indulge either in siri or tobacco. This is saying a good deal, for the Kayans, like the Dyaks, prefer going without rice to depriving themselves of tobacco.

The camphor tree of the Kayan country attains a great size. Its bark is of a dark colour, and comes off in thin flakes. At the base the trunk is wider, but does not throw out true laminar buttresses or *banner*. Botanically, the tree must be considered a true *Dryobalanops*, but it is specifically different from that which produces camphor in Sumatra, and from any other hitherto described. It may be distinguished under the name of *D. Kayanensis* (P.B., No. 3,734). The camphor it produces is found both in large and small trees, and no external sign indicates its presence. In a large tree as much as fourteen or fifteen pounds of the drug may be found; but this is a rare and fortunate occurrence, for Borneo camphor has a value about twenty times greater than that of the Chinese drug. At Bintulu the price of a katty (1⅓ lb.) then varied from nine to ten pieces of *blaju* (common white unbleached calico). The pieces of red cotton cloth (*sumba mera*) have a higher price, whilst yellow cotton cloth (*sumba kuning*) is less valuable than the red, but more so than the white.

We slept in the forest, and early next morning began to climb the hill, which is far less formidable than it had been described to me. Camphor trees abounded all the way up. We reached the summit in a couple of hours, and found its elevation to be about 1,574 feet. The thermometer stood at 77° Fahr., and the aneroid marked 721·3 millim. In a streamlet which flows down the side of the hill I collected three species of Gasteropod molluscs. The hill is of argillaceous sandstone, very friable and easily decomposed, and in consequence the waters of the brook were turbid, an unusual thing in Borneo. Finding nothing of much interest, we soon descended to the plain, following the way we had taken on our climb up, and returned by the river to Tubao village. That evening I gave my guides the compensation I had promised them, and distributed glass beads, or *manet*, to the women and children, which made them very friendly towards me, indeed, rather too much so.

As I was talking with the Kayans around me I heard weeping and loud lamentations issuing from a house next to the one I occupied, and on inquiry I learnt that an old man who had been long ill was then dying. The corpse was left lying on the mat that night; but the next morning it was dressed up in the deceased's best clothes, and placed in a sitting posture, with siri and a cigar in the mouth. The body was to be buried three days later, and in the interval the wooden coffin was made. I was told that the bodies of chiefs are kept exposed thus in their houses eight days before they are buried. After some time, as far as I could make out, the body is exhumed; the bones are collected and enclosed in a new coffin, together with a part of the belongings of the deceased. There is also the singular custom that, if on returning from a burial the women meet men, they bespatter them with mud, or any kind of filth that they can lay hands on. Another strange custom is called "*Bolen*," and consists in a fine in merchandise, varying in value from ten to twenty dollars, which the first traveller or trader who arrives in the village after a death is obliged to pay.

The Tubao Kayans appeared to me a finer and more vigorous race than the Dyaks. Not a few were tall and as well-proportioned as any Greek statue. Their usual dress consists merely of the *jawat* of cotton cloth, and this is the only garment they wear when engaged in rice cultivation or hunting in the forest. When on a war expedition they put on a curious coat made of goat's skin, or, more rarely, of that of the bear or leopard, which serves as an efficient protection against the poisoned arrows of the sumpitan. In shape it may be compared to a short South American poncho, being oblong and with a hole in the middle through which the head passes, one half hanging down in front the other half behind, thus leaving the arms free.[1] This war dress is completed by a singular cap

Fig. 48.—A KINYA ; WITH EYEBROWS AND EYELASHES
EXTIRPATED.

or hat ornamented with big feathers, usually those of the hornbill. The above-described poncho is also often covered with similar feathers. Ear ornaments, often of gold and of fine workmanship, are commonly worn ; and, like the Punans, the Kayans are very

[1] We may regard this species of poncho as the primitive type of dress, worn on ceremonial occasions alike by the fakir of the Far East, and by the Pope, when he officiates in St. Peter's at Rome!

rarely without two big canine teeth, either of the bear or leopard, passed through the upper portion of the cartilage of each ear, with the point turned outwards and downwards, imparting a singular ferocity to the aspect of these men. I have seen facsimiles of this peculiar ornament made of gold and retained in the ear by a sort of head or button, which was very finely and artistically worked. I was unable to learn whence the Kayans get so

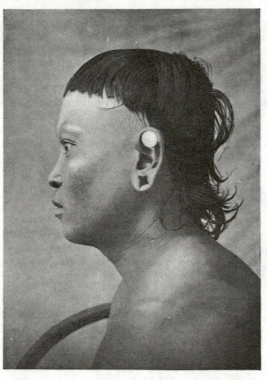

Fig. 49.—A KINYA (SAME SUBJECT IN PROFILE).

many canine teeth of the tree leopard (*Felis nebulosa*), which, according to my experience, is quite rare in Borneo. Probably it is more abundant in the interior of the north-east portion of the island than in the parts I explored, but, no doubt, many of these ornaments must have been handed down from father to son for many generations.

The Tubao Kayans do not file their teeth to a point as the Dyaks do, but they shorten the upper incisors and stain them black. This is done with a vegetable dye, the juice of the large fleshy leaves of a Melastomacea (*Medinillopsis Beccariana*, Cogn., P. B., No. 4,004). The hair is cut short in front, but worn long behind, flowing down over the shoulders. They often wear rings of plaited fibre or of brass below the knee.

Tattooing is in general use, and is practised as an ornament, or as a sign of tribal distinction. The men are usually tattooed on the hands, and the pattern consists of transverse bands, equal in number to that of the heads obtained, beginning from the wrist and going towards the fingers. Many have stars or dragons tattooed on the arms and chest. The women are much more tattooed than the men. I saw some with the hands and lower half of the forearm covered with designs, and the feet and legs up to the knee. A full tattooing may cost as much as twenty-five to thirty dollars' worth of bronze objects. Thus the greater or lesser extent of the tattooing may be looked upon as in a measure representing the wealth of the individual.

The dress of the women is more complicated than that of the men. As usually worn it consists of a cotton cloth, often parti-coloured, tied round the waist and open on one side. They also use, but not always, a baju or jacket, and at night a sort of sarong as a wrapper.

The Kayans, when they wish to cement a solemn tie of friend-ship, undergo the ceremony of blood-exchange. This is, however, less imposing than might be imagined, for it merely consists in getting a few drops of blood by a slight puncture in any part of the body, and placing them in a cigarette. The two neophytes of friendship exchange cigarettes and quietly smoke them, and this comprises the whole ceremony.

The singular operation of " perforatio penis " performed by the Kayans is well known,[1] and another of their peculiarities, prac-tised both by men and women, is carefully to pluck out any hair which grows on their bodies, including eyebrows and eyelashes (Fig. 48–49), the latter operation often causing inflammation of the eyes. Depilation, indeed, appears to be one of the main occu-pations of this people. From what I was led to understand, this custom appears to have arisen from a desire to differ as much as possible from evil spirits, whom they believe to be hairy, like an orang-utan. During subsequent travels in Celebes I found a similar horror of hairiness, and in that island, as in Borneo, a hairy woman is believed to bring bad luck.

The Kayans use the sumpitan and arrows poisoned with upas,[2]

---

[1] Those seeking full particulars on this subject may consult a paper by N. von Miklucho-Maclay, in *Berliner Gesellschaft für Anthrop. Ethnol. u. Urgeschichte*, Meeting of January 19, 1876.

[2] Low (*Op. cit.* p. 53) mentions a poison more powerful than upas,

which, however, they do not make themselves, but get from the
Punans. These are the only kind of arrows used in Borneo, where
the bow appears to be quite unknown. The possibility of obtaining
such a deadly poison as upas must have caused the sumpitan to
supersede the bow. Without this or some similar poison the sumpitan is a harmless weapon and something more efficacious becomes
a necessity. As a proof of this I may instance certain tribes in
South America, who, as is well known, make use of a deadly poison
known as curare, urari, or wourali, prepared from some species of
Strychnos, and are also furnished with a blow-tube, whilst all
the other primitive native tribes of the same region use the bow.

In order to prepare upas poison, the milky sap of *Antiaris toxi-*

Fig. 50.—SHOOTING MONKEYS WITH THE SUMPITAN.
(From the Sculptures of the Boro Budor Temple, Java.)

caria is collected by making incisions in the bark, and is then condensed by exposure to the sun until sufficiently thick to adhere to
the palm leaves on which it is poured. These leaves are folded so
as to cover the gummy sap, and hung up over the fireplace so that
complete desiccation is obtained. When the poison is wanted for
use, the dried sap is dissolved in the juice of the roots of those plants
used for catching fish by poisoning the water generically known as
tuba by the Malays. My informers specified these by the names
of *tuba rabut, tuba tedau*, and *tuba bennar*. The upas must be dissolved
in the juice of one of the above-mentioned kinds—whether fresh or
not does not matter—until the mixture becomes of the consistence
of a paste, and this is spread on the points of the diminutive sum-

the product of a creeper which grows in the Bintulu region. I was, however,
unable to get any further information on this plant, which may possibly
belong to the genus *Strychnos*, of which I found several species in Borneo.

pitan arrows. Other solvents for·the dried sap of the upas are tobacco juice, the sap of the *Hoya imperialis*, and of Dyak gambir, or *kayu seddi*, a Tiliacea of the genus *Elæocarpus*, from which it appears that an astringent juice can be obtained like that of *Uncaria gambir*. Arrows thus prepared preserve their deadly effect for two or three months, and if *kaju seddi* has been used, for as much as a year. I have been told that the Kayans also fix the fangs of poisonous snakes at the extremity of their sumpitan arrows, which are split for their insertion, the fang being secured by a ligature.

The use of upas as a poison (known in other parts of Malaya under the name of *ipo*) is not limited to Borneo, but extends to Java, the Malay Peninsula, and Cochin China.[1] I imagine that the sumpitan was known in a very remote epoch to the primitive populations of the Asiatic continent, whence it must have passed to Borneo. Thus in the grand work on the temple of Boro Budor, published by the Dutch Government, a savage of Aryan type is figured using a sumpitan in plate cix., and on plate clx. men are depicted shooting monkeys with this weapon (Fig. 50).

The sumpitan is not simply a blow-gun, but it is also a spear, being provided with an iron blade in the shape of an olive leaf, with double cutting edges. In war the Kayans, in addition to the sumpitan with its small bamboo quiver for holding the arrows and the parang-ilang already mentioned, carry a large shield of light wood, the *utak*, garnished with tufts of human hair and variously ornamented with arabesques, and usually with a grotesque face with huge eyes and tusks. When fully armed and equipped, wearing the above-described war dress, the singular cuirasse and the cap with tall feathers, the Kayan warrior, with flowing black hair, fine carriage, and fierce expression heightened by the white leopard teeth projecting from his ears, is indeed one of the finest types of savage.

The Kayans are, perhaps, next to the Dyaks, the most numerous of the Bornean people. They are spread over the central portion of the island, and are found on the Bintulu, the Baloi, the Barram, the Limbang, and especially on the Upper Banjar, the Pasir, and the Koti or Kutei. On the Barram river they are very numerous, and some of their villages have a population of 2,500.

The Kayans have great personal courage, are warlike and very enterprising, and they are thus greatly feared by the tribes with whom they are in contact. They have, however, a special fear of firearms, and by means of these weapons the Dyaks, who possess a few, have made themselves respected. They often undertake

---

[1] The sumpitan with which the Semangs of the Malay Peninsula shoot their ipo-poisoned darts is formed by a single internode of the *Bambusa Wrayi*, Stopf. In Cochin China the Moys are said to use ipo.

war expeditions against remote tribes, whom they conquer. Thus
it appears that the Barram Kayans came from the Baloi, and that
previous to their invasion the Barram was inhabited by Kinias.
According to Mr. St. John (*Op. cit.* i. p. 87) the Barram Kayans were
in past times in the habit of attacking villages near Bruni for the
purpose of capturing slaves, whom they carried off. It need, therefore, cause no surprise if several of the tribes inhabiting North-east
Borneo, such as the Muruts, Bisayas, Idahans or Dusuns, and also
the Tedongs and Kajans, have been described by the distinguished
author now quoted as very similar to the Kayans. Moreover, we can
scarcely expect to find uniformity of type in a people who, through
slavery, have for centuries assimilated varied and heterogeneous
elements. It would be interesting with regard to this point to know
whether the Kayans have ever had intercourse with Celebes by the
Koti river ; or, conversely, if the natives of Celebes have had communication with those of Borneo.

On certain occasions, as during the above-described excursion
in quest of camphor, the Kayans deduce omens from birds ; while in
more important ones they also seek them in the entrails of animals,
and especially in the heart of the pig, a practice also in use amongst
the Sakarrang Dyaks.

The Tubao Kayans do not now offer human sacrifices, but I was
assured that the Boajan Kayans of the Upper Banjar sacrifice a
slave when one of their chiefs die, and bury his corpse with that of the
dead chief. I have also heard that certain tribes of the interior,
when about to construct a new house, sacrifice a virgin, burying
her under one of the main piles.

The Kayans are passionately fond of their children, whom they
load with ornaments in the shape of necklaces of differently coloured
glass beads, and especially with large gold, or, more frequently,
brass or tin earrings. These are of great weight in order to distend
the perforation in the lobe of the ear as much as possible, this being
considered a great beauty.

On the Tubao, in addition to the rice and sugar cane, various
kinds of fruit trees are cultivated. I noticed durians, rambutans,
and lemons. The *Coix lachryma*, or Job's Tears, is also sown, the
seeds being used to ornament different portions of ordinary dress,
or for war costumes. The domestic animals of the Kayans, besides
poultry, are a few goats, whose flesh they eat, but which they keep
more especially for the sake of the skins, which, as I have already
mentioned, are used to make war coats or cuirasses.

When not occupied with agricultural work, the Kayans hunt the
boar, or search for camphor, guttapercha or rubber in the forest.
Honey and wax is also found in their country, bees' nests being
abundant on certain trees, such as the tapang (*Abauria excelsa*), the
minuang (*Octomeles Sumatrana*), the mingris (*Dialium* sp.), and the

plai (*Alstonia*, sp.). These trees are considered tribal property, and cannot be felled. This is not the case with the camphor trees, which belong to the finder.

Various Kayan tribes are great collectors of edible birds' nests, but not those of the Tubao, there being no caverns in their territory. The caves inhabited by the small swifts (*Collocalia*) are only found in limestone hills, and these appear to be wanting in the basin of the Bintulu and Rejang rivers. On the other hand, they are frequent from Barram to the Limbang, as well as in the Sarawak district.

The Kayans are able workers in iron, and make finely tempered parangs ; but the notable thing is that they do not work imported iron, but extract it themselves from ore found in their own country.

I have already mentioned the parang-ilang as the characteristic weapon of the Kayans ; but it must be understood that it is not merely a war implement or weapon, but also their ordinary cutting instrument, in common daily use. It is intermediate between a sword and a big knife ; the blade is about twenty inches in length, widest at the end (two to two and a half inches), and narrowing down to the handle. The back of the blade is thick and straight, but the rest is slightly convex on one side and concave on the other, which enables the skilful striker to inflict very deep cuts. I used always to carry one of these parang-ilangs on my excursions, and had acquired some skill in using it, so as to cut off even big branches at a single stroke. But for the Kayans, as well as for the Dyaks, the envied stroke is that which severs a head at a single blow. In unskilful hands the weapon may prove dangerous to the holder, for, on account of the curve of the blade, the cut can only be given in a certain direction, otherwise it is apt to rebound off the object struck, and may then wound the striker.

Parang-ilangs have different names according to the various kinds of accessories and ornaments attached to them. In some, the blade is quite plain ; in others, the back of the widened extremity is cut and worked in ornate patterns, while along the thicker portion, towards the back, bits of brass are often let in. In the common ones the hilt or handle is of wood ; but in the finer sort it is of stag's horn, elaborately carved, and always adorned with tufts of human hair. Every ornament has a meaning and a special name. The scabbard is made of wood, in two longitudinal halves, secured by neat, elegant whippings of rotang. It is also sometimes carved and ornamented with emblematic signs and charms.

The Tubao Kayans take good care of their dogs, which are well fed, and not famished bags of bones as those of the Dyaks. They possess many of them, and use them in chasing the boar, which they kill with spears, never having recourse to traps as the Dyaks do.

The evident prosperity, I might say opulence, of the Tubao Kayans was due to their camphor and guttapercha, which they trade for cotton cloth, glass Venetian beads, and especially for gongs and thick brass wire, which are highly valued by them. Elephant tusks are also articles of very great value in their eyes, one being worth a very large sum. Perhaps this ivory is not an importation, but the produce of elephants run wild, small herds of which are said to roam in the northern portion of the island. Nipa salt is also in high estimation, but less so than amongst tribes who live farther from the sea.

I must say that the reception given me by the Tubao Kayans could not have been more friendly ; but I was beginning to wish to get away from their never-ending visits and everlasting queries, queries which I had often answered for the hundredth time. For every newly arrived Kayan must at once visit the " Orang puti," who had, *nolens volens*, become the lion of the district, and every fresh arrival wanted to see my strange things and ply me with interrogations on them and their uses. I was, therefore, not sorry when my provisions were nearly at an end, and the time came for me to return to Bintulu. To complete the object of my trip to Tubao, however, I still had to secure specimens of the iron ore, and, if possible, see it *in situ*. I had gathered reliable information on the subject, and had also found two Kayans who offered to guide me to the place where the ore was obtained. Accordingly we left Kam Laksa's house early on the morning of the 28th, the two Kayans following in a small boat. Descending the Tubao, we soon came to an affluent, where I left the sampan with my men and got into the Kayans' boat, the former being too heavy for the ascent of the affluent, which is named the Pusso, and is said to be navigable for two days. We had not, however, very far to go, and after two hours' paddling landed on the left bank of the stream. About a quarter of an hour's walk through a jungle of secondary growth took us to a brook with very turbid water, and here the two Kayans, searching in the mud of the bottom, produced several concretions very like roots or rhizomes in shape, from three to six inches in length, and as thick as one's finger. They were crooked and warty, and externally of a brown colour, but on being broken they showed a radiated silvery fracture. Evidently they were concretions of carbonate of iron. This is the ore from which the Kayans extract the iron with which they make their weapons. I regret to say I did not see the process of extraction.

Amongst the few animals collected during this excursion I must mention a big toad, which lives on trees along the rivers and has a loud and singularly cadenced cry, " *Cok-cok-ko-go*," which is heard usually at night. The species, according to my men, is also found in the Sarawak river. Unfortunately, my specimen was lost along with other interesting animals collected during this trip, and I never afterwards got another one. I also found two new palms : one a small very dwarf kind (*Licuala Borneensis*, Becc.), the other also a *Licuala* (*L. olivæformis*, Becc.), but of a very unusual character. The stem was very robust, short, root-like, tortuous, and ringed, covered with the bases of old leaves, and rising from the ground to the height of about two feet. From the midst of the fan-shaped leaves a large branched spadix issued, loaded with fruits as big as olives, of a light yellow colour, and in shape resembling those of *Livistona chinensis*.

Having got back to the Tubao with my booty, I paid the two Kayans and sent them off. We continued to descend the river, and were soon back on the main branch of the Bintulu. Here I got my men to paddle slowly, and we stopped now and then so that I could carefully search the banks for any interesting specimen.

My attention was soon called to a clump of fine palms, with stems some twenty feet high, and six or eight inches in diameter ; the stems were not smooth, but covered by the bases of the old fronds. These palms turned out to be a new and most distinct species of Arenga (*Arenga undulatifolia*, Becc.). Like the common *Arenga saccharifera*, the Kayans call it "Appin," and use it for a variety of purposes. The fact that both yield timber explains the native name, for "Appin" is evidently derived from the Malay word for fire. The wood of *A. undulatifolia* is hard externally, but soft and rich in fecula within, so that it yields a species of sago. The central bud, or cabbage, is excellent eating, and from the hard cortical layer of the midrib, which splits easily longitudinally, the Kayans make their sumpitan darts or arrows.

It is a most important peculiarity of the Bornean forest that it possesses a large number of useful and food-yielding species which require no culture. Thus in Borneo the savage can live on forest produce : a thing which cannot be said of any other Asiatic island, including New Guinea.

We camped for the night a little below the entrance to the Tubao. The current was then slight, but during spring tides their effect is felt up the Bintulu as far as this point.

On the 29th we continued our way down the river ; and on getting to the part already mentioned where the banks are high and picturesque and covered with fine and varied vegetation. I noticed at a considerable distance a very showy plant, with large leaves, and a stem about three feet high terminated by spikes of brilliant red flowers about two inches long. It was a new plant of the order Melastomaceæ, which Dr. Cogniaux has recently named after me *Beccarianthus pulcher*.

I met for the first time, too, a very singular bird, which my men called " Undang-undang." When I first saw it, it was perched on a tree, and as it was out of range, I fired to make it rise, which it did, soaring like a hawk. The tail was long like that of a hornbill ; the neck, which it moved continuously, was also long and very slender; indeed, on account of its neck, I at first thought the bird had a snake in its bill. My men said it was an aquatic bird, that it dived, and had webbed feet. Although I was most anxious to secure it, this time the coveted prize escaped me.

Along the banks of the river cleared of forest minuangs (*Octomeles Sumatrana*) are frequent—a tree I have already mentioned which belongs to the " tapang " group; that is, those on which honey bees build their nests. One isolated specimen I could see from the boat showed long brown spikes hanging from the ends of the smaller branches, and on getting near it I perceived from the fragments on the ground that it bore female flowers. I was, therefore, anxious to secure specimens, as the plant was not well known to botanists ; but when, after fully an hour's labour, we had felled the tree, I discovered to my regret that the flowers were over, and utterly useless for scientific investigation.

On the morning of the 30th, in order to save time, I had the rice for the day cooked before starting. The most notable plant I saw was a Dipterocarp (*P.B.*, No. 3,755), a splendid tree, literally covered with large flowers of a light yellow colour, giving off a sweet vanilla odour. The *Daun balik angin*, the fine *Clerodendron discolor* which I had observed on the Sarawak river, was very common here, as elsewhere on the banks of the Bintulu.

The river flowed through a plain from which the forest had been cleared for some hundreds of yards from the waterside. These were the fields of the Labbang Mellanaos, whom we found at work on them, preparing to plant rice. Some were engaged in burning the jungle, and this being of secondary growth contained many bamboos, which exploded when on fire with reports like musket shots. When the ground is thus cleared, a man with a long pointed pole makes holes in the soil, in which a woman, who follows close behind him, throws a few grains of rice. It rained nearly the whole day. We slept at Pandan, a small village at the mouth of a stream which bears the same name, on the right bank of the Bintulu. The village consisted of ten or twelve houses, and was inhabited by Bintulu Mellanaos intermingled with Pennans.

The Pandan can be ascended in boats for six days, and it is on the upper portion of its course, or " ulu," as the Malays say, that the Pennans are numerous. It is there, also, that the *kajatau* (probably *Eugeissonia utilis*), which produces a good quality of sago, the principal food of the natives, is said to be plentiful. The Pandan at a certain place divides into two branches : the principal one appears to trend eastwards; the other, called the Bigno, turns, it is said, in an opposite direction, and is stated to be navigable for four days. I was afterwards told that it issues from a lake in which sea fish live, and whose waters during the dry season are salt.

The Pennans, like the Punans and the Buketans, have no settled dwellings and do not cultivate rice. They live mainly on the sago produced by the *kajatau* and on wild animals, which they kill with the sumpitan darts, poisoned with upas, which they prepare themselves. They wear the canine teeth of the tree-leopard passed through the upper portion of the ear, as the Kayans do; indeed, they resemble these latter in many ways.

My collections went on increasing by the addition of many interesting specimens. On the last day of August I got a new species of durian (*P.B.*, No. 4,019). It was a great isolated tree, rising in a cleared spot, evidently an old forest giant which had been preserved when the land had been cleared all round for cultivation. It was then in blossom, the flowers being, as in the true durian, on the big branches, and having a delicious perfume of ripe apples. In my remarks on the durians (Cf. *Malesia*, vol. iii.), I have considered the one found on this occasion as referable to *D. carinatus*, but, nevertheless, as a distinct variety (var. *Bintulensis*, Becc.). However, the typical *D. carinatus* does not produce edible fruits, and as the specimen I have just described had been evidently preserved when its forest companions had been without any exception destroyed, there are good reasons to suppose that this was done by the natives because they knew it to be a useful tree. Thus when the fruits of the wild durian of the Bintulu are known, it may be that we shall have to add a new species to the long list of trees growing wild in the forests of Borneo which produce edible fruit.

When we were approaching the sea, on the muddy banks where the river had formed a small island I noted some clumps of *Licuala paludosa*[1] about sixteen feet high, which, with their colour and the elegant shape of their fronds, brightened the monotonous aspect of the vegetation, here composed almost entirely of nipas. I found, also, some specimens of *Cyrtostachys Lakka*,[2] another handsome palm, easily remarked at a distance on account of the bright red colour of the ensheathing portion of its fronds which covers the upper portion of the stem. During this excursion I found but few orchids; and such as I got were only species with small and inconspicuous flowers.

At 4 p.m. we came in for another deluge, but after a couple of hours' paddling we at length reached Fort Bintulu.

[1] This is one of the few palms I met with on the Bintulu which is not peculiar to that region. *Licuala paludosa* is found on the Malay Peninsula and in Siam; its presence in Borneo is explained by its aquatic habits, enabling its seeds to be carried afar much more easily than those of other palms.

[2] This species is also found at Singapore, and is nearly allied to the *Cyrtostachys Rendah* of Sumatra. The observations made above concerning *Licuala paludosa* are applicable to this tree also, for it grows in flooded tracts subject to the influence of the tides, and its seeds are able to resist the action of salt water, so that it has every facility for a wide dispersal.

CHAPTER XIX

SAGO MAKING AT BINTULU—DEPARTURE FOR THE INTERIOR—A PRIMITIVE
BOAT—UP THE BINTULU RIVER—A DANGEROUS ADVENTURE—WE
ARE FORCED TO RETURN—THE UNDANG-UNDANG—AN AQUATIC FERN
—THIRD DEPARTURE FOR THE INTERIOR—SUBAQUEOUS SOUNDS—A
FORTUNATE MEETING—THE PAMALI ON THE TUBAO—I FORCE THE
PASS—WITH THE KAYANS—NOVEL KIND OF IDOL—ASCENT OF THE
TUBAO—DISEASES OF THE KAYANS—INFLUENCE OF FLOODS ON PLANTS
—THE BELLAGA HILLS—ON THE REJANG.

THE first days of September were employed in drying and
arranging the plants collected on the last excursion. Meanwhile my zoological collections were enriched by several novelties,
amongst others a fine squirrel I had not seen before, which had been
captured and dropped by a hawk. Having some spare time, I took
the opportunity of going over to the Bintulu houses to watch the
sago-making operations which were going on. At any hour of any
day one was pretty certain to find some one thus engaged.

At Bintulu an adult sago palm is worth from one to three dollars,
and can give from three to fifteen *passos* (eighteen to ninety gallons)
of " *lamanta*," or pure sago, three *passos* of which cost one dollar.
The Bintulu sago is of the finest quality, and is in great request,
even in Sarawak.

The palm which produces true sago has a thick stem from
twenty-five to thirty-five feet high, which can hardly be encircled
by a man's arms. It blossoms only once in its lifetime, and dies
with the ripening of its fruits. The natives have discovered that
the time when the nutritive pith is accumulated in greatest
quantity amongst the fibres in the stem is just before the blossoming.
The tree is then felled, its trunk cleaned of the leaves, and cut in
sections about three feet in length. These are carried to the river,
tied together, and, being very light, are easily floated down the
stream. When they are got to the houses they are split in
halves lengthwise, and are then ready for the operation called
" *palo*." This consists of breaking up the soft fibrous tissue
filled with fecula which occupies (with the exception of a thin,
hard external part) the entire mass of the stem. For this purpose a wooden implement shaped like a hoe is used.[1] The next

[1] In the Molucca Islands, and in New Guinea as far as Humboldt Bay,
on the north coast, I have observed the same kind of implement employed

process is called "*chinchian*," and its object is to separate the fecula from the fibres detached by the *palo*. This is done by placing the triturated contents of the emptied trunk on a wide wooden board, and beating them for a long time with a big wooden knife. Then follows the "*tindjak*," which consists of washing the mass broken up by the "*chinchian*," which is done in a large and peculiar basket made with plaited strips about half an inch in width, and cut from the huge ribs of the fronds of the sago palm itself. Instead of baskets, large mats made of the same material are sometimes used.

The operation of "*tindjak*," or washing, is performed by placing the pith in the mat or basket, and treading it steadily with the bare feet while an assistant pours water over it from time to time. Even the pails used for this purpose are constructed from the sago palm. They are conical in shape, and are made from the thin laminar and coriaceous portion of the base of the fronds where they encircle the stem. This method of treading the baskets with the feet causes the stuff expressed to be carried off by the water through the meshes of the mat or basket, and to collect in a vessel placed beneath, which is usually a small canoe. Here it settles down, and after the water has been drained off constitutes what the natives call "*lamanta*." After it has been dried and reduced to a granular form (pearling) it becomes the sago we all know. All the above described operations are performed in the outhouses or sheds, which, as I have already mentioned, are connected with the Mellanao houses on the river-side.

My preparations once more to ascend the Bintulu river, and to pass from this river to the Barram, were by this time nearly finished. The object of the excursion was Gunong Julit, of which I had heard all sorts of wonderful stories. They also told me that a species of wild tobacco was to be found, and this I was, of course, anxious to get. From information I had received this mountain lay half-way between the Bintulu and the Tinjar rivers ; the latter a branch of the Barram, which I had resolved to descend to its mouth, and to get thence to Miri.

On the fourth of September I went in a canoe to the Mellanao houses, to see whether I could get a large and sufficiently commodious boat for my journey to the Tinjar. Returning to the fort I noticed a singular floating object in the middle of the river, and on getting nearer I found that it was a diminutive house, or rather the facsimile of one, embellished with tassels and streamers made with the young white leaves of the nipa palm. Curiosity impelled me to ascertain its contents ; but the natives who were with me begged me not to

in this same work ; but the implement differs. Thus in the Moluccas the "business end" is made with a piece of bamboo, whilst in New Guinea it is of stone.

touch it, for the " Antus," or spirits, to whom the Mellanao had
dedicated the little house to obtain some favour would be irritated
by my profanation and seek revenge. Another time I think I shall
abstain from meddling with any such object, and pretend to believe
in what the natives tell me, but on this occasion I was determined
to get hold of the thing and examine it, in spite of the protests of
my men, and, as it turned out, I had a smart attack of fever that
very evening. This made me reflect that fever is easily caught in
Bintulu, and that the spirits must find it an easy matter to revenge
themselves on unbelievers. Anyhow I was sorry that, through my
want of faith, I had involuntarily contributed to intensify that of
my men in their superstitions.

From the time I arrived at Bintulu we had heavy showers of
rain each day, and even on the morning of the 6th, on which I had
arranged to start for the Tinjar, it deluged. At Bintulu I did not
succeed in finding a sampan adapted for my journey, but I was
told that I should certainly get one without difficulty at Pandan ;
so having found a boat to take me and my belongings as far as this
latter place, and the weather having cleared up, I finally got off
an hour after noon.

When I got to Pandan, a difficulty arose with my men, who
now declared that they did not want to proceed to the Barram, as
they had just learnt that the country was no longer safe, war having
broken out between Tummuson and Kam Lia, two influential Kayan
chiefs. I thought it probable, however, that this was only a *canard*,
and later it turned out that the news had been brought by a Buketan,
who was evidently insane. This individual had recently arrived at
Pandan in a boat made of a sheet of bark. I did not see him,
but I saw his canoe, which was, indeed, a most primitive concern.
Its construction had merely required a middle-sized tree with smooth
tough bark devoid of cracks and easily detached from the wood,
and such trees abound in the forests of Borneo. The tree being
selected, it is ringed with two circular incisions at the distance
required by the length of the canoe ; the bark between the two
cuts is then carefully detached for two-thirds of the entire circumference, and has naturally the required shape. The extremities
are sewn up with strips of rotang, the gunwales are kept apart with
a couple of transverse sticks, and the canoe is ready. Should any
cracks appear they are closed with clay.

I sent my guide in search of a boat, but the Orang-Kaya Laghin,
who was not anxious to let me have it, used every possible argument
to dissuade me from going to Tinjar. After much palaver I was,
however, able to get a decent sampan ; but when it was ready,
covered with the *kadjans*, and loaded with our supplies and luggage,
I found to my dismay that it would not hold us without capsizing.
I was thus obliged to waste more time to find a second boat in order

to divide the load. It was 2 p.m. when at last we were ready. I entered the larger boat with five men, and the three Kayans embarked in the other.

That evening we stopped to cook our dinner on the banks of the river, but slept in the boats and had a bad night. In the middle, where I lay down, the edge of the sampan was only an inch or two above the water-line, and we were obliged to move with great caution to avoid capsizing. And here the danger was not merely that of an unpleasant nocturnal bath in the river and the loss of traps and provisions, but of becoming food for crocodiles, which were both numerous and ferocious in this part of the river. My guide told me that at that very spot a few days before a woman paddling in her boat had been carried off by one of these voracious reptiles; while on another occasion a man, likewise in his canoe, had been seized by the arm, but he managed to draw his parang with the other hand, and, with a vigorous cut on the crocodile's snout, succeeded in freeing himself. His arm was literally bored through and through by the creature's fangs, and he was besides badly scratched on the back by its claws.

We had violent rain during the latter part of the night. These everlasting deluges annoyed me, because I foresaw that the river would swell and our progress be rendered slower and more difficult. We reached Labbang at 10 a.m. on the ninth of September. Although early, we stayed there to cook our rice, knowing that we should not find a convenient spot higher up until late in the evening. The whole day we continued to ascend the Bintulu, and found a suitable place, high and dry, for passing the night more comfortably than in the boats; but again rain came to spoil our plans. Even the next day we did not succeed in reaching Tubao. The river continued to rise, the current increased, and so did the indolence of my men; indeed, more than once I lost all patience with them, but with little or no effect. The worst of all was a rascal named Bakar, not my faithful Malay boy, but a man of the same name engaged at Bintulu, who was to act as guide and interpreter. He was an undersized youth, as stupid as an owl, out of whom I could scarcely get a word. He spent most of his time in rolling nipa cigarettes, and then lighting them with his flint and steel.

Towards evening we got to the mouth of the Tubao, but could not enter it on account of the violence of the current. As it was getting late, we entered a bend of the river close by, where we found a lanko on a dry part of the bank, and, as the place was also sheltered from the strong current, I decided to pass the night there. We all dined on shore; but I went with two men to sleep in the boat, which was secured to a branch projecting over the water. I had slept badly for several nights, owing to fever and rheumatic pains, but that night I felt better, and turning in under my mosquito curtain was soon sound asleep. In the middle of the night I was suddenly awakened by water pouring into the boat on one side. I rushed to the other to find water coming in there also ; and at the same time discovered that the stern was being submerged. It was rather a critical moment : the night was as dark as pitch, the river running with a very strong current, not to mention the crocodiles, while to make matters worse I was entangled in the mosquito curtains, from which I had some difficulty in freeing myself. As soon as I did so I rushed forward, and catching hold of the projecting branch scrambled ashore. In vain had I called out to my men for help ; they slept like tops, including the one who ought to have been on guard in the fore part of the boat, who had quietly slipped ashore directly I had fallen asleep. The only one who had remained with me had gone to sleep in the stern, and had been capsized head foremost into the water without being able to understand what had happened. Once safe on shore I soon found out the cause of the mishap : it was simply that the river had subsided during the night, and, as the rope which secured my boat to the projecting branch was too short, the boat had risen out of the water by the bows, and had, consequently, soon brought the stern under water.

When the disaster happened it was a little past midnight, and happily no rain was falling. I endeavoured at once to save my things, but many were lost or else spoilt by the water. Fortunately, my gun and revolver, a Dyak tambuk in which I kept various instruments, the medicine chest, and the more important objects, had got entangled in the mosquito curtain and were saved. My ammunition and botanic paper were, happily, stowed away in a tin case in the fore part of the boat, and did not suffer at all. We lighted a big fire to dry ourselves, and huddling up round it waited for morning.

Next day we were fully occupied in drying our things and replacing them in the boat. Greatly to my dismay I found that all our supply of rice had been spoilt, and, as I could not replace it in any of the nearer villages, I was obliged once more to return to Bintulu. The three Kayans continued on their way to Tinjar, and at 2 p.m. I began to descend the river.

In my various journeys up and down the Bintulu I had always been struck by the paucity of animal life. On this occasion I met with a couple of *undang-undang*, the strange bird which I had noticed on a former occasion on this river. When I saw them they were perched on a branch projecting over the water. I chased them for a long time, but they always flew away just before I got within range. They never took to the land, and certainly cannot run or walk conveniently on account of their short legs and long tail. When in the water only the long slender neck and head, which are held straight up, are seen, the body being entirely submerged. At last I was able to hit one of them; but it was only wounded, and dived, and, after some trouble, I was able to secure it. It fought vigorously with bill and claws, using these very much as a bird of prey would. Not being able to skin it I prepared the skeleton. I found fish in its stomach, and a lot of curious parasitic worms in the gullet. As I had before suspected, it turned out to be the singular but well-known Darter (*Plotus melanogaster*, Gm.).

I was anxious to get to Bintulu as soon as possible, and my men were even more so, and continued paddling far into the night. On the morning of the 12th we were early astir, but I was unwise enough to make them a present of a big heron I had shot for their breakfast, and they took quite three hours to cook it. It was 9 a.m. before they were ready to start.

We stopped for a meal at Silas, where a few houses of an abandoned village yet remained. Growing in the water I found a remarkable fern, *Ceratopteris thalictroides*. Its sterile fronds vegetate perfectly under water, but as long as it remains in that condition it does not fructify, and this only takes place when the waters are low, and a few fronds emerge and develop sporangia.

I reached Fort Bintulu at 7 p.m., and Mr. Houghton at once informed me that during my absence the Tuan Muda and other European residents at Sarawak, with some of the more influential native chiefs, had assembled here in Council. The object of this meeting was to ask reparation of the Sultan of Bruni, who had allowed the Sarawak flag to be insulted, and had also sent his tax-gatherers on Sarawak territory. The Council had therefore decided that an indemnity should be required from the Sultan. In this condition of affairs, the Tuan Muda had expressed a desire that I should postpone my trip to the Barram river, which was within the Sultan's dominions, in order to avoid any disagreeable complication, and he had written me a letter to this effect, which I had not received.

This was very disappointing to me; yet I felt that I could not abandon the project of going to Gunong Julit, and intended in any case to avoid all communication with the Bruni people. Nevertheless the difficulties with regard to the journey increased each day. Even with the help of the Resident I failed to obtain a guide and interpreter, all declaring that they dared not go amongst the Barram Kayans, though I believe this to have been a plot of Pangerang Rio, because I would not take as guide his brother-in-law, the rascal Bakar, who had been so utterly useless on my previous unfortunate expedition.

On the fifteenth of September, however, I managed to get off. Just as we were about to start one of my canoemen was found to have bolted; but the Resident came to my help, and I got a man in Government employ as a substitute. I had no guide and interpreter, and only a small boat with four men. I had with me a good supply of rice, but left behind everything that was not absolutely necessary. This was the third time that I had ascended the Bintulu, and I was determined not to do so again. If I did not succeed in getting to Gunong Julit or to Tinjar I determined to go somewhere else, and on the way I hoped to find some one to guide me towards the interior which I so longed to visit.

At Silas we made our first halt; and here I noticed a strange dull vibrating sound, something like that of a muffled Jewish harp, which seemed to come through the bottom of our boat. My men told me that this sound is produced by a fish, which the Brunese call "*Ikan umbulong-umbulong*," and the Malays of Sarawak, "*Undangkara*." The Malays, however, use the word "Ikan," not only for fish, but also for many water animals used by them as food.[1] The sound lasted a good while, but although I tried to catch a glimpse of the mysterious sub-aqueous performer, it was in vain— the waters were too deep and turbid. Our progress up the river was slow, for we were undermanned and the current was strong, and we also had a violent storm. On the 17th we reached Labbang, where I learnt that a party of about thirty Kanowit Dyaks, led by Jeomakkei, were coming up the Baloi. They had been sent by Mr. Cruikshank, Resident on the Rejang river, to meet and escort me, as he had heard that it was my intention to cross the Kayan country and descend the Baloi. This was indeed a most fortunate circumstance, and induced me to give up the idea of going to Tinjar. But how was I to ascend the Tubao river, which I must do to get to the Baloi, if the "*Pamali*," or "*Mattang*," a true kind of taboo, was then in force on that river?[2] It was this very thing which had determined me to explore the Barram basin first, and to defer the Baloi expedition till later. When but a few days previously I had been obliged by the mishap which happened to my boat to leave the Tubao, I had been informed that the "*Pamali*" was about to commence on that river, and that it would last twenty-five days—that is, until the operations connected with rice cultivation were over. During that period no stranger was permitted to ascend or descend the river.

Meanwhile we continued our journey up the river, and on the 18th met a boat-load of Malay traders from Bintulu, who had started to get to the Baloi, but had been turned back on reaching Tubao. They told me that the Kayans would allow no one to pass, and that they had barred the river across opposite the village with

---

[1] Besides this species there are other well-known estuarine fish belonging to the family of the Sciænoids which produce a strange drumming sound.

[2] I have heard the term Mattang used for Pamali, but it more properly signifies a sacred place, a place inhabited by spirits.

stakes, leaving only a narrow passage sufficient to admit one boat at a time. These Malays made a proposal to join forces and attempt to get through. I accepted their offer with pleasure, for they would be most useful to me as interpreters and guides, having often gone that way.

We got close to Tubao village without being discovered by the Kayans, as I knew the place well. When we got to the bend in the river just before the village came in view, I ordered my men to paddle with all their might, and gave the same directions to the Malays, who followed me closely, telling them above all, not to be stopped by any kind of intimidation. We thus shot through the opening of the barrier of stakes before the Kayans were able to close it, and in a moment had also passed the village, dropping our paddles only at the opposite end. As we paddled frantically past the village I saw some of the Kayans rush along the shore gesticulating as if they would speak and signing us to stop; but I pretended not to see them.

When we came to a halt beyond the village, one of the old chiefs came up to speak to us. He told us that it was a period of strict mattang with them, and that I could not then enter their country. The old man said this, however, in a deprecatory tone, endeavouring to point out to me all the evils which would befall his tribe if the taboo were violated. He also tried to excite my commiseration, dwelling on the effects of the wrath and vengeance of the spirits who preside over and protect the fields and the harvests.

I gave the good old man to understand that for me there could be no question of passing through, or not passing through; through I had come and back I would not go. As to the spirits, it was different; but considering the very friendly terms I was on with them, I thought that it would not be difficult to arrange matters. I added, to reassure him thoroughly, that far from harm being caused by my passage, his country would derive benefit therefrom, and that the ensuing harvest would be more abundant than in ordinary years.

The old Kayan appeared to be greatly quieted and consoled by what I had told him. It is rare to find savage people who will not believe anything that is unlikely or marvellous; indeed, with them faith appears to grow in ratio of the improbability and strangeness of the thing asserted. But, truly, one need not go among savages to have proof of the popularity of anything supernatural, or of the ease with which the masses are led to believe in such things !

Meanwhile the entire population had crowded down to the riverside. They showed no hostility, but would not allow any of us to go up to their houses, which, after all, I did not particularly want to do. After a long palaver, or " bichara," as they call it, with the chiefs, we came to an agreement as to what was to be done to appease the spirits. I began, as a preliminary, and acting on a happy inspiration, by presenting them with an entire piece of red cotton cloth, which had an excellent effect. Then, following the suggestion of the more influential Kayans, I took two glass beads and placed them in a glass of water, throwing the contents in the direction of the fields. They next brought me a living fowl, which I paid for. They cut its throat and took some of its blood and the head, but left the rest, which I had for supper that evening. In this case the spirits were generous, taking the smallest and worst part and leaving me the best. I was unable to learn what they did with the blood and head of the victim.

These doings appeared to have dispelled all anxiety and quieted the population. But my success as a friend of the spirits and a magician was to go further than I expected. For as the fowl which lost its life and head in my cause was being roasted, my eye fell on some sweet-potatoes which were amongst my supplies, and the thought suddenly occurred to me to complete my success and fully establish my prestige amongst these good credulous Kayans. Acting on this I took up a knife and began to carve small idols from the potatoes. This pleased the Kayans immensely, and I impaled the idols on small sticks and distributed them amongst the principal chiefs, instructing them to place them under a diminutive shed to guard the paddy fields. I told them that as long as those divinities, over whom my power was great, remained in the fields, no evil spirits would dare approach their plantations.

My manufacture of potato idols caused such pleasure that they begged me to make some of a more durable material, such as wood, that they might keep them and wear them as amulets tied to their parangs. But I was anxious to pursue my journey. Matters had gone far better than I could ever have expected, and it was wise to be off lest some incident should occur and show me up as a false prophet. Permission to ascend the Tubao had been freely granted on condition that I should neither enter the houses nor stop at the rice fields. It was pouring with rain, but as soon as leave was given I gave orders to start, and we paddled up the river until it was quite dark, when we drew our boats up on the river bank and slept that night in them.

Next day, the 19th, we continued our way up, the Tubao assuming more and more the aspect of a torrent, and it now became much blocked with tree-trunks, which often entirely obstructed our passage, and caused us much loss of time. In some places the depth decreased so much that we had to substitute poles, or " suar," for our paddles, and a little farther on we had to haul our boat bodily through a very long rapid. We passed many rice fields, in each of which was a lanko, but perched on piles, for fear of the Katibas Dyaks, who often come thus far on head-hunting expeditions.

On the banks a very small palm was frequent ; it turned out to be a new species of *Pinanga*, the pygmy of the genus (*P. rivularis*, Becc.). Its fronds have long leaflets, very flexible and nearly linear. It is a species which shows a special adaptation for living on the banks of rivers which are frequently flooded. Several other plants in this region show a similar conformation, including some which belong to families whose members have usually broad leaves.

The country we were crossing was mostly deprived of old forest, and where there were no paddy fields the ground was covered with jungle of secondary growth, more or less dense according to the number of years that the land had been out of cultivation. In some places, however, the primeval forest was yet intact in all its grandeur and picturesque beauty. I saw some trees which were new to me, but I could not then stop to collect specimens. Amongst others I noted a splendid Dipterocarp with very large leaves, provided with numerous and parallel robust ribs. I never afterwards met with this species, of which I have only preserved the memory.

Towards 3 p.m. we reached a village called Tunei. The people would not allow us to enter the house, but we were permitted to occupy a lanko similar to those we had seen in the rice fields on the way, and only accessible by means of a notched tree-trunk.

I was anxious to obtain men to carry my luggage and supplies overland to the Bellaga, in the Baloi basin. The Tubao river could be ascended for another day, but no more villages were to be met with. Kam Diam, the Orang Tua of Tunei, was absent, but his wife, Hat Hipon, was at home. She was civil enough, but asserted that she could not give me men as carriers, giving as a reason the *mattang* then in force. However, I was not easily put off, and after much insistence managed to obtain five carriers, who, for a recompense of two " depa " of red cotton cloth each, were ready to go with me to the Bellaga, where I expected to meet the escort which Mr. Cruikshank had sent for me.

The Tunei Kayans, with Hat Hipon at their head, came at sunset nominally to pay me a visit, but in reality to beg medicines. I should very soon have emptied my small travelling medicine chest had I given to each and all the remedies they asked. It was also rather difficult to guess what ailments afflicted people who looked so vigorously healthy. But I knew their ways, and that a flat denial on my side might have caused trouble ; moreover, these natives have a belief that a medicine once taken is a valid preservative, and takes effect on any kind of future malady. Quinine, whose virtues as a febrifuge were then widely known in Borneo, even to savage tribes, was what they more especially wished to have. I got out of the dilemma by dissolving a few grains of sulphate of quinine in acidulated water, to which I added a small quantity of fish-sauce. A bottle of this stuff, which was appreciable both by the eye and the palate, was quite sufficient to content all my patients.

That evening we retired to sleep in the lanko, taking care to draw up the notched pole which served as its staircase, for we had been told that the country was insecure, and that head-hunting parties of Dyaks were prowling about. But at the time I was too young and too thoughtless to bother much about any such danger ; indeed, I may say that an adventure of this kind with Dyaks would rather have pleased me, and as to my Kayans they were quite excited at the idea of the possibility of such a thing, for they had great faith in my rifle, believing that the bullet, once fired, will follow the person aimed at until it has overtaken and killed him. I always slept with a revolver and a parang-ilang in my waistband, and my gun within reach.

The Kayans are not head-hunters in the true sense of the term. I mean that they do not collect heads or skulls as trophies, and they have not got, as have the Land-Dyaks, special head-houses. However, even with them to obtain a head is a highly appreciated proof of bravery, and, as I have already said, confers the right to certain marks of distinction.

We had decided to leave early on the 20th in order to reach the landing place where the overland journey was to commence, but the rain during the night had swollen the river, and we found it very hard work paddling against the current. Towards evening we reached a lanko where, as my men were worn out and the current was still very strong, we decided to stay for the night, although the *pangkalan*, or landing place, was quite near.

It did not rain in the night, and next morning we found that the waters had greatly decreased. One might almost say that these streams are subject to daily periodical floods, like tides ; for their waters rise and fall at short intervals, in consequence of the violent and sudden rain which falls nearly every day. In Borneo rain is so heavy and the quantity of water which falls is so great that floods are very sudden, and the levels of the streams vary considerably within the space of a few hours. This may be the cause of the special adaptation already mentioned in plants growing on the banks of these torrential rivers (Fig. 51).

In another half-hour we came to the landing place, and began our march. For some distance our path was simply the bed of the torrent, here no longer navigable. Our direction was generally south-east. We climbed a hill about 600 feet high, and descended the opposite slope in an easterly direction, crossing several torrents which ran into the Sepakko, an affluent of the Bellaga. The hill we crossed was thus the true water-parting between the basins of the Bintulu and the Baloi.

Our road lay mostly through primeval forest, where I saw many

new and peculiar plants ; but of very few was I able to get frag-
mentary specimens. Towards noon we reached a village on the
Bellaga, consisting of several big houses quite similar to those seen
on the Tubao. The Bellaga is a large stream about sixty yards
wide where we came to it, and very deep, and it was navigable
for another five days, penetrating farther inland than do the
branches of the Bintulu. Indeed, on reaching the place where it
ceases to be navigable for canoes, one day's tramp overland takes
the traveller to the basin of the Barram.

The inhabitants of the village we had reached are called
Kadjamans, but they did not appear to me to differ from the
Kayans.

On the 22nd I went to the hill near the Bellaga to get specimens
of some interesting plants which I had noticed in coming, but being
then loaded and anxious to get to camp, had not collected. Amongst
the more notable new species of plants got on this hill I may mention
a singular Anonaceous plant (*Enicosanthum paradoxum*, Becc.) ;
and two small but most graceful palms, one a true pinang in miniature (*Areca furcata*, Becc.), the other a *Licuala* (*L. cordata*, Becc.),
remarkable for its entire leaves, which resemble an open Chinese
fan. I was surprised, also, to find in a quite limited area no less
than five distinct forms of begonia, a genus which is by no means
rich in species in Borneo. But on this excursion I did not meet with
many plants in blossom. I returned to the village thoroughly
exhausted, for I had had a bad attack of fever on the way.

Meanwhile, Kam Diam, chief of one of the nearest villages on
the Baloi, came to Bellaga. He was unlike any of the Kayans, or
even Dyaks I had yet seen, and was certainly the stoutest and
fattest man I ever saw in Borneo, though obesity is less rare amongst
the Malays than amongst the inland tribes. From Kam Diam I
heard that the escort sent to meet me by Mr. Cruikshank had waited
a long while at Baloi, but the men having had no news of my arrival
were that very day going back to their homes. To say the truth,
their company was now not so much wanted, for it looked as if I
was not to meet with any great difficulties in accomplishing my
journey. But as a bodyguard they would certainly have been
useful in several ways, for although the Rajah's authority was great
over the settled communities of Kayans and other tribes in the
interior along the Rejang, especially after a severe chastisement
inflicted by the Tuan Muda, it could then hardly be expected to
extend to wandering parties of head-hunters.

I passed the evening nursing my fever, and was tormented by
a crowd of dogs, attracted no doubt by the smell of my supplies.
In the house where I had taken up my quarters there must have
been at least forty of these brutes. I was quite unable to get rid
of them, and during the night they devoured nearly all the supply

Fig. 51.—LEAVES OF BORNEAN STENOPHYLLOUS PLANTS
(UNDER SURFACE).

1. *Fagræa stenophylla.*   2. *Garcinia linearis.*   3. *Psychotria acuminata.*   4. *Eugenia riparia.*   5. *Syzigium nerifolium.*   6. *Nauclea rivularis.*   7. *Erycibe longifolia.*   8. *Eugenia saligna.*   9. *Sauraja angustifolia.*   10. *Tetranthera salicifolia.*

of dried fish for my men, although it had been stowed away in a place apparently out of their reach.

On the 23rd I was able to engage two Kadjamans from Bellaga, and three men, his own Kayans, were procured by Kam Diam to escort me as far as Baloi. With such guides the journey was not so difficult, but without them it would have been next to impossible, for the Bellaga is obstructed in several places by rapids, which cannot be traversed by boats. Thus, to reach its junction with the Baloi, part of the journey must be performed on foot.

My attack of fever had left me very weak, but with a good dose of quinine, taken in time, I hoped to keep off any new access for some time. The Kadjamans had willingly let me have a boat, in which we started down the river, and my men paddled vigorously. We passed two rapids safely, but at 11 a.m. we came to one which was quite impassable for our canoe, so we were obliged to leave it and march overland to Baloi.

As we were descending the last navigable portion of the Bellaga we met with two *kidjans*—very diminutive and graceful little deer. They suddenly appeared on the river bank, but so rapidly moved out of sight again that I had no time to get a shot. For the Kayans, who are extremely superstitious, this was an ill-omened meeting, and they asked me to stop whilst they performed a ceremony to avert the evil prognostic. They manufactured a diminutive hut with sticks and leaves, put a large stone under it, and placed on the stone, as peace-offering to the spirits, a pinch of rice, tobacco, siri, and pinang.

Stretched across one of the small affluents which we frequently passed on our way down I observed a rope, from which hung various objects. This signified that a party was in search of camphor along the stream, and the objects were to prohibit any one from going that way, and indicated besides the penalty he would have to pay if he transgressed. They consisted of a wooden disc, which represented a gong, and two or three wooden models of parangs.

For six hours we tramped in an easterly direction; then we climbed, and crossing several streams, or perhaps a single but very tortuous one in various parts, we at last came again to the Bellaga a short distance from where it joins the Rejang or Baloi. The rocks in the rapids and the hills we crossed were all sandstone. We camped in the jungle, on a sandy flat which adjoined the riverside. I found here a gigantic aroid with enormous heart-shaped leaves, on a stem about four feet high and as thick as a man's leg. Its flower was quite warm, and its high temperature could be felt by placing the hand on the spathe, which had the shape of a horse's ear, and was of a vinaceous colour. I only preserved a spadix of this plant, which I believe, from several of its characters, to be probably an *Alocasia*, allied to but distinct from *A. indica*.

Early next morning Kam Diam's Kayans followed the course of the river to their village, which was not very far from the place where we passed the night, to get a boat. They returned with it, and towards noon we were on our way down the Bellaga. We had to pass one more rapid, and at last, after many days of travel by stream and forest, with the endless jungle constantly limiting the view, our eyes feasted once again on a noble expanse of open country and a wide sheet of water. We were on the Rejang.

CHAPTER XX

DOWN THE REJANG—THE KAYANS' KNOWLEDGE OF THE INTERIOR—STENO-
PHYLLISM AND ITS CAUSES—CAMPHOR TREES—TAMA DIAN AND HIS
ESTABLISHMENT—THE WILD SAGO PALM—A KAYAN MASQUERADE—
THE BANTENG AND OTHER BIG GAME—ON THE RAPIDS—FRESHWATER
ALGÆ OF MARINE TYPE—SHARKS AND RAYS IN THE RIVER—THE
TANJONG—IN THE DYAK COUNTRY—THE KETIBAS—KANOWIT—A DIS-
HONEST TRADER—AT SIBU—THE TRIBES OF THE REJANG—FROM SIBU
TO THE SEA—BLACK FLOWERS—ADVENTURES WITH CROCODILES—NEW
PALMS—MOUTH OF THE IGAN—MOSQUITOES AND OTHER INSECT PESTS
—WILD ORANGES.

WE passed beyond the house of Akim Diam, which was built
on the bank of the Baloi just where the Bellaga pours
its waters into the main river, and halted opposite a big house
a few hundred yards lower down, at a place called Skapan. The
inhabitants are called " Orang Skapan," and consider themselves
as a distinct tribe, but I cannot see in what they differ from the
Kadjamans and the Kayans. All these tribal names in the Kayan
country are, I think, nothing more than family distinctions, in
short, what might be termed "clans." I could not otherwise
explain how, a few hundred yards from this locality, houses of
Kadjamans, Skapans, Punans, and Kayans are found mixed up
together. I believe that the Punans just mentioned must be
considered distinct from those of the Bintulu, being much more
civilised. I cannot feel quite sure that the names Punan, Puanan,
and Pennan, heard on the Bintulu, are those of distinct tribes,
or merely different ways of expressing the name of one and the
same tribe.

Senahan and Sematto, the two chiefs of Skapan, showed every
wish to help me, and gave me a cordial reception. Naturally, the
first thing I asked for was a boat and an experienced crew to enable
me to continue my journey, for the navigation of the Rejang is
difficult and even dangerous, on account of the formidable rapids
which obstruct its course in several places. These two kindly
disposed chiefs immediately furnished me with a large and commodious boat, and ordered fifteen men to accompany me as far
as the next village ; they also gave me some fowls and a small
quantity of rice, although they were very short of the latter. My

supplies were beginning to give out, and I was obliged to measure carefully the rice I gave to my men, and to let them have it only for one meal a day. We had, however, some sago in the granulated form, to which I had got accustomed, and which we all used to munch as we went along. It is a most convenient kind of food for such journeys, and is a good substitute for bread or biscuits, but, unfortunately, far less nourishing.

The village of Skapan was in bad condition. It consisted of a long house thatched with the leaves of an *Alpinia*, or other allied Zingiberaceous plant. The old village of well constructed houses had been burnt by the Dyaks a few years before during one of the famous expeditions of the then Tuan Muda. A short distance from the house of the Skapans was one belonging to the Punans, who were then in a state of great excitement, having heard two days before that the inland Dyaks had killed one of their own people and carried off his head. I saw in this house several persons with sores, and was unable to satisfy myself as to their origin; whether the disease was of a hereditary nature, or caused by bad climatic conditions. I believe the former hypothesis, however, more likely to be the true one. Several of the villagers were also afflicted with bad eyes, but I think that the strange custom of plucking out the eyelashes contributed to this.

The natives of this part of the Baloi are well acquainted with the topography of the interior of Borneo, and traced for me on the sand the courses of the principal rivers; they also offered to pilot me down the Banjar or down the Koti, but such a project was quite impracticable, on account of the absolute dearth of provisions. I questioned my informers on the existence of a high mountain which is said to rise in the very centre of Borneo, and from which its principal rivers are reported to flow. Mr. St. John (*Op. cit.* ii. pp. 35 and 47) mentions this mountain, calling it Gunong Tilong. Its summit is described as being white with snow, and the same author tells us that from its slopes a salt spring flows which gives rise to the Banjarmasin river.[1]

The natives whom I questioned on the subject, however, asserted that the central mountains of Borneo were two, not one, though close together and forming one group. The northernmost they call Batu Tibang, and from it they say the Barram river flows; the other, more to the south, is called Batu Puti, and from its western slope the Rejang flows; and the Koti, the Batang Kayan, and the Banjar from its eastern side. The latter is

[1] " Banjar " may be interpreted " which floods," " which spreads out "; and " masin " means salted. " Banjar masin " would thus mean " the salt river which spreads," and is probably so named because on account of the tides its waters are brackish for a large part of its course, overflow their banks, and flood the country over a wide area.

also called the Makam by the Kayans, and near its source the Silikao.

If a mountain of any great height existed at the source of the Rejang I feel sure I ought to have heard something about it ; indeed, I ought to have seen it from some of the hills to whose summits I had climbed. I see no reason for admitting the existence of an elevated group of mountains in Central Borneo. From the tests of comparison to which I submitted the intelligent natives from whom I was seeking information, and especially referring to Gunong Baloi, which rises behind the Skapan house, I am led to the conclusion that the greatest elevation that can be assigned to the two peaks of the central mountain group of Borneo can hardly be much over 7,000 feet. An erroneous interpretation of the native name Batu Puti, i.e. " White rock," may have led to the inference that the mountain was capped with snow.

Borneo—which, in proportion to its area, is of all countries of the world one of the best provided with great rivers—can be travelled all over by water, so perfect and so extensive is its river-system. A day's, or at the most a two days' walk overland will enable the traveller to pass from the basin of one river to that of another. This is due to the special orographical conditions of the island, which does not gradually rise from the coast towards the interior to reach a great elevation in the central portion. Instead, nearly all the mountains of Borneo rise abruptly from the plains, and thus the rivers have no great fall, and can be navigated by boats nearly up to their source. The action of the tides facilitates also in no small degree the navigability of Bornean rivers. For the reasons above given the tidal influence extends far up each river.

The big house of the Skapans was built on an elevated bank of the river, which had a sort of extensive inclined beach on which canoes were landed, repaired, and also constructed, this being one of the principal boat-building yards on the Rejang.

The river was then low, but the banks showed that when full it rises several yards. At Skapan the bed of the Rejang, which ought properly to be called the Baloi, is narrow and hemmed in, as it were, between the hills which form its banks ; but its width is not less than 330 feet, and it is extraordinarily deep. In some places Sematto assured me that 60 *depa* (about 300 feet) of cord were required to reach the bottom. They informed me that it abounds with fish, and some caught by my men were excellent, and belonged to species I had not seen elsewhere. I was repeatedly told that a species of shark and a ray are caught here in the river. I had too often heard about these two fish—the first being called " Yu," the second " Ikan pare " by the Malays—to entertain any doubt as to the veracity of my informants ; but yet I should have liked to have had more positive proof, and had even planned a great fishing battue, but the scarcity of my supplies and of the more necessary commodities obliged me to shorten my stay. Besides, I could not possibly have preserved specimens of fish.[1]

On the morning of the twenty-fifth of September I took leave of Sematto and Senahan, the two courteous Orang Tuas of Skapan, and got into the big and comfortable boat they had so kindly procured for me, which, manned by twenty-four paddlers, seemed literally to fly over the water. The landscape was fine, varied by hills and low mountains, the highest of which, Gunong Baloi, rises just behind Skapan, and may possibly have an elevation of some 2,000 feet.

Below Skapan the Baloi widens considerably, and divides to form several islands, which are covered by water during floods, though now clothed with the densest vegetation. The plants growing on them belong to very different families, but all have very flexible stems and branches and narrow leaves, which can easily bend to the current without breaking when the waters rise and cover them. Such plants are represented by the willow kind with us, which grow on river banks, and are liable to be flooded at certain seasons.

The action of running water, according to my views, represents a natural force which has brought about a special adaptation in the leaves of many fluviatile plants. To the modification thus produced the term " Stenophyllism," or " narrow-leavedness," may be conveniently applied. This special adaptation, however, is not only caused by running water. Constant and steady air-currents may, I think, have promoted the stenophyllism which occurs in a large number of trees and shrubs growing on the banks of the Rejang and neighbouring rivers, as well as in other countries, but which I did not notice along the Sarawak, the Sambas district rivers, or the lakes of the Kapuas. Not a few of the plants with narrow leaves which I met on the Rejang and Tubao are endemic species, and it might even be said that they still occupy the localities where they were plasmated (Fig. 51). This would prove that no geological perturbations have occurred in this region at least from middle Tertiary times to the present day; for if any such changes had taken place it would be difficult to explain how perfectly local species could have become modified in accordance with stimuli equally limited to these rivers.

In the forest bordering this part of the Rejang river the camphor tree (*Dryobalanops*) which I had found on the Gunong Sedaha was common. I wished to procure a few living specimens

---

[1] I have since learnt that both sharks and rays enter the rivers of Southern Asia and are found hundreds of miles from the sea, and the same thing has been observed in the great rivers of tropical South America.

for Mr. Teysmann, who had asked me to get them for the Botanic Garden at Buitenzorg, in Java ; and as along the lower course of the Rejang this tree is no longer found, I stopped at a hill whose base rose directly from the river, on which I saw several big trees. They had neither flowers nor fruit, but in the shade under their fine crowns of foliage I found quite a number of young plants growing up, about six or eight inches high. I dug up several very carefully, and remembering what I had seen done at the Peradeniya gardens, I placed them in sections of bamboo, which made excellent pots. I afterwards had the pleasure of seeing these plants again at Buitenzorg, grown about a hundred times bigger. Now they are great trees.

The weather was splendid, and the waters of the river, now low, were of limpid clearness. Notwithstanding the stoppage, we did not do a bad day's work, covering, I should say, not less than thirty-five miles.

I saw only small remains of the primeval forest on the banks of the river : a sign that the land was or had been utilised for rice cultivation, and that the district was relatively populous, although we had not yet come to a single village since leaving Skapan. Towards sunset, however, we sighted a Kayan house on the river-side, and from signals visible we found that it was under " pamali," and that we should not be allowed to enter it. But I pretended not to have seen anything of the kind, and, landing, went straight up the ladder, certain that if I once succeeded in entering they would not easily send me away.

It was the house of Tama Dian, i.e. "the father of Dian," the latter being the son's name.[1] The house was large, new, and strongly built, raised on stout squared piles. I saw quite a number of persons about, but learnt that, except the family of the chief, all the rest were " Ulun-ulun," or slaves, probably descendants of Dyaks captured in raids. It was not very easy to distinguish the masters from their slaves, but in countries where dress is reduced to a minimum, social differences are less apparent than elsewhere, for dress is beyond doubt one of the greatest factors in maintaining class distinctions.

The Skapans who had accompanied me from the house of Sematto and Senahan went farther down the river to the village of some Punans to see whether they could find men to go with me as far as Kanowit.

Tama Dian and his people were not offended at my infraction of the pamali ; on the contrary, they appeared glad of my arrival, for many of them had never seen a white man. Only the

---

[1] Amongst the Kayans, and also amongst the Land-Dyaks, a father often drops his name and assumes that of his eldest son.

Tuan Muda had come up thus far some years before. That evening the young men and girls favoured me with one of their dances, or " main pajat." I found that in the art of Terpsichore they had progressed further than the Dyaks, and that in their dances, which are a kind of pantomime, they use masks. I saw some of these being carved out of a soft light wood then and there. I slept badly in Tama Dian's house on account of the dogs, which were, as usual, unbearable.

These Kayans have splendid boats, hollowed out of single tree-trunks, some of them being between sixty and seventy feet in length and five feet in breadth. But I could not find men to go with me, because of the pamali. The day (September 26) also happened to be a fête day for the Kayans, and, if I had stayed in their house, custom would have obliged me not to leave for eight days. Fortunately the Skapans returned in the afternoon with several Punans, who had consented to accompany me, as far as Sibu, and the Kayans having given me one of their big boats I was able to leave towards evening ; but I only descended the river as far as the houses of the Punans. Even next day I did not get fairly started on my journey, for the boat had to be put in order, covered with kadjans, and so forth.

Moreover, the Punans had no rice, and were obliged to go to the forest to get in a supply of kadjattao sago. Here for the first time I had an opportunity of seeing and collecting specimens of the palm which produces this peculiar kind of sago, which I had so often heard mentioned and only seen from a distance. It is a *Eugeissonia*, but different from that which I had found on Mount Mattang, turning out to be an undescribed species, which I have since named *Eugeissonia utilis* (cf. *Nuov. Gior. Bot. Ital.* iii. p. 26). Some specimens of this palm grew near the Punans' house, because, although it abounds in the forest, it is to a certain extent cultivated on account of its usefulness, being grown and the young plants protected in the vicinity of the houses. It is easily grown from seeds, which fall when perfectly ripe and germinate spontaneously. In good soil a tree can be cut in five years, so that growth must be extremely rapid. The trees are cut when in blossom, and before they have borne fruit, and they have then reached a height of as much as fifty feet. The stem is bare for some thirty feet, cylindrical, regularly ringed, and about the size of a man's thigh. It is covered with numerous spiny projections, the result of a transformation of adventitious rootlets. The stem is raised from the ground on many short roots, thus differing from the other species of the genus, which all have long and slender roots, raising the stem much higher from the ground. The fronds are large, forming a regular and ample crown on the top of the stem ; they are much arched, and in their midst rises the inflorescence in the shape of a narrow cone, often six or seven feet high.

The fecula which is extracted from the Kadjattao is of a quality superior to that produced by the common sago palm. Even the pollen, which has the aspect of a violet-coloured meal, is utilised, being eaten as a condiment both with rice and sago.[1] The flowers of the *Eugeissonia* are formed in such a manner as to offer an efficient protection to the pollen, which, on account of its nutritious properties, might be sought after by different animals and thus destroyed before the flowers open. Indeed, the flowers of *Eugeissonia utilis* hardly come up to the usual conception of a flower at all. They are very slender, but as much as three inches and a half in length, and their petals are extremely hard and of a dark funereal colour, much resembling leather. The corolla forms a sheath to the stamens of great toughness, and at the same time does not attract the attention of animals.

The rude cultivation of the Kadjattao appears to me to be a most instructive instance of how plants useful to man have come to be reduced to a state of domesticity or cultivation. If primitive inhabitants of the forest happened to find a locality where there grew in abundance a plant from which, with a slight amount of labour, they could extract a quantity of food, they would certainly take advantage of the boon Nature offered them, and would build their rude shelters or huts at that spot, and settle there as long as these advantages continued. Meanwhile the seeds of the plant which had been so useful to them would become scattered round their huts, where, in the rich soil necessarily accumulated, these young plants of the species would grow up under most favourable conditions, and would bear better fruit and yield food substance in greater abundance than the forest grown specimens. Thus a system of mutualism would be initiated between Man and the species useful to him. The hypothesis that Man may have been, so to say, the creator of those domestic plants and animals which are no longer found in a wild state, and which cannot subsist without his protection, implies the further hypothesis that such plants and animals became associated with Man at a time when there was still a wide field open to variation, and when the plasmative force was yet active. This further renders necessary the acceptance of the hypothesis that Man—possessed of intelligence nearly on a par with that with which he is at present endowed—existed at a time far more remote than that which is generally admitted. For my part, I certainly see no objection in assigning to man an antiquity at least equal to that of other

[1] Sir J. Hooker tells us that the inhabitants of New Zealand make bread with the pollen of *Typha* (cf. *Flora Novæ-Zelandiæ*, i. p. 238). I do not remember any other cases of pollen being used as food.

still existing animals, though it is unnecessary to enter upon the
subject here.

In the case of the Kadjattao, however, the greater facility of
reproduction, the extremely rapid growth, the protection of the
stem by the spines, not to mention that of the flowers by their
tough envelope, have amply insured the preservation of the wild
plants also ; and thus *Eugeissonia utilis* is not in the strict sense
of the word a domesticated species, for it is not entirely dependent
on Man for its existence.   In Borneo there are several other plants
in the same case as that of the Kadjattao, such as *Pangium edule*,
Sagus, *Arenga saccharifera*, several *Caryotas*, *Anthiaris toxicaria*,
etc., all of which, like the Kadjattao, may be considered as semi-
cultivated and anthropophilous plants.   But I must put an end
to this digression, and resume my journey.

That evening, September 26th, at about five o'clock, a Kayan
masquerade paid me a visit, on purpose to show themselves off
to me. They call this fête " Nugal," and it occurs twice in the year ;
the first (the one I witnessed) takes place immediately after the
planting of rice ; the second, I believe, after the harvest.   It was
highly interesting, the procession being numerous and varied.
The instruments used were most singular, as were also the wooden
masks which hid the faces of the performers.   I was sorry not
to be able to make sketches, but that was not possible, for they
did not stay long enough.   I believe that an accurate study of
the masks and instruments used on such occasions would throw
much light on the question of the origin of this people.   From
what I saw I am more than ever inclined towards the opinion that
the people of the Bintulu and the Upper Rejang originally came
from Indo-China.

The 27th was a wearisome day for me, passed in the Punan's
house superintending the getting ready of the boat.   I also prepared specimens of the Kadjattao for my herbarium, and secured
a few living young plants, which I afterwards had the pleasure
of seeing again in the Botanic Garden at Buitenzorg, fully grown
and bearing fruit.

To supplement the Kadjattao sago for the journey the Punans
went into the forest with their dogs on a hunting expedition.   A
few hours later they returned with a large boar.   This was, however, of no·advantage to me, as I was unwilling to force my cook,
Sahat, a Mussulman, to cook pork, having always deference
to the religious principles of these people.   The Punans may
be skilful hunters, but, judging from the immense number of
boars' jaw-bones (about 300) which I saw in long rows suspended
as trophies of the chase in the house, I should think that these
animals must be very abundant in the forest.

We were off at seven o'clock next morning, but the paddlers

were few for our boat, which, although not one of the biggest, was quite sixty feet in length. We accordingly stopped at two other Kayan houses to recruit men. One of these houses was empty, all the inmates, women and children included, being away either in the fields or hunting in the forest. A wag in our party, catching sight of a big gong, began to beat it in the manner these people do when some danger, notably an attack by enemies, is imminent. We had not long to wait to see the effect. People began to appear from all sides in a state of alarm and excitement. First came the women, with the smaller children on their shoulders ; and, following close, the men, panting and excited. But as soon as they saw our inoffensive selves and their inoffensive neighbours, they took the joke goodnaturedly, and burst into a hearty laugh. Possibly this little joke may have helped to induce some of the young men to join my party, though another good reason may have been the cause of their willingness to accompany me to Sibu, the capital of the Rejang. A journey down to the sea is not an easy undertaking for the Kayans ; for, in addition to its length, it is rendered perilous by possible Dyak hostilities, notwithstanding the relative security which the Government of Sarawak had succeeded in establishing along this river, mainly through the energy of the Tuan Muda. Thus the natives felt a greater amount of security in being with me, and I was also quite an excellent opportunity for them in another way, for with the pay I promised them on my arrival at Sibu they would be able to procure various articles they coveted, and especially salt, of which they were then much in want, and which they usually buy from traders at an exorbitant price. I was thus able to get together twenty young and vigorous paddlers, some of them well experienced in handling a boat through rapids, and shortly after noon we took our seats amid much merriment and started at racing speed, the men keeping excellent time with a song, or emitting shrill cries in chorus, just as if they were off on some war expedition. The warlike sentiment is common, and always easily awakened in all these people, for whom war, or, rather, predatory expeditions, are, as it were, a natural instinct, fostered and transmitted from generation to generation.

The river became more and more majestic as we proceeded. The mass of water it carries is imposing, although it was evident from the nature and look of the escarped and high banks that we saw the stream at its lowest level. Towards evening one of the paddlers directed my attention to some large animals which were grazing on the river bank to our left. These turned out to be a small herd of wild cattle. I at once ordered my men to paddle noiselessly, and to approach a spot where I could land unperceived. I had with me the excellent gun which had done such good service

in my hunt after orang-utans, but it was loaded with big shot.
Not to lose time I dropped a bullet into one barrel without removing the shot, and jumped ashore, followed by two of my smartest
Kayans. But the place where I alighted was soft mud, and without
the help of my two companions I should have stuck there. We
scrambled up, however, and to approach the animals without
being seen by them made a long detour, and I managed to get
within twenty-five yards of the herd. A fine large bull, entirely
black with white feet, showed its side, and as I fired the creature
fell, but rose again at once and started at a rush for the jungle,
followed by four others, evidently cows or calves, that were feeding
with it. We then showed ourselves, but one of the herd, which
had been grazing at a distance from the others, on perceiving me
at once lowered its head and charged. At ten yards off I fired
my second barrel, which, unfortunately, was only loaded with
shot. The creature came down on its knees and rolled over. I
thought I had got him, but he was up again in an instant, and
made for the jungle like the others. My Kayans, thinking that
it must be blinded or at least badly wounded, having received the
contents of my barrel full in the front part of the head, followed
its spoor for a while, but were unable to come up with it, and we
reluctantly had to abandon the chase.

The wild cattle of Borneo, or "banteng," as the natives call it
(*Bos sondaicus*), is, after the rhinoceros, which is only found in the
interior, the largest of the indigenous Bornean mammals, the
elephant having been beyond doubt introduced by man on the
island. I once heard that the carcase of a rhinoceros had been
seen in the Sarawak, carried down by the current, but I have
never seen any portion of one got in Borneo. Elephants are
found in the north-east portion of the island, but Mr. St.
John (*Op. cit.* i. p. 95) writes that it is believed that they
are the descendants of some which were presented by the
Hon. East India Company to the Sultan of Sulu about 150
years ago, and which at his request were landed at Tanjong
Unsang. They are now said to be numerous in that district,
doing much damage to the plantations.

The banteng is also called by the natives tambadao, or tam-
madao, and appears to be more frequent in North Borneo than
elsewhere, especially on the Limbang and the Barram. Mr. St.
John (*Op. cit.* i. p. 283) writes that in Kimanis Bay, in British North
Borneo, herds of banteng are met with which are of smaller size than
the wild cattle found on the banks of the two rivers just mentioned.
I was told that the banteng has a special predilection for young
bamboo shoots, and thus prefers keeping in the jungle or secondary
forest, where that plant abounds, whilst it is rarely met with in the
primeval forest. The country we were then crossing appeared to

be rich in game, for I saw deer time after time on the river banks, but always out of range.

The same day we found coal in big seams on the left bank of the river. At dusk we selected a dry spot on the bank to cook our dinner and to pass the night. The Punans cook their sago in earthern pots, which they make themselves. Both they and the Kayans with me were afraid of the Ketibas Dyaks, and kept a strict watch through the night. A heavy storm, too, helped to keep us awake, and we could very well have done without it, for we were camped in a most awkward place.

At 7 a.m. on the 29th we were once more paddling rapidly on our way. Two kidjans (*Tragulus*), and then two fine white-tailed pheasants, very probably the beautiful species subsequently described as *Lobiophasis bulweri*, were seen on the edge of the jungle, but we were going too fast for me to fire at them ; besides, the river was very wide. Wild boars were also seen, but they proved very shy, and turned back into the jungle as soon as they sighted us. Two darters (*Plotus*) had captured and carried ashore a large fish, which certainly must have weighed seven or eight pounds. We secured it, and it was an opportune addition to my breakfast, and to that of several of my men. This bird may well be considered as the most rapacious of its kind, a true web-footed bird of prey. It appears to grasp the fish with its feet, and to despatch it with its sharp-pointed bill. The big fish which we took from the two birds had evidently slipped from their claws on account of its great weight. Its head was quite riddled with holes made by the birds' bills.

We had now reached the most dangerous part of the river, for there are here three rapids at no great distance apart which have to be passed. The waters were then low and the rocks numerous, threatening no little danger to the boats. When the water is high, navigation is less difficult, for the difference of level in the rapids becomes much less, and the danger of being driven on rocks is also greatly diminished. The increasing roar caused by the falling water warned us of the close proximity of the rapid, though we had heard it a long way back. At the first big fall we unloaded our boat, carrying everything on the men's shoulders along the shore beyond the dangerous part ; but we all returned to the boat to make our dash through the foaming waters. For me it was quite a new sensation ; and, indeed, I felt it was quite possible I might never have the opportunity of narrating it. I had full faith in my Kayans, however, and especially in the expert who wielded the steering paddle at the stern. Drawn up to his fullest height, he looked eagerly for the best passage. This was no easy task, for not only has the steersman to avoid the rocks which are above water, but those just covered by it, which are still more

dangerous, capsizing the canoe in an instant. At first the current
seemed nothing out of the common, but as we approached it increased in force until there seemed almost something uncanny in
its overwhelming strength. About fifty or sixty yards from the
rapid our steersman had already made up his mind as to the line
to be followed. His great object was to keep the boat with plenty
of way on in the current; for woe betide us if we but swerved an
instant—we should have been at once capsized and done for ! As
we approached the bigger part of the fall the paddlers redoubled
their efforts, and our long, light, narrow boat shot like an arrow
down the swell, and in an instant was righted in the bubbling
waters of the pool beneath, in a cloud of pulverized water which
formed a mist-like column around us. I feel that it would be
attempting the impossible to endeavour to translate into words the
emotions of that moment, which came and went like a flash of
lightning !

When we got into the comparatively tranquil waters beyond
our boat was full, and would inevitably have sunk but for the
rapid and able manner in which the Kayans baled the water out.
Some of them jumped overboard to lighten the boat at once.

It requires the *sangfroid* and experience of the Kayans to shoot
such rapids. The feat is partly accomplished by taking the fall at
such a pace that the canoe reaches calm water beyond almost
before it has time to sink. It is all important that the paddlers
should not get frightened at the amount of water shipped, but
continue to paddle with all their strength until the danger is well
past. Then comes the work of baling and emptying the boat,
which requires to be done carefully and quickly, most of the crew
springing overboard as soon as possible in order to lighten the boat.

We had thus successfully passed the first rapids, but our experience had been such that we did not feel equal to tackling the second,
to which we came very soon after in the canoe, for it was said to be
even more dangerous than the other. We were accordingly prudent, and made a portage along the shore. At the third rapid the
passage was easy, or, rather, without obstacles: a smooth sheet of
water plunging over into the basin below, with a fall of about seven
feet only. It was here, nevertheless, that the Tuan Muda lost
several of his men on an expedition against the Kayans. On that
occasion more than one of the boats were capsized, and several of
the Dyaks who formed the crews, in spite of being expert swimmers,
disappeared and were seen no more. It was said that the sharks
took them. I should have thought that they more probably fell
victims to crocodiles; but the natives assured me that these reptiles
are not found there, though the eddies below the rapid are frequented
by sharks resembling those found in salt water.[1]

[1] Mr. St. John (*Op. cit.* i. p. 136) tells us that sharks are found in the left

Along the banks of this last rapid, on rocks constantly wet with the spray, I found a small alga growing in profusion, and covering with a violet veil the mosses and Hepaticæ amongst which it grew. It turned out to be a new and undescribed species of *Bostrychia* (*B. bryophila*, Zan.), which has a special interest, as it belongs to the *Florideæ*, a group of algæ all but exclusively marine. In Sarawak I had found another alga of this kind growing in fresh water, the *Delesseria Beccarii*, Zan., previously mentioned, which, like the above cited *Bostrychia*, is one of the *Florideæ*, and belongs to a genus in which not only all the other species are marine, but are also the most elegant and brightly coloured of seaweeds. *D. Beccarii* lives in the perfectly fresh and limpid waters of the Sodomak stream, many feet above sea level. We have here, then, two plants which may be supposed to be of marine origin, but now live in fresh water far away from the sea.[1]

If the presence of such typical sea fish as sharks and rays be proved in that part of the river where I found the seaweed, the coincidence would certainly be suggestive, and offer us an example of adaptation to fluviatile life of essentially marine organisms, caused, perhaps, by ancient changes in the level of land in Borneo. But before proceeding further on the hypothesis thus suggested, it would be well not only to confirm beyond doubt the presence of these sharks and rays in the Upper Rejang, but to determine the

branch of the Sarawak river, *above the rapids*. Moreover, in the *Sarawak Gazette* for 1887, p. 164, two sawfishes are mentioned as having been caught at Lubok pangkalan Singhi, above Kuching, in fresh water, but within the tidal influence.

[1] The fact is not new, for in 1839–48 Leprieur, an apothecary in the French navy, discovered in Cayenne several small Florideæ, known previously as exclusively marine algæ, in mountain streamlets as much as fifty miles inland, and at an elevation of up to 600 feet above sea level. It is worthy of remark that three of them were *Bostrychias* of different species (cf. Montagne · *Sur la station insolite de quelques Floridées dans les eaux douces et courantes des ruisseaux des montagnes à la Guyane*, Ann. des Sc. Nat. 1850, p. 283). At Cayenne, also, in rivers within the action of the tide, Leprieur found another *Bostrychia*, together with a small *Delesseria* (*D. Leprieurii*, Mont.) which is so like the Sodomak plant that it might well be looked upon as a variety of it. In Borneo I also found a *Delesseria* (*D. adnata*, Zan.) and a *Bostrychia* (*B. fulcrata*, Zan.) growing on the big stems of the nipa palms in waters alternately salt and fresh. These are eloquent instances showing how seaweeds of two genera have become adapted gradually to a change of station from salt through brackish to fresh water. In *Bostrychia bryophylla*, the adaptation to conditions of existence different from the original ones would be even more extended, for it has become nearly a land alga. The above mentioned facts reveal a remarkable analogy between the physical conditions of the rivers of Borneo and those of Guiana ; because in both countries, remote as they are from each other, a similar change in the biological conditions of certain seaweeds has occurred, which can alone have been caused, I think, by a similar process of adaptation, brought about, no doubt, by an upheaval of the land.

species to which they belong. As I have already remarked, the statement that they exist here, which at present rests entirely on native authority, is not so strange, for it is well known that certain sharks (*Carcharias*) and rays (*Trygon*) inhabit the Ganges and other rivers in Southern Asia as well as tropical America. I am, however, puzzled to explain how sharks big enough to seize a man can live in the pools below the rapids, unless there is an extraordinary abundance of other fishes there. It may be, however, that the expedition of the Tuan Muda being a numerous

Fig. 52.—TANJONG WOMEN WEAVING TAMBUKS WITH STRIPS OF ROTANG.

one, sharks had followed it, as they sometimes do, and had remained in the deep pools below the rapids.

After the three cataracts the river widens out considerably, and forms a series of small rapids and shallows, dangerous on account of rocks just awash, which are only avoided by using great caution. Just as we were in the most difficult part of this a sudden storm came upon us with torrential rain; so, to avoid a catastrophe, we beached our boat on a small island, and camped there for the night.

Next day we paddled away without stopping from 7 a.m. till

noon, when we halted at some houses belonging to the Tanjongs—one of the many tribes living on the Rejang, but belonging, from what I could discover, to the great Kayan family. Together with these Tanjongs some Buketans had recently come to live, and had begun to plant rice.

The Tanjongs are more tattooed than the Kayans. In most of those I saw the breast, chin, and part of the shoulders were covered with tattooed designs. The women now dress as the Bintulu females, in black cotton cloth, and have the lobes of their ears enormously distended by the heavy tin, brass, or copper rings, some as big as bracelets, which they wear in them.

We had got now to the Dyak country, and on both sides of the river the hills were covered with well cultivated rice fields, the old forest having been utterly cleared away. Many isolated houses were seen. The commonest tree I noticed on the river banks was the " kayu bayor," a species of *Pterospermum*, which produces large white flowers. We passed the mouth of the Ketibas, along whose banks still live the most dreaded and savage Dyaks of the Rejang, inveterate head-hunters. Only the year before they took those of two Chinamen who were trading up the river. For this misdeed they were duly and severely punished by the Tuan Muda, but it appears that the lesson had not been sufficient, for even then they were sending out parties in search of heads. I stayed the night at a Dyak house, the inmates of which appeared to me not to differ from the Dyaks I had met with on the Batang Lupar.

On the following morning, October 1st, I had not much trouble in getting my Kayans to start, for they were anxious to reach Sibu, and soon after dawn we were *en route* once more. We stopped at the small fort of Nongma, then the farthest inland station of the Sarawak Government, but I found no Europeans resident here. At 2 p.m. we reached Kanowit, a village at the mouth of a river which bears the same name. The people here are different in appearance both from Kayans and Dyaks. They wear the *jawat* like the latter, but are offended if they are compared with them. The women are dressed in the usual Malay fashion.

The Kanowits were once a race of ferocious head-hunters, but are now peaceful and inoffensive. Before Rajah Brooke and his nephew used their energetic civilising influence, giving peace and prosperity to these people, it was considered a duty, when a Kanowit died, for his kindred to obtain a head at any cost, and on such occasions they did not hesitate to take that of the first person they met, man, woman, or child, were they even members of their own tribe, and even, it is said, relatives. This is certainly a queer way of understanding " duty," a word which can only express a hereditary form of sentiment, corresponding to the social condition of a given people at a certain epoch.

I saw some Buketans here also, who had settled amongst the Kanowits. The river at Kanowit is very wide, and the high hills which bank it in all the way from the village of the Tanjongs cease here. The majestic aspect of the Rejang is now much increased, owing to the addition to its waters of two such important affluents as the Ketibas and the Kanowit. The current is moderate, but thanks to the energy of my Kayans and our light and gracefully built boat, we got along famously; and having left Kanowit shortly after sunrise, we reached Sibu about five hours later.

During this journey from the Bellaga to Sibu I met with several tribes of natives, whose very names were new to me. Others I only heard mentioned by the Kayans who accompanied me. It would be as well, perhaps, to give here a general *résumé* of the information I gathered concerning the people living on the Baloi or Rejang and in its vicinity.

In addition to the Malays, Chinese, Mellanaos, Dyaks, and Kayans, the following tribes inhabit this region :—

Sigalang, once a numerous tribe, but now greatly reduced. The few survivors, who no longer speak their language or dialect, live at Siriki.

Sirus, also once a powerful tribe, now reduced to a few families.

Bilions, only a few left, who wander in the forest; they have a special dialect.

Minkilon, Banjok, Tanjong, and Sidoan, (Fig. 53), small allied tribes, now assimilated by the Kayans, and having lost their own dialects.

Buketan, a nomadic forest tribe.

Pennan and Ukit, allied to the Buketans, and also wanderers in the forest.

Krian and Sian, also nomadic forest tribes akin to the Buketans.

Punan, Skapan, Kadjaman, and Lanan, tribes all speaking peculiar dialects, now conquered by the Kayans.

Punan tana, or Punan batu, who live principally on the Baleh.

Kinya, a far inland tribe, who inhabit the country near the sources of the Kapuas, Barram, and Koti.

The following tribes live beyond the boundaries of the kingdom of Sarawak :—

Sibu and Malo, dwelling on the Kapuas. I met a few of the latter on the Kantu.

Butan, who live on the upper course of the Koti and Banjar, and are said to be more civilised than the Kayans.

Klai and Taman; tribes known to my Kayans, living on the Upper Banjar.

The fort of Sibu is the most important in Sarawak after that of Kuching. Its position is well chosen at the apex of the delta formed by the two great branches of the Baloi, which are the Rejang, properly so-called, and the Igan.

The fort commands an immense expanse of water, the Baloi being here no less than a mile and a half in breadth. The country is quite flat; not the slightest hillock breaks the uniform line of the horizon. Behind the fort, marshes covered with swampy grounds and primeval forest extend right away to the sea. The river here is very deep, and its waters, which are turbid, are of a dirty greenish colour.

Mr. Cruikshank, the local Resident and commandant of the fort, was absent; but Mr. Skelton, his lieutenant, received me as an old friend, and treated me with the most generous and cordial hospitality.

For eighteen days I had lived and fared like a Kayan. Sago and rice, with curry and a few sardines as condiments—and especially the first, for rice was scarce till we got to Kanowit—had been practically my only food.[1] It is true that I often had fish, for my cook, Sahat, was clever with the " jala," or casting net—a round net weighted with lead plummets all round, used in many countries. When I was in Borneo I always carried one of these nets with me, finding it most convenient for catching fish, and thus varying our very monotonous diet; in fact, in these regions I found it much more useful than my gun, which, on river journeys, can hardly be used without much loss of time. With a net, on the other hand, a haul of fish was easily obtained in the shallows hard by while the rice was being cooked.

When I reached Fort Sibu my personal luggage was greatly diminished. My shoes and socks were gone, and my dress was reduced to a jacket, a pair of trousers, and a sarong in a condition which I dare not describe. My utensils consisted of a single pot for cooking rice. But I had safely brought to my journey's end a large package of dried plants, many of which I afterwards found represented endemic species mostly new to science, even generically. The living plants of camphor and of Kajattao had also arrived in perfect condition.

Notwithstanding my meagre diet of rice and sago, I had had no more attacks of fever after leaving the Bellaga. I felt perfectly

---

[1] Bad hygienic and nutritious qualities are usually attributed both to rice and sago, but I believe this to be a mistake. It is true that sago is not very nutritious, but it is easily digested, and can be safely eaten in large quantities. I may say that during our journey down the Rejang we used to munch pellets of sago the whole day long; and certainly my paddlers never showed signs of losing strength, but worked energetically all the time, and they ate hardly anything else. Physiologists have now shown that carbohydrates, such as feculum, sugar, etc., facilitate and keep up muscular energy and force, on which nitrogenous food has little or no special influence.

well and strong; but I should be guilty of an untruth if I asserted
that I did not relish and appreciate the luxuries of my friend
Mr. Skelton's table, and that I failed to do them full justice.

Sibu, nevertheless, was not the end of my journey, for I
had planned to follow the Igan branch of the great river down to
the sea. I remained a couple of days at the fort, however, to take
a little rest, to replenish my supplies, and to allow a Chinese tailor
sufficient time to make me something new in the way of clothes.

On the fifth of October, having procured a boat without difficulty,
and added the necessary number of paddlers to my four Malays, I

Fig. 53.—SIDOAN WOMEN OF THE LOWER REJANG MAKING BASKETS, ETC.

started at 3 p.m. on my way down the northernmost branch of the
Rejang delta, distinguished as the Igan. The forest of tall straight
tree-trunks rose like a gigantic wall on either side, the width of the
river being several hundred yards. The ground level was so low
that in some places we entered with the boat into the forest. Few
of the trees were then in blossom, but the aspect of the vegetation
was different from that of the Upper Rejang, and plants with
narrow leaves were no longer to be seen. The effects of sudden
periodical floods on the river banks are not felt here, nor those of

constant currents of air. We were now in a region where variable winds reign, alternating with calms.

Although the entire delta of the Rejang may be considered as an unbroken swamp, it has no such aspect, for the plants which grow there cannot be called aquatic in the true sense of the term. For while the tall forest-vegetation which covers every bit of ground is practically aquatic, herbaceous aquatic plants, and especially floating species, are entirely absent. The Araceæ, Pandanaceæ, palms, and an infinite number of other plants besides, whose feet are always in water, become truly aquatic. This is the reason why many of the tropical plants belonging to the above mentioned families do not thrive in our hothouses, or only do so when they are treated as aquatic plants, and the pots in which they grow are immersed in water kept constantly at a high temperature.

Few, indeed, were the brightly coloured flowers which I saw in the forest through which we were paddling. In that never-ending mass of green only a few scarlet Ixoras met my eye. I found a new species of *Momordica* (*M. racemiflora*, Cogn.) pretty common, remarkable for its large flesh-coloured flower and a black calyx—a *true* black, that is to say, which is a colour very rarely met with in flowers. Many are very dark, but there is always a tendency towards violet or purple. For the moment I can only recall one other instance of true black in a flower, and this is also that of a Bornean plant, an orchid, *Cœlogyne pandurata*, in whose flower the labellum has large patches and veins of a deep black colour.

Stillness, heat, sandflies, horseflies, and mosquitoes reigned supreme, but did not combine to make our journey an enjoyable one. The absolute silence and solitude are startling. Not a hut, not a single boat did we meet with for hours and hours together. Towards noon Nature appears asleep; not a bird's note, not a sound of any kind breaks the profound stillness. The very water appears to move on as a solid mass, and not the slightest breath of air moves its polished shining surface. The atmosphere is heavy and oppressive to an extreme, loaded with aqueous vapour, invisible on account of the high temperature.

The silence was only broken by the cadenced sound of the paddles dipping in the water, at long intervals, to the sleepy chorus of my men. But a sudden shock and the lifting of our sampan from beneath awoke us from the drowsiness into which we had fallen. We at first thought that we had struck some snag or tree-trunk floating on the water. It turned out to be the back of an enormous crocodile, but I could not make out whether we had struck him accidentally, or whether he had tried to capsize the boat.

Shortly after this adventure I perceived another huge crocodile sunning himself on the muddy bank. His posture was comical, for there he lay stretched out immovable on the mud, and looking as if he were dead, but the mouth was open to its widest extent, the upper jaw nearly at a right angle to the lower one, showing all the teeth and the yellow colour of the inside. I contemplated the monster for some little time, wishing to see how long it would preserve this absurd attitude, but it never moved, and looked exactly like a stuffed museum specimen. I cannot understand how such a posture can be comfortable, but for crocodiles it appears to be a common attitude of repose. My Malays said that the animal had just gone to sleep, and certainly its eyes were closed, possibly the result of some unusual digestive effort. When crocodiles lie thus with open jaws, small shore birds, especially waders of the sandpiper kind, which are always running about on the banks in search of food, enter the huge reptiles' mouths to capture any such small fry as may have sought refuge amongst the teeth or in the folds of the mucous membrane of the mouth or pharynx. Indeed, if I remember right, I have witnessed the thing myself; but now as I write I cannot feel quite sure that it was not one of the many stories told by my men.[1]

But to return to the one which has given rise to these reflections. I thought that I would disturb its slumbers with a bullet, and aimed at the inside of its mouth. I do not know whether I hit it, but it certainly awoke as suddenly as the report of my gun, and dived into the river's depths forthwith. This, and other shots fired at the crocodiles we met now and then with their snouts sticking out of the water, were the only incidents of the day. I was never able to make out whether I hit the animals or not, for they invariably plunged under water and disappeared at once. On one occasion only, on the Sarawak river, was I able to secure a small crocodile which I had shot. It is very difficult to kill at the first shot creatures whose vitality is so tenacious, and whose skin is so admirably protected by its scales, whilst the brain in the massive skull is nearly inaccessible to a bullet. It is said, however, that even a slight wound is eventually fatal to crocodiles on account of worms which take possession of the sore. This may be partially true; but all the same, one often meets with animals which have been more or less mutilated in fights amongst themselves, which are alive and active enough.

Crocodiles are more abundant in places such as those I have just described than elsewhere. Perhaps this may be accounted for by the fact that they find an easy prey in the wild pigs, which are extremely numerous in these forests when the fruits ripen, and often cross the river in troops. The scarcer the wild animals on which they prey, the more dangerous do crocodiles become to

---

[1] Cf. *Herodotus*, Bk. II. lxviii., where the same story is told. I have also heard it from the lips of a Malay in Celebes.—ED.

human beings. Where wild pigs abound they are the principal food of these huge reptiles, and it is in the estuaries of rivers, where the receding tide leaves large tracts of uncovered banks, that wild pigs find their favourite food, and easily supply that of the crocodiles.

Although numerous enough in the rivers of Borneo, I have never seen crocodiles herded together, as the caimans are said to herd in South America. Many were the crocodiles I met with, but never did I see even two together.

The stillness of the day had its contrast during the night. A violent wind arose, carrying away the matting which roofed the sampan, whilst the rain fell in torrents. This rendered the air less oppressive, and made us feel less languid and indolent, but it was impossible to put up any kind of shelter, and we remained as we were until morning, drenched to the skin.

I was able to collect but few plants of any interest, partly on account of the great width of the river, which prevented me from keeping inshore, and partly again from the difficulty of always catching sight of blossoming plants when paddling along. Amongst those which attracted my attention, even from a distance, were two " pinang-utan," a name which the Malays give to all the forest palms which resemble the true pinang (*Areca catechu*). This time, however, one of these pinangs, about twenty-five feet high, turned out to be a genuine *Areca*, an undescribed species peculiar to Borneo (*A. Borneensis*, Becc.), distinct but allied to a species widely diffused in the Malay Archipelago.[1] *A. Borneensis* is also called by the natives " pinang umbut," because its cabbage is edible. The other species of palm, which was quite a small one, I had already found at Bintulu ; it was a variety of *Pinanga patula*, Bl.

Towards evening we arrived at Igan, a village near the mouth of the river, almost exclusively inhabited by a colony of Mellanaos, who speak the same dialect as those settled at Muka, and different from that of the Bintulu Mellanaos.

On the 8th I made an excursion to the mouth of the river and the sea beach, but I found no novelties. The most remarkable plant met with was a species of *Hoya*, or an allied genus (P.B. No. 3,926).

Igan is considered unhealthy, and is also renowned for the number of its mosquitoes. According to a Malay expression, the air is so thick with these insects that they can be cut with the parang. The place had so little interest that next day I commenced my return journey up the river to Sibu. This trip was even more tiresome than the down-river one. The mosquitoes formed, without exaggeration, veritable clouds, and we had to put up with horse and sandflies besides. It would be interesting to know why

[1] This is the *Areca triandra* v. *Bancana*, Scheff. (cf. *Malesia*, i. pp. 22, 97).

in such deserted regions these small vampires are so numerous.   In
other parts of the world, as in the Bogos hills of Northern Abyssinia,
I subsequently found these pests abundant; but there, at least, they
had cattle in large numbers from which they could quench their
thirst for blood.   In the forests of the Rejang, however, the only
large animals on which they can feed are monkeys and wild pigs,
and these are scattered over an extensive area, though the latter,
indeed, at certain seasons are said to congregate in the delta in
great herds, coming from all parts of the country, and swimming
across small and big branches of the river alike.   This, as I have
already said, takes place when the wild fruits are ripe, and the
ground in the forest is literally covered by them.

On the 10th we continued our monotonous journey, harassed as
usual by myriads of mosquitoes.   For two days we paddled through a
continuous mass of these insects.   Truly, their quantity is incredible.
On our way towards the sea we progressed much more rapidly, and
the mosquitoes were less trying; but going up the river against the
current it was far more difficult to rid ourselves from their attacks.
It may be that when a swarm has once taken possession of the boat
it sticks to it.   To lessen their numbers I made my men smoke,
and throw pinches of tobacco on a small fire kept burning at the
prow.   But this was of not much avail, and I had to remain all day
under my mosquito net, and not having gloves to protect my
hands, I covered them with a pair of socks.   The night brought us
even worse torments than the day.   Though my men had rolled
themselves in their sarongs, they were unable to sleep a wink.   I
had, besides, an attack of fever, so that my condition was not a very
enviable one.

Three days had now passed without our meeting a single living
creature, excepting, of course, the mosquitoes.   At length it rained,
and they were less troublesome.   On the 12th we had fine weather;
but the current was strong, and we did not reach Sibu till the
13th October, and right glad were we to do so.

I remained six days at Sibu to finish drying and arranging my
plants, to take some rest, and to make preparations for continuing
my journey across the State of Sarawak.   Of those days of rest
and comfort, thanks to the kindness and pleasant companionship
of Mr. Skelton, I still retain a very pleasing recollection.   And
this is quite unassociated with any affection for the locality; for
Sibu can hardly be called a pleasant place, although there is a
certain grandeur in the immense extent of water, the endless forest,
and especially the wide expanse of horizon, which in Borneo is
usually so limited by the exuberance of the vegetation.

During my stay I visited some of the Dyak houses, and made
several short excursions into the forest.   In a locality near the
fort I found a species of wild orange quite abundant.   The fruits

are larger than those of a common orange, which they resemble in shape and colour, but not in taste, for they are very bitter, quite as much so, indeed, as the so-called Seville oranges. The rind is very thick. The Malays call the plant " Limau antu," which means " Spirit's lemon," but in a truer sense signifies " Devil's lemon," an appellation better suited to its flavour. This Citrus formed little groups by itself in the forest, in places where the ground was evidently liable to frequent inundation, and where few other species of plants grew. Amongst scientifically interesting forms I found in tolerable abundance, and growing nearly above ground, a Hymenogastræa (*Clathrogaster Beccarii*, Petri), one of those fungi which live in the ground like truffles, and have been rarely met with in tropical countries.

Mr. Cruikshank, being aware of my wish to cross from the basin of the Rejang to the Sakarrang, had, before leaving Sibu, asked Mr. Skelton to get me some trustworthy Dyaks to accompany me as far as Simanggan. Meanwhile, I had furnished afresh my scanty and dilapidated wardrobe, and had procured the necessary supplies of rice and dried fish for the journey. I had also bought from Chinese traders various indispensable articles to be used as presents or for barter, such as tobacco, thick brass wire, glass beads, and cotton cloth. I consigned to Mr. Skelton my limited but precious collections, which he had kindly offered to send on to Kuching by the first safe conveyance.

My Baloi Kayans, well satisfied with what I had given them, took their leave, and returned to their own country.

CHAPTER XXI

ON the morning of October 19th, as previously arranged, Ladja,
with eight other Dyaks, came to the fort duly equipped
for the journey. Ladja (i.e. "Sumpitan arrow") was the son of
the Orang Kaya of Pulo Kaladi, the island which lies opposite to
the fort of Sibu, right in the middle of the Baloi. He was a handsome young man, tall like most of his companions, slender, and
beautifully made. His profile was nearly regular, the nose perfectly
straight, but the cheek bones rather too prominent and the chin
rather pointed. His complexion was very light. Similar types
are not at all infrequent amongst the Baloi Dyaks, amongst whom
one seldom sees cases of "kurap" (a skin disease allied to itch),
which is so disfiguring and so prevalent amongst the Land-Dyaks.[1]
Ladja presented himself to me in his picturesque costume—a
short jacket of red cloth and the "jawat"; a parang was stuck in
his belt, and in his hand he held a sumpitan. From his ears hung
large pendants made out of the huge red beaks of the great hornbill
(*Buceros rhinoceros*). A large number of rings of brass, gradually
decreasing in diameter, covered his legs below the knees, whilst on
his arms he wore two rings of white shell.

Having taken leave of Mr. Skelton who had been so kind to me
and done so much to facilitate my journey, I went over to Pulo
Kaladi to Ladja's house in order to exchange the boat I had for a
more commodious one. In the house I saw a Mayas Tjaping's
skull, well smoked, and hanging up with numerous human skulls.

---

[1] "Kurap" (see footnote on p. 60) is the same as the common and
widely-distributed skin disease of the Pacific known as Tokelau ringworm,
and is caused, not by an Acarus, but by a fungus (*trichophyton*).—Ed.

I should like to know why these Dyaks placed the skull of an ape amongst their war trophies. Perhaps they, too, have an inkling of the relationship existent between Man and the anthropoids, and in one of their war expeditions, having failed to secure human heads, brought back what they may have considered a substitute. Orang-utans, it should be remarked, are rare on the Rejang, and are thus regarded more or less as objects of curiosity.

On the twentieth of October I commenced my journey towards Simanggan. The Rejang, where its two branches enclose Pulo Kaladi, is, perhaps, about 1,100 yards across from bank to bank. At daylight we were all in the boat, but just as we were starting an accident happened which might have had serious consequences. A Dyak, unskilled in the use of firearms, in sitting down, removed my gun loaded with big shot which was lying by my side, causing it to go off. Ladja was just behind me, and at first I feared that he was badly wounded; but, fortunately, between him and the muzzle of the gun was a native rotang basket or tambuk containing some of my clothes, a package of tobacco, and a pair of shoes; these received the full force of the discharge, and Ladja, fortunately, was merely struck in the legs by a few spent pellets of shot which had gone through, and hardly penetrated beyond the skin. I did not know how Ladja would take the occurrence, but neither he nor any of his companions for a moment thought of attaching any blame to me. I feared that such an accident, taking place just as we were about to start, might be regarded as a bad omen, auguring against our departure. But it was just the opposite. Ladja, far from being discouraged by the mishap, considered it as a patent proof of his invulnerability. Not having been killed then, he felt confident that he was proof against all bullets. Meanwhile, with my taxidermists' tweezers, I extracted the shot from Ladja's legs. The operation was a simple and easy one, the more so as the young Dyak was as impassive as if I had been taking the shot out of the soles of my shoes instead of from his muscles.

Towards evening we left the Rejang, here quite 700 yards across, and entered the Kanowit. We halted for dinner, but resumed our journey immediately afterwards. Rain fell in the evening, all the more disagreeably as it increased the force of the current against which we were paddling.

Ladja's Dyaks, active and obedient to their chief, did not require much persuasion, as the Malays do, to take up their paddles, nor was their next morning's toilet a lengthy business. At dawn they were up, and when, very shortly after, the sun rose—for here the dawn is brief—we were again on our way.

The country we were now traversing was most uninteresting to me; the banks were high and the land in consequence was dry. The primeval forest covered the land no longer, and jungle of secondary growth was to be seen wherever there were no rice fields. The rain had caused the river to rise, and we proceeded slowly. But the Dyaks are very clever in taking advantage of any counter-currents formed by projecting points. For such portions of the river placed between two reaches the Malays have a special term, "rantao."

We met with a big crocodile of the kind called by the natives "boaya katak," or frog crocodile, so called because it has a shorter snout than the common species. The boaya katak prefers shallow, clear-running water, whilst the common long-snouted species keeps to the big rivers.

The banks of the Kanowit continued to be uninteresting because deprived of the old forest, a proof that the country was populous, although few houses were to be seen from the river. I noticed several fine tapangs, and some specimens of the ruddy monkey (*Semnopithecus rubicundus*), which is also met with on the Batang Lupar and Sadong rivers, though I had never seen them on the Sarawak. The local restriction of an animal which can easily travel long distances is remarkable. The Dyaks call this fine monkey "Julu mera," and assert that in it is found a bezoar stone, here known as "Batu belliga," to which they attribute great virtues. Up to that time I had been told that the bezoar was hidden in the head of the animal, but Ladja assured me that it is found in the *prut*, i.e. abdomen. Possibly it is a urinary calculus, and occurs in the bladder. Most of these bezoars come from the Kayan territory. The Malays set a great value on them, and pay extravagant prices for them, using them for medicinal purposes. One kind, more highly esteemed than the others, is said to be found in the porcupine.

We halted next day for the usual culinary operations at a place called Aboi. The long house-village was not visible from the river, and is reached by ascending a streamlet, hidden by vegetation and barely accessible to a boat, for a few hundred yards. Sahat got here a good haul of fish with the casting net.

The Dyaks at this house struck me as peculiar. Some of their women had goîtres, which I had never seen before in Borneo. I also met an albino—the second I had seen, and similar to the one I had met at Marop. Several of the children, I noticed, had fair hair. I cannot explain why in this house I should have found such an assemblage of abnormalities. I do not believe in accidental characters in organisms, when such a term is applied to a character produced independently of physiological or hereditary causes. The cause may be unknown, difficult of recognition, and possibly even not capable of explanation in the present state of our knowledge ; but even the smallest modifications in living beings, every line in the physiognomy, as well as every variation in the proportion or form of any part of the body, except those of pathological origin, I take to be the result of hereditary influences, for I have little or no faith in the acquisition of new characters in the present period of evolution.

Perhaps albinos and fair-haired persons in tropical countries serve to show how, from little-known but climatic influences, a dark race may assume the complexion of Northern races ; or possibly the phenomenon is merely a case of a return to a character possessed by a remote ancestor, traces, in short, of interbreeding with a race different from that which now occupies the country. The girls at Aboi were the handsomest I had seen amongst the Dyaks ; fair in complexion, with full, rounded forms and busts, and none of the usual angularities.

Hitherto we had been going through flat country under the usual Dyak cultivation, which consists in not replanting rice in a field before an interval of six or seven years after its first sowing. Now hills reappeared, and the river was more broken and torrent-like, the water was shallower and the banks more picturesque. We passed the night of the 23rd at the mouth of the Sungei Matto, one of the branches of the Kanowit, and next day continued our ascent of the latter river. The country was populous. We passed numerous Dyak house-villages, partly hidden by areca palms and big fruit-trees. At each house, or village, as it may aptly be called, they invited us to stay ; indeed, at each they wished me to pass the night, which would have pleased my Dyaks greatly, but I was too anxious to get on with my journey to accede.

The bright complexions of the Kanowit Dyaks are no doubt the effect of their prosperous condition, the abundance of food they have, and the salubrity of the country ; but not a little must also be owing to their frequent ablutions. Indeed, we never passed one of these houses without seeing a lot of women and children bathing in the river. After the bath the women rub their bodies all over with the root of a *Zingiber* or of a *Curcuma*, which gives a yellow tint to the skin, and to my eyes was far from adding to their beauty, making them look as if they were suffering from a severe attack of jaundice. The colour is, however, easily removed by a wash. I do not know whether this part of the toilette of the Kanowit ladies has a hygienic object, or whether it is adopted from æsthetic reasons.

That morning we saw on a branch projecting over the river a beautiful bird, called *burong papu* by the natives. The feathers are thick and peculiarly soft, black on the breast, brilliant carmine on the abdomen, and light brown on the back. It is the *Pyrotrogon kasumba*, and one of the birds whose appearance is considered a good omen by the Dyaks, especially if they are starting for a " munsu," or head-hunting expedition. But to meet it is always a sign of good luck, and my Dyaks asked me to allow them to stop a little while in token of respect, to which I readily consented. They stopped rowing, and remained a few minutes quite still with their paddles lifted, and then cheerfully resumed their labour.

It was nearly noon on October 24th when we left the Kanowit and entered the Entabei. Here we found the current stronger, but as the water was shallow we made good progress with the " suars," i.e. by poling. Ladja's men were very clever at this work, and could push a boat rapidly up shallow streams with strong currents in a way unknown in the Malay Islands east of Borneo. The study of poling-methods in various countries would be not without its interests. Our Arno boatmen in Tuscany always pole where the river is shallow, and use their poles exactly as the Dyaks do theirs, only they certainly cannot compare with the latter in the length of the journeys thus performed with their light canoes. Ours literally flew over the surface of the water, handled with incomparable dexterity by my six young savages. There is to my mind no lighter and more pleasant method of progression, and certainly no kind of work displays so well the elegant movements and perfect proportions of these young Dyaks, who, practically unencumbered with clothing, are truly splendid specimens of humanity. Timing their movements with marvellous precision, one stands erect and raises his *suar*, while his neighbour bends low over his as he thrusts it into the bed of the torrent, and so alternately. Anyone inexperienced in the work would very soon be overboard.

Several villages were passed, but as it was still daylight we continued on our way, only halting when the shade of the trees of both banks, which now nearly touched each other overhead, had deepened into darkness.

The morning of the 25th was delicious ; a cool gentle breeze wafted to us the sweet scent of the blossoming trees in the neighbouring forest. The sun, in spite of its tropic fierceness, hardly managed to pierce the dense mass of foliage overhead with a few of the slenderest rays, which, reflected by the limpid crystalline waters of the river in dancing shafts of light, fitfully illumined the green tunnel through which we made our way. The clear water ran over a bed of gravel, at times sloping enough to form a series of small rapids, covered over a wide area by a singular plant having purplish leaves with sheeny reflections. This was a small aroid (*Cryptocoryne bullosa*, Becc.), belonging to a genus the species of which live mostly under water. The leaves of this plant are most remarkable. Their surfaces are not flat, but pitted beneath and with corresponding protuberances above, as in some varieties of the common cabbage. What is the cause of such a conformation in an aquatic plant ? All structural peculiarities in an organ must have, or have had, some cause or reason—for adaptation, as I understand it, is merely the result of the action of stimuli on organisms at one time endowed with the faculty of modifying themselves according to their environment. Admitting this, what stimulus can have produced the singular conformation of the leaves of this *Cryptocoryne*? Perhaps it was the need of enlarging the assimilating surface of the leaves (the plant living in shady places) without increasing too much the resistance to the water current, which might have torn it. Or was it due to the current itself exercising a continuous tension on the surface of the leaves in the spaces between the longitudinal and the transverse ribs, and distending the tissues in these parts, as the wind would a sail. Or have both the above mentioned causes contributed to render hereditary a character which was at first accidental, but of daily occurrence? There are some plants in which the tension of water against the leaf surface has acted more energetically, lacerating the least protected places so as to produce complete perforations. This is the case with some of the *Uvirandras*.

The above-mentioned *Cryptocoryne*, the cause of this digression, was then in blossom, but the inflorescences were submerged and all closed. Probably they only expand when the waters are very low, or else the plant is one of those termed by botanists cleistogamous, i.e. producing flowers which never open, not even when fecundation is taking place.

I searched most carefully on the rocks, both submerged and awash, for Podostomaceæ, as such places looked likely for these plants, but I found none. The absence of members of this family through the entire Malay Archipelago excepting Java is singular, for several are found in Ceylon, whose flora offers so many affinities with that of Malaysia. All the rocks we had seen so far were sandstone.

We camped for the night on a projecting tongue of land which lies at the confluence of the Mintei and the Entabei. On the bank, exactly at the point where the two rivers meet, rose a most majestic tapang (*Abauria excelsa*), one of the finest specimens of this gigantic tree. I had never been able to ascertain the height of these giants on account of their surroundings. But here was an excellent opportunity for taking a measurement, for the tongue of land was perfectly level and flat, and gave me the means of measuring a base. With this datum, a very simple trigonometrical operation enabled me to determine the height of the tree, which proved to be 230 feet from the ground to the top of its immense crown of foliage.[1] Six

---

[1] I am of opinion that the heights of 450 feet and more attributed to some Australian trees (*Eucalyptus*) are unreliable. [Mr. W. Ferguson, Inspector of State Forests, measured a fallen Eucalyptus on the Watts River which by the tape was 435 ft. from base to a point where it was fractured. Here its diameter was 36 inches. "Before it fell," he writes, "it must have been more than 500 feet high." (v. A. Trollope's *Australia and New Zealand*, vol. I, appendix iv.)—ED.]

Fig. 54.—DYAK METHOD OF BORING A SUMPITAN.

feet from the ground the circumference of the trunk was 69 feet; but this was not the girth of the cylindrical part, or trunk proper, but of the buttresses as well. Such expansions or buttresses in the *Abauria* are at times so large and flat as to furnish the immense planks which I saw during my stay with the Tubao Kayans. The trunk, covered with a light-coloured smooth bark, rises perfectly straight without a branch, like an immense column, for at least two-thirds of the total height of the tree. Only at that great height does it spread out its vast branches, on which honey bees build their nests in preference to any other tree. The crown is immense and dome-shaped.

On the 26th we continued to ascend the Entabei. In some places the water was very low, but my Dyaks, strong, active, and always good-humoured, got out and dragged the boat for long distances. The weather continued fine, but the country was less picturesque. With the exception of some fields covered with green rice, we passed through nothing but land clothed with jungle of secondary growth. Whilst we were passing a village I noticed an object which I could not explain. It looked at first something like the scaffolding for putting up a statue (Fig. 54). When I learnt that it was the apparatus for making sumpitans I stopped on purpose to examine it, and had the good fortune to see it working, for one of these weapons was then being made. The piece of wood selected to be bored is always of a hard, tough kind, usually tapang or mingris (*Dialium*). It is cut about the length required, some six or seven feet, but the thickness is considerably greater than the ultimate diameter of the tube. This long log of timber is fixed vertically on a kind of platform, which is raised on four stout wooden pillars planted in the ground and held firm by slanting stakes; they are also bound together by transverse bars, so that the whole structure is exceedingly strong. The raised platform, on which the log rests vertically, is about seven feet above the ground. As soon as the log of wood is fixed firmly in its perpendicular position, so that it cannot possibly move, the Dyak artificer places himself beneath the scaffold and strikes with a uniform and measured stroke the centre of the lower end of the log, using a round iron rod a little longer than the log, nearly as thick as the calibre of the sumpitan, and sharp at the end like a chisel. This is continued until the log is bored right through. To polish the bore and render it perfectly uniform in diameter, a rotang of adequate length and diameter is passed through and worked up and down as long as is necessary. The method of boring is similar to that used for making blasting holes in mines, only the work is done from beneath upwards. The iron borer has a wooden handle fitted to it to facilitate working, and this handle is run down the iron rod as the work proceeds.

That evening we reached the *pangkalan*, or landing-place,

where our overland journey was to commence. My Dyaks appeared very much pleased, not because their labour was at an end, for owing to the transport of the baggage the land journey was far more fatiguing than that on the water, but for the change which is always welcome to these people. We lighted a fire to cook the rice for our supper, whilst some of my men went into the woods in search of young shoots of bamboo, of ginger, edible fern (*Asplenium esculentum*), leaves of trees, or other *sayor*, as the Malays call such kinds of vegetable condiments. Others went along the river and managed to catch some fish. These Dyaks are so well acquainted with all kinds of useful forest produce, that they do not require to take a quantity of provisions when on their journeys. I was also struck with the fact that they never appear to be tired, even after paddling from sunrise to sunset, with less than an hour's rest at noon. That night, naked as they were, they preferred to sleep ashore on the pebbles of the riverside to lying in the boat. But during the night it began to rain, and the water of the swollen torrent reached their sleeping place, and obliged them to seek shelter under the matting covering the boat.

Under heavy rain we next day commenced our march overland from the basin of the Baloi to that of the Batang Lupar. It is a most tiresome journey, the road for the greater part of the way being the actual bed of the Kammaliei torrent. Half that day we marched through the water on slippery pebbles covered with algæ. At intervals we left the bed of the torrent and went up and down small hills, in order to make short cuts or to avoid places where the water was too deep for wading. The forest was very fine, and would, no doubt, have yielded grand botanical novelties if I had only had time to stop and collect. Amongst the notable plants I found was a singular Anonaceous shrub (*Unona flagellaris*, Becc.), whose flowers are neither on the branches nor on the trunk, but on underground offshoots. These flowers are about two inches in length, of a conspicuously bright liver-red, and highly perfumed. It is most strange to see them emerging isolated from the ground a foot or more away from the base of the plant to which they belong. In one place a little streamlet formed a waterfall, and I found the rocks wetted by its spray covered by a diminutive Aracea. The entire plant hardly attains the height of three-quarters of an inch. I have named it *Microcosia pygmæa*, for it is the smallest member of the family, which has some gigantic species, such as the *Amorphophallus titanum*, which I discovered later in Sumatra.

From the Kammaliei we got into the Attoi, another torrent, and thence into the Blangun, which is quite a streamlet where we struck it. After a short rest for dinner, we started once more, climbing a hill of about 1,000 feet to begin with. Such a path it was, too ! It took us through land which had once been cultivated, but had been long since abandoned. We marched along under a sun of truly tropical intensity, at the very hottest hour of the day. The heat in the forests of Borneo is always moderate,[1] but in the open it is most oppressive. There were no trees, and the ground was covered with the detestable lalang grass and by rassam (*Pteris arachnoidea*), a tall and thickly matted fern. This is the vegetation which invades clayey soils, when, after the forest has been cleared and after the first cultivations, the heavy rains have washed away the superficial layer of humus. The hills covered with lalang grass look well from a distance; indeed, with the clumps of trees which are scattered about, they have quite a park-like appearance. But this is only another kind of mirage, and the illusion passes away as soon as one sets foot on them.

The hill which we had to cross was steep, and the miserable pathway we followed was as slippery as ice from the morning's rain. Now and again we came across prostrate tree-trunks hidden in the grass, over which we fell. After two hours of this far from pleasant exercise we at last reached the summit, where it was some compensation to get an extensive view over the surrounding country —a rare thing in Borneo. In the distance we could see higher hills on the misty horizon. I was also able to form an idea of the kind of country to the S.S.E., which we had to cross in order to reach the Sakarrang or S'krang river.

We got down the hill by a pathway no better than the one which had led us up, and after three hours of a very fatiguing march we reached the torrent Meliet. Half of my men had remained in the rear to wait for an old Dyak who had joined us from one of the houses on the way. Although he was a Dyak, he felt the weight of his many years, and our pace was rather too quick for his old legs. Rain was threatening, and the sun was nearing the verge of the horizon. Only a portion of our luggage was with us, and it looked as if we should have to pass an uncomfortable night in the jungle, when one of Ladja's Dyaks, who had been this way before, suddenly remembered that there was a house in the neighbourhood. We accordingly followed his indications, and got there when it was quite dark.

Happily, amongst the things with our detachment of the party there was a vessel for cooking rice. The house was empty, the inmates having probably gone to look after their rice fields, where, when they are far from the house, temporary shelters are always built. We found rice in the house and honeycombs, from which my Dyaks extracted some excellent honey, clear and very fluid.

---

[1] Not every traveller, perhaps, will subscribe to this statement. Some of the most unbearable temperatures I have ever experienced in any part of the world have been in the Bornean forests, especially trying on account of the extreme airlessness.—ED.

This is the product of the tiny bee called by the Dyaks "nuang" (*Apis nigrocincta*), which is found in the forest, but can easily be domesticated. We had thus an excellent supper of rice and honey; and we hoped, also, to have a good sleep, after the tiring march and the heat, from which I at least had suffered, and apparently my sturdy Dyaks as well. But we were doomed to disappointment, for the sandflies were simply insupportable, and, not having my mosquito net with me, I never closed my eyes. In all my excursions in the Bornean forests I would always prefer to do without food than without that most excellent of inventions. But we should have fared still worse had we not found the house, for the rain came down in torrents throughout the night.

Whilst we were waiting for our laggards at the Meliet torrent, I saw the Dyaks who were with me hunting amongst the pebbles of the torrent for a peculiar stone, which they greedily nibbled as if it were a sweetmeat. It was a kind of clayey schist, soft and brittle, and greasy to the touch. I brought a few specimens away with me.

Next morning the rest of our party joined us. They had camped in the bed of the torrent; but when it rained the waters rose, and they had to fly, and passed a miserable night on the bank, for they were not even able to light a fire. The old Dyak who had been the cause of this delay, discouraged by so unpleasant a commencement of his journey, had thought it wiser to turn back.

None of the inmates of the house had returned, but Ladja and his men, without much ado, helped themselves to all they cared for, knowing that they were amongst friends. They prepared a luxurious breakfast, consisting of fowls, rice, sago, and honey, of which I partook with zest. For once in a way we made a late start, and it was ten o'clock before we were off. We marched in the bed of the torrent in six inches of water. This is the most tiring kind of locomotion that can well be imagined, and is quite as unpleasant to the Dyaks, whose feet become tender from such constant soaking, and are more liable to get wounded afterwards in walking through the forest. In my wanderings I found that a three days' tramp in these forests disabled a third or half of the natives who were with me. Most undoubtedly Borneo is not the land that has caused an anthropoid like the orang-utan to exchange his arboreal locomotion for a terrestial one!

Leaving the torrent we climbed a hill of some 1,300 feet, which was entirely planted with rice, not the smallest tree remaining to shade us from the merciless sun. When I got to the top I was once more rewarded for the fatigue and heat I had endured by an extensive view of the hills of the Sakarrang, the Batang Lupar, and the Seribas. These lay in front of us, whilst looking back over the way we had come I could see those of the Kanowit. Sadok, too, famous in the wars of the Tuan Muda, boldly dominates the landscape. All the hills near and around us were under rice cultivation, or covered with lalang. For miles and miles around there was no old forest, or only small patches on the steeper slopes of some hills. It was in one of these patches that I found a shrub whose leaves when rubbed emitted a strong smell of lemon-scented verbena (*Aloysia citriodora*). It is the only plant which I found in Borneo with that kind of scent. It was without flowers or fruit, and from the leaves alone I could not even attempt to guess its systematic position.

We descended the hill by a very steep path, and from the clayey nature of the soil slid down the greater part of the way, it being most difficult to stand erect and preserve one's footing. The sun was in the zenith, and I felt as if I were in a furnace. I endeavoured to shield my head with the broad leaves of wild bananas, whenever we came across these plants. A few pieces of the leaves folded and placed on one's head inside the hat are an excellent defence against sunstroke. We reached the right bank of the Sakarrang at a place called Rantu N'karas, about two hours after noon. Travelling, as I did, Dyak fashion, constantly in and out of the water, or drenched to the skin with rain, it was useless to carry a watch ; it would very soon have been *hors de combat*. But in a country so near the equator the division of the meridian circle into twelve equal parts is no very difficult matter, and with a little practice it is easy to tell the hour during the daytime within an error of fifteen to twenty minutes. Even the length of one's shadow can be easily and with considerable accuracy turned to account in ascertaining the time.

Just opposite the spot where we had struck the Sakarrang we could see the village we were bound for. Its name was Ruma Sale, and, as usual, it consisted of one large and very long house, for many families lived under its roof. It takes its name from that of the headman or Orang Tua, which was Sale, and it was once a famous nest of pirates. Ruma Sale is built on a kind of land-spit or promontory, which commands a sudden curve of the river, and thus dominates the stream on both sides ; it is, therefore, impossible to approach it without being seen from a good distance. The big house is partly hidden by fine pinangs and big fruit-trees. I also saw there several upas trees and fine kadjattao sago palms, grown from seeds brought from the forest.

The Sakarrang is a large and rapid river, which here describes a tortuous course amongst picturesque hills. From Rantu N'Karas it can be ascended in boats for three days, after which in one day's overland journey the Katibas basin can be reached. The hills which form the dividing range between the Katibas and the Sakarrang are probably under 3,000 feet.

At Ruma Sale I again saw some Dyaks eating with evident relish the clay schist which I alluded to just now as having seen at the Meliet. It certainly was not eaten to appease hunger, but as a delicacy, or, perhaps, to assuage an instinctive craving of the stomach for some alkaline substance.

As there were many upas trees here, and as the natives are very proficient in preparing the well-known poison, I wished to witness the process used in its manufacture. It is a very simple one. With a parang they first make a deep oblique incision in the bark of the tree, and then place just below it a bamboo joint, in which the milky sap, which exudes in abundance from the cut, is collected. In this manner, from a upas near the village, I myself collected sufficient sap to fill a joint of a medium-sized bamboo in a very short time. The fresh sap of the upas is quite harmless, and thus no precautions are necessary whilst collecting it; a fact I can amply confirm, for whilst tapping the tree my hands were splashed all over. I have explained elsewhere the way in which the poison is preserved in palm leaves hung over the fireplace, and when required for use dissolved and applied to the points of the sumpitan darts.

No European had previously been in this part of the country, and I was therefore an object of the greatest curiosity, especially to the women, and amongst these the most importunate were the elderly ones, of whom there was an ample and scarcely attractive collection. I had few things with me, my personal necessaries forming only the load of one man, for travelling as I did I could not take much luggage with me. And yet every object was passed in review, handled, and commented upon. These old hags would have taken possession of everything had I let them do so. In no other place was I so much pestered with questions, and nowhere were they as absurd as here ; especially those relating to elementary cosmography. But there was a reason for this, at least it appeared to me so. These Dyaks, who, by the way, do not differ from the other Land-Dyaks I had seen, consider the earth to be a flat surface, whilst the heavens are a dome, a kind of glass shade which covers the earth, and comes in contact with it at the horizon. They, therefore, believe that, travelling straight on, always in the same direction, one comes at last, without any metaphor, to touch the sky with one's fingers. Now as they know that Europeans come from far away over the sea, the supposition that we are nearer heaven comes naturally to them. It seemed to them, therefore, nearly impossible that I had not been in the moon, and they wanted to know if in my country we had one or several moons, and if we also had only one sun. It was most amusing to see the signs of incredulity which my negative answers elicited amongst my audience. Had I told them the story of Jules Verne's *Voyage to the Moon* I should certainly have been believed. It was with real sorrow that they heard me assert that in Europe the sky was quite as far from the earth as in Borneo.

But who can say that the belief of these Dyaks was not that of many people of the West in prehistoric times during the Stone Age? Or that the idea of the possibility of the gods descending to the earth may not have had its origin in the above-mentioned notions as to the shape of heaven and earth? The gods of Olympus may have been in origin nothing more than invaders from the East, who profited by the beliefs of the primitive peoples of the West to inculcate in them greater respect. It is a mistake, I feel sure, to believe that the present-day savage populations of Southern Asia and its islands are inferior in point of intelligence to the primitive peoples of Europe. Far from this being the case, I imagine that, making allowances for differences in climate, the manner of life of the two peoples must have had great analogy.

At 10 a.m. the next day we began to descend the Sakarrang, which for many miles below Ruma Sale is an almost unbroken succession of rapids, and has to be navigated with great care. My party was a numerous one, and as large boats were dangerous we divided into two. In each of these boats were two experienced hands from Ruma Sale. We passed, almost at starting, two very dangerous places. My boat, skilfully handled, shot past the rocks in the boiling and foaming waters, but we were very nearly swamped, and got into calm water only in the nick of time. The boat which followed, and which carried our supplies, was prudently dragged over the rocks by the crew, a longer and more fatiguing, but much safer operation. After this we passed the other rapids very successfully, and the rivalry between the two crews sent us along at a prodigious rate.

At noon we reached a village, where we found quite a number of people assembled. A meeting of the neighbouring chiefs was being held to give judgment in the case of a man who had married a second wife, the first one being yet alive. This appears to be a very grave offence against the established customs of this tribe, for I was told that the guilty person ought to be punished with death. I found the chiefs squatting in a circle on mats, each having in front of him a dish and a cup, both of which were empty, while around the assembly gongs, drums, and especially tajaus, were disposed.

I do not know what was the verdict given by the judges, because our arrival interrupted the proceedings, and I only stopped for the time necessary to change my boat and crew. I was also able to buy some fowls, eggs, and rice, which were abundant here. At every village we came to we changed boat and crew; it appears that such is the custom of the Sakarrang Dyaks, and that they

accompany friendly travellers only as far as the next village. It is
a kind of posting by water, which, however, causes much loss of time,
although we got along very fast on account of the strength of the
current. We passed the night at a house which contained very
few inmates, having changed boats and crews four times *en route*.

Ladja at each village came out in gala costume. He removed

Fig. 55.— SEA-DYAK OF THE SAKARRANG.

the breeches he wore in the forest, or when he was paddling in the
boat, and wore the jawat only. He then put on his enormous
hornbill ear-pendants, passed his numerous brass rings on his arms
and legs, and put on his red jacket. He liked to show off at full
advantage before the girls, and I could see that they looked on him
with admiring eyes. Ladja was not only a handsome young fellow,
but an excellent *parti* for any girl; and I can fully understand he

was a good deal more killing when his muscular and well-shaped legs were not encased in a prosaic pair of trousers.

On the 30th we were early in our boat, and passed through a very populous region, where no trace of the old forest had been left. We were obliged to change boats and crews six times, and at each village we were forced to stop and answer the persistent questions as to who we were, where we had come from, whither we were going, and so forth. The hills now disappeared, the river became deeper, and there were no more pebbles in its bed. All those I had examined in the region we had crossed were of sandstone. I did not see any trace of limestone or of granite. Greatly to my annoyance —for I wanted to follow the entire process of the preparation of the poison—I found that the bamboo joint containing the upas had been left behind at the house where we had slept. When I discovered the loss it was too late to turn back, and besides we should have had to paddle up stream, which would have required at least twice the time. We halted at 5 p.m., having covered not less than seventy miles in the two last days.

On the thirty-first of October, favoured with a full flood, we entered the Batang Lupar and reached Simanggan in the afternoon. At the fort I found the Tuan Muda, who had just come from Kuching. To my delight I found that he had kindly brought my letters and newspapers, of which I had been deprived for several months.

CHAPTER XXII

SIMANGGAN Fort is built on a very slight eminence rising
from the river bank, but it is quite sufficient to afford a view
over a large extent of country. The surrounding district is covered
by a swampy forest of high trees, whose bases remain all the year
round in water. This kind of forest is the most tedious to cross, but
it is that which offers the greatest harvest to the naturalist, on
account of the enormous variety of species which form it, a fact
which I am inclined to attribute to the ready dissemination of fruits
by the water. As most of these fruits float, they are easily carried
about during floods by the current ; and if the forests are invaded
by water they find favourable conditions for germinating.

From Simanggan there is a good pathway leading to Undup,
with which I was already acquainted, having traversed it twice ;
the first time with the Bishop of Labuan the year before, the second
when I came to Simanggan, in March, on my way to Marop. But
the pleasure of being able to walk comfortably and dry in a Bornean
forest was too great for me to resist the temptation of going there
again.

The forest would doubtless have rewarded me with many things
of interest if I had been able to stay and work it, but a mere excursion through it can hardly be expected to give important results,
since it is impossible to have trees climbed or felled in order to
get specimens. Nevertheless, I found submerged beneath the water,
which remains permanently in the lower hollows of the forest,
another very distinct species of *Cryptocoryne* (*C. longicauda*, Becc.,
cf. *Malesia*, i. pl. 27, Fig. 6), of which I had the misfortune afterwards to lose the only specimens collected, though I fortunately
have a drawing made on the spot. This genus of aquatic plants is
of especial interest, on account of the multiplicity of its adaptations
to a subaqueous life. I have already mentioned *Cryptocoryne*

bullosa, which lives in the clear and rapid waters of the Entabei. I found other species of the same genus on the muddy banks of the Bintulu and Igan ; and another and very large species (*C. ciliata*, Fisch.) is abundant on the slimy mud along the banks of the Sarawak river, where at low tide it is partially out of the water. The *Cryptocoryne* of the Simanggan forest was evidently adapted to live in the limpid waters of the densest forests, and thus in perennial deep shade. The spathe in species is very long, and terminates in a long filament which resembles that of the European *Arisarum proboscideum*, and serves, perhaps, to guide fecundating insects into the nuptial chamber when the waters are low. Another species (*Cryptocoryne pallidinervia*, Engl.), found at Simanggan, grows under conditions resembling those in which *C. longicauda* occurs, and is an instance (which I believe to be hitherto unrecorded) of a subaqueous plant having leaves variegated with white along the midrib.

I remained for a week at Simanggan Fort as the Tuan Muda's guest, and was thus able to finish drying and arranging the plants which I had collected. They were not numerous, but were of exceptional importance.

At that time of the year to return by sea to Kuching was a serious undertaking in a small boat, for the north-east monsoon was blowing strong on the coast. I was very desirous, moreover, of visiting and exploring the country between the Batang Lupar and the Sarawak rivers, a region quite unknown to me. I therefore decided to return to Kuching overland. Of the Dyaks who had accompanied me thus far, Ladja and one other alone expressed the wish to go on with me, the others remaining at Simanggan. I had, besides, my two Malays, Sahat and Bakar, who had followed me from Bintulu, and the Tuan Muda kindly gave me a boat and a few more Sea-Dyaks to accompany me as far as Banting (Fig. 56).

We left Simanggan early on November 8th, but shortly after noon a most violent storm burst over us, obliging us to seek refuge in a small stream until the wind abated. The river, which was very wide at that spot, assumed the aspect of a tempestuous sea, and would have been very dangerous for our fragile boat. That evening we reached Lingga, and I took up my quarters in the old fort.

Early next morning I went up to the mission-house at Banting, where Mr. Chambers gave me a most cordial and hospitable reception, repeating the kindnesses he had shown me a year before when I visited him with the Bishop of Labuan. The next day was a Sunday, and I took a quiet stroll on the hill, leaving my gun at home. Banting Hill is entirely covered with great fruit-trees, mostly durians, amongst which the Dyak houses are built.

From Banting one has a fine view of Gunong Lingga, or Gunong Lessong, thus named on account of its shape—a truncated cone with a wide base, which resembles an overturned mortar, to which article the Dyaks and Malays apply the name "lessong."

On the 11th, in company with Mr. Mesney, the other resident missionary at Banting, I started to make the ascent of Mount Lingga, which was no very difficult undertaking. We left at 2 p.m. in a

Fig. 56.—SEA-DYAKS OF THE BATANG LUPAR.

sampan, in order to get the assistance of the inflowing tide. For about eight miles we paddled up the right branch of the Lingga river, and then entered a small stream which led us to Kranji, a Dyak house-village, where we passed the night. We were off again early next morning. The road up towards the mountain led through land once cultivated, but now abandoned. The ascent was not so bad, and pretty easy walking, but most of the hill-side was covered with the usual uninteresting vegetation which springs up on abandoned lands. We reached the summit of Gunong Lingga at 10 a.m., after a few hours' continuous but easy climbing, during which we were able to keep up a good pace. Only near the top was there any true old forest, and here I noticed several species which I had collected on other mountain summits, such as *Dacrydium*, *Podocarpus*, *Dammara*, and the Mattang *Eugeissonia* (*E. insignis*, Becc.). There was a fine view of the tortuous course of the river lying beneath us. On the rocks at the summit, which, like the rest of the mountain, were of sandstone formation, I found some nests of *Collocalia*, but they were not of the edible kind, being composed of moss with only just sufficient of the gelatinous substance to hold it together.

The descent only took us about three hours, and at 3 p.m. we were back at Kranji. There we had not long to wait for the ebb tide, and with its aid we reached Banting in another three hours, in time to have supper with Mr. Chambers.

All I now required was a guide and a boat large enough to take us a one-day's journey to the landing place, whence our overland march across to the Samarahan was to commence. But the good missionaries were unable to procure this for me. I must confess that this surprised and disappointed me greatly, for I had had no such difficulty whilst travelling amongst remote and savage tribes. Everywhere boats had been freely and willingly given to me ; and I certainly never should have expected a refusal of so small a favour at Banting, where for years missionaries had dwelt and exerted their influence. When I bid good-bye to my otherwise most kind hosts I felt rather ruffled and indignant.

With my men, Sahat and Bakar, and the two Dyaks from the Rejang, I went down to the Dyak houses by the river, where I had seen the sort of boat I wanted. Without further ado I had it put into the water by my men, placed my small amount of luggage in it, and telling my men to take the first paddles they found, got in and started. Meanwhile people had gathered on the bank, and the owners of the boat protested ; but a " ringgit " (dollar) I threw them was sufficient to quiet them, and I ordered my men to paddle on.

I had certainly overcome the main difficulty, but without a guide my journey was no easy one, for the Lingga river soon loses itself in a maze of swamps, splitting up into innumerable intricate channels, through which without a guide it is almost impossible to find one's way. I hoped, however, to meet some one who could act as pilot on the way. After having paddled up that portion of the river which I had gone over on my trip to Gunong Lessong, as the time of flood tide was near we stopped at a lanko to await the tidal "bore." This came at 4 p.m., and was rather imposing, only instead of being a single wall of water it was followed by several waves in succession. We started again with the tide in our favour, and paddled for five hours, as long as it served us, in fact ; when we made fast the boat to a tree, lit a fire, had our supper, and then lay down to sleep in the boat, there being no dry spot ashore. Our slumbers were not quiet, for the boat caused us continual anxiety, being in bad condition and very leaky. The river was very full, and the water was perfectly clear, but of a dark colour, like that of strong tea, just as I had seen it in the Kapuas lakes.

On the 15th we continued to ascend the Lingga river, which now widened and spread over the forest, completely inundating it. At one spot the vegetation was entirely composed of pandani, through which we with great difficulty found a passage. We often heard the bellowing of orang-utans, but did not see any.

Since we had left Banting we had not fallen in with a single living soul, and we were beginning to get anxious regarding the direction we were following, for the regular course of the river could no longer be made out, and we had got to a kind of lake, where all view around was impeded by a thick growth of pandani. But in the nick of time, when a guide had become an imperative necessity, we met with a boat paddled by a single Dyak, happily a pagan, who readily offered to pilot us.

We had fortunately not yet got off the track, and after a little time we came to a part where the course of the river was plainer. It was nevertheless still so full of plants and floating tree-trunks that our progress was very slow and fatiguing. Towards evening, after having got drenched to the skin by a very heavy shower, we found a little sort of hill raised above the waters, where we passed the night as well as we could.

I left there next morning the boat which I had taken at Banting, for it was too large for the river, which was now reduced to a mere torrent. Two men with my luggage accordingly got into the small canoe we had met, whilst I with the other two and our guide proceeded by land along the bank of the stream, following a pathway which led to the dwelling of some Subumban Dyaks, which we reached at about 11 a.m.

In this house I noticed for the first time a very ingenious instrument for husking rice (Fig. 57), an operation usually performed in a wooden mortar, as I have previously mentioned. But the instrument I now saw was a form of mill, and consisted of two cylinders of very hard wood, about a foot in diameter, which were placed one over the other. The top one was shaped like a funnel at its upper end, and bored through, the bore having a diameter of about 4 inches. Its lower end was concave, and had deep grooves radiating from the

centre to the circumference or outer edge The bottom part was a
solid block, equal in diameter to the upper cylinder, very heavy, and
furnished with a peg on which the upper block revolved. It was
convex at its upper end, and cut into radiating ridges which corre-
sponded to the grooves of the lower end of the upper piece. The
rice to be husked is poured into the upper cylinder at the funnel-
shaped end, and passes out where the lower end of the first and
upper end of the second cylinder meet with their grooved and ridged
surfaces, the husk being rubbed off the grains by a semi-rotating
movement given to the upper cylinder, which has lateral handles
for that purpose, whilst the lower one is held firm and upright by its
great weight.

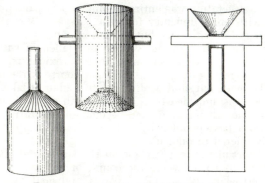

Fig. 57.—HAND-MILL FOR HUSKING RICE.

As it was not my intention to travel any farther that day, I
determined to make an experiment with the upas poison. In
exchange for a "ringgit" the Dyaks sold me one of their dogs for the
purpose. Since the first of November I had myself prepared a few
sumpitan darts, or ladja, dipping their points into some dry upas
sap, which I had obtained from the Sakarrang Dyaks and dissolved
in tobacco juice. I gave the poor dog that was to be the victim
a little rice, and as it was eating I gently blew one of the little
darts into its right thigh. The wound was so slight that the dog
hardly shook itself, and went on eating its rice ; only the skin
had been penetrated and not a drop of blood appeared. After
a few seconds, the dart being still in the wound, the creature showed
signs of slight uneasiness, such as might be occasioned by the bite
of a flea, and after the ladja had been about thirty seconds in the
wound, drew it out with its teeth. After about a quarter of an hour,
during which time the dog showed no further signs of being affected,
it retired to a corner as if to sleep. Half an hour later it was seized
with several accesses of vomiting, after which it went out of the

house and had an evacuation. It then came up again and curled up as if to sleep on the floor, showing no signs of pain, though it appeared exhausted, and its breathing was very feeble and infrequent. After two hours it was still in the same condition, looking as if it would die at any moment; but in about three hours after having been wounded it began to recover slightly, and dragged itself towards the fire.

Next morning the poor dog was still alive, but still under the influence of the poison. It made frequent attempts at vomiting, its circulation was evidently profoundly affected, and the pulsations of the heart were very irregular. Considering how slight and superficial the wound was, the effect of the upas appeared to me very energetic, and I have no doubt that it would have been fatal had the dart penetrated further and carried the poison directly into the circulation.

On the 17th I had hoped to make an early start, but only managed to get off towards 9 a.m. I had been able to recruit four men, for I had very energetically impressed on the Dyaks that it was their bounden duty to accompany Europeans who were travelling through their country; a thing which I believe the missionaries have never thought of teaching them. For some time we marched up the Subumban torrent, walking in its bed, and then crossed over some hills about 1,600 feet high, following a fairly good path which traversed an old forest, where, judging from the abundance of their nests, orangs must have been common. Large blocks of granite were strewn about the forest.

As we descended the hill I came across a kulit-lawan tree (*Cinnamomun Kulitlawan*), a species then new to me, which is akin to the true cinnamon, and also produces an aromatic bark which is highly esteemed. The leeches were more than usually abundant and troublesome, and I could not protect my feet from their attacks. My men chewed tobacco and squirted the juice over them, when they fell off. If they are violently detached the bite gets inflamed, and may then easily become a tiresome and even dangerous sore— as I can amply testify from personal experience during the first period of my sojourn in Borneo.

We next crossed a small plain, with an isolated Dyak house in the middle of it, built on the Seppas torrent, which empties itself into the Sumundjang river farther on. We had thus crossed the water-divide; but instead of following the course of the torrent, which is a very tortuous one, we climbed over another sandstone hill, and found ourselves again in the Sumundjang valley. We then crossed a marshy tract, and after seven hours of rapid and continuous marching, fatiguing even to the Dyaks, we reached the Ramin pangkalan.

We put up in a house belonging to the Sabuyo Dyaks, who

were as much surprised to see us as if we had fallen from the clouds. They appeared to be people of very stay-at-home habits, and to know next to nothing of the country beyond their own district, at all events landwards, for at sea these Dyaks were once famous for their piratical cruises. Ladja and his companion were never tired of narrating the story of our wanderings over and over again, with the minutest particulars. In all the houses where we had stopped for the night in the latter part of our journey, the Dyaks used to assemble and squat down in a circle around me, staring in silence at me and watching every movement I made, whether I was dressing, washing, or taking my meals. Then came a flood of questions—some of them most absurd—concerning Europe, our ships, railroads, etc. Then Ladja and his companion would sing, extemporising in Dyak verse our wonderful adventures during the journey. They always began with a shrill and ear-piercing scream, which was kept up as long as their breath lasted ; then followed cadenzas, much after the fashion of our own peasants' songs. The Sabuyos appeared to enjoy this music exceedingly, which I cannot say I did.

At 7 a.m. on the 18th we left for the pangkalan, or landing place, where we were to find boats to descend the Sumundjang as far as the village of that name. We crossed some marshy ground by one of the most awful of Dyak pathways—the very worst I had ever met, which is saying a great deal. On account of the rain the water in the marshes was higher than usual, the branches and tree trunks on which we had to walk were rotten, and to add to our discomfort the terrible *Scleria*—a kind of sedge which always covers these tracts of swampy land—covered my hands and half-naked legs with scratches. There was no shade, and the heat was intense ; and, to crown all, the fierce red ants abounded. As we could not avoid disturbing their nests in passing, they revenged themselves by swarming all over us, and inflicting particularly painful bites.

On our way we came to a pool on whose borders grew quite a number of the same wild orange-trees which I had found at Sibu. The conspicuous feature of the marsh vegetation in these localities is a species of *Pandanus*, which appeared to me identical with that which I had met with on the Umpanang.

When we reached the landing place we all got into the boat, but it was a very small one and could hardly carry us. We were therefore obliged to move with the greatest caution, so as not to capsize. The water was black and with hardly any current, the river here spreading over the forest in all directions, and looking as if it had no proper bed of its own. We saw again a lot of Mayas' nests, and at last caught sight of one of these creatures not more than thirty yards off. I fired two shots at him, and apparently hit him badly ; but I was obliged to leave him, for he fell in the midst of a lot of pandani, whose young shoots he had been eating, and these formed a hedge so dense and prickly as to be practically impassable. I might have spared the poor brute's life, and should have done so had I stopped to think ; for even had I got him our boat was too overloaded already, and we could not possibly have added any further weight to it, unless we desired to serve as a repast to the numerous crocodiles, whose snouts we saw sticking up above the water in all directions. At 3 p.m. we reached Sumundjang.

From Sumundjang to Samarahan a Dyak path, consisting of the trunks of trees placed end to end, had been made a few years before across the forest, principally, I believe, for the use of the workers in a coal mine in the neighbourhood, which was later abandoned. Reduced as I now was to the shortest of commons, and obliged to get to Kuching as quickly as I could, I thought it best to take this path as being the shortest, although we were warned that it was almost impassable on account of the rotten batangs, and the creepers and shrubs with which it was overgrown. It was, however, a sort of furrow in the vast mass of the primeval jungle which might serve us as a guide ; and certainly without its aid I should not have ventured to penetrate such forest as lay before us, having heard only too often of people who had done so, in search of gutta or rotang, and had never been seen again. This kind of half-submerged forest, where the subarboreal vegetation is very dense and intertwined, offers almost insuperable obstacles to the traveller, and a mile of road such as this entails more fatigue and more time than ten miles under ordinary conditions. But trusting in the path in question, which in seven or eight hours of travel should bring us to Samarahan, I started early with my four men, none of whom had been that way before, without taking anything more than a little cooked rice in the way of food.

Very soon the going became really atrocious; the forest was flooded everywhere, and we followed along the edge of the old path as best we could. On it we could not go, for densely matted vegetation of new growth had completely blocked it up. When we were obliged to diverge from it, we carefully marked the direction with the compass, cutting our way with the parang through masses of *Pandanus* and *Mapania*. Both these plants abounded, and were most troublesome on account of the thorns with which their long leaves are provided. To add to our difficulties rain fell incessantly throughout the day.

Meanwhile, it was getting dark, and we saw no possibility of reaching Samarahan that evening. We had had to go along slowly during the latter part of our journey, for one of my men had wounded his foot, and it soon became evident that we must camp in the forest. We therefore constructed one of the usual hasty shelters or lanko, lifted from the ground, taking advantage of a small space amongst the roots of some trees, the only spot sufficiently dry on which to light a fire and dry our clothes. Here we had a meagre supper on the small quantity of cooked rice we had brought along, whose sole condiment was a little salt. Even when we came to light the fire we found it no easy matter. There was no dry wood, and so soaked was everything with the rain that my men vainly tried to get a blaze with their strike-a-lights and tinder. I managed to succeed, however, with the wadding of my gun, which I fired for the purpose.

I need not dwell upon the tedious length of that night. With a half-empty stomach and the cramped position in which I was forced to lie, I never slept a wink. It rained incessantly all through the night, and as we had not been able to cover our lanko sufficiently, for it was dark when we finished setting it up, the water poured in on us in streams.

At last daylight came, but no sun with it ; on the contrary, a minute penetrating rain continued to fall. I could not find my compass. Apparently I must have dropped it the preceding evening whilst collecting branches for the lanko. As there was no sun we could not get our direction. We were, in fact, for the time being completely lost, for all trace of the old path had become obliterated, and we wandered about for a long time, vainly trying to find it. At length, by carefully watching the water that covered the ground, we were delighted to find it slowly flowing in a definite direction. This meant a stream somewhere, and following up the hint given us we at length came to a place where the natives had been working at a tree to make a canoe. Here we found a little path, which brought us at last, after wandering for several hours in the forest, to a stream. No houses were in sight ; the river banks had been cleared of forest, and were covered by tall coarse grass, through which we made our way with difficulty. The rising tide, however, carried past us a large nipa crown, big enough to carry one or two persons. Bakar and one of the Dyaks immediately jumped into the water, got on it, and having made a couple of extempore paddles, set off down the stream. They soon found a small boat, returned with it to fetch us, and towards noon we reached the village of Samarahan, where we found fowls and rice in abundance to make up for our enforced abstinence. I also took some rest, of which I was in great need, whilst we waited for the ebb tide to continue our journey. I had no difficulty here in finding a boat and the requisite men, and we got to Kuching at eleven o'clock that night. The journey from Bintulu to Kuching across the State of Sarawak, in its then greatest length, had lasted from the fifteenth of September to the twentieth of November. I had taken nine days from Bintulu to the Bellaga ; eight days descending the Rejang, stoppages included ; twelve days in going from Sibu to Simanggan ; and six from Banting to Kuching, not losing much time on the way.

CHAPTER XXIII

AT Kuching it rained nearly incessantly for a whole month (from the 20th November to the 20th December), but from the latter date to the 30th December the sky was clear. This abrupt passage from an excessively wet to a dry season soon showed its effects on the vegetation. Thus, opposite my house, a mango tree renewed all its foliage and got covered with flowers in twelve days, and many other trees as quickly underwent a similar change. Such abnormalities in the prevailing course of the monsoons are not rare in Sarawak.

About this time—unfortunately too late, because the day was approaching on which I had resolved to leave Sarawak—a most capable trapper came to offer me his services, bringing several interesting species of small mammals which I had been unable to get previously. The manner in which he captured them was simple and efficacious. He enclosed a portion of the forest with a small stockade, leaving narrow openings at intervals, at which he placed his nooses and traps.

New Year's Day of 1868 found me at Kuching, assisting for the third time in the festivities of the season, but in very different spirits from those I had enjoyed on the preceding occasions. My health, which up to the last few months had been excellent, had now completely broken down ; no doubt in consequence of the fatigue and exposure, not to mention the privations, which I had gone through, especially during my last journey. Fever attacks were now frequent and violent, and elephantiasis, which had shown itself some months before, was evidently increasing rapidly. My strength and energy were ebbing, and I now felt that the time to leave the country and return to Italy had come, and, indeed, was an absolute necessity. More than once the desire for home had come upon me, but never so strongly as then. Yet before leaving the field of my researches I felt that I must pay another visit to the auriferous and antimony districts of the Upper Sarawak river, to collect samples of the minerals and ores. Accordingly, when I felt a little better, I started for Busso, going along the same route I had followed on a previous occasion, and thence proceeding to Grogo.

The geological formation of the Grogo mountain had a special interest for me, and I was able to ascertain that it is of a crystalline and eruptive nature, like that of the Pinindjao and Singhi mountains. So, at least, say the notes I made on the spot in my journal.[1] I collected specimens of the rocks in order to have them more carefully examined on my return to Europe by some competent specialist, but, unfortunately, they were lost, together with most of the other rocks and minerals I had collected in Borneo.

Singhi, Pinindjao, Grogo, and, I believe, Santa, which, however, I did not visit, are the only examples of crystalline and eruptive geological formations found in the vicinity of the antimony mines.

At Grogo amongst the more remarkable plants which I met I may mention a *Costus*, with a fine orange-yellow flower, borne on a short radical stem. On the cliffs, in the most inaccessible places, I observed a lot of honeycombs, which I think belonged to the same species of bee which usually resorts to the tapangs. The Grogo Dyaks brought me several specimens of a bivalve (*Alasmodonta Vondembuschiana*) which lives in the streamlets near their village, and which not infrequently contains small pearls. From Grogo I went through Busso to Paku, to examine the alluvial formations from which the Chinese extract gold ; and from them I bought samples of the auriferous sand. Gold is also found on the bottom of caves, in isolated particles, or adhering to the sides and jammed into the fissures of the limestone rock. I was able to get some good samples of this peculiar auriferous formation.

It has been thought difficult to account for the presence of gold in caves, and in the neighbouring limestone rocks, but to me the explanation appears an easy one. I have previously remarked how, in the Busso district and in that of Bau (where gold and antimony are found), isolated peaks rise up from the plain, formed of cavernous limestone, which I believe to be of madreporic origin, and thus of slow submarine formation. Moreover, the vicinity of mountains formed of eruptive rocks (like those mentioned above) in the same districts with the limestone hillocks, would point to volcanic action having taken place in the same sea that witnessed the madreporic origin of these limestone hills. Under such circumstances the disengagement of sulphurous gases was probable, and how these may have formed chemical combinations with the antimony, the arsenic, and the mercury which occur in the same area is easily imagined. The sulphurets thus formed would crystallize in the fissures and

---

[1] The compact soil, of a clayey aspect, often perfectly white and similar to kaolin, which forms the hills of Kuching, appears to me to be the product of the decomposition of the rock of which these three mountains are formed.

other hollows of the eruptive rocks, and also through eruptive action be eventually injected, as it were, into the hollows of the limestone formations. If all this be admitted, and the presence in the neighbourhood of the caves of cinnabar, i.e. sulphide of mercury, be taken into account,[1] it is easy to understand how gold may be found in caves. My explanation is the following :—The heat due to volcanic action reduced the cinnabar, freeing metallic mercury. This, in contact with particles of gold, would at once amalgamate with them, carrying them off to where its fluid condition and weight allowed it to rest, namely in the fissures of caves. Any further evolution of heat would volatilise the mercury and leave the gold as it is found, i.e. in more or less dendritic masses of varying but always small dimensions, adhering to the limestone rock on the sides or in the hollows of caves. Or, again, the action of carbonic water dissolving portions of the limestone rocks may have further contributed towards fixing the particles of liberated gold in their mass. Amongst the specimens I collected, which were afterwards lost, was a fine and most interesting one, showing native gold in the fragment of the limestone rock.

The cave of Paku, which I went to see, was very difficult to get at. In addition to gold, edible nests of *Collocalia nidifica* were to be got there. The wooden props and steps by which access to the cave was rendered possible, were, however, in a rotten condition and quite useless, so I had to give up my attempt to explore its recesses. I was told that some time before a large quantity of human bones, especially skulls, had been found in this cave, and that they had been broken up by the Dyaks. In another cave, too, not far from that of Paku, bones had been found, but very friable, and reduced to semi-fossilised fragments. The limestone of these caves is sometimes white, sometimes dark in colour, crossed with veins of flint or chert, and often containing fossils, which are conspicuously visible.

This was my last excursion in Borneo. Before returning to Europe I had intended paying a visit to Java, starting from Pontianak, whither I had decided to go overland from Kuching. Everything was ready for my departure on the 20th January, 1868, when a violent attack of fever completely prostrated me. Meanwhile the mail steamer arrived, and as I had lost all hope of regaining sufficient strength to undertake a fatiguing journey overland, I decided to give it up, and took my passage on the steamer to Singapore, the first step on my journey homeward bound.

[1] A cinnabar mine in that district was worked with profit by the Borneo Company.

CHAPTER XXIV

Sarawak ten years later—The " Astana," Residence of the Rajah—
A Glance at the History of Sarawak—Rajah Sir James Brooke
—The Chinese Rebellion—The Present Rajah—Extent and Boun-
daries of the Kingdom of Sarawak—Our Present Geographical
Knowledge of the Interior of Borneo—Wild Tribes—Absence
of Negritos in Borneo—Cannibalism and Human Sacrifices—
Population of Sarawak—Intercourse of the Chinese with the
Island—Archæological Discoveries in Sarawak—Stone Adzes—
Archaic Writing—Products of Borneo—Agriculture—Preserva-
tion of the Forests—Earthquakes and Volcanic Phenomena—
Mineral Wealth of Borneo—Kuching—Political Divisions of
Sarawak—Commerce—Revenue and Customs—Form of Govern-
ment—Religions and Missions—Conclusions.

WHAT I have written in the previous chapters refers to many
years back, and Borneo has in the interval made marked
progress towards a more civilised condition, while its political and
commercial importance have enormously increased since my first
visit. I have therefore thought it best to give in this last chapter
a short summary of the present conditions of Sarawak. Some of
the changes which have taken place since I left the country in 1868
I have been able to witness myself, but for more recent events
I have chiefly had recourse to the *Sarawak Gazette*, the official
publication, which since 1870 has been uninterruptedly issued at
Kuching.

At the end of 1877, after a hurried journey across Northern
India and Burma, I happened to be at Singapore with my friend
Captain Enrico A. D'Albertis, awaiting a steamer to convey us
to Australia, viâ Torres Straits. We had a few days to dispose of,
and as the mail steamer for Sarawak was in the roads ready to start,
I proposed to my friend that we should profit by the occasion and
pay a visit to the dominions of Rajah Brooke. It was to me an
unspeakable pleasure to be able to revisit Sarawak. Ten years had
elapsed since I first landed at Kuching—ten years spent in almost
constant travel in New Guinea, the Moluccas, Celebes, and Java,
as well as in Abyssinia.

We reached Kuching on the last day of 1877. The next, the
New Year, was welcomed with similar festivities to those in which
I had taken part when I was last in the country, a period which
I still look back to as the happiest of my life.

The regattas on the river were most successful, and the assembly of European and native notabilities at the Astana, or house of the Rajah, afforded me the pleasure of meeting several of my old friends. I was also delighted to find sundry old Malay acquaintances, and their friendly greetings proved that I had not been forgotten and that they had preserved a kindly recollection of our former friendship. It is pleasant to record the general reciprocity of good feeling which is such a characteristic feature of the Sarawak community, cordially uniting Europeans and natives in bonds of mutual consideration and esteem. The barriers of race and rank are obliterated in this mutual and cordial good will. Together with representatives of the people, there was at the Astana a large sprinkling of the Malay aristocracy, which has always shown itself faithful to the enlightened government of the Brookes, even at the most critical times. This aristocracy has conformed itself entirely to the new order of things and has cordially accepted the reigning dynasty as a natural and improved substitute for that which for two centuries previously had ruled over North Borneo.

Usually on the first day of the year the Rajah and Ranee receive personally the European and native notabilities, but this year they had thought proper to hold their levée at one of the distant stations of the State. They returned to Kuching next day however, and I went at once with D'Albertis to the Astana to present my respects to their Highnesses. It was with very great pleasure that I again shook hands with the Rajah, Sir Charles, and made the acquaintance of the Ranee, Lady Brooke.

Old Government House exists no longer; the new residence of the Rajah, the Astana, is built on the small hill covered with fruit-trees, where stood the bungalow in which Doria and I had stayed. On the Astana hill the Rajahs of Bruni once lived, and their tombs are still there. There, too, Sir James Brooke had his residence, until it was burnt to the ground by the Chinese during their memorable rebellion.

I feel that I should be failing in a bounden duty towards a truly great and noble man, who founded a civilised kingdom in one of the most barbarous countries in the world, if in writing a book on Sarawak, I omitted to give a sketch of the principal events of his remarkable career.

Sir James Brooke, founder of the dynasty which for half a century has now ruled over Sarawak, was born at Coombe Grove, near Bath, on April 29th, 1803. When quite a youth he entered the army and went as a cadet to India, where he distinguished himself in the Burmese War and in Assam. Severely wounded by a bullet which went through his lungs, he was invalided home to England. In consequence of the wreck of the vessel on which he was going out to India again, he exceeded his furlough, and was thus unable to resume his service in the Indian army. He took the opportunity to travel to China, and during the voyage saw something of the islands of the Malay Archipelago, the beauty of which made such an impression upon him that he then and there determined to explore them.

In October, 1838, he left England for the China seas in his yacht the *Royalist*, a schooner of 142 tons, with a crew of 20 picked men, whom he had fully tried during a cruise in the Mediterranean. On arriving at Singapore he heard that at Sarawak there was a Rajah very friendly towards the English. This decided him to visit that place, and he anchored with his yacht off Kuching on August 15th, 1839.

Muda Hassim, the Rajah at that time, received Brooke with great cordiality, partly, no doubt, because he well knew how advantageous his assistance would be in restoring order in his State, which was then troubled by a revolt of some of the inland tribes. Brooke consented to assist him, and it was mainly owing to his aid that the Rajah was able to quell the rising and capture the rebel chiefs, whose lives were spared at the request of Brooke. But it appears that Muda Hassim was tired of ruling his small State, and accordingly on September 24th, 1841, he made a regular cession of it to Brooke, who thus became the legal Rajah of Sarawak, in which high position he was solemnly invested and confirmed by the Sultan of Bruni in the following year.

During the first succeeding years, in conjunction with Captain, afterwards Admiral Keppel, commanding H.M.S. *Dido*, Brooke was busily engaged in the suppression of piracy, at that period the scourge of the coasts and rivers of North Borneo. A fatal blow was finally given to these hordes of pirates by the flotilla commanded by Sir Thomas Cochrane, and Brooke took a prominent and very active part in all the operations. Meanwhile Omar Ali, the Sultan of Bruni, who had at first invoked the help of the British in the suppression of piracy, treacherously had Muda Hassim and several other prominent men put to death, as being too friendly to Europeans. When he heard, however, that the British fleet was on its way to Bruni to punish him, he fled into the interior, hoping to escape the consequences of his treachery.

After Sir Thomas Cochrane had left, the suppression of piracy was continued by Captain Mundy and Rajah Brooke, who had also been given the task of restoring order in Bruni by the Admiral. Brooke succeeded in getting from Omar Ali an abject letter craving forgiveness, and he was eventually allowed to return to his capital. But his prestige was hopelessly shaken, and went on declining until at his death, which took place on May 30th, 1885, he being more than 100 years old, his kingdom was reduced almost to vanishing point.

Fig. 58.—THE ASTANA, KUCHING.

Rajah Brooke had now acquired the power which comes from success, and his authority over the natives was complete. Sarawak awoke to new life, and was quietly developing and improving its natural resources with that rapidity of progression which is the outcome of civilised and orderly government. The regenerated State was in this prosperous condition when, in 1857, the Chinese rebellion suddenly broke out, menacing its very existence and nearly destroying the noble work done by Rajah Brooke. The causes of that revolt were in the main doubtless due to the ill-feeling aroused amongst the Chinese by the measures taken to repress opium smuggling. It was, however, a combination of circumstances which led the chiefs of the Kunsi, the Chinese society, working at the gold mines on the Upper Sarawak, to believe that a *coup d'état* would be an easy matter.

It was on the night of February 18th, 1857, that the Chinese rebels, numbering about 600, descended the river, and arriving unexpectedly, proceeded to attack the residence of Rajah Brooke, which was situated on the same hill as that on which the Astana now stands. The Rajah was in bed, and there was only a single European servant with him in the house. Suddenly awakened by the noise, he at once realised what had happened, and knowing that defence there was impossible, was fortunately able to leave the house before it was completely surrounded. Favoured by darkness, he reached the river unperceived, and being an excellent swimmer contrived, in spite of the width of the stream and the strength of its current, to gain the other bank in safety. Meanwhile, the Chinese, believing that the Rajah had perished, attacked and burnt the houses of the European residents, several of whom were killed or wounded. They also got possession of the small fort, which was defended by a single European and a few Malays, who all sold their lives bravely, but having been taken by surprise were soon overcome.

The rebels were now masters of Kuching, and proceeded to set on fire the houses of the Malays, most of whom, having put their women and children in safety, were preparing to encounter the Chinese insurgents. The Rajah had rallied them and placed himself at their head, but he soon saw that for lack both of men and arms, he could offer no great resistance to the Chinese, much less defeat them. His chance of success was to get to Fort Lingga, where a sufficient force might be collected to vanquish the rebels. A fugitive, and with only a few faithful followers around him, the Rajah had reached the Maratabas mouth of the river, when the Borneo Company's steamer was sighted, entering from the sea, and at the same time the first Dyak reinforcements appeared coming from Fort Lingga and led by the Tuan Muda, Charles Brooke, the present Rajah. The latter, as soon as he had heard what had taken place at Kuching, had started, taking with him all the fighting men he could collect at the moment, and leaving behind directions that all those who would join him were to follow at once.

The meeting at Maratabas was indeed a fortunate one. The steamer towed up the boats containing the Dyak warriors, and came unexpectedly before Kuching. The rebels were taken by surprise, and when the guns of the steamer opened fire on them with grape, they scattered and gave way, although they were supported by their fellow-countrymen settled in the town, numbering no less than 4,000.

The Kuching Malays, encouraged by the unlooked-for help, at once resumed the offensive, obliging the Chinese to retreat towards their head-quarters on the Upper Sarawak. They were now closely pursued and attacked by a strong party of Sakarrang Dyaks, who had by this time joined those from Lingga and from the nearer villages. In the end most of the Chinese rebels perished, and only a small number succeeded in reaching the Dutch territory of Sambas.

Thus, by a happy chance, with the exception of material damages and losses, the Chinese revolt did nothing to lessen the prestige and authority of Rajah Brooke. Sarawak soon shook off the effects of that memorable episode which had come so near to destroying the young State and the master-mind under whose rule it was developing in so wonderful a manner. The insurrection was in a certain way useful in showing the advantage arising from the ethnic and religious diversities of the population of Sarawak, which by maintaining an antagonism amongst the various communities renders a joint action against the ruling power practically impossible.

As is always the case, there have not been wanting those who, short-sighted and narrow-minded, or worse still, moved by envy or still baser motives, have severely blamed the actions of Rajah Brooke's Government, and, unwilling to recognise the civilising action resulting from the suppression of piracy, have stigmatised the latter as a barbarous waste of human life. But the evidence of facts soon silenced these calumnies, and the name of Brooke will always have an honoured place in the history of the development of civilisation in the Far East.

Sarawak, before Brooke came, was in a state of complete anarchy, and laid waste by continual wars. Malay fought against Malay, and one tribe of Dyaks against the other ; whilst from without piratical expeditions scoured its coasts with fire and sword, now siding with the Malays, now with the Dyaks. And if at the present day strife, pillage, and murder have ceased, and peace reigns and trade flourishes, it is all due to the enterprise, wide views, and integrity of Brooke, whose iron will and perseverance have made the country what it is. Sir James Brooke was fortunate in living long enough to see his work so far advanced as to feel sure of complete success in the end. From 1863 ill-health obliged him to remain in England, and he placed the Government of his State in the hands of his nephew, Charles Brooke, the present Rajah, who became his successor in 1868, when death ended his adventurous and remarkable career.

But if it is owing to Sir James Brooke that Sarawak is now a civilised State, his nephew, the present Rajah, has the high merit of having completed and extended that work, following out the humane and liberal views of his uncle.

H.H. Sir Charles Brooke arrived at Kuching on July 21st, 1852, being then quite a youth, but having already attained the rank of Lieutenant in the British Navy. This he has himself told us in a book in which—far too modestly—he relates the story of his expeditions against the inland tribes who had rebelled against the check placed by the Rajah's Government on their piratical and head-hunting propensities.[1] His brilliant operations against the Sakarrang and Batang-Lupar Dyaks, as well as against the Kayans of the Rejang—ascending this river far beyond the farthest point then reached by any European—resulted not only in completely subjecting and pacifying these wild savages, but in converting them into friends and faithful allies. And it is owing to the energy and wise administration of Sir Charles Brooke that the ancient custom of head-hunting is now all but extinct, and that the territory of Sarawak can be travelled over in every direction in perfect safety. Nor has this latter the modest dimensions it formerly had. Even at the time of my first visit to Sarawak, the dominions of the Rajah had been extended to Cape Kedurong, beyond Bintulu. Subsequent agreements with the Sultan of Bruni added, in June, 1882, the entire course of the Barram, and at the beginning of 1885, the Trusan. Finally, on March 27th, 1890, to put an end to a condition of things which threatened the tranquillity of Sarawak, Sir Charles Brooke occupied and annexed the Limbang district.

Thus the Sultanate of Bruni, which fifty years ago extended from Tanjong Datu over all North Borneo as far as the Sibuko river, the boundary with the Dutch possessions on the east coast, is now reduced to the city of Bruni and a small territory around it. What has not been ceded to or incorporated with Sarawak has become the property of the British North Borneo Company, which also took over the administration of Labuan in 1890. At present Bruni has no trade of its own, and the people live miserably on the produce of the fishery, while hundreds of families have left to escape the rapacity of the chiefs. The boundary between British

[1] C. BROOKE, *Ten Years in Sarawak*. London, 1866.

North Borneo and Sarawak is in lat. 4° 57′ N., long. 115° 13′ E.; for to the latter belongs the entire basin of the Trusan, which empties itself in Bruni Bay.

Inland the boundaries of Sarawak are as yet rather vague, but geographically the demarcation is simple, Sarawak claiming all the territories between Tanjong Datu and the mouth of the Trusan which are traversed by rivers flowing into the China Sea.

I believe that the area of Sarawak amounts approximately to some 70,000 square miles, which is greater than that usually assigned to it,[1] for hitherto the calculation has been made on Dutch charts, and in these the watershed from which flow the rivers emptying into the China Sea is placed much too near the coast. The rivers which debouch on the north and north-east coasts have thus short courses, whilst those which run into the Java and Celebes Seas are inordinately prolonged, causing a considerable augmentation of Dutch and a corresponding diminution of Sarawak territory. I therefore consider that the central chain, of which Batu Puti and Batu Tibang are the highest points, should be placed a degree farther to the east; the water-parting thus coming almost in the middle of the island.

In the maps which are given in Dr. Posewitz's excellent book,[2] the results of the observations of recent travellers in North Borneo have been used, but even in these it appears to me that the area of Sarawak is less than it ought to be. Dr. Posewitz could not allow the Rejang river a course of less than several hundred miles, and he has thus been obliged to make it run a short distance from, and nearly parallel to the coast. But I must add that the course of this river in Posewitz's map is traced according to the map published in the *Proceedings of the R. Geographical Society of London* (vol. iii., No. 5, p. 256, 1881), to illustrate a paper of Mr. Crocker's, who writes (p. 193) that the information regarding the upper course of the Rejang was furnished by me. In fact, on my return from the exploration of that river, I left a sketch-tracing of its course at Kuching, which sketch is the one I used in compiling the map of my wanderings.

I find, after carefully reading Posewitz's book, which is in most things extremely accurate as regards the present state of our knowledge of the geography of the interior of Borneo, that little indeed has been added thereto since the account of my travels in Borneo which I published in 1868 in the first volume of the *Bollettino* of the Italian Geographical Society, and which naturally corresponds to what I have written in a more extended form in

---

[1] The total area of Borneo is given as 285,700 square miles; being thus more than twice and a half the area of Italy.

[2] POSEWITZ, *Borneo : its Geology and Mineral Resources* (English translation). London, 1892.

Chapter XX of the present work. The few further details obtained amply confirm what I noted and observed more than thirty years ago, namely, that no very high mountains form the water-parting, where the rivers which flow in opposite directions through Borneo have their sources in the very heart of the great island. If mountains of any considerable height exist in that central region, they would have been undoubtedly recorded by recent explorers, for of late the watershed has been crossed with tolerable frequency.[1]

The Kayans of the Baloi and of the Batang-Kayan frequently pass from one versant to the other, and between the natives of the rivers on each side reciprocal head-hunting is carried on.[2] In 1884 some Ukits of the Makam (Koti) came to settle on the Rejang.[3] Rival feuds and hostilities have existed from time immemorial between the Peng Kayans of the Makam and the tribes of the Upper Rejang, also between the natives of the Barram and those of the Batang-Kayan. In 1885 a party of Peng Kayans and Ukits from the Makam came to Kapit, one of the forts recently constructed on the Rejang.[4] Kinya Dyaks from the Koti also have reached Bintulu by way of the Tubao, carrying rhinoceros horns and bezoar stones for trade.[5] Finally in March, 1900,[6] a party of about 500 Kayans of the Batang Bulungan, belonging to the Leppu Jalang, Leppu Bams, Leppu Teppus and Uma Tukon tribes, arrived at the upper stations of the Rejang river. This party had travelled about five months, with frequent halts to build canoes, and to collect food and forest produce. The expedition was led by Pingang Sorang, who with other of the principal chiefs was invited by the Rajah to visit Kuching. They thus can boast of having crossed Borneo nearly in its greatest width, from the Celebes to the China Sea. The trade which was done by these people at Kapit and at Sibu was very considerable. They brought guttapercha and indiarubber of excellent quality, valued at thousands of dollars, taking in exchange salt and various goods. Notwithstanding the great distance they had come, they asserted that as long as they were on good terms with the Hivan Dyaks they found

---

[1] In the *Geographical Journal*, London, July, 1901, p. 87, is an account of Dr. Nieuwenhuis's journey to the Sarawak frontier. He ascended the Makam to the mouth of the Rata and reached the source region of that river, whence a route leads to the Nyangeyan, a tributary of the Rejang. Batu Tibang was seen directly to the eastward, and estimated at over 6,500 feet, and the boundary of Sarawak—in other words the water-parting between the Makam and the Nyangeyan—consisted of a ridge from 2,300 to 5,200 feet in height.

[2] ' Mr. Low's Diary ' in *Sarawak Gazette*, June, 1884, p. 51.

[3] Cf. *Sarawak Gazette*, November, 1884.

[4] Cf. *Sarawak Gazette*, April and June, 1885, p. 56.

[5] Cf. *Sarawak Gazette*, March, 1885, p. 24.

[6] *Sarawak Gazette*, March 1, 1901.

the Rejang markets preferable to the more prosperous and more accessible markets of their own country.

I do not believe that from Bellaga the distance in a straight line to the foot of the mountains which form the central water-parting of Borneo can be more than 60 miles, only time is required to reach that spot on account of the rapids which have to be passed, and the strong current of the river. At the time I visited these parts the journey might have been easily performed in six or seven days, for no feud then existed between the tribes on the two slopes. A state of war or feuds between the tribes are the only difficulties now likely to be experienced in crossing Borneo from the Rejang or Bintulu to the eastern sea.

Mr. Hugh Brooke Low, whose lamented death occurred in 1887, has left a narrative of his journeys along the Rejang.[1] It was mainly through him that the majority of the Kayans were peaceably induced to pay Government taxes. At present, with the exception of a few tribes near the head-waters of the Koti and Banjar, all the others have submitted to the Rajah of Sarawak, and very little absolutely unknown country remains in that part of Borneo. Of all the great rivers of the northern part of the island, the least known is the Barram; but even this river has been recently explored by Dr. Hose.

Although we have still a good deal to learn concerning the physical conditions and natural productions of Borneo, I do not think it probable that any race or tribe of mankind is to be found there in a more primitive stage of existence differing greatly from those we are now acquainted with, as the assertions of some travellers might lead one to suppose. The most savage tribes of Borneo are the Buketans and the Punans, often called Ukits, and some other smaller tribes which are now disappearing. But even these do not seem to differ essentially from the Kayans, who are indeed more advanced than the others in civilisation and have come more in contact with the tribes living on the coast, especially with the Mellanaos, and perhaps in remoter times with the Chinese and the Annamites. With the Kayans must be grouped the Kadjamans, the Skapans, the Sians, and others.

The Ukits or Punans and the Buketans are savages in the true sense of the word, but they are neither degraded nor inferior races in the series of mankind. Their primitive condition depends more than anything else on their nomadic or wandering life, and on the ease with which they live on the produce of the forests and on that of the chase, which the sumpitan procures them. This has no doubt contributed to keep them from associating with their fellow-beings and from settling in villages or erecting permanent

[1] Cf. *Sarawak Gazette*, April 1, 1885. Mr. H. B. Low was the son of Sir Hugh Low.

houses. I believe that these, although they must be considered as the remnants of an ancient Bornean people, are not descended from autochthonous savages, but are rather the present-day representatives of a race which has become savage.

It is difficult to deny that Borneo has had older and perhaps more primitive human inhabitants. In most of the great islands in proximity to the Asiatic continent, and in some of the smaller ones also, from Ceylon to the Philippines, as well as on the Malay Peninsula, there are found people with crisp or woolly hair who may be regarded as having more or less affinity with the Negrito race, which has pure representatives in the Andaman islanders, the Sakais and Samangs of Perak, and the Aetas of the Philippines. In Borneo I have no recollection of having seen anything of the kind, but I must confess that during my earlier journeys in the island I did not make special anthropological investigations, nor had I that experience and knowledge of crisp or woolly-haired peoples which I was to acquire in my later travels amongst the Papuan islands. However, in none of the narratives of journeys and explorations in Borneo subsequent to my own have I found any mention of traces, much less of the existence, of Negritos in that island. I am, nevertheless, much inclined to admit the hypothesis that Southern Asia and its islands were once inhabited by Negroid races. These would have been substituted in process of time by immigrants from the more central parts of Asia. The dark skin and crisp hair would in all cases reveal a trace of the primitive Negroids. But it appears that in Borneo no such traces are to be found.

A recent author has asserted that cannibalism exists in Borneo, and accuses the Punans of the Upper Koti and Rejang of that practice. I never heard anything of the kind when I was in that part of the country, nor have I seen anything to confirm such an assertion in narratives or reports of recent explorations. It appears, however, that amongst the Kayans and Mellanaos human sacrifices were practised up to quite a recent period.[1] And it is not improbable, as I have already remarked, that in some of the more remote tribes of the interior such a practice still exists. It certainly exists in Sumatra,[2] and about forty years ago was extensively practised by the Khonds of Central India, being only put an end to by the energy of Major Campbell.

The motive of human sacrifices has always been one and the same in all times and in all countries—the offer to the Divinity

---

[1] W. Crocker (*Proc. R. Geogr. Soc.*, April, 1881, p. 200) tells us that, on the death of a Mellanao chief, a slave was chained to the hollow wooden post containing his corpse, and left there to die of hunger, so that he should be ready to follow his master, and to serve him in the other world.

[2] E. MODIGLIANI, *Fra i Batacchi indipendenti*, p. 184. Rome, 1892.

of what is best and most precious to man, and is considered therefore most acceptable to the gods, with the idea of propitiating
them, of obtaining new favours or the pardon of past offences ;
and above all to avert pestilence and epidemics, always considered
by primitive people as a visitation brought about by the anger
of the Divinity.

Much has been done to complete our knowledge of the life
and manners of the natives of Borneo, and extensive ethnographical
material has been collected by the Rajah of Sarawak in the museum
at Kuching. But nowadays it is not sufficient to know that such
and such an object belongs to the Kayans, to the Dyaks, or to
whatever tribe it may be, because the natives along each river,
I might say of each village, although belonging to the same " gens,"
have peculiarities of their own in the shape and ornamentation,
etc., of weapons and implements of all kinds. An exact,
methodical, and comparative examination of these is a crying
need before the increasing facilities of communication and the
influence of Western civilisation renders the task impossible.

I have already given a brief notice of most of the various tribes
and peoples of Sarawak ; but as to their origin and as to how they
came to inhabit Borneo, little indeed has been added to our meagre
knowledge of thirty years ago. Archæological discoveries in Sarawak
are also extremely restricted in their results. At Santubong a
primitive rude statue representing a human figure lying prone
with extended arms, has been found, but the epoch cannot be
determined. From the same locality come two monumental
stones, also of unknown origin and age, which are now in the
Kuching Museum. They are carved with leaves in relief. At
Pankalan Ampat some antiquities have been discovered, amongst
others a large gold Persian coin of the year 960 of our era, together
with some gold jewels.

The hypothesis that the Chinese knew and traded with Borneo
at a very remote epoch has gone on gaining ground, supported by
new facts which all tend to prove its truth. Dr. Posewitz (*Op. cit.*,
p. 312) mentions that in the year 977 A.D. a Bornean Prince, ruling
a State lying between the Sambas and Landak rivers, sent an embassy to the Emperor of China. In 1888, at Santubong, at the
entrance of the Sarawak river, fragments of gold jewellery, crockery
ware, glass beads, stone crucibles and ancient Chinese coins, some
of a period as far back as 600 B.C., were discovered.[1] The
tajau jars, so precious now to the Dyaks, and especially the
varieties known as " Gusi," " Russa " and " Naga," and perhaps
certain ceramics found amongst the Mellanaos, also come under
the head of Chinese antiquities.

Although the Chinese have no doubt influenced and modified

[1] *Sarawak Gazette*, 1888, p. 87 ; and 1889, p. 23.

the ethnic type of many inland tribes, such as the Muruts, Kayans, and others, yet it appears that there are no traces of their peculiar monosyllabic language in the dialects of the above-mentioned tribes. Mr. Low, however, in his *Journal*, already quoted by me, notes that the songs of the Kayans, whose meaning he did not make out, had a singular resemblance to the inflections of the Chinese language. But however great and undeniable be the ethnic affinities between the less civilised people of Borneo and those of Indo-China, it is not less obvious that the dialects spoken by the former have nothing in common with those of the latter. The Indo-Chinese are all derived from the Chinese languages, the Bornean from the Malay.

Remains of Buddhist or Brahman monuments or idols, have not, as far as I am aware, been found in Sarawak, with the exception of those mentioned by Mr. St. John (*Op. cit.*, i., p. 227) consisting of a *Yonê*, and the mutilated body of an animal, which might have been a " Nandi " or sacred bull of the Hindoos. Dalton, quoted by Crawfurd,[1] appears to have found ruins of temples similar to those of Java, on the Upper Koti, and, like these, showing highly finished workmanship, with the peculiar emblematic ornamentation of Hindoo temples. At Negara near Banjarmasin and in the neighbourhood of Pontianak, remains of Hindoo antiquities are also found. This would prove that in Eastern and Southern Borneo a higher civilisation gained a footing in the past than is shown by documentary evidence to have existed in the other districts of the islands.

After my residence in Borneo I visited several of the wild tribes of head-hunters in Celebes, and found there natives who in very many respects resembled the Dyaks and Kayans.[2] This would seem to show that it was by the Koti river that communications were kept up in the past between Celebes and the interior of Borneo. But the Kayans, in spreading from the east towards the west and the north of Borneo, came in contact (perhaps not for the first time) with the Chinese and Mellanaos living along the coast. The Sea-Dyaks, on the other hand, have had more constant contact with the piratical tribes of the Sulu Sea and with the Malays.

I think there can hardly be any doubt that Borneo was invaded by various civilised races coming from different countries at a very remote epoch, so remote as to explain the great rarity in Borneo of those implements which characterise that primitive stage of human culture known as the " Stone Age," and which are found in

---

[1] *A Descriptive Dictionary of the Indian Archipelago*, p. 62.

[2] On the origin of the name Kayan only conjectures can be made. An interesting statement is made by Fea (*Op. cit.*, p. 446), that the name of the Karins of Burma is also pronounced Kayn or Kayen, showing a singular analogy to Kayan. The manners and customs of the Karins are also very similar to those of the Land-Dyaks of Borneo.

most countries. It would thus appear that stone implements, if such were ever made and used in Borneo, ceased to be so perhaps long before this was the case in Europe. Whatever be the explanation, it is a fact that stone implements are excessively rare in Borneo, whilst they are not so in Java and in the Malay Peninsula. Perhaps the reason why they have not been found lies in the luxuriance of the vegetation, which covers most of the island and virtually prevents or renders exceedingly improbable any such finds. Not merely small stone implements, but even great temples might easily thus be hidden for ages to come in the depths of the jungle.

Dr. Shelford, in his Report on the Sarawak Museum, dated February 1901, states that he bought from a Malay a stone axe found in the house of a Dyak on the Upper Sadong, where it is probable that others may be found ; and adds that similar implements of various shapes and sizes have been discovered by Dr. Hose and Dr. Haddon amongst the tribes of the Barram district. The first stone axe discovered in Sarawak was found by Mr. A H. Everett in the gravel in the banks of the Sinyawan river.

On the Malay Peninsula stone implements are rare, but a stone axe was found at Singapore, and has been described by Mr. Ridley. In Perak and Pahang they are called " batu linta," which means literally " leech-stone," probably in allusion to their usual shape.

Mr. St. John (*Op. cit.*, p. 190), mentions stones or pebbles of a dark colour considered by the natives as sacred. Some such, found at Quop, were said to have been lost during the civil wars. They are possibly palæolithic implements.

Sarawak, up to the present, has derived its wealth more from Nature's spontaneous products than from agriculture or human industries of any kind. Agriculture has hitherto been less successful than might have been expected in a country whose soil has a reputation for great fertility. Sago has alone yielded good profits in the hands of Europeans, pepper and gambir to the Chinese. The sago palm is a plant whose cultivation, more than that of any other, is likely to give profitable results, and it can be extended to low swampy and flooded land which is otherwise unproductive. Hill-rice succeeds well in Sarawak, but the present system used in its cultivation keeps large areas of ground in a fallow condition for years, for rice cannot be sown again in the same field under an interval of six or seven years. The reduction to " sawas "—a series of irrigated terraces—might, however, be tried wherever possible.

All over Borneo agriculture is in a very primitive stage The cultivation of rice is no doubt extensively practised, but it is undertaken, as I have shown, in the rudest manner. In Sarawak the plough is unknown, although it is used in North Borneo. As I have suggested, the Javanese " sawas " system of rice-cultivation might be adopted with advantage, using the requisite implements and employing buffaloes. But it would, I think, be vain to expect in Borneo the grand agricultural results which are obtained in Java, where the soil is so different. In Borneo fertility is in very great measure due to the humus accumulated in the forests, and when this is used up, or carried away by rain or floods, the soil which is left could scarcely be productive unless it were properly worked and manured. It is therefore doubtful if it would suffice to support a large and dense population, living exclusively or mostly on the produce of the land, and in a very limited degree on the results of its own industry. On the other hand, in Java the continual decomposition of lavas and volcanic rocks under the constant influence of a hot and moist climate yields a soil of inexhaustible fertility, capable of supporting a very large population even if practising only primitive methods of agriculture. The true reason of the scanty population of Borneo may probably be looked for in the above-mentioned facts. Had the mountains of Borneo been volcanic, I think there can be little doubt that it would have been from the remotest times quite as populous as Java, for it lies in a position of easy access to civilised peoples migrating from Continental Asia.[1]

With the system of rice-cultivation now practised in Borneo, any extension would lead to a corresponding destruction of forests, and thus lessen those forest products which at present certainly form one of the main resources of the country. A glance at the most populous and fertile countries near Borneo will show that these are the islands which form the volcanic chain around it, the denser population being in the districts where the volcanoes are situated. This is the case, not only in Java, but also in Sumatra, Celebes, the Philippines, and the Moluccas. Ceram, on the contrary, which stands with respect to the nearest volcanic islands in relatively the same position as Borneo does farther to the west, has a scanty population, and is almost entirely covered with forest.

The reasons here adduced to explain the relative agricultural poverty of Borneo explain also the non-success of the various attempts which have been made to cultivate the sugar-cane, coffee, tobacco, indigo, and other tropical products. I do not mean to say that these do not give any results in Borneo, but that their

---

It is doubtful whether this can be looked upon as the sole reason of the undoubtedly small population of Borneo. The natives doubtless use the land recklessly because vast areas of unworked soil lie at their very door, and the absence of the domestic animals is against manuring. But so prolific is nature in the untouched soil that the inhabitants of six crowded huts on the Kinabatangan have been known to draw their entire subsistence, day after day, from a little plot under two acres in extent (v. Stanford's Compendium, *Australasia*, vol. ii., p. 242).—[ED.].

cultivation does not pay, at all events not sufficiently to compensate
the expense of outlay and of European supervision and adminstra-
tion.   The natives, and better still the Chinese, for whom a minimum
outlay of capital is sufficient, who are good field-labourers, and to
whom their own manual labour is money, can obtain paying
returns from various kinds of cultivation in Sarawak, foremost
amongst which are pepper and gambir.

Were it not dangerous for a small State with a limited military
force, perhaps the best way of improving the agricultural output
of Sarawak would be to encourage Chinese immigration as much as
possible, for the Chinese do not suffer from the climate,[1] are good
agriculturists, and can make the land pay where it would give little
or no profit to the European capitalist.   Borneo, like most tropical
countries, is a region where the European labourer cannot work
his own land, thus prosperity deriving from agriculture can only
be obtained by an adequate development of Asiatic labour.

The efforts of H.H. Rajah Sir Charles Brooke to introduce
new agricultural resources in Sarawak have been unceasing, and
he has spared neither time nor money.   Certainly it was neither
owing to want of energy on his part nor of the active co-operation
of the persons he employed, if success did not always crown his
efforts.   When I was first in Borneo attempts at rearing the silk-
worm were made, and in this I helped to the best of my ability,
having been familiar with the industry in Italy.   I have still a
skein of silk spun from cocoons produced in Sarawak in 1867,
which in quality is all that could be desired.   But the want of well-
defined seasons, and especially the all-prevailing dampness, rendered
the results very uncertain, the silkworms being often and easily
decimated by the various maladies to which they are liable.   The
mulberry-tree grows well, especially at Lundu, hence there would
be no lack of the leaves for feeding the worms.

Coffee-planting, as I have said in the beginning of my narrative,
was first attempted whilst I was in Sarawak on the Mattang
mountain, around my hut " Vallombrosa," and was a failure as
regards the ordinary species, *C. Arabica*, which produced no berries.
It was, however, the beginning of a sort of experimental plantation
on a large scale, where, from what I hear, Liberian coffee, cinchona,
and tea plants, thrive and produce well.   No less than 650 acres
are now cultivated with Liberian coffee, which, from the prosperous
condition of the young plants, promises to be highly successful.
Another extensive coffee plantation, also belonging to the Government, is now thriving at Satop.   At " Vallombrosa " an elegant
bungalow now occupies the old site of my hut in the midst of
extensive plantations, and on the grounds which for centuries were

---

[1] This is not invariably the case.   The Chinese working in the plantations of Borneo have always suffered considerably from beri-beri.—[ED.]

covered by primeval forest, rose-bushes yielding a wealth of flowers now grow. Higher up, where the air is pure and the climate temperate, the Rajah has had a small house built, which is used as a sanatorium for the European residents in Sarawak.

Other cultivations have been tried in Sarawak with various and varying results, such as that of the oil-palm (*Elæis Guineensis*), tapioca, kapok (*Eriodendron anfractuosum*), the nutmeg, cinnamon and cacao. Many others might be tried, for tropical plants grow splendidly as long as the forest humus can be supplied.

I do not know whether at the present period, when the cultivation of what are generically termed colonial products has undergone so great an extension in many parts of the world, it would pay to employ European capital on a large scale in Borneo on agricultural speculations. I am, however, fully persuaded that the Government of Sarawak will reap manifold advantages and largely benefit the population by promoting and encouraging amongst the natives the cultivation of those plants which experience has shown to be profitable.

In order to attain this result in Sarawak, the establishment of small agricultural stations in different localities, where culture experiments of various kinds could be undertaken on a small scale, would be very useful. Without being in the ordinary sense of the term botanical gardens, they would be quite as advantageous. Another suggestion I should like to see adopted is that a considerable extent of primeval forest be preserved in proximity to the capital, in its natural condition, somewhat on the lines of the National Parks in the United States. For this purpose the tract of country between Kuching and Gunong Mattang might be chosen, where if the forest were cleared the soil would in all probability after a short time become unproductive and get overgrown with lalang grass. It should be remembered that if the destruction of the forest diminishes the frequency and the abundance of rain, it would nevertheless cause a notable increase of temperature around the capital. Such portions of the forest as offer favourable conditions might be utilised for the cultivation of forest products, such as the different species of Sapotaceæ and Apocynaceæ, which produce gutta percha, india-rubber and solid oils ; certain choice kinds of rotang, as " rotang sega," " rotang jernang " (dragon's blood), " rotang semambu " (Malacca cane), etc., etc., which are now getting very scarce in the jungle.

There are good reasons to suppose that the existence of gold and diamonds in Borneo was known in remote times, both in India and in China. This fame of former days has helped considerably to maintain even to the present time an erroneous and highly exaggerated idea regarding the mineral wealth of the country. Gold in the dominions of Rajah Brooke is only found on the

Upper Sarawak river towards the head-waters of the Sadong and on the Batang-Lupar at Marop, though some time ago its existence in small quantities was also demonstrated on the Binatang river, one of the affluents of the Rejang. Up to quite recently only Chinamen worked on the Sarawak goldfields, the yield not being sufficient to attract European enterprise. Lately, however, the Borneo Company has undertaken the extraction of gold on a large scale with the cyanide process, extensive machinery, electric lights, and a numerous staff of European employés, on the Upper Sarawak river. It is not possible, however, to give the precise amount of the gold annually won, on account of the facility with which any supervision of the results of native work can be eluded, whilst the gold collected by the Borneo Company does not figure in the official reports, as the company pays a fixed sum for its mining rights to the Sarawak Government.

Diamond seeking under European direction on the Sarawak river has always given poor results, and it has consequently remained entirely in the hands of the Chinese and Malays. It is certain, however, that many of the stones found in Sarawak are smuggled out of the country without any one being the wiser. Rubies have recently been discovered in the Barram district, but I know of no other precious stones having been found in Sarawak.

The famous antimony mine which existed on the Upper Sarawak river, and was at one time one of the riches of the country, is now exhausted. Antimony ore is still found in the Sadong district at Siring, on the Batang-Lupar near Marop, and on the Pelagus, Kanowit, and Silalang, affluents of the Rejang. At present the metal is extracted only by independent miners on a small scale, but it still yields a profit to Government of over $20,000 per annum.

A vein of cinnabar had been discovered on the Upper Sarawak river when I was in Borneo, and was worked with profit by the Borneo Company, but it is now exhausted. Other deposits of mercury ore have been subsequently found in the Samarahan and Sadong districts, on the Batang-Lupar at Kumpang and Marop, and in larger quantities at Tegora and Gading in the so-called Sarawak district, but it appears that they have been nearly worked out, for the exportation of mercury from Sarawak is now very small.

The iron ore found in the Kayan country, which I have spoken of in a previous chapter, has not been worked except by the natives themselves for their own use. Traces of copper, in the shape of azurite and malachite, have been met with in the antimony veins of the Upper Sarawak. In the same localities lead ore has also been found, but in very small quantities.

Contrary to what has happened with other mineral products,

the output of coal has become increasingly important. Coal abounds in several localities in North Borneo, but at present only two mines are worked in Sarawak, both by Government. One of these is on the Sadong river ; its daily produce was calculated at 100 tons reduced in 1900 to only 65 tons. The other is at Brooketon on the Limbang river, in a district rented from the Sultan of Bruni. It yielded 50 tons daily at one time, but for the last two years it has been worked at a loss, producing 10,774 tons in 1899, and only 7,058 tons in 1900. Most of the Sadong coal is exported to Singapore, whilst that of Brooketon goes to Labuan. Mineral oil has also been found in some places in Sarawak, but it is only lately that attempts have been made to obtain it.

Kuching, which when I was first there consisted merely of the Malay kampongs on the banks of the river, a Chinese bazaar, and a few bungalows for Europeans, has now developed into a fine city with broad, well-kept streets, elegant villas, and public edifices. Amongst the latter are the new museum, the Protestant and Catholic churches, the mosque and several Chinese temples or joss-houses, besides the Government buildings, the Court of Justice, the prison, markets, hospital, dispensary, etc., etc. I do not know whether at present Kuching is the most populous town in Borneo,[1] but it is certainly the first city in Borneo so far as civilisation is concerned. The climate, considering its proximity to the equator, is exceptionally mild and healthy, and above all uniform. Rarely does the thermometer rise above 85° Fahr., and it never descends below 67°. Intermittent and remittent fevers are not wanting, it is true, and diarrhœa and dysentery are frequent, but with simple hygienic precautions Europeans can live there for a long time in good health. There are, however, in Sarawak districts where malaria is far more frequent than in and around Kuching, but usually it does not assume a malignant form. Other diseases are not of frequent occurrence.

In Borneo storms are common, with strong electric discharges, particularly at the time of the change of the monsoons, but I have never seen them accompanied by hail.

The island is entirely beyond the range of typhoons, and also beyond the influence of the plutonic forces which affect the adjacent regions. Even earthquakes are rare and not severe. The only signs of volcanic activity are thermal springs. In Borneo only one small extinct volcano, the Melabu, of the nature of which there can be no doubt, is known. It is in the Montrado district, in the extreme west of the island, and according to a Dutch engineer, M. van Schelle, who discovered it, is only about 230 feet high (POSEWITZ, *Borneo*, p. 246). It has also been asserted that Kina Balu, the great

---

[1] The population is now about 12,000.

mountain of North Borneo, formed of crystalline rocks, has a large central crater (*Scottish Geogr. Magazine,* December, 1887), but I think that before admitting the volcanic nature of the mountain, further information is required. Fragments of lava are also said to have been found on one of the small islands to the north of Borneo.[1]

Regarding the population of Sarawak we possess only very uncertain data. Mr. Crocker, in his paper, which I have already quoted, assigns 240,000 inhabitants to the old territory of Sarawak, which extended from Tanjong Datu to Tanjong Kedurong, a little above the mouth of the Bintulu river. In a recent report of Mr. Keyser, British Consul in Sarawak, to the Foreign Office, a population of 500,000 is assigned to the dominions of Rajah Brooke within their present limits, but this appears to me too high a figure. It must be remembered that in Sarawak, and, indeed, throughout the whole of Borneo, human habitations and villages are only found near rivers, so that all the remaining area may, so far as man is concerned, be considered a desert. Allowing to Sarawak two inhabitants for each square kilometre, we have a population of 360,000, which is, I believe not far from the truth.

According to my calculations, this population may be approximately divided as follows :—

Malays	50,000
Chinese	15,000
Land-Dyaks	25,000
Sea-Dyaks	120,000
Kayans	100,000
Mellanaos	20,000
Other Tribes (Native)	30,000
Total	360,000

A steamer, which at present flies the German flag, keeps up regular weekly communication between Kuching and Singapore. The Rajah possesses a flotilla of seven or eight small steamers which run between the coast stations, and which constitute at the same time a naval force.

Several Europeans are in the Rajah's service, divided between the public departments and the central administration at Kuching, whilst others, bearing the title of " Residents," represent the authority of the Rajah in the ten provinces into which Sarawak is divided, being invested with full civil and military power. The provinces correspond more or less to the basins of the principal

---

[1] Quite recently Dr. Nieuwenhuis appears to have found that the central range of Borneo is of volcanic nature (*Tijdsch. v. het K. Nederl. Aardr. Genootsch.* No. 3, 1901); but this assertion requires to be confirmed. It would be truly strange in Malaysia to find so important a volcanic chain so far from the sea.

rivers; they are, beginning from the west: 1, Lundu; 2, Sarawak; 3, Sadong; 4, Batang-Lupar; 5, Oya; 6, Muka; 7, Bintulu; 8, Barram; 9, Limbang; 10, Trusan.

The principal forest products of Sarawak are guttapercha, indiarubber and rotangs, of which guttapercha is the most important export, being in great demand and fetching high prices. The larger portion of that which arrives at Kuching to be exported to Singapore now comes from the Rejang. The Government makes a large profit from this valuable product, for the export due amounts to $16 per pikul, but is only $10 per pikul on indiarubber.[1]

The export of rotangs from Sarawak has lately shown a decrease when compared to what it was a few years back, which may be explained by the high prices obtained by guttapercha and indiarubber, which give larger profits, and are thus more sought after. The exportation of timber has recently attained large proportions on the lower Rejang, where ships from Hongkong now constantly call, the supply appearing to be inexhaustible. In the lower districts of Sarawak (Sadong and Sarawak) a small duty on the export of timber has been recently established, with a view to diminish the felling of forest trees. Elsewhere the export is free, with some restrictions on that of bilian wood, on account of its value.

Amongst the forest produce of a certain value must be included the edible nests of the *Collocalia*, or "bird's-nest swallow," from which the Sarawak budget obtains an annual income of about $3,000, the lease of caves which belong to the State; but most of the nest-yielding caves are the private property of natives.

The principal agricultural products exported from Sarawak are pepper, sago, and gambir. Pepper at present, owing to the great demand on the Singapore market, is one of the most important agricultural products in the country; its plantations, cultivated by Chinamen, have attained a large development and are on the increase. Sago is always the main product of the soil in Sarawak, and in 1900 336,173 pikuls were exported. The cultivation of gambir, which was at one time quite extensive in the neighbourhood of Kuching, appears to have given place largely to that of the pepper-vine, which pays better. Rice has not yet been grown in sufficient quantities for the local demand; but as a result of the great encouragement now given to Chinese immigration on the Rejang river it is hoped that the produce of that staple food-supply of the entire native population of Borneo will increase, and eventually contribute also to the export trade.

The internal trade is entirely in the hands of the Chinese, who

[1] A pikul is equal to 133⅓ lb. English.

Fig. 59.—CULTIVATION OF PEPPER IN SARAWAK.

import for that purpose brass-wire, gongs, earthenware, and common sorts of cotton cloth.

The main sources of revenue are the farming of opium, gaming-houses, sale of spirits, and pawn-shops ; which together yielded $282,535 during the financial year 1900.

Direct taxation in Sarawak is very slight. There is a family tax for Dyaks and Kayans, which was estimated for 1901 at $39,000. In Kuching there is a house-tax of 5 per cent. on the rent, when it is over $20 per annum. Revenue is also derived from the sale of licences, registration, plantation concessions and many other minor sources.

The Government of Sarawak is absolute, in the hands of H.H. Sir Charles Brooke, aided by a Council of six members, viz. two high European officials, and four Malays, elected by the native notabilities. Besides this Supreme Council, there is a General Council of fifty members, contributed by the principal Europeans and native representatives from the various districts. The General Council meets rarely, being only convoked on very special occasions. Justice is administered on the basis of English law, somewhat modified to adapt itself to native and Mohammedan traditions.

The military forces of the Rajah consist of a body of 300 men, the " Sarawak Rangers," principally composed of Dyaks, and of about 100 constabulary. However, internal security is mostly based in Sarawak on the diversity of races forming the population, and on the possibility of profiting, should occasion require it, by the bellicose instincts of the large masses of Dyaks.

Sarawak is a free and independent State in the true sense of the words, although a portion of its territory has passed under the dominion of the Brookes by a pecuniary agreement with the Sultan of Bruni. The independence of Sarawak and the legitimacy of the sovereignty of H.H. Sir Charles Brooke and his descendants has been sanctioned and guaranteed against the danger of any possible foreign interference, by a Convention concluded with the British Government in 1888, in which Great Britain accepted and assumed the suzerainty without the right of interfering in the internal administration of the State, the Rajah of Sarawak binding himself to consult the British Government in case of any difficulty arising between his State and a Foreign Power.

The Rajah considers himself the father of his people, who have all his thought and care, and he does his utmost to lead his subjects along the road of progress and civilisation, though without sudden or violent changes, to which he is absolutely opposed on principle. He has no wish that the country he rules should be taken advantage of by unscrupulous speculators of European nationalities for their own special benefit alone. He leases land on advantageous conditions to all persons who desire to cultivate it, and he is not opposed to investment of European capital in Sarawak, in undertakings of a rational kind, as has been wrongly asserted. But he has legitimate reason to decline to protect mere adventurers who swarm in new countries solely to fill their empty purses without the least consideration for the consequences which may accrue to others and to the country through the effects of their speculations. Any honest trader, and better still any able agriculturist, who earnestly wishes to deal well with the natives, may always be sure of a hearty welcome in the dominions of Rajah Brooke.

At present, with the exception of the Borneo Company, which holds several important mineral and commercial trusts, the entire trade of Sarawak is in the hands of Chinese, under the direct control of the Rajah's Government. As is well known, Europeans cannot possibly compete with Chinamen in small trades and industries. The latter easily penetrate the interior, living amongst Dyaks and Kayans, and grow rich by exchanging articles of scant value, but appreciated by the natives, for valuable forest produce.

The Rajah's Government is eminently impartial towards the many and varied races it has to rule. In Sarawak all religions are tolerated and equally protected. There are at present in the country several Protestant missionary stations, which are dependent on the Bishop of Singapore and Sarawak. There is besides a Vicar Apostolic who resides at Kuching, with several Roman Catholic priests. The Mohammedans have various mosques, and the Chinese joss-houses and temples at their many settlements. A certain number of Dyaks have been converted to Christianity by the missionaries, but perhaps a still larger number are becoming assimilated by the Malays, adopting the Mohammedan religion, which, when free from fanaticism, as it usually is when practised by Malays, is perhaps more consonant with the manners and customs of the peoples of the tropical portion of the Far East, and with the climate of those countries.

Most of the territory of Sarawak is still in a wild and primitive condition, and immense forests will continue to cover it for centuries to come, but the natives of the greater portion of Rajah Brooke's dominions can no longer be termed mere savages, for peaceful trade between the different districts is now fully and perfectly established. Head-hunting has entirely ceased, and slavery is abolished everywhere. It should also be stated that most of the customs of the Dyaks, and even of the Kayans, although in many cases opposed to our ideas of morality and civilisation, are not such as to present an insurmountable obstacle to the material progress of the native populations, nor are they thus contrary to the prosperity of the State.

And on his part, the second European Rajah of Sarawak, devoted to the sole task of increasing the welfare of his native subjects, by directing the energy of the Dyaks and Kayans towards peaceful avocations, by favouring Chinese immigration, and by developing trade and encouraging agriculture—has given to the country he rules a prosperity which could hardly have been hoped for, when one looks back at the condition of Sarawak prior to the advent of the Brookes.

Appendix

THE BORNEAN FOREST

ON several occasions in the foregoing pages I have mentioned some of the more notable features of the magnificent forest which covers nearly the entire surface of Borneo, yet I think that a general sketch of the vegetation in Sarawak from a biological and physical point of view may not prove uninteresting to the reader, premising that it is not within the scope of this book to attempt, even on the most general lines, an account of the Flora of Borneo, a vast subject, which in the present state of our knowledge cannot possibly be treated as it deserves.

If it be true, as it seems to me, that each climate has stamped its special mark on the organic productions which live under its influence, what is it that characterises the Bornean vegetation as a whole?

Before answering this question, it is necessary that I should give some account of the climate of Sarawak, which is indeed practically that of the larger portion of the lowlands of Borneo.

The Climate of Sarawak.—It has been already stated that the kingdom of Sarawak is within the region of the monsoons; that from April to November these winds blow from a prevalent N.E. direction, and during the remaining months of the year from the S.W. The seasons are, however, somewhat irregular, for although the monsoons are constant, and as a general rule the N.E. brings rain and the S.W. fine weather, it cannot be said that the year has only one dry and one wet season, for rain is pretty frequent during each month of the year.

The average temperature in Sarawak, considering its latitude, is a relatively low one, and at the same time peculiarly uniform, which is to be attributed not only to the insular condition of Borneo, but also to the fact that it is covered with dense vegetation, which prevents the ground from getting heated and favours an abundant condensation. Another factor in maintaining a low temperature is the extensive evaporation. Nor is the shortness of the days without its effect, for the sun does not remain on the average more than twelve hours above the horizon throughout the year.

The highest temperature observed during my stay at Kuching was on August 31st, 1866, on which day the thermometer in the verandah of my house rose to 91° Fahr. The lowest temperature, at sea-level, was noted by me at Bintulu on August 16th, 1867, when the thermometer stood at 67° Fahr. During my sojourn in Sarawak I did not keep a regular meteorological record, for I never made long stays in the same place, but I have been able to avail myself of the meteorological observations registered regularly at Kuching of late, and published in the *Sarawak Gazette*. From these we find that during the years 1891–92–93 the maximum temperature registered at Kuching was 95° Fahr., the minimum being 82°, on March 31st, 1893. The very same extremes are given on the following April 1st. For this reason I suspect that there must have been some error in the reading or in the printing of the temperature data of those two days. Putting these aside, therefore, the maximum temperature during the three years mentioned would be 92° Fahr., and the minimum 69° Fahr.

From the records mentioned it is evident that there is a singular constancy and uniformity in the minimum temperatures of Kuching throughout the year, as they vary between 69° and 75° Fahr. It also appears that the warmer months are from May to September inclusive, with maxima of 88° and 92°. January and February are the coldest months, the maxima being 82° and 85°. Thus in Kuching there would be at the most a difference of about 10° between the maximum temperatures of all the months in the year; and again, differences exceeding 18° almost never occur in the twenty-four hours, and when they do, it is especially in the warmer months.

The amount of the rainfall in Kuching over a period of seven years is given below—

Years.	Number of Rainy Days.	Rainfall in Inches.
1886	246	173·37
1887	225	166·45
1888	176	107·41
1889	249	154·33
1890	255	147·30
1891	254	144·29
1892	266	163·93

This shows the exceptional relative dryness of the year 1888. The most rainy months of the year are usually December, January, and February, and in a lesser degree November and March; the dryest months are July, August, and September. In July, 1889, an extraordinary minimum rainfall—1·95 inches—was observed. The maximum rainfall was in February, 1886, when 43·83 inches fell.

During some years abundant rain fell also during the fine (or so-called dry) season. Thus during May, 1886, 12·38 inches were registered; in August of the same year, 11·08 inches; in June, 1887, 14·47 inches; in July, 1889, 12·84 inches; and in the following September, 14·38 inches; in May, 1890, 12·15 inches; in June, 1891, 10·43 inches; in August, 1892, 11·16 inches. This is sufficient to prove that during the so-called dry season a prolonged absence of rain is quite exceptional in Sarawak.

Nature of the Vegetation in Borneo.—With these data before us, we may now pass on to a consideration of the question raised at the beginning of this chapter. A tropical country, which has a climate like that above described, and in which the growth of vegetation is continuous and active throughout each day of the year, must necessarily be clothed with a high, dense, and luxuriant arboreal mantle, with evergreen foliage, from the seashore to the summits of its mountains. And this, indeed, is the marked feature which I would call the " physical characteristic " of the flora of Borneo. There being no season during which the vegetative functions are quiescent, either on account of a low temperature or by reason of a prolonged drought, it is easy to see why in Borneo neither annual (forestal) plants, nor terrestrial bulbous plants, nor thickened tree-trunks, nor fleshy ground-plants are to be found.

A sort of correspondence to the above-mentioned physical forms of plants is to be met with in the world of Epiphytes, where, on the naked trunk and branches of the trees, alternate periods of dampness and dryness occur, corresponding with the climatic periods. Similarly amongst the epiphytes in Borneo, on the better lighted and higher parts of trees, we meet with plants termed " Xerophiles " or lovers of dryness, which are so organised as to be able to exist for a longer or shorter period without water, but which are at the same time provided with special adaptations enabling them to take advantage of it when it does occur on any occasion and under any physical condition.

The soil which nourishes the forest trees of Borneo, especially in the plains, is always loaded with moisture, and at the same time is never too much heated, being sheltered by the dense foliage of the trees themselves. For this reason the greater portion of the tropical sylvan plants, living on the sea level, only flourish under a moderate temperature, say from 70° to 90° Fahr. When I use the term forest, I refer only to that which is really primeval, which in Borneo is characterised by the great size of the arboreal vegetation, by the infinite variety of species which form it, and by the great number of peculiar forms. In Borneo, except along the coasts where mangroves and casuarinas are found, woods entirely formed of one or a few species of trees are entirely wanting.

The vegetation which covers an area where the primeval forest has been destroyed is utterly distinct from that of the latter, with its rich and specialised primitive forms. The species thus establishing themselves are quite different and are mostly those which have an extensive geographical distribution. I have adopted the term " secondary forest " for this assemblage of vegetation, when, as is often the case, it is formed of timber trees, which, however, never attain the size of those which constitute the primeval forest. From a botanical point of view I cannot insist too strongly on the difference which exists between these two kinds of forest.

Secondary Forest.—This kind of forest in Sarawak is characterised by trees of small size, among which predominate the *Euphorbiaceæ* with the genera *Mallotus* and *Macaranga* ; some *Ficus* and other *Urticaceæ* (*Sponia, Pipturus, Leucosyke*) ; and shrubs such as *Eurya, Adinandra Glochydion, Phyllanthus, Pavetta, Mussænda, Callicarpa, Memecylon, Melastoma*, etc., amongst which various creepers trail their flexible stems, mostly belonging to the genera *Uncaria, Tetracera, Artabotrys, Uvaria, Vitis*, etc., together with some ferns. Amongst the small trees of the secondary forest in Sarawak a composite of the genus *Vernonia*

APPENDIX

deserves special mention.[1] It is only to be expected that the flora should not be rich in the Bornean secondary forest, and that the plants which form it should belong to the commoner sorts, for being of easier adaptation to the conditions of existence and to the nature of the soil, these are more widely diffused in the neighbouring regions. The secondary forest in Borneo always owes its existence to human agency, which has destroyed the primeval forest ; but in volcanic countries it may be the consequence of an eruption, which may cause the entire vegetation of a mountain to perish.

In a country where the forests are formed of few species, and the trees are gregarious, the destruction of the primeval vegetation does not produce a great alteration in the flora ; but in a tropical country covered with virgin forests, where hundreds of species of trees, lianas, and epiphytes can be found crowded together in an area of a few square miles, a clearance of the forest produces a complete change in the character of the flora, and should such destruction be extended and continued, there can be no doubt that not a few species would be rendered totally extinct.

It is very probable, indeed almost certain, that in the long run the truly forestal species would regain possession of the secondary forest, once more forming a forest of the primitive type.

Primeval Forest.—The species of trees which go to form the lofty, primitive forest of Borneo are extraordinarily numerous, and belong to very different families. Those which predominate belong to the *Dipterocarpeæ, Leguminosæ, Elenaceæ, Sapotaceæ, Cupuliferæ, Arctocarpeæ, Bombaceæ, Tiliaceæ, Dilleniaceæ*, etc. ; but many other trees of moderate dimensions live in the shade of these giants, and contribute to the whole. They belong more especially to the families *Myristicaceæ, Meliaceæ* and *Guttiferæ*, and principally to the *Lauraceæ* and *Euphorbiaceæ*. This last family, with the exception of a few herbaceous forms, adventitious in inhabited localities, is represented in Borneo entirely by woody species, but few of these are relatively big trees, most of them being shrubs forming the lower growth of the great forest.

In the primeval forest a large number of the trees and shrubs which live in the shade of the forest giants are naturally young specimens of the latter, but a large proportion of small trees also exist which, even when they attain their full development, never reach the lower branches of the greater trees. Some of these have slender stems, often undivided or but slightly branched, and not many metres high, crowned with scanty but large leaves, simple or pinnate in form. Beneath the shade of the great trees, even those plants which would naturally be herbaceous often become diminutive trees. Even those which are really herbaceous are, without exception, never annuals.

In some cases the soil of the primeval forest is covered by a thick

[1] The members of this family (herbaceous or woody) are certainly wanting in the primeval forest of Borneo, and only a dozen of adventitious species are found in the vicinity of habitations and cultivated grounds. It thus appears that the damp region of the monsoons is not favourable to the plants with feathery seeds. The *Asclepiadeæ*, especially epiphytic species, nevertheless form an exception ; but in these the feathery appendage of the seed is of such a nature that the slightest difference in the hygrometric conditions of the atmosphere render it fit to act as an organ of flight, whilst contact with a wet or even merely damp object causes it at once to adhere.

APPENDIX

layer of dead leaves, and is almost devoid of any minor vegetation ; more frequently, however, especially in the lowland forests, in the mountain gorges, along rivulets, and in all localities where, on account of the dampness and the nature of the decaying leaves, humus is rapidly formed, herbaceous plants are both numerous and varied. They belong principally to the families of the Ferns, *Zingiberaceæ*, *Marantaceæ*, *Araceæ* (particularly *Schismatoglottis*), *Gesneraceæ*, *Acanthaceæ*, *Urticaceæ* (with the genera *Pellonia*, *Elatostoma* and *Procris*). Common enough, too, are some species of *Argostemma* and *Ophiorrhiza* among the *Rubiacæ*, of *Sonerila* among the *Melastomaceæ*, together with other small forms of this fine group of plants, various orchids, commelinas and begonias. Of the *Cyperaceæ* only a few *Mapania*, *Hypolytron* and *Scirpodendron* are forest species, and of the *Graminaceæ* only *Leptasis urceolata*, R. Br., a widely spread plant within the tropics.

Whilst the herbaceous plants of the Bornean primeval forest are mostly endemic forms, or in any case limited to a restricted geographical area, those of the districts in which the primitive forest has been destroyed, or occupied by cultivation, are without any exception adventitious and often cosmopolitan species, or at least widely diffused in Southern Asia. Amongst the herbaceous plants of Sarawak there are found only two or three *Euphorbia* and some *Phyllanthus*, only four or five *Labiatæ*, some *Lythraceæ*, *Hedyotis*, *Desmodium*, etc. I collected twelve species of *Cyperus*, but none of these was peculiar to Borneo or the Malay Archipelago, though everywhere common, growing amidst the rice or on the sandy sea-beaches. Some are common even in Europe. Amongst other *Cyperaceæ* several *Fimbristylis*, *Scleria*, but only two *Carex*, are found in Sarawak. Of the Graminaceæ I collected about 60 species, but except the already mentioned *Leptasis*, I found none living in the primeval forest, although some appear in the clumps of fruit-trees which surround the Dyak houses. The majority of the grasses in Borneo are to be found in plantations around habitations, on the river banks denuded of forest, on the islands of the larger torrents when left dry for some months, and lastly on the sandy sea-beaches ; here are also found species of *Convolvulus*, *Crotalaria*, *Indigofera*, *Phaseolus*, *Vigna*, *Tephrosia*, *Desmodium*, etc.

The families of plants most largely represented in the primeval forest of Borneo are the following, mentioned approximately in accordance with their richness in species :—*Rubiaceæ*, *Orchidaceæ*, *Euphorbiaceæ*, *Leguminosæ*, *Anonaceæ*, *Melastomaceæ*, *Palmæ*, *Urticaceæ*, *Myrtaceæ*, *Araceæ*, *Guttiferæ*, *Dipterocarpeæ*, *Meliaceæ*, and *Anacardiaceæ*.

The physical characteristics of the trees which form the primeval forest of the island are of the same nature as those met with in the trees of all tropical forests, in which, as in Borneo, growth suffers no interruptions, but is continuous all the year round. The vegetative characters of such a forest may be summed up as consisting of the great height attained by the trees, and of certain special peculiarities of the latter, viz., the perfect straightness of the trunks, which are bare and only branch high up ; the huge expanded head which crowns them, and the great laminar " banners " or buttresses, which very frequently augment their stability.

APPENDIX

The large quantity of humus accumulated in the forest predisposes, even in great trees, to the development of numerous superficial roots. This, perhaps, is one of the reasons why the forest species can only thrive in the secondary forest after many years, when a thick stratum of humus has been formed. For the smaller plants of the underwood this kind of soil must be an essential condition of existence, as is proved by the fact that most of them cannot exist elsewhere.

As trees in these forests find abundant nourishment in the humus, it appears natural that their roots should not penetrate vertically into the ground, but extend along its surface. This is, I think, the true cause of the development of " banners " or laminar expansions from the base of the trunk. The stability of these giant trees which, owing to the lack of deeply penetrating roots, is rather deficient, is thus greatly augmented. The banners have been called " laminar roots," but in reality they cannot be thus described, except in some cases when they extend along the ground, reaching far from their trunk. In most cases however these laminar expansions grow out at a considerable height above the level of the ground. One meets with trees, especially in localities where the forest is habitually flooded, whose trunks appear as if lifted above the soil by their roots. The best instance of such stilt-like roots in the Sarawak forests is that shown by *Plojarium pulcherrimum*, Becc., whose stem is provided below with laminar expansions, and raised in the air by branched roots, just as if the entire plant was hoisted out of the soil for six or eight feet or more. This form of roots is quite different from that which may be termed " fulcral," peculiar to the screw pines and some *Eugeissonias*, and especially to mangroves. In these plants new adventitious aërial roots are constantly being produced from the stem or trunk *pari passu* with the growth of the tree, or else secondary roots grow from the older ones, and all eventually penetrate into the soil.

The abundance of creepers and rope-like palms such as *Calamus* and allied genera are salient features of the great Bornean forest, as are also the large number of epiphytes and parasitical plants on the tree-trunks and branches ; the rich collection of undergrowth plants ; the multitude of humicular species, of ant-harbouring plants, and of urnigerous or pitcher plants (*Nepenthes*) ; and the existence of species producing flowers and fruit on the trunk or around its base, on the main branches, and even on underground growths. But all these find a perfect correspondence in analogous forms to be met with in the equatorial forests of the New World.

Amongst the plants which live under the shade of other vegetation, those that have leaves with a large surface area often predominate. In this category are found not only herbaceous plants, both terrestrial and epiphytic, *Araceæ*, *Gesneraceæ*, *Marantaceæ*, *Zingiberaceæ*, etc., but also many shrubs peculiar to the underwood, which flower and fruit protected by the larger trees, and often show large leaves. To this group belong many *Anonaceæ*, *Magnoliaceæ*, *Euphorbiaceæ*, *Lauraceæ*, *Myristicaceæ*, etc. Many of the underwood shrubs which have not large simple leaves, have composite leaves, such as many *Leguminosæ*, *Meliaceæ*, etc.

The majority of the giant trees have medium-sized or small leaves,

Fig. 60.—A FOREST CLEARING IN NORTH BORNEO.

APPENDIX

mostly entire, coriaceous, and shining on the upper surface. Big leaves, however, are to be seen in certain *Sterculiaceæ*, *Bombaceæ*, and *Diptero-carpeæ*, etc. On the summits of mountains in Borneo most of the shrubs have small leaves. Acicular, narrow, long, rigid or phyllodiform leaves, so frequent in plants of Australasia, are very rare.

The surfaces of the leaves of the plants of the primeval forest vary greatly. Often they appear as if coated with varnish above and covered with small scales or dense wool beneath. It does not appear to me impossible that similar structures, besides having a moderating action in regard to evaporation, are useful as a defence against parasitical fungilli, preventing the penetration of spores into the tissues. If the plants of our climes had to pass a summer in an atmosphere like that of Borneo, they would at once be invaded by cryptogamic vegetation, as indeed happens in our own country when we have a warm, damp summer. Within the tropics fungilli affecting the inner tissue of growing leaves are rare. At every step in the forest, however, minute forms of inferior plants are to be seen, such as lichens, mosses, *Hepaticæ*, or *Algæ*, which vegetate on the surface of living leaves, without damaging the tissue on which they grow.

Plants with Variegated, Metallic, or Brightly Coloured Leaves.—The plants which are most beautiful on account of their variegated leaves, and bright, metallic, or intense green coloration, live in the humus where the forest shade is dense. To their number belong various species of *Araceæ*, *Melastomaceæ*, *Cyrtandraceæ*, *Rubiaceæ*, *Orchideæ*, etc., which show a leaf-coloration far more brilliant than congeneric species which grow in the sunshine, a fact which appears to be in direct contradiction with another, for it is well known how plants kept in the dark fade and lose their colour. Yet whilst plants generally fade and become etiolated when kept from light, those with leaves of a deeper green and more bright coloration prefer shady spots.

It is well known that the green coloration in plants is caused by an immense number of minute granular corpuscules enclosed in the tissue cells, which owe their colour to a pigment known as chlorophyll. These corpuscles are a product of the protoplasm, viz. of the essential living and sensitive portion of the vegetable cells, and have the faculty of moving about within the walls of the cell which includes them, and of modifying their shape, by reason of the vitality and sensitiveness of the protoplasm in which they are embedded. A very strong light causes the chlorophyll granules to hide away, crowding together in the deeper portion of the tissues, whilst diffused light is favourable to a uniform distribution of the granules. It is well to bear in mind these details of the minute and microscopic structure of plants, because it seems likely that leaves naturally silver-spotted, marbled, or variegated owe their peculiar coloration to the faculty possessed by chlorophyll granules of grouping themselves together in various ways according to the manner in which light influenced the leaves *during the most remote plasmative epoch.* According to this hypothesis, marbled and variegated leaves would be merely the hereditary reproduction of the above-mentioned phenomenon, which must have occurred when (in the period when the stimuli could produce permanent effects on organisms) the thin solar rays struck the surface of the leaves of a plant on the ground after filtering through the foliage of a dense forest. To the migration, then, of chlorophyll from the superficial layers of leaves under the action of a strong light, leaving the cells full of air, may be attributed the first origin of silvery leaves, though possibly in other cases the necessity felt by leaves to assimilate in localities where light was scanty and unequally distributed, may have caused the chlorophyll to accumulate in certain spots and to absent itself from others.

On the vividly-coloured leaves of plants living in shady places purple and violet tints are often found to predominate. Such colours are caused by special pigments, and to these the function of moderating the action of light on chlorophyll has been attributed. But as such pigments are frequent in leaves which grow in the shadiest places, where such a function would be not only unnecessary, but harmful, the theory is one which may well be called in question. It is a fact worthy of note that the lower surface of the leaves is that which is usually more brightly coloured. I am thus more inclined to believe that the violet pigments may serve as a sort of sensitising filter to green rays, which are not very active in assimilation. In fact the solar rays which have filtered through a dense foliage are wanting in actinic rays, for these are absorbed by green. The violet pigment may in a way make up for this deficiency and excite and aid the assimilating energy. It does not, in fact, seem too much to say that the protoplasmic granules, which in certain plants and in special organs are charged with pigment, may be a sort of embryonic stage of those organs which in more highly constituted beings are those of vision.

Various ground orchids belonging to the genera *Anœctochilus*, *Nephelophyllum*, *Vrydagzinia*, *Odontochilus*, and especially *Goodyera*, have purple, velvety, or metallic leaves, often with veins of a rosy, golden, or silvery tint. Variegated with green and white are those of *Schismatoglottis asperata albomaculata*, Engl., and of *S. Beccarii albolineata*, Engl., amongst the *Araceæ* ; of *Pinanga variegata*, Becc., amongst the palms ; of *Didymocarpus kompsobœa*, C. B. Clarke, and *D. Clarkei*, Becc. amongst the *Gesneraceæ*. Variegated leaves, too, are frequent amongst the *Acanthaceæ*, and numerous are the tiny forest species of this family which show the above-mentioned peculiarity. One species (P. B., No. 889) is particularly remarkable for the marked contrast in its leaves of a deep metallic green with silvery white and yellowish lines. Very noticeable for their leaf-markings are two *Rubiaceæ*, an *Argostemma* (B.P., No. 1658) and an *Acranthera* (P. B., No. 3794). Amongst the *Marantaceæ* the leaves of a *Phrynum*, which I discovered on the Bellaga Hills (*Ph. Zebrinum*, Becc. P. B., No. 3785) are very beautiful ; they are of a deep green with light lines, recalling those of *Maranta Zebrina*. Another species of *Phrynum* (P. B., No. 1493), which I found on Mount Mattang, has similar markings, but less distinct. One of the *Cyperaceæ*, which I found in the dense shady forest on the slopes of Mount Mattang has its narrow leaves green with metallic violet sheen (the only example, I believe, of such a coloration in the entire family). It is a new species of *Mapania*, to which the name *M. versicolor* is aptly given (P. B., No. 1414 and 27). I have already recorded the singular example

APPENDIX

of *Cryptocoryne pallidinervia*, Engl., which lives in stagnant waters in the forest, and is the only known aquatic plant with variegated leaves.

Saprophytes.—There can be no doubt that the plants of the Bornean forest have been perpetually engaged in a struggle against numerous enemies, who have ceaselessly striven to destroy or to damage not only their aërial parts, but also those which lie beneath the soil. At the present time, as in the far remote past, the struggle for existence in plants, even beneath the surface, against micro-organisms and the mycelia of a host of fungi must have been incessant. The final result can only have been the extinction of all those vegetable forms which did not possess a sufficient power of resistance, or which were unable to adapt themselves to their surroundings, modifying themselves so as to be victors in the battle. In the latter condition were probably many of the forest ground plants, which might almost be said to have come to an agreement with their foes, conceding to them a hospitality which appears ultimately to have proved of service to them, for the outcome of the struggle is a condition of mutualism advantageous to both parties. The presence of mycorhizæ in the roots of plants may have had such an origin.

Humicular saprophytal plants are frequent in Borneo ; it is sufficient here to mention the genera *Burmannia, Thismia, Geomitra, Triuris, Salomonia, Petrosavia*, and some orchids (*Lecanorchis, Aphyllorchis*, etc.).

Parasites.—True parasitic plants in Borneo may be divided into two classes, viz., the aërial, and those which may be termed terrestrial, since it is on the roots of plants that they have established themselves.

Except the well-known and wide-spread *Cassytha*, a type of the common *Cuscuta*, the aërial parasites in Borneo all belong to the family of the *Loranthaceæ*, and, with the exception of some species of *Viscum*, all to the genus *Loranthus*, largely represented by conspicuous species with brightly coloured flowers, in which red and yellow predominate, and bearing large bracts almost equally resplendent. The *Loranthaceæ* are true parasites, preferring to attach themselves to the higher branches of trees, where their flowers are more exposed. In Borneo, however, I also found a terrestrial *Loranthus, Macrosolen Beccarii*, Van Tiegh (P. B., No. 610), a humble forest shrub, which is apparently non-parasitic. I have been able to ascertain positively that the " burong unparu " (*Trachycomus ochrocephalus*) feeds on the fruits of *Loranthus* ; but probably many other birds feed on them also. It is also probable that some slender-billed birds, and perhaps some butterflies, are attracted by the brilliancy of the flowers of plants of this genus, and that they take part in their fecundation, but I have no personal observations on this subject. Nearly all the *Loranthaceæ* have thick fleshy leaves, or else are clothed with woolly down ; the above-mentioned *Macrosolen Beccarii* alone has glossy and thinly coriaceous leaves. They are the despair of botanists who have to prepare specimens for the herbarium, for whatever precautions are taken they break up during the process of drying.

The species of terrestrial parasites known to me from Borneo are only two species of *Balanophora*, the *Brugmansia Lowii* and *Rafflesia Tuan Mudæ*, Becc.

The genus *Rafflesia* only contains a restricted number of species,

APPENDIX

very localised in the thickest parts of the forests of Java, Sumatra, the Philippines and Borneo. They are beyond doubt amongst the most marvellous products of Nature in existence, and I can only compare them to vegetable monsters which undoubtedly afford evolutionists a good deal of material for conjecture. I really cannot understand by what process the progenitor of the *Rafflesia* can have lost roots, stem and leaves, concentrating all in one gigantic flower, parasitic on a creeper, and devoid of apparent relationship with other families of plants. If it be true that the various forms of living species have always made their appearance by gradual and slight modifications one from the other, where are now the intermediate forms which acted as the connecting link between *Rafflesia* and the normal plant ? If *Rafflesia* is now so very different from the other forms of the vegetable world, the transitional types, according to the theory of slow and gradual evolution, ought to have been infinite. It thus appears very extraordinary that none of those extremely numerous intermediate types should have survived. May it not be that the *Rafflesia*, and a host of other aberrant species, both animals and plants, are examples of the autocreation of organisms (derived from exceptional circumstances of the environment) and suddenly appeared *à l'improviste*, as it were, in that primitive epoch during which organic matter was easily plasmated, so as to adapt itself with facility even to extraordinary conditions of existence ?

Size, Colour, and Scent of the Forest Flowers.—A considerable number of the trees which form the great Bornean forest have small and insignificant flowers, often of a greenish colour. I am not acquainted with any big tree in Borneo producing flowers in any way comparable to those of a common magnolia. The largest flowers of arboreal plants of the first magnitude are perhaps those of the *Durio*. Amongst trees of the second and third magnitude, flowers of notable dimensions are borne by some species of the following :—*Talauma, Dillenia, Gardenia*, some *Anonaceæ* (*Sphærothalamus insignis*, for instance, and some *Goniothalamus*). Amongst shrubs, the flowers of *Dillenia* (*Wormia*) *suffruticosa* are perhaps unsurpassed by those of any other plant in Borneo. Large and beautiful flowers are produced by many epiphytes ; I need merely mention those of numerous *Orchideæ, Fagræa, Rhododendron*, etc.

Amongst the minor trees and shrubs which are conspicuous in the dense forest on account of their flowers, although not frequent, *Plojarium pulcherrimum*, already alluded to for the singularity of its stem and for its masses of red flowers, which recall those of *Nerium oleander*, merits the first place, and following come several *Ixoras*, with their bright bouquets of scarlet flowers, and various species of *Saraca*. Smaller plants, remarkable less for the dimensions of their flowers than for their brilliant colours and the way they are grouped and rendered conspicuous, are various kinds of *Clerodendron*, some *Æschynanthus*, and more especially numerous *Zingiberaceæ* (*Costus, Alpinia, Amomum*, etc.). I can remember only one tree, *Mussændopsis Beccariana*, Baill., which has large white bracts, analogous to those of the shrub-like *Mussænda*. The predominating colour of the flowers of the trees, not taking into consideration the more common greenish, is white ; then follows yellow, then red.

APPENDIX

Blue and violet are less frequent, and are to be found in some *Melastomaceæ*, in a few *Gesneraceæ* (*Didymocarpus*), and *Acanthaceæ* (*Eranthemum*).

I have noted about sixty species of trees and shrubs in Borneo which produce flowers with a fragrant odour, which in not a few cases is extremely pleasant. This occurs especially in the following families— *Rubiacæ*, *Anonaceæ*, *Dipterocarpeæ*, *Orchideæ*, and *Bombaceæ*. Amongst the *Rubiaceæ* some species of *Randia* have pleasantly scented flowers, but those of two species of *Gardenia* (P. B., No. 1986, 3230), which recall the well-known perfume of *G. florida*, are especially sweet. The odour of the flowers in some of the *Anonaceæ* greatly resembles that of certain fruits, especially melons ; while that of the flowers of a *Xylopia* (P. B., No. 3488), of *Goniothalamus suaveolens*, Becc. (P. B., No. 2527), of a *Drepananthus* (P. B., No. 2543), and of several *Artabotrys*, is peculiarly grateful. At least two species of *Talauma* have flowers smelling much like those of some *Anonaceæ*. Amongst the *Dipterocarpeæ*, whose flowers are often delicately scented, those of *Isoptera Borneensis* are peculiar for their vanilla-like scent. Fragrant flowers are also met with in some of the Garcinias, and in various *Meliaceæ* and *Connaraceæ*. An *Apocynea* (*Epigynum ?* P. B., No. 1858) has flowers which in odour and appearance resemble those of white jessamines. None of the *Euphorbiaceæ*, a family so largely represented in Borneo, produce flowers, as far as I can remember, which are in any way odorous.

Plants with fœtid and disgusting flowers are not wanting in Borneo, but they are far less numerous than the fragrant ones. Amongst the more unpleasant I may mention first *Bulbophyllum Beccarii*, Reich., whose flowers smell strongly of putrid flesh ; next a *Kantium* (P. B., No. 3482 and 3916), and *Mussændopsis Beccariana*, both *Rubiaceæ*, whose flowers have the stench of excrement.[1] Thus it is amongst the *Rubiaceæ* in Borneo that the greatest number of species with fragrant flowers is met with, and at the same time some of the most fœtid.

Odorous, but unpleasantly so to us, are the flowers of a *Parkia* (P. B., No. 1447) and of *Horsfieldia* (*Myristica*) *reticulata*, Warb. Distinctly fœtid too are those of *Palaquium rigidum*, Pierre, *Helicia*, sp. ? (P. B., No. 3216), a *Taraktogenus* (P. B., No. 3972), some *Mangifera*, a *Cryptocarya*, several *Elæocarpus*, etc.

Regarding the relations of the odour of flowers and their colours, I have come to the conclusion that in Borneo the more fragrant flowers are white. I have no recollection of any bright red flower in Sarawak which is notably fragrant ; but *Unona flagellaris*, Becc., which is brownish-red in colour, has remarkably sweet-scented flowers.

Lianas.—In the tropical forests all over the globe lianas abound, a fact which may be regarded as not unnatural, since shade has the effect of lengthening the tissue cells in plants, and consequently the stems also. There has always been in forests a tendency in most plants to attempt to outgrow each other in order to get above the tree-tops and expose the leaves and flowers to the air and light.

[1] A wood called by the Malays " Kayu tai " (dung wood), has the same offensive odour, but the plant which produces it is unknown to me. This wood is more fœtid when wet, though the specimen I possess has with time almost lost its smell, even when wetted.

APPENDIX

Lianas, in the proper sense of the term, are plants with rope-like stems, which, rooted in the ground, manage to raise themselves by means of the neighbouring plants, and often ultimately to overtop the highest trees with their fronds. I do not, therefore, consider as true lianas those creepers which in their early stages find a support in tree-trunks, but afterwards, when sufficiently high, become free and independent. I have not yet been able to draw up a list of the true lianas of Borneo, and cannot therefore give the numeric relation in which they stand with regard to the other plants forming the flora of that country. There can be no doubt however that lianas are very abundant in the island, and that species belonging to very different orders are represented in the group, though if we include the rope-like palms (*Calamus*, and allied genera) amongst them, both for number of species and in many localities for that of individuals, these stand at the head of the list.

The more typical lianas are however all dicotyledonous plants. Particularly abundant are the *Leguminosæ* of the genera *Spatholobus, Entada*, and especially *Bauhinia*, several species of which are characterised by their spiral stems; the *Melastomaceæ*, represented by *Marumia, Dissochæte, Amplectrum*, etc.; the *Apocynaceæ*, amongst which several kinds of *Willoughbeia, Urnularia* and *Leuconotis* are valuable on account of the caoutchouc they yield; the *Anonaceæ* of the genera *Uvaria, Ellipeia, Artabotrys*, etc.; many *Rubiaceæ*; some *Cannaraceæ*, which with their rich bunches of flowers often show bits of vivid colour along the river banks. Among the larger lianas, in some localities very abundant, I must not forget to mention *Gnetum*, several *Menispermaceæ*, not a few *Vitis*, and some *Strychnos*, etc.; but I omit a host of others, in order not unduly to prolong my list. I must not, however, pass over a *Bambusa* (P. B., No. 2292) which I found in the vicinity of Kuching. It has thin stems, not thicker than the finger, with filled-up internodes, and climbs over trees by means of its stiff branches, which turn downwards and act as hooks. To this bamboo, which is the only climbing species in the Old World, and which has besides the peculiarity of solid stems, General Munro has assigned in my herbarium the name of *Bambusa solida*.

Lianas in Borneo are not only numerous as species, but extraordinarily abundant as individuals, for in some parts of the forest nearly every tree has one climbing its trunk and hanging from its topmost branches.

It is plain that no other reason but the tendency to struggle upward in search of light can have transformed a slender shrub into a liana or a thin straight palm into a climbing rotang. Even now if a plant is cultivated in a shady spot where it gets light only from above, it will lengthen out in an extraordinary manner—will become " drawn " as gardeners say. This fact, well known and of daily occurrence, illustrates how in nature a palm, for instance, has become a creeper. If however at the present day an erect *Calamus*, or other straight slender palm be cultivated under the conditions favourable for lengthening out, a creeper will not be produced, for adaptation has now become nearly impossible. Erect-growing plants cannot now be turned into creepers, nor can a liana become a tree, just as none of own indigenous plants transported to the tableland of Mexico will turn into fleshy species.

In various root-climbing plants the leaves produced at the earlier

APPENDIX

stages of growth are small and very different from those which are formed later. They are also flattened against the bark of the tree to which the plant adheres. But when the creeper has gained strength its upper leaves change their form, detach themselves from the supporting trunk, and may even acquire considerable dimensions, as in the case of some *Araceæ* of the genera *Raphidophora, Epipremnum, Scindapsus,* etc.

Stenophyllous Plants.—I have adopted this term for certain plants growing on river banks, or in the beds of torrents, which have linear or else very narrow leaves—narrower than those of congeneric species growing in the forest. By this I do not mean that every plant with narrow leaves must of necessity grow by the side of rivers, nor that it is only on Bornean rivers that such are observable. That plants with linear leaves have such a habitat is well known, and I need only mention as an example the many species of *Salix* so frequent in such localities. In Borneo however, along the inland rivers, stenophyllism appears to me much more accentuated, and more instructive by reason of the fact that the plants exhibiting this characteristic are numerous, and in many cases very strictly localised. They thus give one the idea of growing on the spot where they were originally plasmated ; where, submitting to local influences, they modified their structure, and more especially their leaves, in compliance with the stimulus received. I am inclined to ascribe the stenophyllism as due to the action of the continuous currents of air, so constant along rivers, and, secondly, to that of periodical floods. In the latter case stenophyllism is associated with great flexibility and toughness of the stems and branches, such as that exhibited by several species of *Salix*. To this type I refer *Croton viminalis*, Becc. (P. B., No. 3824) ; *Nauclea rivularis*, Becc. (P. B., No. 3827), which is allied to *N. angustifolia*, Haviland ; *Tetranthera salicifolia*, Becc. (P. B., No. 3826) ; and two *Antidesma* (P. B., No. 3829, 3831), besides some sub-herbaceous plants, such as *Osmoxylon helleborinum*, Becc., and *Pinanga rivularis*, Becc., and perhaps an orchid (*Arundina*, P. B., No. 3839).

To the group of stenophyllous Bornean plants resulting from the action of fluviatile air-currents one may, I think, refer *Garcinia linearis*, Pierre, from the rapids of the Rejang and the banks of the Entabei ; *Fagræa stenophylla*, Becc. (P. B., No. 3863), and *Erycibe longifolia*, Becc. (P. B., No. 3832) of the same region, where I also found, belonging to the same type, *Syzygium Nerifolium*, Becc. (P. B., No. 3862), *Eugenia riparia*, Becc. (P. B., No. 3880), *Psycotria acuminata*, Becc. (P. B., No. 3840), *Saurauja angustifolia*, Becc. (P. B., No. 3774), a *Milletia* (P. B., No. 3828), and *Pinanga calamifrons*, Becc.

It is certain that in my necessarily rapid exploration of the Rejang and other rivers of that region, I cannot have collected all the plants of a stenophyllous type which grow there, and I have no doubt many additions will be subsequently made to the species I have enumerated. I believe also that, although these species appear to be highly localised forms, they may be found along other rapid rivers subject to sudden inundations in the central parts of Borneo. But it is certain that plants of this type are not frequent on the west side of Borneo visited by me, and I can only recall a *Ficus* (*F. riparia*, Becc., P. B., No. 2781), from

APPENDIX

the banks of the Upper Sarawak river, which should come under the head of stenophyllous plants.

Fici.—The collection of the genus *Ficus* made by me in Borneo, consisting of 55 species, has been accurately determined by Sir George King (v. *Annals of the Roy. Botanic Garden*, Calcutta, vol. i., 1887–88), which circumstance gives me an opportunity of commenting on some of the more salient biological peculiarities of the species of that genus which are found on the island.

The topmost leaf-mass in the forests is largely composed of the foliage of trees of the genus *Ficus*, whether springing from a separate unsupported trunk rising straight from the ground, or from some gigantic epiphyte which has later become arborescent. But species of *Ficus* are found everywhere in all kinds of situations and all sorts of forests, the vegetative adaptations of these plants being infinite. Some species of *Ficus* are diminutive epiphytes (*F. diversifolia*, Bl. ; *F. Borneensis*, P. B., No. 1246 and 274=*F. diversifolia Borneensis*, King ; *F. linearis*, Becc., P. B., No. 2501). Others climb at first on tree-trunks and on rocks (*F. adhærens*, Miq. ; *F. crininervia*, Miq. ; *F. punctata*, Thunb., etc.), and mount up to the tops of the most lofty trees. These adhering species, as already stated, often have the leaves of the first period of growth applied against the bark of the trees or to the surface of the rocks on which they creep, and different from those developed later and higher up. Some of the creeping kinds grow first as an epiphyte on a high tree, and then develop large rope-like roots very much like the stems of lianas, which reach the ground. These produce at various heights large brightly coloured fruits (*F. callicarpa*, Miq.). A few species become big trees of the primeval forest, whilst several, which do not attain a large size, abound in the forest of secondary growth, along the river banks, and on the coast. Many are epiphytes. Some are so at one period and not at another. Some enclose their hosts in meshes of colossal size (*F. glabella*, Bl. and *F. caulocarpa*, Miq.) and become themselves gigantic trees. Others develop numerous roots from their branches, which either become secondary trunks or else remain cord-like (*F. retusa*, L. ; *F. Benjamina*, L.).

The remarkable biological relations subsisting between insects (Hymenoptera) and the *Ficus* during fecundation, and the constant presence, in the receptacula of all the species of this genus, of galloid flowers which contain the larva of a hymenopterous insect, or which, even when such a larva is not present, maintain through the force of heredity a galloid shape, shows how great an influence insects must have had in the morphological plasmation of the receptacula of *Ficus*.

The production of male flowers in this genus, like the impregnation of the ovuli, is biologically so bound up with insects, that I do not think it improbable that the present flask-shaped receptacula are due to deformation caused by insects, during the epoch of greater energy in the plasmative forces, in flat receptacula similar in nature to those of a *Dorstenia*.

The species of *Ficus* in Borneo have leaves of diversified form and aspect. Most are entire, sometimes lobate, rarely pinnatilobate, polished, opaque, coriaceous, herbaceous, membranaceous, rough, verrucose,

APPENDIX

smooth, hairy, but never lepidote. But whatever be their nature, and however great their variability, a *Ficus* can always easily be recognised as such even by its leaves alone.

All of them in Borneo have a white milky sap. As far as I know, there is only one *Ficus* in Malaysia, *F. leucantotoma*, Poir., which has a watery sap, but this species does not appear to have been as yet found in Borneo. Those species which attain large dimensions always have a light and soft white wood.

Of the 55 species of *Ficus* which I have .collected in Borneo, only sixteen are apparently peculiar. What a difference from the palms, of which only eighteen to twenty species out of 130 are found elsewhere, even including the domesticated forms ! The explanation lies in the fact of the facile dissemination of the various species of *Ficus* through the agency of birds, an explanation which applies to all trees which produce edible fruits specially relished by animals. The species of *Ficus* preferred by birds, particularly pigeons, hornbills, and buccos, are those belonging to the section *Urostigma*, which includes sixteen species known to me in Borneo, of which only two are not found elsewhere. On the other hand, of ten species belonging to the section *Covellia*, which develop their fruit on the lower portion of the trunk or on underground offshoots—in short in more or less hidden or inconspicuous positions, so as to be with difficulty discovered by birds which are migratory, or of powerful flight—six at least are peculiar.

Such facts show that, in tropical countries, the various kinds of *Ficus* are to a large extent biologically connected with birds, which perhaps on their part also owe some of their peculiarities in the shape of the bill, or in the plumage, to the nature and coloration of the fruits which form their food. In the many bird-skins which passed through my hands I have very often found that a relation existed between the colour of the fat on their bodies and that of the fruits on which they habitually fed.

The Bornean figs have usually globose or pyriform fruits, the size of which varies from that of a small pea to that of a large lemon (*F. callicarpa*, Miq.). Exceptionally small is the fruit of *F. linearis*, Becc., hardly one-eighth of an inch in diameter. Their colour is mostly yellow, but red and even black are frequent. Such colours are easily seen by birds. The fruits are generally fleshy and tasteless, though often sweetish, and in only one instance acid (*F. acidula*, King). In most of the species, and in all the *Urostigmas*, the fruits are placed in the axillæ of the leaves on the terminal branchlets. They are on the bigger branches in *F. acidula*, King ; and on the trunk in *F. Miquelii*, King ; *F. condensa*, King ; and *F. Hensleyana*, King. No less than six species in Borneo produce fruits half hidden in the ground, or inserted on hypogeal flagelliform offshoots, which radiate from the base of the plant. Four of these, viz., *F. Beccarii*, King ; *F. stolonifera*, King ; *F. Treubii*, King ; *F. uncinata*, Becc. (P. B., No. 2458=*F. geocarpa*, Teysm. *v. uncinata*, King), are peculiar to the island.

With regard to the general geographical distribution of the Bornean figs, it may be said that two-thirds of the species are also found in the Malay Peninsula, in Java, or in Sumatra, or else that they are very

APPENDIX

nearly akin to others from these regions. Several are widely diffused forms inhabiting an area which extends from the base of the Himalaya and Southern China to New Guinea.

Palms.—Amongst the vegetable forms of a markedly tropical type which greatly predominate in Borneo the palms are conspicuous. Of what I may term gregarious species, giving a special aspect to the landscape I can, however, only mention two—the Nipa (*Nipa fruticans*) and the Nibong (*Oncosperma filamentosa*), both of which are restricted to the lowlands along the estuaries and mouths of rivers. The *Eugeissonias*, in the somewhat limited areas where they grow, can also to a certain extent be considered gregarious palms. No palm in Borneo overtops the level of the forest, as in other regions. Although some have very tall stems (*Pholidocarpus Mayadum*, Becc.; *Oncosperma horrida*, Griff.), their crowns remain always beneath the shadow of the great forest giants. But the long rope-like palms, such as *Plectocomia*, *Korthalsia*, *Dæmonorops*, and *Calamus*, do manage to make their way up to, and above the topmost level of the forest mass.

The Bornean palms at present known, for the most part found by me in Sarawak, number about 130 species, divided amongst twenty-five genera. Of these only about twenty grow in neighbouring countries; the rest appear to be peculiar to the great island. The majority of the palms in Borneo are climbers, and such are almost all of the genus *Calamus* (which includes 32 Bornean species); 21 *Dæmonorops*, 8 *Korthalsia*, 1 *Plectocomia* and 1 *Plectocomiopsis*.

Amongst the non-climbing Bornean palms are some notable forms of *Arenga* and of *Zalacca*, which thrive along torrents in narrow valleys ; the highly characteristic *Teysmannia altifrons*, which I found abundant only on the slopes of Mount Mattang, but which occurs also in Sumatra and on the Malay Peninsula ; *Cyrtostachys Lakka* with its flame-coloured leaf-sheaths, *Areca Borneensis*, and *Licuala paludosa*, which last three species prefer the edge of the marshy forest, along rivers. The more abundant palms in the primeval forests of Borneo are however small and even diminutive species, always elegant, of *Pinanga* and *Licuala*, (the former being represented by fifteen, the latter by twelve species), of pygmy *Areca*, *Iguanura*, and *Didymocarpus*. Two of the *Pinangas* (*P. rivularis* and *P. calamifrons*) are stenophyllous, and occur on the banks of rapid torrents in the interior of the island. The *Gigliolia* is the only genus of palm peculiar to Borneo.

Pandanaceæ.—These contribute not less than the palms to characterise the tropical vegetation, on account of their very peculiar foliage. I collected about twelve species of *Pandanus* in Sarawak, and six or seven *Freycinetias*, but both the former and the latter are as yet undetermined.

Some kinds of gregarious *Pandanus* form impenetrable thickets in certain marshy localities, whilst others with their singular candelabra-like trunks supported on numerous stilt-like roots, grow isolated on rocks by the sea-shore, or on the edge of littoral forests. Several are small species which thrive in the shade of the primeval forest. There are besides in Sarawak two true epiphytic Pandani, notable for their long and abundant mass of leaves, which are often seen associated with the great *Platycerium* and other ferns and orchids high up in the fork of some giant forest tree. The *Freycinetias*, combined with big *Araceæ*, twist around the trees, and help with their tufts of long leaves to give that exotic aspect which is so fascinating in the equatorial forests.

Epiphytes.—To endeavour to treat, even in the most general manner, of the Bornean epiphytes would require a volume, so numerous are the adaptations and special modifications which these plants have assumed to succeed in surmounting the enormous difficulties besetting the mode of life they have chosen, and to find the means of maintaining themselves in situations where water and nutritive matter is either wanting or deficient. But the necessity of avoiding the competition of other plants has enabled them to get the better of these difficulties, and to establish themselves on different ground from that occupied by more powerful competitors.

For many plants the thirst for light may be supposed to be the cause which has determined their migration from the ground ; but the epiphytes which love shade and live on the lower and bare portion of the tree-trunks are numerous. A great many orchids, screw-pines, and Freycinetias, as well as aroids, ferns, etc., show the same tendency. Those epiphytes which live on the elevated parts of trees derive their nourishment from the air and rain, but probably in a greater measure still from the maceration and moisture of the bark of the tree to which they adhere. Such epiphytes very frequently take root on their host among mosses and minute ferns, not requiring much more than the point of attachment and profiting by the small amount of humus which slowly forms there, often augmented by ants, who take advantage of the shelter afforded by the roots of epiphytes to accumulate round them heterogeneous particles primarily for their own use, but ministering at the same time to the requirements of the plants under which they have sought cover.

No one will deny that epiphytes must have derived their origin from terrestrial plants. When the forest rendered the development of certain plants impossible, by reason of the shade which stunted their growth, and perhaps the dampness of the soil, or else on account of that tendency, so common amongst living beings, to strive to get above each other, a given number found their salvation at higher altitudes where, though they were able to satisfy their craving for light, they were nevertheless compelled to struggle against hunger and thirst.

The deficiency of water which all epiphytal plants must have experienced in passing from a terrestrial to an arboreal existence has been the origin of a multitude of adaptations for procuring it, or for storing up what came to them in the shape of rain or aqueous vapour. Indeed one of the principal conditions of existence in epiphytal plants is the economy of water, which they attain in many and various ways, but especially by preventing, or at least rendering difficult, all evaporation from their tissues by the thickening now of one, now of another organ, in which they accumulate the necessary amount of fluid; or, on the other hand, by means of special adaptations for facilitating the absorption of aqueous vapour.

Amongst the Bornean epiphytes are to be found all the most varied forms of adaptation which this group of plants can show within the

APPENDIX

tropics. Some are hygrometric or hygroscopic, able to resist drought for a long period, and to profit by ever so slight an amount of rain or aqueous vapour suspended in the surrounding air. To this category belong several ferns (*Hymenophyllaceæ* mostly) and various other vascular and cellular Cryptogams. Many epiphytes have thick and rather fleshy leaves, others have stems or roots with tuberous, bulbiform, or otherwise thickened enlargements. In some the vegetative organs are clothed with a waxy or varnishy layer, more rarely with hairs (*Eria* amongst the orchids). All these modifications are simply means for diminishing evaporation and maintaining the vitality of the protoplasm of their tissues. A great many epiphytes have the property of condensing atmospheric aqueous vapour, especially on their roots. It is thus that many orchids manage to grow, having most of their roots suspended in the air.

The condensation of aqueous vapour is one of the most important conditions for the existence of epiphytal plants, and it is perhaps for this reason that many, for instance a large number of orchids, prefer smooth barks in trees, which being inferior heat-conductors to cork-like barks, condense more readily the aqueous vapour with which the air is laden.

One might well describe the epiphytes as the misers of the vegetable kingdom, for they economise every thing, seeking to spend as little as possible, and utilising even the smallest resources in the way of food and drink.

The epiphytes of Borneo belong to the following families :—*Orchideæ, Asclepiadeæ* (*Hoya* and *Dischidia*), *Melastomaceæ* (*Medinilla* and *Pachycentria*), *Rubiaceæ* (*Myrmecodia, Hydnophytum*), *Araliaceæ* (*Heptapleurum*), *Loganiaceæ* (*Fagræa*), *Urticaceæ* (*Conocephalus*). Some plants of the genera *Vaccinium, Diplicosia, Rhododendron, Nepenthes, Pandanus,* and *Freycinetia* are also epiphytes, besides several *Zingiberaceæ,* many *Araceæ,* ferns and others.

From a certain point of view it seems to me that there is a kind of analogy between epiphytes and alpine plants, to which perhaps certain conditions of temperature are not as essential as a given amount of humidity, abundant light, and most probably the necessity of avoiding the neighbourhood of a number of other plants, with whom they could not struggle advantageously on the ground. In many of the Bornean epiphytes this resemblance is great. It is sufficient to mention the rhodendrons, amongst which *R. Brookeanum* flourishes at sea-level on mangroves on the equator ; whilst in the arctic regions *R. Lapponicum* resists any amount of cold.

Orchids.—Amongst the epiphytes of Borneo the *Orchideæ* hold the first rank, both for the number of species and for the beauty of their flowers. Some of the most splendid orchids known are natives of Borneo. It is, however, a mistake to suppose, as many do, that beautiful flowers, and especially those of orchids, are common in equatorial forests forming conspicuous masses of bright colour. One may wander for days in a Bornean forest without seeing a single brilliant flower. If all the Bornean plants bearing brightly-coloured flowers could be collected in a hothouse, and if they could be had in blossom at the same time, the sight would indeed be surprisingly beautiful, but beautiful flowers in Borneo are for the most part hidden from view to the wanderer in the forest. The spectacle of meadows spangled with flowers on our hills, or of rock-plants and bushes resplendent with brilliant colours on some alpine height, are sights unknown in Borneo ; mainly because there no single species of plant occupies entirely any extensive area. At times, however, it is true, the crown of a tree may be seen entirely covered by its own flowers or those of an enveloping liana, forming when viewed from an elevation, great masses of colour in a sea of verdure.

Although, as I have said, Borneo produces some of the finest orchids now cultivated in European hothouses, the island does not possess the number of species with large and brilliantly-tinted flowers which grow in Upper Burma, in some parts of the Himalayan region and in the forests of the tropical New World. Nor has Borneo any peculiar generic type belonging to this family. Perhaps the most remarkable Bornean orchid is *Arachnanthe Lowii,* which I have already mentioned ; a special type in its own group on account of the two kinds of flowers which it produces on the same spike, the proximal flowers nearest the leaves being quite different from those which grow above. This very exceptional case among orchids justifies in my opinion the formation of a new and special genus for this remarkable and beautiful plant, for which I would suggest the name of *Lowianthus Borneensis*, retaining thus the dedication to its discoverer.

I collected in Borneo over 200 species of orchids, which number perhaps does not represent even half of the species existent on this great island ; but amongst them few indeed would from an ornamental point of view deserve to be cultivated.[1] Amongst the more handsome and commercial forms about thirty are now cultivated in European hothouses. I may mention some fine Dendrobiums, three species of *Phalænopsis*, five or six Cypripediums, the above mentioned *Arachnanthe Lowii*, *Grammatophyllum speciosum*, two or three splendid Vandas, and several kinds of *Bulbophyllum* and *Cœlogyne*. The latter genus is represented in the Bornean forests by many species, some of which are often to be met flowering within hand-reach on the lower parts of trees, on bushes or on decaying prostrate trunks, together with ferns, mosses and other plants. The Cœlogynes with remarkable flowers in Sarawak, are, however, only four or five, and amongst them *C. pandurata* is the most noteworthy, having green flowers largely blotched with a deep black (*Vide*, p. 320.) I need not mention again here the small ground orchids with variegated or metallic-looking leaves (*Anæctochylus, Goodyera*, etc.) which are the gems of amateurs' collections.

Amongst the notable orchids of Sarawak *Bulbophyllum Beccarii*, Reich. deserves a special mention. It is a gigantic orchid which produces a conspicuous bunch of flowers, but the odour they give off is so strongly fœtid that when the hothouse at Kew where the plant was

---

[1] My Bornean orchids, after having remained for over ten years in the hands of Prof. Reichenbach, were returned to me without a single name affixed, Yet they had been worked, and the results will no doubt be found amongst the papers rendered useless to science by the singular testamentary dispositions of that learned but most eccentric botanist and lamented friend of mine.

APPENDIX

grown for the first time in Europe was opened to the public, those who entered were obliged to fly, not being able to endure the pestilential exhalations. *B. Beccarii* appears to grow originally on the ground, or at least to germinate near the foot of tree-trunks, along which its stems grow and take root tenaciously, climbing up spirally, with symmetrical, equally-distanced coils, to a great height. Its enormous coriaceous leaves, some of which measure over twenty inches in length and fourteen in width, follow the spirals of the stem at regular intervals, forming as a whole an object of great beauty, which one cannot but admire whenever one has the good fortune to come across it.

The antithesis of this colossus amongst the *Orchideæ*, perhaps the biggest in the entire group, is a pygmy orchid which I discovered also in Sarawak. It is the smallest known, and strange to say it also is a *Bulbophyllum*, which Professors Reichenbach and Pfitzer have designated as *Odoardi*, kindly naming it after me. On this species Professor E. Pfitzer has written an instructive memoir, showing some interesting and remarkable structural peculiarities which characterise this diminutive orchid. It is one of those species which adhere to the naked and nearly smooth bark of the big branches of the highest trees, and it is most difficult to find, unless one can minutely examine the parts its prefers to grow on. I discovered it whilst carefully searching the big branches of a great tree which had been felled near Kuching on a spot where a plantation was being established.

Bulbophyllum Beccarii, as we have seen, is a muscarian orchid, viz. one of those which give off a putrid stench, thus attracting flies, who unconsciously perform the important function of aiding fecundation. This method of attracting insects is very rare amongst orchids, whose flowers are usually extremely fragrant, and appeal rather to the tastes of butterflies and moths. It is not only through the scent of their flowers, however, that orchids attract insects, but also—and very considerably—by their strange shapes. No flowers resemble insects, especially the Lepidoptera, more closely than do those of certain orchids. I need only mention *Phalænopsis* amongst Bornean species. Orchids, indeed, may well be termed the butterflies of the Vegetable Kingdom. And this is a certain proof of the connexion which exists, or has existed, between insects and the flowers of these plants, a subject on which Darwin made his well-known and highly interesting investigations. Yet up to the present, but little is known regarding the insects which visit and fertilise the flowers of the more gaudy orchids of tropical lands. It is true that we are now acquainted with a great number of beautiful orchids which are cultivated in our hothouses, where they blossom abundantly. Indeed, no other family of tropical plants is better known in the living condition. But in our hothouses those insects which in a state of nature have biological relation with the flowers of orchids are not to be found, whilst collectors have as yet told us little or nothing on this subject, and this for many reasons, amongst which the more important is perhaps the fact that orchid-hunters often get their plants through natives. Moreover, to do good work on this subject collectors ought to be equally good botanists and entomologists. And even the true botanist has rarely occasion to make observations and researches on the subject, for the flowering of orchids

APPENDIX

is capricious and not of frequent occurrence, while, as I have said more than once, their flowers are often high up on the trees, beyond reach. With the exception of *Bulbophyllum Beccarii*, which attracted flies, I have personally never seen in Borneo an orchid in flower on which a butterfly or any other insect was posed. Probably some of the insects which visit the flowers are nocturnal or crepuscular, which is another obstacle to observations on the interdependence of insects and the flowers which they frequent.

If the flowering of orchids is infrequent and capricious, as a compensation their blossoms in most instances last a long while, which is in itself a proof of the difficulties which beset their fertilisation. The flowers last long because they have to wait long for an opportunity of fecundation, and this circumstance tends to show that for some cause or other insects are not naturally too prone to visit them. Many orchids under natural conditions hardly bring to maturity a single fruit of the many they bear. And this difficulty and the long delay in fecundation may account for the surprising mechanisms which the flowers reveal in their reproductive organs. It appears to me to be almost a general rule that the more a plant is provided with anomalous, complicated, and uncommon contrivances, the more precarious and difficult must have been its conditions of existence in past evolutive periods. It is a fact that plants so provided are rare and localised. They have been, as it were, dissatisfied with their position, and have endeavoured to better it by special adaptations, but the complications attending these have finally proved a disadvantage rather than an advantage to them.

Passing now to the forms of Bornean orchids, it is worthy of note that, both in their foliage and their stems, these show a remarkable polymorphism, exhibiting all the ways and means known proper to epiphytes to enable them to live in the peculiar physical conditions which they have chosen.

Although various terrestrial orchids are found in Borneo, none, as far as I am aware, are provided with underground tubers, a character which appears to be peculiar to members of the family living in localities where terrestrial vegetation has alternate periods of activity and rest. Many of the epiphytal orchids of Borneo, however, possess basal enlargements, which may be looked upon as aerial bulbs, for the plants find on the branch of the tree on which they grow that marked diversity in the conditions of alimentation, absorption, and assimilation between the inferior part of the stem and the leaves, that bulbous plants find in the soil—a diversity of conditions which may indeed have been the first origin of bulbous plants. Amongst all the various structural forms in the vegetative parts of the Bornean orchids, there is one which has specially surprised me—the rush-like form which is assumed by some few, for it corresponds to a type frequent in marsh-loving plants. It would be interesting to know what is the physiological connexion existing between plants which live in localities where water abounds, and these xerophil epiphytes, which have to battle with drought. This analogy of existence between epiphytal and paludal plants exists also between the various species of *Nepenthes*, some of which are epiphytes, while others are aquatic.

APPENDIX

Flowering Trunks.—In the Bornean primeval forest the eye is often struck by the singular sight, not only of plants, but trees, in which the flowers, instead of showing in normal positions, appear on the cylindrical portion of the trunk, or form bunches or masses at its base close to the ground, or again, in rarer cases, emerge from the ground from hypogeal branches. Such abnormal situations for flowers, indeed, are not unknown in a few plants in other countries; notable examples of this being the American calabashes (*Crescentia*), the African *Omphalocarpum*, and the Asiatic Jack-tree (*Artocarpus integrifolia*) with its enormous pendant fruits hanging from the trunk and the bigger branches. But in the Malayan region species with flowers in abnormal positions are perhaps more frequent than elsewhere, and I have noted at least fifty kinds of trees and shrubs in Borneo which show this peculiarity in a marked degree.

In Borneo we find two principal categories of plants with abnormally-placed flowers; in one these appear on the trunk, in the other on the roots, or rather on underground branches, the flowers expanding just above the level of the ground. Amongst the plants belonging to the first series besides trees and shrubs, are not a few lianas, *Leguminosæ*, *Anonaceæ*, many species of *Gnetum*, some *Ficus*, several *Menispermaceæ*, etc.

The majority of those with flowers growing on the trunk are shrubs, but there are also trees of great size. Amongst the latter the most remarkable is *Durio testudinarum* or "Durian kakura"[1] a singular tree, for it hardly differs from the cultivated durian, except that its flowers and succeeding fruits (which are about half the size of the true durian) are crowded together round the knobby trunk in great numbers on a level with the ground. The very same thing was observed by me in a small tree, *Goniothalamus lateritius*, Becc., already mentioned (p. 233), and in a Sapotacea (*Palaquium Beccarii*, Pierre). There is a big tree belonging to the *Bixaceæ* (*Taraktogenus*, P. B., No. 2644) which produces on its trunk very hard woody fruits as round as cannon-balls, four inches in diameter. I have also described another Anonacea, *Polyalthia anomala*,[2] which I often meet with at Mattang, in which the flowers always appear on excrescences at the base of the trunk. The flowers of this *Polyalthia* are of a greenish colour and not large, but the fruits which follow are very big, of a beautiful golden yellow and very conspicuous, and therefore must be visible to animals even at a distance. There are also some species of *Polyalthia* whose otherwise naked trunk is for many feet literally clothed with largish flowers of a very brilliant salmon colour. These are the trees which Wallace has referred to under the description of "Flowering trunks."[3] Two palms, *Pinanga brevipes*, B., and *P. crassipes*, B., produce flowers and fruits on a level with the ground, whilst in all the other species of the genus these grow from the upper portion of the stem.

More numerous than those with flowers growing from the trunk are plants in which they develop from the larger branches; certain species

[1] Cf., *Malesia*, vol. iii.
[2] Cf. *Nuovo Giornale Botanico Ital.*, vol. iii., p. 188.
[3] Cf. *Tropical Nature*, pp. 34–35.

APPENDIX

of *Ficus* and several *Myristicaceæ*, *Bombaceæ*, *Lauraceæ*, *Bixaceæ* and others, come under this head.

The cause which has made flowers grow on the big branches instead of amongst the leaves at their extremities, must be the same which has made them grow on the trunk. The abnormal position of the reproductive organs in " Flowering Trunks " has been attributed by Wallace to the circumstance that in the tropics many butterflies and other insects fly in the lower part of the forests, beneath the great mass of foliage. He therefore opines that flowers are thus placed low down and conspicuously in order to attract them. This may be true for some species. But if it explains how flowers which have grown for the first time on the stem (and not in the usual places) should continue to appear in an abnormal position on account of the advantages thus obtained by the plants producing them, it nevertheless does not give the physiological reason of the first deviation from the general rule ; it does not explain why such flowers, which habitually were produced at the vegetative extremities, should suddenly have appeared in the axial parts.

With regard to this point I would draw attention to the fact that some of the *Anonaceæ*, for instance, have flowers of a rather peculiar structure, which in the phenomenon under examination might lead one to suspect another and somewhat different cause than that suggested by Wallace. There are abundant reasons to show that, in various *Anonaceæ*, fertilisation takes place with perfectly closed flowers, in which insects, not being able to enter, have no part—in other words, belong to the category of what are technically known as cleistogamous plants. It is noteworthy, too, that many flowers of this family are thick and fleshy and often sweetly fragrant, with a perfume which recalls that of ripe fruit. It is true that odours of this kind may have been equally attractive to insects, but it appears to me even more probable that they may have been the means of attracting animals, who ate the flowers, mistaking them for fruits. I suggest therefore that when, in the ancestors of the present *Anonaceæ*, the flowers grew on the upper portions and smaller branches of the tree, the continual destruction of them by animals may have been the stimulus which caused their growth on another part of the plant. Such is the reason which I have already given to endeavour to explain what may be termed the caulifloral condition of *Durio testudinarum*.[1]

In support of Wallace's opinion it might be argued that certain plants which could not emulate in height the giants of the forest, and would thus have been obliged to expand their flowers in the shade, hidden amidst the foliage, and thus remaining unfertilised, being neglected by insects whose aid is necessary to insure this operation—it can be argued, I say, that as an expedient, such plants produced flowers where they were most easily noticeable. In this case the non-fecundity of the flowers normally placed would be equivalent to my suggestion of their destruction by animals. The structure of plants is such that it is perfectly possible that a stimulus felt by an individual in a given spot should produce its effects in another part of the same plant.

Of all the tissues which exist in the higher plants, the cambium is that which possesses the greatest sensibility, and the faculty to multiply

[1] Cf. *Malesia*, vol. iii., p. 224.

and transform itself into the various secondary tissues. There is a period in the life of plants during which the protoplasm of the cambium, and especially that contained in the perforated vessels under the cortical layer, appears to be in communication with the cambium existing in all the vital parts of the plant. And it may be admitted as certain that, during the period of organic activity (which, with us, occurs in the spring), the elements for the production of reproductive cells, i.e. of those cells which can give origin to the flower, are found in every portion of that tissue. If, therefore, at the moment when, in the fibrous-vascular bundles, the cells which are to be transformed into the reproductive organs are becoming specialised, an impediment occurs to their formation in the normal places, it may well happen that that which cannot take place in one part of the plant may occur in another.

And for this reason, if, during the epoch of the forming of species, which for brevity's sake I have called the " creative " or " plasmative " period, the normally-placed flowers of a plant got destroyed, and consequently no fruits and seeds were developed, that plant may have been able to produce flowers elsewhere, and especially in those parts of the bark which correspond to original vegetative centres, viz. where eyes or latent or potential buds exist, precisely as buds or gemmations appear where no previous trace was visible, when the trunk or big branches of a tree are cut or lopped.[1]

Among herbaceous plants in Borneo are also some which produce flowers on subterranean leafless branches, among which are not a few *Zingiberaceæ*. I, however, know of only a single woody plant in Borneo which produces true flowers emerging from the ground on hypogeal branches far from the main trunk—the *Unona flagellaris*, Becc., already mentioned.

In various species of *Ficus* the receptacula with the reproductive organs spring up from the ground, being inserted on long underground stolons, sometimes at a distance of several yards from the trunk from which they branch ; and on one occasion, having discovered one of these plants, or rather its fruits, I was unable to find the main stem to which they belonged. I have already mentioned that not a few species of *Ficus* produce fruits on their trunk and even at its base, on a level with the ground, or on the bigger branches. As in the case of true " flowering trunks," I believe that such an anomaly in the position of the floral receptacles of *Ficus* must be accounted for by their previous destruction in the upper parts of the plant, more accessible to animals such as monkeys, squirrels, etc.

Ant-harbouring Plants and Nepenthes.—Amongst the most marvellous

---

[1] Actual experiment shows precisely the process which I have postulated. In grafting vines already adult and producing fruit, I have seen several small bunches of flowers appear, growing from the naked stem, doubtless because the head of the plant had been cut off. In the *Revue Horticole* for 1882 (p. 430, fig. 93), is described and figured a vine-stem bearing several berries on its bare portion, thus also reproducing exactly the case of fruits growing from the trunk. My hypothesis has further corroboration in the experiments of Professor Mattirolo (*Malpighia*, xiii., p. 20, extract) on *Vicia Faba*, in which the continued ablation (disantholization) of the flowers, as they were developed in their normal position, caused the production of other flowers in abnormal places on the lower portion of the plant.

APPENDIX

productions of the vegetable kingdom, more largely represented in Borneo than elsewhere, are the Pitcher-plants or *Nepenthes*, and those ant-harbouring species to which I have applied the term of "hospitating plants."

The *Nepenthes*, which I have had occasion to mention more than once, are now so well known in their general characters, for they are everywhere successfully cultivated in Europe, that I shall here merely note some of their many peculiarities. I shall begin by stating that of about forty known species of *Nepenthes*, half at least are to be found in Borneo, and of these about a dozen are exclusively confined to its soil.[1]

The term "hospitating plants" is applied to certain singular species which constantly shelter (in cavities specially destined for that purpose) insects, which are nearly always ants. In this category various epiphytal *Rubiaceæ* belonging to the genera *Myrmecodia* and *Hydnophytum*, both comprising numerous species, are most conspicuous.

The genus *Myrmecodia* is represented in Borneo by a single species; *Hydnophytum* by two. In Sarawak these strange plants appear to have struck even the imagination of the natives, who have given them the fantastic name of "anak antu," or "children of the spirits." Both the *Hydnophytum* and the *Myrmecodias* are provided with a large bulbi-form enlargement, formed by a thickening of the basal portion of the stem. In *Hydnophytum* this organ sometimes acquires the size of a child's head, whilst the remainder of the plant is reduced to a few twigs and leaves. In *Myrmecodia* the enlargement is also voluminous, but the stem is single, rather large, and continuous with the swollen part, terminating in a tuft of good-sized leaves. The tuber or bulb both in *Hydnophytum* and in *Myrmecodia* is formed mostly of cellular tissue, soft and watery, and is highly adapted to store up a large amount of sap. The structure of the outer layer or skin of the bulb is such as to render evaporation difficult, for which reason, in a country with such frequent rain and an atmosphere so constantly saturated with moisture, that organ is sufficient to retain in the tissues the quantity of water necessary to keep the plant in a condition of active vegetation even during the time intervening between a wet and a dry season. The basilar swelling of *Myrmecodia* and *Hydnophytum* cannot properly be called a bulb or tuber, because it is not, as true tubers are, a store of alimentary reserves, but merely a reservoir of water.

Interiorly these organs of the above-mentioned plants show a singular structure. If cut across they are not found full, but excavated in all directions and crossed by canals and sinuous galleries, in which ants are constantly sheltered. The insects have in fact permanently established their home in these galleries, where they breed in prodigious numbers. And this is the reason why I have proposed for this class of plants the name of "hospitators"[2] in preference to that of "formicarians," for the latter qualification applies equally to quite another series of plants, which, instead of possessing receptacles or homes of shelter for ants, present small spaces secreting saccharine fluids which are a great attraction

[1] Cf. *Malesia*, vol. iii., p. 1.
[2] For further and more complete information on these plants I would refer to my memoir on "Hospitating plants," published in the second volume of *Malesia*.

APPENDIX

to such insects. However, the biological connexion which exists in either case between the plants and the ants is similar, being a symbiosis for reciprocal advantage. In the one case as in the other the plants tolerate and act as hosts to the ants, because these insects are useful to them as a defence against other insects and hurtful creatures of various kinds.

At first I thought that the ants, by the irritation they produced on young budding plants of *Myrmecodia*, favoured the swelling of the base of the stem, and were the direct cause of such an hypertrophy. Further investigations and researches and the observations of Dr. Treub have, however, convinced me that from the very beginning these swellings appear independently of any action of the ants, and that when the latter are absent the tubers develop much in the same manner. I do not however think it equally certain that ants have no part in the formation of the internal galleries. My observations tend to prove that in some cases, in non-Bornean species of *Myrmecodia*,[1] ants take an active part in the formation of the galleries and especially in that of the apertures which lead to them. But be this as it may, the hospitating *Rubiaceæ* live on a footing of reciprocal utility or mutualism with their inhabitants, which act as a formidable army of defence, for no animal dares to meddle with a plant guarded by a host of biting ants, ready to assault the imprudent invader in myriads.

The globose form and succulent substance which make the tubers of formicarian *Rubiaceæ* resemble big fruits, would be a sufficient attraction to not a few animals, monkeys for instance, as food ; but it is certain that on account of the ants no animal dares to touch them. I suppose that this is the reason why, in nature, no individual of *Myrmecodia* or of *Hydnophytum* is found uninhabited and deprived of its useful dwellers, because undoubtedly in this case it would be immediately destroyed. It remains, however, to be ascertained whether in the natural condition ants, besides serving as an alert militia for the defence of the tubers, confer indirectly some other advantage on the plant which shelters them. Whether, for instance, it is not possible that the mass of detritus, excreta, and humus which the ants accumulate in the galleries, is not utilised for alimentary purposes by the plant.

In order that such material may be utilised by the plant, the latter must be able to assimilate the nutritive elements from the surfaces of the internal galleries. Now it is true that in the tubers of some species of formicarian *Rubiaceæ*, not living in Borneo, I have found on the walls of the galleries small roots, which might serve for the aforesaid function ; but both in the *Myrmecodia* and in the *Hydnophytum* of Borneo, no such internal rootlets have been found, although it has been observed that the internal walls of the galleries are dotted with small but numerous cellular prominences similar to so-called "lenticellæ" with which, in fact, Dr. Treub has compared them, considering such "pseudo-lenticellæ" as aërating organs of the plant. Without wishing to deny this, I cannot, however, exclude the hypothesis that these are more probably subsidiary organs of alimentation, analogous to those which are found in the

[1] In *Myrmecodia alata* and *bulbosa* ; *Malesia*, vol. ii., pl. xxv., xxvi.

APPENDIX

external wall of the basal tumefied part of *Balanophora*, a part which is always in contact with the humus, from which I suspect that *Balanophora* and allied plants combine parasitism with saprophytism. By analogy the formicarian *Rubiaceæ* would be both epiphytes and saprophytes, for it appears to me quite possible that the surface of the galleries of their tubers may serve for the direct absorption of nutritive substances for the plant. The galleries might also act as subsidiary organs for the absorption of water, as Dr. Treub opines, it being not impossible that at certain moments the aqueous vapour diffused in the atmosphere may condense in them.

In any case I consider the tubers of hospitating *Rubiaceæ* to be complex organs which primarily originated from a thickening caused by the position which those plants have sought, and by the necessity of having a reserve of liquids against a dry season. All the other advantages which I have enumerated have come afterwards, and must be considered as secondary adaptations obtained in an indirect way. The tubers of these *Rubiaceæ* may thus be organs which originated through the action of simple physiological causes inherent in vegetation, were enlarged later by the hypertrophy produced through irritation caused by the ants, and finally became hereditary.

The *Myrmecodia* and *Hydnophytum* just mentioned are not the only hospitating plants found in Borneo. There are not a few others, and very interesting ones, but these I need not dwell on here. For further information I must refer my reader to my special memoir on the subject already quoted. I must not omit, however, to mention *Clerodendron fistulosum*, Becc.,[1] a handsome plant which has a stem about five feet in height bearing a few big opposite leaves of a purple colour beneath and a terminal bouquet of long tubular white flowers. Each internode of the stem is swollen and shelters internally a colony of ants. Of a similar kind is a euphorbia, *Macaranga caladifolia*, Becc.,[2] a small tree with few branches, which are hollow and formed to shelter ants. This plant has also, like the *Clerodendron*, large glands on the leaves which secrete a sweet juice, and act as an attraction for the ants, so that they may appreciate and not abandon the plant. Or perhaps it may have been the presence of these glands which first attracted the ants and induced them to form a safe refuge within reach of the prized delicacy.

There are also palms in Borneo which are provided with permanent shelters for ants. These are the *Korthalsias*, rotangs or creeping palms, which along the stems, at the insertion of each frond, at the end of the sheath, have an appendage called an " ocrea " or sock, of a paper-like structure, swollen out so as to form an entirely closed receptacle in which certain species of ants find a home, making an entry into the cavity by using their mandibles. These ant-shelters in the inflated ocreæ of *Korthalsia* are permanent and constant organs, undoubtedly not now produced by ants ; but I feel sure that originally (I mean during the plasmative epoch) it was irritation caused by ants which occasioned them. The swollen ocreæ of the *Korthalsia* would thus be hereditary pseudo-galls or ant-homes. In Borneo several species of hospitating

---

[1] *Malesia*, vol. ii., pl. iv.
[2] *Ibid.*, vol. ii., p. 45, pl. iii.

APPENDIX

Korthalsias occur—indeed, it is in their ant-shelters that the characters are found which serve to distinguish the formicarian species of this most difficult genus.

Amongst the *Korthalsias* one species surprised me when I first met with it near my house on Mattang, because I could not at first account for a peculiar noise which I made out to be coming from one of these plants. It was a sonorous rustling sound, which I afterwards found was produced by the passage of a colony of ants inhabiting the vesicular organs and inflations of the *Korthalsia*, which, being by nature rigid and dry, produced in a certain measure the effects of the resonators of a stringed musical instrument.[1]

Amongst the hospitating plants in Borneo must also be included *Nepenthes bicalcarata*,[2] one of the most marvellous species of that singular genus, because to the already surprising structure of its pitchers, it adds the prerogative of a formicarian plant. In its case the ants inhabit the stalks sustaining the pitchers, which are enlarged and hollow for the purpose.

I could not ascertain whether any connexion exists between the ants sheltered by *N. bicalcarata* and the insects which fall into its pitchers ; nor was I able to verify what has been asserted by others, namely, that the insects imprisoned in the pitchers attract that singular little lemur *Tarsius spectrum*, said to show a desire to prey on insects so detained, were it not prevented from introducing its head into the pitchers by the two appendages in the shape of walrus-tusks, which protect their mouths.

It is impossible not to marvel at the shape and distribution of all the appendages which surround the rim of the pitchers or ascidia of the *Nepenthes*. In this respect a *Nepenthes* which I found near Kuching, and which Sir Joseph Hooker has distinguished with the specific name of *echinostoma*,[3] deserves special mention. In it, instead of edges, crests, or projections, the rim of the pitchers is fringed with rigid points directed inwards towards the cavity, which must serve admirably to lead insects to the very edge of the precipice, make them fall over, and prevent their escape.

It cannot be doubted that insects must be attracted towards and induced to visit the pitchers of the *Nepenthes*, considering all the artifices and inducements brought into play, the strange shape of the pitchers, their bright colours, and, above all, the glands disseminated around, affording all kinds of sweetmeats, to tempt and lure the insects to perdition. Of this kind are the glands which are on the inner part of the lid of the pitcher, where if a greedy and imprudent insect tries to rest, it is almost certain to be trapped. But where Nature has shown all her refinement of perfidy is in the disposal of these baits within and around the rim of the pitchers. All the ornamental appendages, grooves, enlargements, rings, points, etc., found there, have no other end than that of leading the insects toward the lower inverted portion within these appendages, where is a gland secreting nectar, placed in such a position that if an insect reaches it, it almost certainly loses its balance

[1] Cf. *Malesia*, vol. ii., p. 62.
[2] *Ibid.*, vol. ii., p. 231, pl. 55.
[3] *Ibid.*, vol. iii., p. 27.

and falls into the well prepared to receive it. Once in there it cannot escape, and is drowned in the liquid always accumulated therein, which has been secreted by the plant even before the opening of the pitcher.

The plan followed by Nature in the production of the ascidia of the *Nepenthes*, is, as I read it, the following one :—Originally the primordial dilatation of the leaf organs, from which the pitcher is derived, was caused by the necessity of storing water, supposing that the *Nepenthes* were aquatic plants in early epochs, transformed later into epiphytal or terrestrial species.[1] According to this view the ascidia would have been merely internal reservoirs for water, swollen by tension, which eventually breaking at a given point, formed the lid or operculum, in a manner analogous to that of the " urns " of the mosses. Into the open cavity containing water thus formed, insects accidentally fell, and subsequently the stimulus of organised matter in contact with the walls of the pitcher may have produced in the protoplasm of its peripheral cells (by reversion towards primitive voracious instincts) an avidity for nitrogenous substances, whilst the visits and stimuli of insects would have induced the development of glands secreting saccharine substances, and would have given origin to the appendages which surround the lips of the ascidium.

Formerly it was thought that the insects fallen into the pitchers of the *Nepenthes* by putrefying in the liquid therein collected, indirectly furnished to the plant nitrogenous substances useful for its alimentation. But recent investigations have proved that this is only exceptionally true, and that normally the *Nepenthes* secrete, by means of certain glands placed internally in the lower part of their " pitchers," a digestive fluid, and the same glands afterwards subtract the assimilable matter from the bodies of the ants and other insects captured, not through putrefaction, but by a true process of digestion. The *Nepenthes* are thus to be placed among those plants which have been aptly termed carnivorous. It is not however proved that in order to live and prosper the *Nepenthes* must necessarily digest animal substances, and many a time these plants are found without a single insect caught in their pitchers, and yet they do not appear to suffer. This nearly always happens to the *Nepenthes* cultivated in European hothouses.

Carnivorism in plants is, I think, to be considered rather as a vice than as a functional necessity. Indeed, it does not appear that they have derived any great and special advantage over normal-feeding plants by this extraordinary faculty, which in a certain way brings them near to the higher animals. Animal food is beyond doubt a luxury for carnivorous plants, and they can perfectly well do without it, precisely as a number of human beings have existed until now, and could still continue to exist, without spirits, tea, coffee or tobacco.

Floral Areas in Borneo.—The Bornean Flora assumes multiform aspects, and its components are of a varied nature according to the localities, the elevation, and the physical conditions of the soil. Thus distinct areas of varied extent can be recognised, some much restricted, on which a special vegetation grows, different from that of adjoining lands. Such floral areas, which might even be styled " botanical

---

[1] Cf. *Malesia*, vol. i., p. 233.

APPENDIX

regions " if their extension were not at times extremely limited, are very numerous in Borneo. The following appear to me to be the principal ones :—

1. Sea-beaches, composed of a dry, sandy tract, where the casuarinas form a small fraction of a special kind of forest, composed almost entirely of one species. In such localities grow bushy and herbaceous plants generally distributed within the tropics. Behind the casuarinas usually extends a forest rich in endemic forms mixed with others which are not so. Rotangs, screw-pines, etc., abound there. (See p. 94.)

2. Dry rocky sea-beaches. As there is no sand the casuarina cannot grow. The first line in such localities is held by trees with a wide geographical distribution within the tropics, such as *Barringtonia, Terminalia, Pongamia, Hernandia*, various species of *Ficus*, etc. This kind of vegetation is to be met with along extensive tracts of coast in the more western portion of Sarawak. (See p. 224.)

3. The swampy and estuarine coastal region, completely invaded by nipas and mangroves. In this zone the sago and other palms, especially the " nibong " (*Oncosperma filamentosa*) grow. (See p. 81.)

4. The river banks within the influence of the tides, such as those of the Sarawak around Kuching, where the *Sonneratia* is the prevailing tree. (See p. 80, and *footnote*.)

5. The river banks above the tidal influence, as those of the Upper Sarawak. When in such localities the primeval forest has not been destroyed, they are characterised by a rich and peculiar flora. (See pp. 123-4.)

6. The fluviatile region of stenophyllous plants, which I met with on the banks of the Rejang and other rivers in districts remote from the sea. (See page 298.)

7. The great primeval forest in lowlands constantly watered, immensely rich in species, and of enormous extent. To this type belongs the forest in the neighbourhood of Kuching, of the delta of the Rejang, of Undup, etc.

8. The primeval forest of non-watered plains and foot-hills, as rich and extensive as the preceding, and perhaps more so ; it is often in contact or alternating with it. To this type belongs the forest between Kuching and the base of Mount Mattang.

9. The primeval forest on the mountain slopes, such as that on the lower parts of Mattang, so rich in *Dipterocarpeæ, Sapotaceæ, Ebenaceæ*, etc. (See p. 91.)

10. The primeval forest of the middle mountain region, where the number of species is less than in the lower parts, but where certain austral types abound, such as *Dammara, Podocarpus, Dacrydium, Phyllocladus*. Of this type is the forest of Poe, of between 3,000 and 4,000 feet in elevation. (See p. 99.)

11. The primeval forest on the summits of medium elevation (5,500 to 6,500 feet), such as those of Tiang-ladja, Mattang, Poe, where wind and mists prevail. This zone is not so much characterised by its elevation as by its exposed position, much wind-swept, and at the same time subject to frequent condensations of aqueous vapours. The plants do not acquire any great size, and show mostly a small and coriaceous

APPENDIX

foliage. In such localities Mosses and *Hepaticæ* abound, covering the trunks and branches of the arborescent vegetation. (See page 100.)

12. The limestone hills.

13. The so-called " Mattang " (See p. 147, etc.)

14. The secondary forest, composed of small or middling-sized trees, with species mostly of extensive geographical distribution. This type of flora covers very great areas in Sarawak, and appears quickly in all fertile localities where the primitive forest has been cut down, cultivated, and afterwards abandoned.

15. The " Lalang," where common species of small shrubs often grow associated. This is the poorest in vegetable types in Borneo. The lalang grass covers poor soil after the destruction of the primitive forest and when the rains have carried off the upper and richer part of the soil.

16. The marshy region of abandoned rice-fields, invaded by *Scleria*, ferns, or large Graminaceæ. Such are the plains of Lundu and Lingga. (See p. 138.)

17. Cultivated lands in dry situations (mostly rice), where for a short time various herbaceous species have established themselves, practically cosmopolitan or nearly so. (See pp. 131 and 192.) During the first years that such rice-fields lie fallow, wild bananas often spring up, which later give way to the secondary forest.

18. The swampy forest of the Kapuas lakes. (See p. 187.)

19, The swamps covered with screw-pines, which take the place of our *Cyperus*, *Carex*, and *Typha*. As an example I may mention the frequently overflowing rivers of the Lingga and Sumandjang districts. (See pp. 345, 348.)

20. The area of aquatic and submerged plants, which in Borneo are reduced to the *Cryptocoryne*, *Barclaya*, and *Ceratopteris*. As I have previously remarked, floating or natant plants are scarce in Borneo, a notable characteristic of the island flora.

Finally there remains the floral area of the elevated regions of Kina Balu, with which I am not personally acquainted ; but we have a most important work on the subject by Mr. O. Stapf, in the *Transactions of the Linnean Society* (vol. iv., p. 2, 1894). I shall not here refer to the many and important facts connected with the distribution of the plants on Kina Balu given in this memoir ; I shall merely remark that from the point of view of Bornean floral areas, and in conformity with the sketch I have given, one may recognise on Kina Balu, besides some of the zones or areas above-mentioned, two others peculiar to that mountain group, viz. (1) that of the big *Nepenthes*, which reaches an elevation of 11,500 feet ; and (2) that of the summit. The latter, which is the most elevated floral zone in the entire Indian Archipelago, is not what might have been expected on a mountain placed in the centre of a land remarkable for the great variety of peculiar forms. The summits of Kina Balu do not possess numerous types derived from the surrounding Malayan flora of the lowlands, nor are there many forms of the same genus revealing themselves as local creations, like the *Dipterocarpeæ* of the Mattang forest. The plants of the top of Kina Balu are rather a casual medley of heterogeneous types derived from other mountain tops often far away ; a fact which can perhaps be attributed to the

Fig. 61.—MOUNT KINA BALU, FROM THE TAMPASSUK RIVER.

APPENDIX

comparatively recent epoch in which the mountain attained its great elevation.

The special climatic conditions of the summits of Kina Balu may have proved an obstacle both to the derivation of numerous forms from mountains of temperate regions, and to an expansion of those of the low regions above which the great mountain rises. Rains are very copious on its summit, and heavy mists are almost permanent. The temperature is very uniform throughout the year, but always very low at night. If therefore vegetation is favoured by the heat of the day, it finds a permanent obstacle in the constant coldness of the nights, whilst it cannot profit from a period of rest, as happens in cold countries. Such conditions differ from those existing on any elevated mountain of higher latitudes.

If the elevation of Kina Balu to its present height had happened at a very remote geological epoch, when the plasmative period was in full force, I am confident that a large number of characteristic types would not be wanting there. I also believe that under such circumstances even the few types which had gained a footing would have produced numerous adaptation-forms peculiar to the great mountain.

INDEX

INDEX

Banjok tribes, 317
" Banner " (basal buttresses of trees), 88, 269, 385, 386
Bansi village, 141
Banteng, 37, 166, 311
Banting village, 41, 200, 342
Barclaya Motleyi, 259
Barram River, 288, 298, 363 ; Kinyas of, 317 ;
Bat, fruit, 36
" Batang," meaning of word, 40 ; forest paths, 8
Batang-Kayan, 303 ; Kayans of the, 362
Batang-Lupar, 40, 137, et seq. ; watershed of, 186
Batavia, orang at, 195
Batrachospermum Borneense, 192
Batu Lanko, 142
Batu Puti, 304, 361
Batu Tibang, 254, 304, 361
Batu Ujong, 124
Bau, 135
Bauhinia Burbidgei, 70
Beads, Venetian, 263
Beak, Hornbill, a Dyak ornament, 117, 325
Bear, Malay, 37, 106, 158, 159
Beccarianthus pulcher, 284
Beccarinia xiphostachya, 141
" Bedang " (Dyak dress), 44
Bee-eaters, 135
Bees, 106 ; adventure with, 107
Begonias on the Bellaga Hills, 298
Belcher, Sir Edward, lands with Brooke at Labuan, 246
Bellaga river, 296, 297, 363
Bellida or Blida, 53, 135
Berok or Bruk monkey, 30
Bezoar stone, 327
Bidi, 135
Bilian ataps, 79
" Bilion " or Malay axe, 66
Bilion, tribe of, 317
Bintulu river, 256 et seq. ; fort, 286
Binturong, 37
Birds, colouring imitating butterflies, 118 ; protective colouring of, 12 ; used for augury, 328 ; Bornean, 32, 120 ; dissemination of *Ficus* by, 394 ; tame, 32 ; of Kapuas lakes, 188 ; female brighter than male, 116 ; nocturnal, 159 ; plumage coloured by food, 12
Birds' nests, edible, 56, 57, 136, 228, 282, 374
Bishop McDougall, 40
Black water, 182 et seq.
Blood-brotherhood ceremony, 278
Boats of the Kayans, 307 ; of the Mellanaos, 257 ; of a Buketan, 289 ; sampans, 222
Boar, large, 39

Boletus edulis, 113
Bombok village, 56
Bore on the Batang-Lupar, 40
Borneo, former races of , 21, 366 ; knowledge of the natives of its interior, 303 ; recent explorations in, 361 ; its fertility due to rich humus, 368 ; the characteristics of northern, 254 ; origin of name of, 254 ; scarcity of population, 368 ; improbably the home of Man's precursor, 207 ; its geography, 361 ; is without Negritos, 364 ; its useful water-ways, 304 ; Posewitz on, 361 ; lengthy native journeys in, 362 ; trade of, with China, 365 ; Hindu and other antiquities in, 366 ; agriculture in, 367 ; gold and other minerals of, 370 ; forest products of, 374
Borneo Company, The, 371, 377
Boro-Budor carvings, 23, 24, 265, 279
Bos sondaicus, 37, 166, 311
Bostrychia bryophila, 314 ; *B. fulcrata*, 314
Bow and arrows unknown in Borneo, 279
Brackenridgeas of the Kapuas Lakes, 187
Brain in Man, development of, 218
Brenthidæ, food of *Pityriasis*, 116
Bridges, bamboo, 125, 127
British North Borneo Company, 360
Brooke, Sir Charles, 4, 360
Brooke, Sir James, sketch of life of, 355 et seq.
Brookea dasyantha, 57
Brooketown, coal mines of, 372
Brownlowia Beccarii, and *B. Sarawakensis*, 80
Brugmansia Lowii, 247, 389
Bruni city, 249, et seq. ; formerly a dependency of China, 253 ; its houses, 249 ; the Palace, 250 ; Sultan of, 250 ; decay of, 252, 253 ; gives its name to Borneo, 254 ; British Consulate at, 252
Buceros rhinoceros, 117, 325
Bugis in Borneo, 22
Buitenzorg, orang at, 195 ; camphor trees sent to, 305
Bukit Kananpei, 186 ; Bukit Lampei, 186 ; Bukit Tundon, 191
Buketans, 263, et seq., 286, 317, 363
Bulbophyllum Odoardi, 400. ; *B. Beccarii*, 400
Bulungan river Kayans, 362
Buntal, 120
Buprestis, colours of, 76
Busso, 132, 135
Butan tribe, 317
Butterflies, 153 ; colouring imitating birds, 118
Buttresses of trees, 88, 269, 385, 386

INDEX

INDEX

Denison, W., on a former waterway from Sambas to Sarawak, 56

De Notaris, on Hepaticæ of Borneo, 101

Depilation, practised by Kayans, 278 ; by Celebes tribes, 278

Derris uliginosa, 241

Diamonds, 121 et seq., 371

Dichilanthe Borneensis, 187

Didymocarpus bullata, 96 ; *D. rufescens*, 96

Dillenia Indica, 124 ; *D. suffruticosa*, 6, 30

Diospyros, flowering period of, 90

Dipsas dendrophila, 33

Dipterocarpeæ, 91 et seq. ; on Gunong Poe, 99, 102

Dipterocarpus Lowii, 223 ; *D. oblongifolius*, 92

Disantholisation, 404

Diseases among the Punans, 303

Dissemination, of forest species, 68 ; of *Dichilanthe*, 187 ; of ground-plants by earthworms, 112

Divinities of the Sea-Dyaks, 50

Dogs, wild, 166 ; Dyak, 225, 226 ; a pest to the traveller, 298, 188, 150 ; Kayan, 282

Doria, Marchese Giacomo, 109 ; returns to Europe, 85

Draco volans, 35

Dragon's blood, 231, 233, 234

Dryobalanops, camphor-yielding, 272

Duel by water, 177

Dugong, 224

Durian (*Durio zibetinus*), 166 ; wild, 286 ; its place of origin unknown, 25, 60

Durio carinatus, 286 ; *D. dulcis*, 110

Dyak, songs, 48 ; head-hunting, 44, 46, 50 ; albino, 327 ; mission, 41, 344 ; cosmography, 337 ; trial by water, 177 ; love customs, 172 ; mode of climbing trees, 107 ; fear of mountain summits, 62, 110, 158 ; interpretation of dreams, 158 ; stories of orangs, 204 ; backwoodsmanship, 333 ; mode of cooking rice, 157 ; names of, 191 ; justice, 338

Dyaks, Land, 53 ; head-houses of, 54 ; houses of, 54 ; appearance, 60 ; character, 61 ; food of, 61 ; cremation among, 61 ; superstition, 62 ; houses, dress, weapons, etc., 63 et seq.

Dyaks, Sea, 42 et seq.

Earrings, 46, 263, 264

Earthquakes in Borneo, 372

Earthworms, their influence on the distribution of plants, 112

Eggs, of turtle, 98 ; of frog in pitchers of Nepenthes, 96

Elateriospermum tapos, 129

Elephantiasis, 241

Elephantopus scaber, 192

Eleusine Indica, 192

Elœis guineensis in Labuan, 245

Endomychidæ, 115

Enhalus acoroides, 85

Entabei river, 329 et seq.

Environment, action of, 118, 207 et seq.

Epiphytes of the Bornean forests, 397 ; on mangroves, 83

Erect posture in anthropoids, 217

Erotylidæ, 115

Erycibe longifolia, 299

Eucalyptus, giant, 330

Eugeissonia, on Mount Wa, 128 ; on Pulo Burong, 138 ; *E. ambigua*, 189; *E. insignis*, 85, 344 ; *E. minor*, 99 ; *E. utilis*, 249, 254, 307, 308

Eugenia saligna, 299 ; *E. riparia*, 299

Euphorbias inodorous in Borneo, 391 ; ant-harbouring, 407

Euplocomus nobilis, 159

Eusideroxylon Zwageri, 89

Everett, Mr. A. H., finds stone axe in Borneo, 367 ; on wild pigs, 38

Evolution, author's ideas on, 207 et seq.

Excœcaria agallocha, 81

Exports of Sarawak, 374

Eye of *Cymborhynchus*, 134

Facial expansions in the orang, 149 et seq. ; 194 et seq. ; in man, 197

Fagræa stenophylla, 299, 393

Falcon, miniature (*Hierax*), 11

Fea, L., on dress of Kachin women, 44 ; on the name Kayan, 366 ; on mode of obtaining fire in Burma, 236

Fecundation, in *Cryptocoryne bullosa*, 341 ; in *Enhalus acoroides*, 85

Felis nebulosa, 37, 277

Ferns, aquatic, 292

Fertility of soil, near Kuching, 28 ; of Borneo generally, 368

Fête, Chinese, 153 ; Sea-Dyak, 48

Fever, Chinese mode of reducing, 151

Fibre, of *Arenga*, 232 ; of Zingiberaceous plants, 176

Ficus, 12, 394 et seq. ; *F. acidula*, 123 ; *F. Miquelii*, 180 ; *F. pisifera*, 180 ; *F. parietalis*, 180 ; *F. consociata*, 180 ; *F. cucurbitina*, 180. (For the various species *see* Append., p. 394.)

Figs. *See* Ficus

Fire, Dyak methods of obtaining, 235, 236

Fireflies, 75, 76

Fish, a native test for thieves, 240 ; archer, sumpitan, or shooting, 139 ; dungan, 175 ; brilliantly coloured of the Umpanang, 181 ; " talking " or sound producing, 240 ; taking

INDEX

INDEX

INDEX

Sarawak generally, 370; antimony, mercury, and iron in Sarawak, 371
Oreodoxa regia, 232
Ornithoptera Brookeana, 153
Oryza sativa, 229
Osmoxylon helleborinum, 392
Oya Province, 374
Oysters, 253; affected by an *Ascaris*, 254
Paddles, Malay canoe, 223
" Padma," or " Patma," or " Pakma," native name for Rafflesia, 102
Paku village, 352, 353
Palæornis longicauda, 11
Palaquium optimum, 90, 91, 92; *P. rigidum*, fœtid flowers of, 390
Palembang, orang from, 205
Palms, 395; striking species of, 232; oil, 245; sago (*see* under *Arenga*); areca, 27; smallest known, 114; peculiar to Borneo, 395; aquatic, of wide distribution, 286; on the Igan River, 322; climbing, 391: in the Rotang valley, 114; on the Bintulu, 259; hospitating (*Korthalsia*), 406; diminutive, on Mattang, 70, 71; stenophyllous (*Pinanga rivularis*), 392
" Pamali " or taboo, 267, 293, 306
Pandan village, 265; and river, 285
Pandani, 395; at Sibu, 94; marsh, 348
Pandanus dubius, 227
Pangenesis, 216
Pangerang Rio, 269; Pangerangs of Bruni, 21
Pangium edule, 309
Pankalan Ampat, 124, 130, 132; antiquities found at, 365
Papaw fruit (*Carica papaya*), 26
Papuans, negroid hair of, 364
Parakeets, 11
Parang battok, 65
Parang-ilang, 46, 282
Parasitic plants, 388
Paspalum conjugatum, 192
Pelagus, antimony at, 371
Pelidna subarquata, 120
Penis, perforation of, 278
Pennan tribe, 286, 302, 317
Pepper, 374, 375; at Bruni, 253
Perham, Mr. R. J., on Dyak songs, 50; on Dyak traditions of the Deluge, 52
Periophthalmus kolreuteri, 81
Petrosavia stellaris, 100, 388
Pfeiffer, Ida, in Borneo, 186
Phanerogams, marine, 262
Phalanx, ungual, of toe in orang sometimes wanting, 198
Pheasant, Argus, 117; Euplocamus, 159; Bulwer's, 312
Pholidocarpus majadum, 233, 395
Phosphorescence of trees and plants, 76, 158

Phrynum zebrinum, 387
Phyllocladus hypophylla, 99
Pigs, wild, 38, 39, 155, 323; traps for, 61
Pinang, 27, 322, 396. See also under Areca
Pinanga brevipes, 401; *P. crassipes*, 401; *P. variegata*, 387; *P. calamifrons*, 392; *P. patula*, 322; *P. rivularis*, 392
Pininjau, 54 et seq., 352
Piracy, 356; influence on population, 20
Pistia stratiotes, 17
Pitcher-plants. See Nepenthes
Pitchers of *Nepenthes*, 96, 405, 408
Pithecanthropus erectus, 217, 220
Pitta granatina, 159
Pityriasis gymnocephala, 115
Plants, aquatic, 188, 320, 410; with large leaves, 236, 384; with narrow leaves, 296, 297, 299, 392; alpine, analogous with epiphytes, 397; carnivorous, 408 (*see* also under Nepenthes); with flowers on trunks, 401; with variegated or brilliant leaves, 386; cleistogamous, 330; adapted to floods, 296, 305; of the Kapuas lakes, 187, 411; of the primeval forest, 382; of the secondary forest, 381; of the estuarine river banks, 80, 81; domesticated, 308; marine, in freshwater, 314; herbaceous of the coastal flora, 94; formicarian or hospitating, 403; marine, derived from freshwater, 360; marsh, in arid soil, 248; parasitic, 388; climbing, 390; saprophytic, 388; epiphytic, 396; spinous, 114; stenophyllous, 296, 392; living in salt water, 211
Plasmation, theory of, 36; 209, et seq.
Plojarium pulcherrimum, 384
Plotus melanogaster, 291, 292
Podocarpus cupressina, 99, 128
Poe, Mount, 98 et seq.
Pollen, of *Eugeissonia* eaten, 308
Polyalthia anomala, 401
Polypodium dipteris, 16, 96
Pomponia imperatoria, 11
Pongamia glabra, 224
Population of Sarawak, 373
Porcupine, 117
Poronia Œdipus, 248
Posewitz, on Borneo, 361, 365
Posture, erect, in man, 217
Precursors of man, 216 et seq.
Primula Chinensis, 210
Proboscis monkey, 31
Products of Sarawak, 369 et seq.
Provinces of Sarawak, 373, 374
Psychotria acuminata, 299, 392
Pteris arachnoidea, 334, 147
Pteromys, 36; *P. nitidus*, 12
Pteropus, 36, 78

INDEX

Ptilocercus Lowii, 248

Pulo (=island), P. Burong, 137 ; P. Kaladi, 326 ; P. Sampadien, 223

Punai (*Treron vernans*), 53

Punan tribe, 264, 302, 309, 312 ; stated to be cannibals, 364

Pyrocælia opaca, 75

Pyrotrogon kasumba, 328

Python, Bornean, 33 ; length of, 34

Quercus, on Gunong Poe, 99 ; on Gunong Wa, 128

Quop, palæolithic implements found at, 367

Races, aboriginal of Borneo, 364

Rafflesia Tuan-Mudæ, 101 et seq., 388, 389

Rain, in Sarawak, 379, 380

Rajah Brooke, biography of, 355 et seq.

Rajah Muda (Sir Chas. Brooke), 355 376, 377

Rambutan, 25, 130

Rapids, of the Rejang, 312 ; of the Sarawak, 123 ; of the Sakarrang, 338 ; of the Bellaga, 300

Rassam fern, 147, 334

Rays in fresh water, 314

Rebellion, Chinese, 358

Regatta at Kuching, 79, 355

Regions, botanic, of Borneo, 408

Reichenbach and the author's orchids 398

Rejang River, 243, 301, 302 et seq. 317, 326 ; delta of, 323 ; floating islands from, 259 ; course of, 361 ; extraordinary depth of, 304, 305

Religions in Sarawak, 376

Renanthera on Poe, 101

Reptiles of Borneo, 33, et seq.

Resin, Dammar, 99, 258

Rhacophorus Reinwardtii, 36

Rhinoceros, in the Sarawak, 311 ; fossil, 135

Rhinoceros sumatrensis, 38

Rhizophoræ, 84

Rhododendron Brookeanum, 397 ; *R. lapponicum*, 397 ; *R. salicifolium*, 85

Rhodomyrtus tomentosa, 247

Rhyncophorus ferrugineus, 27

Rhyncopyle elongata, 104

Rhytidocerus obscurus, 77

Riam Ledong, 123, 124

Rice in Sarawak, 374, 131 ; wild, 229

Rice mill, 345

Ridley, N., on occurrence of orang in the Malay Peninsula, 205

Rivers, with periodical floods, 297

Roads, Dyak, 8, 349

Rollulus rouloul, 32

Roots, in the galleries of formicarian Rubiaceæ, 405 ; buttress, or " ban-

ner," 88, 269 ,384 ; fulcral, 384, 395

Rotang, 8 ; *R. jernang*, 231, 233, 234 ; rotang kawat, 71 ; rotang tikus, 71 ; the valley of, 115 ; length of, 114

Rotangs, 71, 114

Ruins, Hindu, in Borneo, 366

Saba, State of (British North Borneo), 360

Sabayana, 52

Sacrifices, human, 364

Sadok, 335

Sadomak, 98

Sadong, coal on the, 372 ; source of the, 130 ; province of, 374

Sago (*see* under Arenga), 233, 244, 374, 409 ; making at Bintulu, 287 et seq. ; Kadjattao, 307, et seq. ; as substitute for biscuit, 303 ; its good properties, 318

Sakarrang, Dyaks of the, 47 ; descent of the, 336 et seq.

Salak, 80, 84

Salt, 310

Salvadori, on Bornean birds, 32, 120

Samangs, sumpitans of the, 280

Samarahan, 349

Samatan, 224

Samattang village, 227 ; river, 228

Sambas, confines of, 56, 101

Sampan, Malay, 222

Sand-flies, 180, 335

Sandoricum Maingayi, 131

Santubong, 1, 259 ; plants and trees on, 95 ; antiquities found on, 365

Sapium Indicum, used to catch fish, 241

Sapotaceæ, flowering period of, 91

Saprophytes, 111, 388

Sarawak, 354 et seq. ; former territory of, 242 ; extension of, 360 ; river, 2, 121 et seq., 132 et seq. ; Province, 374 ; Rangers, 376 ; government of, 376 ; products of, 374 ; population of, 373 ; history of, 356, 365 ; area of, 361 ; native tribes of, 363 ; antiquities of, 366, 367 ; agriculture of, 367 ; minerals of, 370 ; coal in, 371 ; capital of, 372 (*see* also under Kuching); climate of, 372, 379 ; exports of, 374

Sargassum angustifolium, 227

Sarong, 23

Satang island, 96, 97

Saturnia pyri, 118

Sauraja angustifolia, 299, 392

Sauropatis chloris, 224

Schismatoglottis asperuta, 387 ; S. Beccarii, 387

Scleria sedge, 348

Scortechini, Padre, 247

Scyphiphora hydrophyllacea, 80

INDEX

INDEX

Tiang Laju, Mount, 155
Tigers in Singapore, 86
Tiles, bamboo, 128
Timber of *Shorea falcata*, 84
Tinder for production of fire, 236
Tjaping, meaning of word, 149 (*see* also under Orang-utan and Mayas)
Toad, Ko-go, 283
Tobacco, Dyak, 174
Togak, Mount, 176
Tolypothrix distorta, 192 ; *T. flexuosa*, 192
Tombs, Kayan, 268
Tomistoma Schlegelii, 188
Toxodes jaculator, 139
Trachycomus ochrocephalus, 388
Tragulus, 38 ; *T. napu*, 30
Trapa natans, 259
Traps, for wild boar, 61
Treacher, Mr. W. H., on the native name of Borneo, 254
Trees, height of, 84, 88, 108, 330 ; fruit, 129, 131 ; mutually support each other, 7 ; age of, 110 ; covered by water, 184
Tree-trunks, flowering, 8, 233, 401
Treron vernans, 53
Trial by water, 177 ; Dyak, 338
Trigonocephalus Wagleri, 155
Trinchese, Prof. on orang fœtus, 206
Trogon, 328
Trousers an ancient form of dress, 23
Trusan Province, 374
Trusans, or estuary channels, 80
Tuan-ku, meaning of word, 10 ; Tuan-ku Yassim, 11, 195
Tuan Muda (present Rajah of Sarawak), 4, 108 ; *Rafflesia* dedicated to, 104 ; excursion to Poe with, 98 ; expedition against Kayans, 313
Tuba (poison for fish), 240, 279
Tubao river, 267, 290, 295
Tubers of hospitating plants, 404 ; colossal, of *Dioscorea*, 131
Tummusong, Kayan chief, 269
Tunei village, 296
Turtles, 98, 224, 227
Tutop, Mount, 176

Ukit tribe, 317, 363
Umbut, or " cabbage " of palms, 69
Umpanang river, 181, 183, 189
Uncaria Gambir, 67, 374
Undup, 42, 341 ; river, 139
Unggan village, 141
Unona flagellaris, 333, 390, 403
" Untut," or elephantiasis, 241
Upas tree and poison, 158, 252, 278, 309, 346

Urari poison, 279
Urnularia oblongifolia, 262
Urostigmas, crowded with birds, 12, 394
Utan, meaning of word, 31
Utricularia exoleta, 192

Vallombrosa, 84, 87, 106, et seq. ; left alone at, 118, 369
Van Schelle, discovers Melabu volcano, 372
Vanda Lowii, 125, 247 ; *V. suavis*, 180
Variability of species, 210 ; checked by the force of heredity, 212, 213
Variation not due to adaptation, 211 ; how occasioned, 210, 211
Vegetation of the estuaries, 80 ; of the Upper Sarawak, 123, 124 ; of the seashore, 94 ; of Poe, 99, 100 ; on Lessong, 344 ; special areas of, 408 et seq.
Venetian beads, 263
Vicia faba, 403
Vinciguerra, Dr., on Bornean fish, 182, 240
Viverra (*V. tangalunga*), 30
Volcanic islands always fertile, 368
Volcano, Melabu, 372 ; volcanoes in Borneo, 372

Wa, Mount, 126, 130
Wa-wa monkey, 30
Wallace, on facial adiposities of orang, 195 ; on orang throwing fruit, 204 ; his visit to the Sadong, 137 ; to Pininjau, 57 ; on flowering tree-trunks, 402
Water, black, 182 et seq. ; trial by, 177
Waterfall of Mount Gading, 104
Waterparting, Central Bornean, 362 ; Batang-Lupar and Pontianak, 172
Whitehead, G., his exploration of Kina Balu, 249
Woods, Tenison, on coal formation, 185
Winds, Cave of the, 132
Wine, palm, 48
Wings, of seeds as navigating organs, 92
Wood, of *Shorea falcata*, 84 ; fossil, 124
" Woodlands," 85
Wymann, on the foot of the human embryo, 207

Zanardini, on Bornean algæ 227
Zannetti, on skull of a Buketan, 263
Zebu hump, analogous to steatoparesis, 197
Zingiberacea, root of, used to rub skin, 328 ; remarkable, 160

Oxford in Asia Hardback Reprints

CENTRAL ASIA

Robert Shaw
Visits to High Tartary, Yarkand and Kashgar
Introduction by Peter Hopkirk

Francis Younghusband
The Heart of a Continent
Introduction by Peter Hopkirk

Francis Younghusband
India and Tibet
Introduction by Alastair Lamb

CHINA

L. C. Arlington & W. Lewisohn
In Search of Old Peking
Introduction by Geremie Barmé

J. Dyer Ball
Things Chinese
Introduction by H. J. Lethbridge

Juliet Bredon
Peking
Introduction by H. J. Lethbridge

Juliet Bredon & Igor Mitrophanow
The Moon Year
Introduction by H. J. Lethbridge

E. H. M. Cox
Plant-hunting in China
Introduction by Peter Cox

E. J. Eitel
Europe in China
Introduction by H. J. Lethbridge

Reginald F. Johnston
Lion and Dragon in Northern China
Introduction by Pamela Atwell

Owen Lattimore
Inner Asian Frontiers of China

C. P. Skrine
Chinese Central Asia
Introduction by Alastair Lamb

INDONESIA

Henry O. Forbes
A Naturalist's Wanderings in the
Eastern Archipelago
Introduction by the Earl of Cranbrook

William Marsden
The History of Sumatra
Introduction by John Bastin

J. W. B. Money
Java, or How to Manage a Colony
Introduction by Ian Brown

Johan Nieuhof
Voyages and Travels to the East Indies
1653–1670
Introduction by Anthony Reid

Urs Ramseyer
The Art and Culture of Bali

Thomas Stamford Raffles
The History of Java (2 vols in 1)
Introduction by John Bastin

Plates to Raffles's History of Java
Preface by John Bastin

Thomas Stamford Raffles
Statement of the Services of
Sir Thomas Stamford Raffles
Introduction by John Bastin

Alfred Russel Wallace
The Malay Archipelago
Introduction by John Bastin

Beryl de Zoete & Walter Spies
Dance and Drama in Bali

MALAYSIA

S. Baring Gould & C. A. Bampfylde
A History of Sarawak under its
Two White Rajahs
Introduction by Nicholas Tarling

F. W. Burbidge
The Gardens of the Sun
Introduction by Francis Ng

Hugh Low
Sarawak
Introduction by R. H. W. Reece

Sherard Osborn
The Blockade of Kedah in 1838
Introduction by J. M. Gullick

Mubin Sheppard
A Royal Pleasure Ground:
Malay Decorative Arts and Pastimes

Walter W. Skeat
Malay Magic
Introduction by Hood Salleh

Spenser St. John
Life in the Forests of the Far East
Introduction by Tom Harrisson

SINGAPORE

Song Ong Siang
One Hundred Years' History of the Chinese
in Singapore
Introduction by Edwin Lee

THAILAND

John Crawfurd
Journal of an Embassy to the Courts of Siam
and Cochin China
Introduction by David K. Wyatt

George Finlayson
The Mission to Siam and Hué 1821–1822
Introduction by David K. Wyatt

Simon de la Loubère
The Kingdom of Siam
Introduction by David K. Wyatt

Carol Stratton & Miriam McNair Scott
The Art of Sukhothai: Thailand's Golden Age